W9-CBV-759

FAVOURITE STORIES
FROM AROUND THE WORLD

FAVOURITE
STORIES
FROM AROUND
THE WORLD

Retold by
Jane Ives and Jean-Luc Billeadeux

Illustrated by
Luděk Maňásek, Vladimír Machaj,
Karel Teissig and Vladimír Tesař

CATHAY BOOKS

First published 1982 by
Cathay Books Limited
59 Grosvenor Street
London Wl

Text © by Octopus Books Ltd. 1982
Illustrations © by Artia Prague 1982
Graphic design by Aleš Krejča

ISBN 0 86178 179 1
Printed in Czechoslovakia by Polygrafia, Prague
1/18/05/51 — 01

Contents

PROMETHEUS

Long, long ago, when the world was young and the earth was green and peaceful, the gods lived in splendour on Mount Olympus. This high mountain with its tip wreathed in clouds looked down over the hills and valleys of Greece. This was a beautiful land created by the gods for their pleasure. The rivers were forever clear, the flowers never faded, the air was filled with the song of birds and the bright flashing wings of butterflies. Even at night while the stars shone down through the velvet darkness, the soaring song of the nightingale and the soft flutter of moths' wings filled the sparkling sky as if in praise of the beauty around them.

The gods looked down through the clouds and saw how lovely the world was. Only the animals of the earth, the fishes of the blue oceans and rivers and the birds of the clear heavens lived there — for as yet no men had been created.

The greatest of all the gods on Mount Olympus was Zeus. He, and his wife Hera, who was the most beautiful of all the goddesses, ruled firmly over the other gods. But the earth had not always been so peaceful. Many years before, when the world was born, there had been a terrible war between the Titans, a huge, warlike race of gods. Father had fought son, brother had fought brother. Finally Zeus, the grandson of the mightiest Titan god Uranus and son of the powerful god Chronos, conquered and forced peace upon all of them. That was why Zeus now ruled so firmly, helped by his brothers Poseidon and Hades. Never again would Zeus allow war to break out between the gods. With Poseidon as the King of the Oceans and Hades as the King of the Underworld they watched over the world. Nothing escaped their notice, no matter how small. Now, once again, trouble was coming to Zeus' peaceful land.

Prometheus, another grandson of the mighty Uranus, loved the earth. He was tired of living on Mount Olympus and wanted to live amongst the valleys and hills of Greece. With his brother Epimetheus they wandered through the countryside. Prometheus noticed that there were always most fish and animals where ever water flowed freely and where the soil was rich and dark.

'Water and soil give life,' he told his brother Epimetheus, 'we could create life from these two things.'

Epimetheus thought that this was a wonderful idea and set to work modelling men out of clay by mixing soil and water together.

Prometheus, who knew more than the other gods about the ways of the animals and creatures of the earth, helped him and soon Epimetheus had made a whole race of men and women. They lay on the ground before the two brothers but they did not move.

'We cannot breathe life into them,' cried Prometheus. 'We are only half-gods. I shall go to Mount Olympus and ask Pallas Athene, the wisest of all the goddesses, to help us.'

Now Pallas Athene, who was indeed the wisest of all the goddesses, often became bored on the cloudy heights of Mount Olympus. She too thought that Prometheus' idea of creating a race of men from clay was a splendid idea. Besides, she was curious to see how these strange little creatures would turn out. She came down from the tall mountain with Prometheus and breathed life into the clay figures that he and his brother had made.

The clay figures stirred, then stretched and stood up, stumbling at first because they had not yet become used to their legs and arms. They looked round them in wonder, for they knew no more than new-born babies, even though they were fully the height of grown men and women.

Prometheus realized that he would have to teach them how to survive, for although Pallas Athene had breathed life into them, she had not made them clever — that was the task for Prometheus.

For many seasons Prometheus lived with the men and women he had created. He taught them how to make houses from the stones of the hillside and the wood from the trees. He showed them how to plant grain and harvest it, how to fish in the streams and the sea. He showed them how to read and write, and how to foretell the weather from the clouds and the sun. He taught them about music and painting, and how to create beautiful and useful things from the tin, gold and silver they found in the caves of the hillsides.

And all the time Prometheus was busy with his teaching Zeus and Hera looked down at what he was doing and became angrier and angrier.

'Prometheus is teaching his men to be too clever,' boomed Zeus. 'These men of his will soon be almost too powerful for us. If they can do all these things, what is there to stop them from climbing Mount Olympus?'

'That is very true, dear,' replied Hera, 'and what is worse is that although Prometheus has taught them to be so clever, he has never taught them to be afraid of us. No, indeed, his men have made no temples or altars to worship us, they offer no sacrifices, no, not even the smallest gold ring or two . . .' sighed Hera, who rather liked the look of some of the beautiful things that Prometheus' men had made.

'I shall teach them to respect us,' roared Zeus, and he stretched his arms wide and clenched his fists.

Immediately the sky darkened, purple and grey thunderclouds rolled in from across the sea. Strong winds whipped the sea into spray at first and then into enormous waves. The waves rose like mountains, dashing against the shores, while the wind roared and

howled across the valleys. Great bolts of lightning sped across the sky, splitting trees and breaking rocks. Then the rain started. It became heavier and heavier until the green valleys of the land were hidden by it and the drops fell like veils across the face of the land. Every single fire that Prometheus had built for his people was put out, every tiny cinder, every lighted torch, every spark of fire.

When the storm was over the land was very still and terribly dark.

'That will teach them,' roared Zeus, who could see that there was not a single spark of fire burning anywhere. 'Let us see how clever they will be without fire.'

Zeus had known all along that the one thing that Prometheus could not teach his people was how to make fire.

All through that dark night the people huddled in what shelter they could find and when the morning came they began to rebuild their houses. At first they did not miss the fire too much, but by that evening, when they could not bake bread or cook their food or even build a fire to keep themselves warm they began to understand what a dreadful thing had happened to them and how important fire was to them.

They went to Prometheus and begged him to help them. Prometheus loved the people that he had made and he was determined to help them. He knew that there was one place in the whole world where he could find fire, but he also knew how dangerous it would be for him to try to go there. He had seen how angry Zeus could be, and how powerful the greatest of all the gods was. Even so he decided that he could not leave his people without fire, so, late that night, taking a hollow branch with him, he began to climb Mount Olympus.

He climbed quickly, knowing that he must hurry before Zeus realized what he was trying to do. He reached the palace of the gods and crept into the sacred chamber where the eternal fire burned. Stealthily he stole several of the flaming embers and placed them in the hollow branch and just as stealthily he crept back down the mountain.

Using the embers he had stolen he brought fire back to his people, but as he looked up through the darkness towards the top of the mountain he knew that Zeus would punish him the next day.

The morning came and Zeus looked down on the land. To his amazement and fury he saw little columns of smoke rising from the houses in the villages and towns. He saw twinkling flames in the blacksmith's forges and the silver and goldsmith's workshops. He realized that somehow Prometheus had outwitted him. He raged through the palace, shaking his fists at the land below.

'Prometheus shall pay for this,' he vowed, and he sent for his powerful brother Hephaestus, the god of the forge and the fire.

'Prometheus has stolen your fire, capture him at once,' he shouted at Hephaestus. 'Bind him with chains to the topmost peak of Mount Caucasus so that he may never escape.'

Hephaestus did as Zeus demanded, although his heart was heavy and he felt that such a cruel punishment was too harsh.

Zeus still had not finished with Prometheus, the half-god who had dared to defy him. Every day for thirty years Zeus sent a gigantic eagle to attack him.

This eagle had a steel beak and claws and every morning tore at the poor chained Prometheus until it reached his liver, and every night Zeus caused Prometheus to be healed, ready for the savage eagle to attack him the next morning.

Although Prometheus was in great pain he would not give up, for he believed that what he had done was right and he was prepared to stand any pain if it would allow his people to keep their fire.

At last Zeus relented. He had come to admire the bravery that Prometheus showed. Zeus commanded one of his mightiest sons, Hercules, to release Prometheus by slaying the monstrous eagle. With a sweep of his great sword, Hercules slew the eagle and severed the chains that bound Prometheus to Mount Caucasus, but as he did he also sheared off a small piece of the mountain. The chains that Hephaestus had made to bind Prometheus were so strong that even the strength of Hercules could not part all of them from Prometheus. So for evermore this brave half-god carried with him a part of the mountain that had been his prison for so long — a reminder of his noble sacrifice in bringing fire back to the world of man.

DAEDALUS AND ICARUS

The ancient city of Athens has always been the mightiest city in Greece. Even today its temples and palaces, squares and meeting places are still impressive. Imagine how Athens must have looked when it was young, when the great Acropolis was first built.

This huge temple to Pallas Athene, the patron goddess of the Athenians, stands on the hill of the Acropolis, overlooking the paved streets and smaller temples of the city. Inside the Acropolis once stood a proud and awesome statue of the goddess. This statue was said to be so lifelike that when the people of Athens prayed to her she bowed her head to receive their prayers. Who built such a statue? Who could have made such a strange and wonderful thing?

This is the story of the man who was believed to have built not only this statue but many of the beautiful temples and palaces of Ancient Greece; the man who built the fabulous maze which surrounded the dreaded Minotaur of Crete. The man whose name meant 'cunningly wrought'. This is the story of Daedalus and his son Icarus.

Even when Daedalus was a young man he began to make wonderful sculptures. Most statues at that time were stiff and straight, their eyes were blank and they looked blindly out at the people who came to see them. The statues that Daedalus made looked as if they might step down and walk among the men and women of Greece. Some of these statues showed men throwing the discus — a popular sport in Greece; some of them showed the athletes and sportsmen who took part in the great Olympic Games that were held every four years. The statues that Daedalus made of the statesmen and leaders of that time showed them as if they were real men, not stiff and unnatural stone models. Their eyes seemed real, their robes looked as if they might move in the cooling breezes that blew through Athens.

Even more than this, the temples, palaces and houses that Daedalus designed were more comfortable than the houses built by any other architect. Their mosaic floors, pillared halls and painted walls proclaimed the genius of Daedalus. Whenever a new temple was built or a great palace was created for the rulers of Athens it was Daedalus who was asked to design it.

No wonder then that Daedalus became the greatest artist in all Greece. Students came from all parts of the ancient world to learn from him, songs were written praising him and his name was known all over Greece.

Daedalus became proud and haughty, and when one of his students, the son of his sister, began to show great promise as an artist, Daedalus began to watch him carefully.

Daedalus' nephew Talus learned fast, and soon there was very little that Daedalus could teach him. Talus knew how to carve the fine marble from the mountains round Athens, how to take a rough block of this milky stone and turn it into a fine likeness of a man. He carved little sculptures of animals; cats and dogs which seemed so real that they might jump down and scamper away. Then he turned his hand to making pottery. He invented a wheel on which beautiful vases could be made: vases which were smooth and shapely, unlike the crude pottery that had been made before. He even made small models of shrines to the gods. Talus became well thought of and some of the rich merchants of Athens began to ask him to design their cool marble villas.

Daedalus watched this and grew more and more jealous. He did not feel pleased that Talus had learned his skills only from him. He didn't listen when people told him how proud he must be of his nephew and how well he had taught him. Daedalus began to forget that he himself could still make fine sculptures, that he was still the greatest artist in Greece. He only looked at what Talus had made. He would not allow Talus to build any of the great temples of Athens and never asked for his help.

He tried to ignore Talus, but wherever he went people spoke so well of his nephew that Daedalus could never forget him. At last he became determined to destroy him.

One evening Daedalus sent a message to Talus asking him to come to a high cliff beside the sea near Athens. He pretended that he wished to ask for Talus' advice about a temple that was to be built there. Talus received the message, and, glad that his uncle, who had seemed so strange and silent recently, wanted to see him, hurried off to the meeting place.

Daedalus was waiting for him, pacing around the cleared space which was littered with blocks of marble ready to be carved into statues of the gods. Below him he could hear the thunder of the waves on the sharp rocks at the base of the cliffs. He looked around. This was a desolate place, a mile or so from the city and far away from curious eyes.

'Yes,' thought Daedalus. 'This place is ideal for my plan. No one can see me and the sea is deep and full of deadly currents.'

He looked down at the crashing waves and for a moment almost changed his mind. 'Talus is so young . . . my sister's only son . . . just a few years older than my own son Icarus . . .' he thought to himself, but then he hardened his heart again.

'There must be only one great sculptor and architect in Greece, and it must be me,' he said to himself. 'The gods will surely forgive me for what I do, I have built many temples to them, surely they will forgive me . . .'

The voice of his nephew broke into his thoughts.

'Uncle, this is indeed a wild and magnificent place for a temple, see how the mountains surround us and the sea stretches before us.'

Talus walked towards Daedalus and stood by him. Daedalus put his arm round the young man's shoulders and turned towards the cliff edge.

'See how far the sea stretches into the distance,' he said, urging Talus towards the crumbling stone that marked the edge of the sheer and fatal drop into the sea.

It was done swiftly; a scuffling of feet, a muffled cry and Talus fell into the darkness towards the hissing waves.

Daedalus turned away from the cliff, sickened at what he had done. Fearfully he looked up into the darkening sky, afraid that the gods had seen him. Pulling his robe round his face he crept back to Athens.

The gods had indeed seen what Daedalus had done and Pallas Athene was determined that Talus should not die. As he plunged downwards she turned him into a bird before he could reach the sea. She had saved him from death and for evermore Talus would swoop and cry round her temple on the Acropolis — one of the white seabirds that forever give thanks to the wisest of goddesses.

Daedalus hardly dared to go out among the men and women of Athens. He was sure that his face must show the dreadful thing that he had done. The days passed and at first Talus was not missed, but then people began to wonder.

'Where is Talus, the nephew of Daedalus?' they asked.

'Why does Daedalus look so pale and frightened?' they murmured in the streets.

'Daedalus was jealous of his nephew, anyone could see that,' they whispered in the alleyways.

'Perhaps Daedalus has . . .' they muttered in the squares of Athens.

Still the body of Talus was not found. Weeks passed and Daedalus began to feel bolder. He began to go out and about again, but wherever he went people stared after him.

'There goes Daedalus,' they hissed. 'His nephew Talus is missing, such a strange thing . . .'

'See how pale Daedalus looks, as if he had a guilty secret,' they said, and their voices followed Daedalus around.

Even the white birds that circled the temple of Pallas Athene seemed to be crying out — Talus . . . Talus . . . Talus . . .

Daedalus was frightened. No one dared to openly accuse him, for the body of Talus was still missing. But now, instead of being the proudest artist in Greece, Daedalus was the man who everybody thought was a murderer, and he knew that they were right. He had to get away, away from the whispering voices and the accusing stares.

He packed his belongings and persuaded one of the Athenian fishermen to take him and his son Icarus far, far away from Athens. And so they sailed far across the stormy waters of the Mediterranean Sea until they came to the island of Crete.

Minos, the King of Crete, was a strange man. He had heard of Daedalus, of the marvellous palaces and temples that Daedalus had built, and he had also heard that Daedalus was thought to have killed Talus. Minos did not care, for he had need of this man. Only Daedalus could help to hide the dreadful secret that this King kept in his heart.

Parsifae, the Queen of Crete, had a son, but this was no ordinary child. He was born with the body of a human but the head and shoulders of a bull. As the child of Minos and Parsifae became stronger he grew into a monster whose terrible rages· could not be controlled. Minos knew that Daedalus was the only man who could build a palace large enough and strong enough to hide his monster son, a palace so complicated and strange that no one could enter it. Even if they did, they would never be able to find their way out again.

'If you build a palace for the Minotaur, you may stay here and I will protect you from the Athenians,' Minos told Daedalus. 'You and your son will have the finest house and everything you could ever want. I will pay you handsomely and you will be safe.'

Daedalus agreed. He wanted Icarus, his son, to grow up without being taunted and bullied for having a murderer for a father.

For five years Daedalus worked at building the most fantastic palace the world had ever seen. Made from the pinkish stone of the island it had hundreds of rooms, countless courtyards and galleries and thousands of pillars. Some of the walls were painted with bright pictures. Carvings surrounded the doorways and windows, the floors

16

were paved with mosaics and patterned slabs of marble, but strangest of all were the passageways. These twisted and turned like a nest of serpents, doubling back on themselves. Some of them led nowhere, some made a complete circle and returned to the outside of the palace.

One of these passageways, so secret that only Daedalus and Minos knew where it was, led to a room at the centre of the palace. Here, far away from the outer walls, the Minotaur, the terrible son of Minos and Parsifae, was to live. The half-human, half-bull monster whose roars and screams would never be heard by the outside world.

When the palace was finished and the Minotaur safely hidden inside, Daedalus was tired. The island of Crete, although beautiful, was not as lovely as Greece. Daedalus was homesick. His son was nearly a grown man and Daedalus wanted to return to Athens.

'Surely the Athenians will have forgotten about Talus by now,' he thought.

He went to Minos and told the King that he wished to leave and take Icarus with him. Minos persuaded Daedalus to stay a little longer; he had no intention of letting this brilliant artist go.

'It is the feast day of my wife, Parsifae,' he told Daedalus. 'Make me a present for her, something that will astonish and amaze her.'

Daedalus set to work again. He made the most magnificent wooden model of a cow, so lifelike that no one believed it was carved.

When it was finished he went to Minos again.

'Now may I leave?' he asked.

But Minos still would not let him go, and Daedalus realized that he must devise a way to escape from Crete, a way that would take both himself and his son far across the Mediterranean to his beloved Greece. Daedalus knew that Minos had hundreds of fast and well armed ships.

'The sea is too dangerous,' he thought. 'The only way to escape is through the air: I must make wings for Icarus and myself and like birds we will fly to freedom.'

Daedalus secretly began to collect birds' feathers. From the wings of the tiniest thrush to the great pinions of the eagle, Daedalus hoarded the feathers until at last he had enough. He built a light framework of the hollow stems of reeds and attached the feathers to this with wax. When one pair of wings was finished he made another pair for his son Icarus.

At dead of night he and Icarus crept to the top of the highest cliff in Crete. They strapped the wings to their arms and launched themselves into the darkness.

The wings worked well and they flew on and on over the sea towards Athens. As dawn broke, Daedalus and his son could see the cliffs and islands of the Greek coast ahead of them in the distance. They looked down and saw the sea below them, wrinkled and blue. They looked up and saw the clouds and the sun above them and curious birds circling around them, wondering what these two strange winged creatures were.

Icarus loved flying.

'Look at me,' he called to his father. 'I can fly higher than you.'

'Come down, come down!' called Daedalus. 'The feathers are only glued to your wings with wax and the sun is too hot. Fly lower where the sea breeze can cool you. If the wax melts you will fall.'

But Icarus would not listen and flew up and up towards the sun, and the wax began to melt. Soon the feathers began to fall and spiral down towards the sea. At last so many feathers had fallen that the wings could no longer hold Icarus up and he fell, like a thunderbolt, down and down towards the blue Mediterranean.

Daedalus looked down at the sea. There was no sign of his son and he saw ahead of him the very cliff where he had murdered Talus.

He realized then that the gods had punished him for the death of Talus by taking the life of Icarus. He had no heart now to return to Greece. Instead he flew on towards Sicily. There he spent the rest of his life. Although he made many statues there he was never happy again. None of the statues he carved ever smiled, and their eyes always looked towards the cliffs of Athens and the sea which claimed the life of his son Icarus.

DEUCALION AND PYRRHA

Perhaps you have read about the story of the great flood in the Bible, but maybe you didn't know that the ancient Greeks had a story about a flood, too. Here it is, the story of the four ages of man, the great flood and of Deucalion and his wife Pyrrha, the couple who survived.

Before the great god Zeus ruled the heavens, Chronos, his father, who was one of the oldest gods of all, was king of the world and the sky. He created a race of men to live on the earth. They were tall and fair and lived a perfectly happy life. They wanted for nothing, the earth gave them all their food, the seas were warm and calm and full of fish. The forests and meadows abounded with fruit and flowers and there was no sickness anywhere. Nobody ever grew old and even death itself was no more than a delicious sleep. When the Age of Gold came to an end it was followed by the Age of Silver. The people of the Age of Silver stayed young for a century, only becoming adult after the hundred years of youth had passed. Unfortunately when they were adult, they changed suddenly and became cruel and un-reasonable. They jeered at the gods who had given them life and would not care for the lands that had supported them for so long. Zeus became angry and turned them all into demons and banished them to the Underworld.

After the Age of Silver came the Age of Iron. The men of this age were created by Prometheus and at first behaved well, but as the years passed they became worse than any who had come before them. War was their favourite sport and they thought no more of killing than they did of eating and drinking.

Battles raged all over the earth, nation fought nation and even families fought amongst themselves.

Hermes, the winged messenger of the gods, was kept very busy flying between Mount Olympus and the earth, reporting what was happening. He told Zeus that the world was in a piteous state and that was why the king of the gods was constantly being asked to give judgement between the warring sides. At last Zeus could stand it no more and he decided that he would come down to earth himself to find out what was happening.

He disguised himself as a man and descended from the Palace of the Immortals to a little town called Lycaon. This town was gov-erned by the king of the Arcadians and even for such a fierce and

warlike region was thought to be the worst of all the Arcadian towns. There Zeus hoped to see for himself just how the men of earth behaved. He discovered that Hermes had been telling the truth, and that not only were the Arcadians cruel and savage, but they also held no belief in the gods. Zeus decided it was time that they were taught a lesson. He caused a great thunderstorm to show the men of Arcadia that he was no ordinary man. He expected them to fall at his feet in fear and trembling, but to Zeus' fury, the king of the Arcadians pretended not to believe that Zeus was really amongst them.

'How am I to know that you are really an immortal as you say you are?' he demanded. 'It is an easy thing to say that you are a god; I should think that you go all over Arcadia pretending to be Zeus, just so that you can feast and drink at other people's expense.'

Zeus held his tongue and waited. He believed that even such a barbaric king would abide by the rules of hospitality and offer a stranger a meal and shelter.

'I will feed you,' said the king sarcastically, 'and it will be a meal fit for a god.' The king commanded that the oldest of his watchdogs should be killed, skinned and cooked and when this was done he served it up to Zeus.

This was too much for the proud father of the gods. He drew himself up to his full height and stretched out his hand; from his fingers flames burst forth and the entire palace of the king was burnt to the ground. Then Zeus turned on the king, who was weeping and wailing and grovelling on the ground. Once again the mighty Zeus stretched out his hand. The king's body stretched and lengthened, his skin changed into a furry pelt, his hands and feet turned into paws and in a trice the king was changed into a wolf. Then Zeus turned his might on the land that harboured such villains. He conjured up a terrible storm. The heavens grew dark and the winds rose. Poseidon, brother of Zeus and god of the sea, sent waves and tides sweeping inland. There they met the boiling waters of the rivers and swept away the trees and grass. As the waters rose men and women struggled to higher land, but the faster they climbed the faster the waters followed. Many days and nights passed and still the water rose steadily until no land could be seen anywhere. Only one place was spared and that was Mount Parnassus. This beautiful mountain rose above the plains of Arcadia, and there, huddling from the rain and the wind-blown spray, were a man and a woman, the only survivors of the human race.

Zeus loved these two, for the man was the son of Prometheus, one of his half-god sons. Deucalion and Pyrrha had never been like the violent Arcadians, but had lived quietly and industriously, looking after their flocks and tending their vineyards. Zeus had warned them of the coming flood and they had built a boat that rose with the waters until it had come to rest on Mount Parnassus. Deucalion and Pyrrha stayed on the mountain until the floods had receded and then they walked sorrowfully down to the drowned plains. Nothing stirred, no animals, no birds, no trees blew in the wind.

'What are we to do, my husband?' sobbed Pyrrha. 'There is nothing to eat and nowhere to shelter.'

They wandered on until they came to the ruined temple of Themis, the mother of Prometheus. There they knelt down and prayed to the goddess.

'Great mother of the earth,' they prayed. 'We cannot live so lonely a life; there are no men and no women but us.'

A strange light began to flicker over the tumbled stones of the temple and a mist gathered round the altar. From the mist came a silvery voice.

'I will help you,' the voice said, 'but you must do exactly as I say. Take the bones of your grandmother and throw them on the ground. Hide your faces while you do this.'

'Great goddess,' replied Pyrrha, 'you cannot mean this. How can I scatter the bones of my grandmother? The gods teach us that we must respect and care for the bones of our parents.'

Then Deucalion spoke, 'Pyrrha, do not be afraid, the gods would never ask us to do anything that was wicked. Is not Themis herself our grandmother and is she not the mother of the earth? Her bones are the stones on which we stand, that is what she means.'

So Deucalion and Pyrrha did as the goddess had told them and scattered stones behind them, hiding their faces as they did so. The stones thrown by Deucalion were changed into men and the stones thrown by his wife Pyrrha turned into women, and the earth was peopled by the men and women made from the bones of the mother goddess — Themis. These people of the earth were strong and honest and worked hard to repair the damage done by the great flood.

Zeus also created another race of men. They were noble and fair, but alas, in time they too perished, just like the three races of man who had gone before them. These men were the heroes of the Greek legends; they were half-gods and when they died they went to a heavenly island — the Island of Happiness where everything was peaceful and no sadness clouded the lives of those who dwelt there.

The people of stone lived on. They were only mortals and so it was their destiny to work and labour to survive, and so it is today for us.

TANTALUS

Zeus, the greatest of all the Greek gods, had many children. Some of them were born to his wife Hera and lived on Mount Olympus, but others were born to women of the earth and were only half-gods. One of these half-god sons was called Tantalus, and ever since he had been a baby he had been a favourite with his father. Like all the earthling sons of Zeus, Tantalus grew up to be tall and handsome and Zeus gave him everything he could ever wish for; lands and riches beyond belief. Tantalus became King of Phrygia, ruler of one of the wealthiest states of ancient Greece.

From time to time Zeus would invite his favourite earthling son to dine with him and the other gods in the marble hall of their palace on Mount Olympus. There Tantalus would eat delicious food and drink the Ambrosian wine that only the gods were allowed to drink. To be sure, Zeus spoiled Tantalus dreadfully, but then, even the gods are sometimes allowed their weaknesses.

Tantalus began to believe that he was as important as the gods themselves. He secretly laughed at Zeus and mocked the other gods, even going so far as to steal a flagon of the sacred Ambrosian wine and bring it back to earth. There he and his friends became very drunk and in their drunkenness sneered and laughed at the Olympians.

Zeus knew how ungrateful Tantalus was, but turned a blind eye to his son's stupidity.

'He is still young,' he told Hera, who was furious that a mere mortal dared to mock the gods. 'He will grow up and become wiser.'

But Tantalus did not grow any wiser. He became more and more haughty, refusing to make offerings to the gods or even to worship them. He began to forbid the people of Phrygia to build temples to Zeus saying:

'Zeus is not so mighty. I know Mount Olympus well and have met all the gods, they are just like us — a little larger perhaps, but they quarrel just like us and make mistakes just like us. Why should you worship them, why not worship me — I am just as mighty.'

Still Zeus did nothing about his wayward son; and then Tantalus went too far.

'The gods are supposed to know everything,' he said to the Phrygians one day, 'but I will prove to you that I can trick them.'

Tantalus then did the most terrible thing. He went to the nursery

of his son Pelops and killed him. Then he ordered his cook to prepare a dish fit for the gods, and he gave the cook the body of Pelops
to use for the meat for the dish. In fear and trembling the cook
obeyed, for he knew that Tantalus would kill him if he disobeyed.
When the dish was prepared, Tantalus took it to Mount Olympus
and presented it to the gods. Zeus was away hunting at that time, but
was expected back that night.

'I bring you a present,' Tantalus said to the gods, 'in thanks for all
your hospitality to me. It is a dish prepared especially for you, but
please save it until Zeus returns and then you may all dine together.'
He placed the dish on the marble table and went back down the
mountain, smiling to himself.

Now it was true that the gods knew everything that ever happened
and they were horrorstruck at the dreadful thing that Tantalus had
done. They also knew that he was trying to trick them. They left the
dish on the table to wait until Zeus returned when he would decide
what to do with his evil son.

Zeus, who in his wisdom knew immediately what had occurred, came back from the hunt early. His anger was terrifying. He hurled thunderbolts about the heavens and split the sky again and again with lightning.

'Tantalus will be punished,' he raged at the other gods, 'you may be sure of that, but first we must bring Pelops back to life.' He called for Clotho, who was one of the Muses and could restore life. She took up the dish and placed its contents in a large bronze cauldron.

'I suppose that no one has eaten of this?' she asked.

'Oh!' said the goddess Demeter in surprise, 'were we not supposed to eat it? I only nibbled a little, but I was so hungry.'

Demeter had just lost her only daughter Persephone to Pluto, the god of the Underworld, and had been quite distracted with grief. Normally she would have known at once what the dish contained, but in her misery had not noticed.

'Well, I shall do what I can,' said Clotho and took the cauldron away with her to a secret place where she chanted incantations and spells over it until Pelops was re-formed and came back to life. Where Demeter had nibbled away at his shoulder Clotho made a new shoulder from ivory, which Pelops in later life showed proudly to anyone who was interested, for, as he would say: 'It is not every mortal who has been nibbled away by a goddess!'

The punishment that Zeus devised for the evil Tantalus was indeed terrible. The wicked king was banished to hell, to the darkest regions of the Underworld. There he was to stay for eternity, standing in a pool of water which reached to his knees. Tormented by thirst, whenever he bent down to drink the water drained away and yet, when he stood up, the water rose again to his knees. Worse even than his thirst was his hunger, and there, dangling in front of him was the branch of a tree, laden with juicy peaches, apples, pears, grapes and olives, all growing from the same branch. The branch seemed just within his grasp and yet, whenever he stretched his hands towards it, it would draw away as if it were alive, until the fruit was a mere fraction beyond his trembling fingertips, so near but never near enough. Above his head was suspended a huge boulder, just on the brink of falling, threatening the terrified king: no matter how many years Tantalus might be there the threat of this heavy rock always hung over him, threatening to fall and crush him. So Tantalus was punished for his crimes — an eternity of yearning, an eternity of hunger and thirst and fear, but what was even worse — an eternity of unfulfilled hope, an eternity of striving and never gaining any peace.

THE TROJAN WARS

This is the story of Paris, the son of the King of Troy, and Helen, the woman he loved so much that he fought a war for her; a war that lasted for many years and finally led to the downfall of one the greatest cities of the ancient world.

King Peleus of Pythia had fallen in love with the goddess Thetis and she had agreed to marry him. Because Thetis was an immortal, all the gods were invited to the wedding feast, all, that is, except one. The uninvited goddess was Eris, the most unpopular of all the goddesses. No one ever invited Eris to any celebrations because she always caused trouble, for Eris was the goddess of discord. In the middle of the feasting and dancing Eris stormed into King Peleus' banqueting hall. She was furious that she had not been asked. She strode up to the top of the table where Zeus, Hera, Pallas Athene and Aphrodite were sitting. Without speaking Eris threw a golden apple onto the table and pointed at Zeus.

'Here is my wedding present to the bride and groom,' she said with a cruel smile, 'and to the guests, both immortal and human.' She then vanished with a clap of thunder.

'How unlike Eris to give anyone a gift,' murmured Hera. 'I wonder what she is up to?'

Zeus picked up the apple and turned it over in his hand. The apple was made of pure gold, and all the guests caught their breath in wonder. They had never seen such a beautiful thing.

'Yes,' said Zeus, 'it is unlike Eris to do anything that does not cause strife and war, and this gift is no exception, see . . .'

He handed the apple to Hera, who read out the words carved round it: 'To be awarded to the fairest of all.'

Immediately there was a hubbub, all the guests craned forward to look at the apple, and above their excited chatter the voices of Hera, Pallas Athene and Aphrodite rose the loudest.

'Well there is no question who should be awarded this apple,' said Hera. 'After all I have always been said to be the most beautiful of all the goddesses.'

'Fashions change, Hera,' retorted Pallas Athene, 'a few years ago golden hair and blue eyes were considered lovely, but you have grown a great deal fatter lately and now people think that tall, dark-haired and slender women are loveliest. I claim the apple.'

'Neither of you deserve it,' chimed in Aphrodite. 'Athene, you are too tall and Hera, you are too old. I am the youngest and fairest of us all. I claim the apple.'

Hera turned to her husband. 'Great Zeus, dearest husband, only you in your wisdom can decide — which of us is the fairest?'

This put Zeus in a quandary. He knew that Hera would give him no peace if he did not choose her and that Athene and Aphrodite would claim that he had only chosen Hera because she was his wife.

'I will not choose,' said Zeus. 'Surely there must be a mortal who can decide for me.'

At this Priam, King of Troy, stood up. 'My son Paris is the handsomest lad in Greece, he is just the person to choose,' he said. 'He is waiting outside.'

Paris was brought into the banqueting chamber. He was a tall, golden-haired young man, with the brightest blue eyes that Aphrodite had ever seen.

'Paris,' said Zeus handing the golden apple to him, 'look well at these three lovely goddesses and tell me which one you think is the fairest.'

First Hera stepped forward.

'If you award the apple to me I will make you the most powerful king the world has ever seen,' she told Paris. 'I am the queen of the immortals and can make your greatest wish come true.'

'I am the wisest of the immortals,' said Athene. 'I can give you wisdom and knowledge greater than any man has ever known. Give the apple to me.'

Then Aphrodite came and stood beside Paris. She placed her little hand on his arm and looked up into his bright blue eyes.

'I am the goddess of love,' she said, 'and if you choose me I promise that the most beautiful woman in the world shall fall in love with you.'

Paris looked at the three goddesses. They were all so lovely, but it was Aphrodite, with her smiling red lips and dancing green eyes, that seemed the most beautiful to him. Falling on one knee he presented the apple to her. Pallas Athene and Hera were furious.

'You will regret this, Paris,' raged Athene. 'Aphrodite may bring you success in love, but you will never have any success in war, Hera and I shall make sure of that!'

'Pooh,' said Aphrodite, 'with the woman you love by your side, what does that matter. Love will triumph over all. You have made the right decision, Paris.'

And she threw the golden apple up and down in the air and caught it in her little rosy hands.

'Where shall I find the woman I am to love?' asked Paris.

'She lives in Sparta,' Aphrodite told him, 'and you will know her the moment you see her. You remember that your father's sister Hesione was stolen away by Hercules many years ago? Why not ask your father to give you a fleet of ships so that you can sail to Greece and bring your aunt back. Greece is only a day's sailing from Sparta and so you may kill two birds with one stone by bringing back Hesione and finding the woman who is destined for you.'

So Paris sailed away across the blue Aegean Sea, down the coast of Greece towards the walled city of Sparta and the woman he was to love.

When he reached Sparta he sent messages to the king to announce his arrival. Menelaus was delighted to welcome him and even sent a troop of horsemen to ride with him from the coast to the city gates. There Menelaus and his wife Helen waited to receive their royal guest.

The moment that Paris set eyes on Helen he knew that this was the woman that Aphrodite had promised to him. It did not matter to Paris that Helen was already married to the King of Sparta. It did not matter to Paris that Menelaus, that very same king, was welcoming him into Sparta. All he could think about was the beauty of Helen's eyes and the way her hair curled softly around her shoulders. His days and nights became full of dreams about the lovely Queen of Sparta.

Helen and Menelaus had a daughter called Hermione and Paris would watch Helen playing with the little girl. He could see that Helen loved her daughter and her husband and although she made Paris welcome she showed no special sign that she was falling in love with him.

Paris prayed to Aphrodite and asked the goddess to honour her promise that he should be loved by the most beautiful woman in the world.

'Be patient, Paris,' the goddess told him. 'In a few weeks Menelaus must go away on a long journey and will be away for a month or more. Then I will make Helen fall in love with you, when it is safe to steal away with her.'

So Paris had to wait patiently. At last, Menelaus left Sparta; he kissed his wife and daughter goodbye and shook hands with Paris.

'Take good care of our guest,' he told Helen, 'treat him royally and see that he lacks nothing.'

Helen kissed her husband and promised to look after Paris.

As soon as Menelaus had left, Aphrodite cast an enchantment on

Helen. The Queen of Sparta suddenly saw the young man in a new light. She fell in love with him and forgot all about her daughter Hermione and her husband Menelaus.

When Paris begged her to flee to Troy with him she agreed and taking no more than she could carry she sailed away in Paris' ship, leaving her kingdom, her crown, her child and her riches behind. She was never to be known as the Queen of Sparta again, just as Helen of Troy, the woman who caused the Trojan Wars because of her beauty.

When Menelaus returned the whole of Sparta was agog with the news. Menelaus was terribly angry. He loved Helen with all his heart and now she had been stolen away from him by a man who he had welcomed and trusted as a guest. He sent soldiers out throughout Greece carrying messages to all the greatest kings and heroes of the land, telling them of the treachery of Paris and asking them for their help and support.

So a huge army gathered. Led by Menelaus and his brother Agamemnon, they prepared to sail for the ancient city of Troy, but before they left Menelaus went to consult the Oracle at Delphi.

People often consulted this miraculous oracle whenever they needed advice or were about to embark on a risky undertaking. Menelaus and Agamemnon made offerings to the gods. Then they asked the oracle what chances of success they had against the Trojans.

The oracle replied, 'Only with the help of Achilles will the Trojans be overthrown.'

This mysterious message pleased Agamemnon and Menelaus very much, for Achilles, one of the great heroes of Greece, had decided to march with them.

'The oracle is never wrong,' said Menelaus. 'We shall conquer and I shall regain my lovely wife. The treacherous Paris will be punished for his wickedness, as will the Trojans who harbour him.'

The great army set off, led by the King of Sparta. They marched to the seashore where they were met by Achilles and Patroclus, both worthy soldiers famed throughout the ancient world. Diomedes and Nestor also joined them, as did Odysseus, the widely travelled and greatly feared King of Ithaca. And so one of the largest armies ever gathered together in Ancient Greece set off across the sea for the city of Troy.

At that time, Troy was the strongest city of the ancient world. Surrounded by towering walls and battlements it guarded the plains and foothills of the peaceful land around it. King Priam was immensely wealthy and the Trojans lived in splendid houses. The Trojan army numbered thousands of men, but they were rarely called on to fight because King Priam preferred peace to war. The Trojans were not pleased that Paris had brought this disaster on them, and they muttered amongst themselves. Paris was hated throughout the city and even though the beauty of Helen was admired, many men thought that even her loveliness was not a good enough reason for war.

The Greek army camped on the plain in front of the walls of Troy. Their tents and campfires were spread across the grass as far as the eye could see, and at the edge of the sea some miles away the masts of the fleet of ships which had brought the soldiers from Greece nodded and swayed as the waves rocked the ships up and down.

For nine long years the siege of Troy continued and in all that time the Greeks could not take the city and the Trojans stood on the battlements and looked down at the army before them. The Greeks raided the cities of the Trojan Plain and it was in one of these raids, on the City of Chryse, that two slaves were taken. They both were beautiful young women; one of them was Chryseis, the daughter of the High Priest of Apollo, and the other was Briseis. These slaves were so beautiful that Agamemnon took Chryseis and Achilles took Briseis and each of the girls was treated with honour and in time came to love their captors.

Now the father of Chryseis was the most powerful priest of Apollo in the land and he grieved for his daughter. He said prayers at the temple of Apollo and asked the god what to do. 'The Greeks worship Apollo as I do,' he thought, 'surely they will return her to me if I ask them in the name of Apollo to do this.'

When the Greek leaders, Menelaus and Agamemnon, heard the old priest's pleas, Agamemnon was angry. He had come to love Chryseis and would not consent to return her. In vain the priest offered a rich ransom for his daughter and in vain he pleaded in the name of Apollo, the god whom they both worshipped. Agamemnon would not give in.

The High Priest returned to his city and prayed once more to Apollo.

'The Greeks have scorned me, even though I asked in your name,' he said. 'Send some sign of your displeasure that will show the Greeks that the gods are not mocked.'

Apollo heard him and sent a terrible plague to the plains of Troy. Only the Greeks were struck down with this and they began to sicken and die. Agamemnon took council with his priests and asked them what to do, for he knew that soon the army would be so weakened that they would have to return to Greece.

'It is the wrath of Apollo,' the priests told him. 'When you refused to return Chryseis to her father you angered the gods. You must now obey the High Priest and give Chryseis back.'

Agamemnon knew that what they said was true, but he loved Chryseis and was loth to part from her.

'If I return Chryseis, I shall do it for the good of the Greek army, and not for myself,' he said. 'What will I be given in return? Surely I am entitled to a further part of the riches that we have taken from the cities of the plain.'

Achilles heard this and became very angry.

'You know full well that the riches we have taken have been shared out among the men long ago. You are not entitled to any-thing further. If you had not been so obstinate before, Apollo would not have been angered,' he shouted at Agamemnon.

At this Agamemnon became angry, too.

'Why should I give up Chryseis while you keep Briseis? I am your commander, I shall take Briseis from you by force and show you who commands here.'

'If you do this, we shall part,' Achilles told Agamemnon. 'I will not fight beside a man I do not trust.' And he turned on his heel and strode back to his tent.

Agamemnon sent Chryseis back to her father and the High Priest prayed again to Apollo, who stopped the terrible plague.

Still Agamemnon's heart burned with anger against Achilles, and he sent his soldiers to Achilles' tent to bring Briseis to him. When Achilles heard what had happened he flung down his sword and gathered his men about him.

'We shall return to our ships,' he told them. 'I will no longer fight for Agamemnon.' And they withdrew to the shore and camped by their ships. Achilles prayed to his mother, the goddess Thetis, and asked her to punish Agamemnon for what he had done. Thetis agreed to avenge her son, although she had to consult with Zeus first, for Zeus had promised to aid the Greeks.

Again the two armies faced each other on the plains of Troy, and this time, Paris, the cause of all the strife, came to the front of the soldiers and hurled abuse at the Greeks. When Menelaus saw Paris his eyes blazed with anger. The Greek king strode to the front of his army and drew his sword.

When Paris saw this his courage failed and he ran back and hid behind the first rank of Trojan soldiers.

'You coward,' his brother Hector shouted at him. 'We are fighting this war because of your deeds, many of our soldiers have been killed and yet you are too afraid to face the man you have wronged.'

At this Paris was ashamed. 'You are right, my brother,' he answered. 'There has been too much bloodshed already. I will offer to fight Menelaus in single combat and the victor shall take Helen and he who loses shall make peace with the other.'

Hector strode forward and conferred with Menelaus. The Greek king agreed and a space was cleared between the two armies where the combat was to take place. The two men stepped forward, each arrayed in his gleaming battle armour. They faced each other and Paris was the first to throw his spear.

It flashed through the air and struck the shield of Menelaus full in the centre. Menelaus staggered, but the spear had not gone through the shield and he was unharmed. Then it was the turn of the Greek king to hurl his spear. As straight as the flight of a hawk it sped towards the shield of Paris, and this spear pierced the shield and wounded Paris in the shouder. Menelaus sprang forward and brought his sword down on the helmet of Paris. The sword shattered but Menelaus would not give up. He took hold of the red plume of horsehair on the crown of Paris' helmet and began to pull Paris towards the Greek ranks. Paris began to choke on the strap of his helmet and would surely have fallen had not the goddess Aphrodite swooped down and carried him away from the scene of the battle back to Troy. Imagine the surprise that Menelaus felt when his foe disappeared. He searched for him among the Trojan ranks, but no one knew where Paris was.

Agamemnon declared that Menelaus was the victor and that Helen should be returned to her husband, and a truce should be arranged. This was agreed, but once again the gods intervened. They were angry that Aphrodite had interfered and were determined that the truce should be broken. Pallas Athene disguised herself as a Trojan soldier and whispered in the ear of Pandarus, the greatest of all the Trojan archers.

'If you kill Menelaus now, you will win great glory, and the favour of all the Trojans.'

Pandarus was swayed by the Athene's words and fitted an arrow to his bow. He drew back the bowstring and let the arrow fly. It was true to its mark and struck Menelaus on his belt. The wound was not fatal but Menelaus fell at the feet of Agamemnon. The Greek soldiers gathered round him and carried him back to his tent on their shields and Agamemnon, full of fury at the treachery of Pandarus in breaking the truce, at once called his men to arms.

'Fight on, noble Greeks,' he commanded. 'The treacherous Trojans have broken the truce. Fight on, fight on to the death.'

For days the battle raged, but neither side could gain a victory. Now Agamemnon greatly missed the strength of his friend Achilles. He remembered that the Oracle at Delphi had said that only with Achilles fighting beside him would Troy be taken and he decided to send a message to Achilles to beg him to join them once more.

The messengers arrived at Achilles' camp.

'Return to the Greek army, Achilles,' they begged, 'Agamemnon will return the beautiful Briseis to you and when Troy is taken you shall have the lion's share of the spoils.'

Achilles would not listen, even though his greatest friend Patroclus, a soldier as valiant as himself, begged him to do so.

'I shall only return to the battle if the Trojans try to burn my ships,' he told the messengers. 'Return to Agamemnon and tell him this.'

The messengers returned and the battle raged on. Patroclus

grieved to see so many Greeks killed and begged Achilles to let him take a troop of men to aid the Greeks.

'Take my armour,' Achilles said, 'and the gods go with you.'

Patroclus donned the armour of Achilles and led his men into the fray. The Trojans were greatly afraid when they saw the battle helmet and breastplate of Achilles, for they did not know that Patroclus and not Achilles was wearing them. Patroclus rushed at Hector, who was leading the Trojans, and drove him back to the very walls of Troy. But at the height of the struggle, Apollo, still angered at the disrespect that the Greeks had shown to him, pulled the helmet from Patroclus' face. When the Trojans saw that it was not Achilles that they were fighting they redoubled their efforts, and Patroclus fell dying at the feet of Hector.

'It is not the Trojans, but the gods who have defeated me,' murmured Patroclus. 'I will be avenged.'

Hector stripped Patroclus of the battle helmet and the breastplate and left his body lying on the battlefield where it was found by the Greeks and taken back to the camp of Achilles.

When Achilles heard of the death of his friend, and was told that his armour had been taken by Hector his anger knew no bounds.

'I will be avenged,' he cried, and prayed to his mother Thetis, who went to Vulcan, the blacksmith of the gods. Vulcan made a golden breastplate and helmet and Thetis took them to her son.

The next morning Achilles led his men into battle. The Trojans fled before him and Achilles drove them back. At last he stood face to face with Hector and they fought hand to hand. Achilles' grief at the death of his friend gave him terrible strength and with one dreadful blow he killed Hector. He commanded that the body of his enemy should be dragged through the Greek camp.

When King Priam of Troy heard of this he sent messengers to Achilles to beg him to return the body of his son and Achilles relented, for Hector had been a brave soldier and had fought fairly. That night the two great soldiers were honoured, Patroclus and Hector, the bravest men of the two armies.

And still the Trojan war continued with neither side winning. The plains of Troy became a burial ground for the brave Greek and Trojan soldiers who had fallen there.

'Will this war never end?' Agamemnon asked his commanders. 'There must be a way to take Troy.'

It was then that Odysseus, the cleverest of all the Greek commanders, spoke up. 'We are equally matched in strength,' he said, 'but I have a cunning plan. We will take the city of Troy by stealth. Once

34

we are inside the walls of the city, the Trojan army will not be able to withstand us. This is what we will do . . .' and he told them his plan.

They would build a huge wooden horse. This horse would be hollow, with enough room inside to hide the commanders of the Greek army. Then they would leave this horse outside the gates of Troy and pretend to leave. The Greek army would pack up their tents and retreat to the ships and sail away; but not back to Greece as the Trojans would think, but only a little way out to sea, out of sight of the watching guards on the walls of Troy. One man only would remain and he would pretend that he had been left behind by accident. He would tell the Trojans that the horse was an offering to the gods, and that if the Trojans dragged it into the city they would never again be attacked by enemies. Once inside, the commanders would leave the wooden horse, open the gates of the city and light a beacon fire to recall the ships.

For the next few days, the Greek encampment echoed to the sound of hammers and saws. The Trojan guard watched from the walls of Troy as a huge horse was constructed. This horse was designed by Epeios, the cleverest of the Greek architects. When the horse was finished on the night of the third day, the Greek commanders crept inside and the Greek soldiers packed up their tents and sailed away, leaving the plain empty and windswept. One man slept by the horse. His name was Sinon, and he was a cousin of Odysseus.

At dawn the next day, the Trojan guards ventured out and came to where the horse stood. They roughly shook Sinon awake.

'What is this?' they demanded. 'Why have the armies left, and what is this great horse?'

Sinon pretended to be surprised.

'Alas,' he said, 'they have left me behind. I surrender to you, I shall tell you whatever you wish to know.'

Sinon was taken to Priam and the horse remained outside the walls in the blazing sun.

Priam questioned Sinon. 'Tell us the meaning of this,' he demanded.

'The Greeks have left,' Sinon said. 'They have given up all hope of conquering Troy. The horse is a gift to the gods; it will protect any city from battle.'

Priam was amazed, but he was a cautious man and he took council with his cleverest advisor Laocoon.

'How do we know that this is not a trick,' Laocoon said, and he thrust a spear into the side of the horse. A booming groaning issued forth from the horse's mouth, and the Trojans trembled in fear. And then the gods intervened for the last time. They, too, were tired of the constant battles and decided that justice must be done. Zeus sent two great serpents from the sea which attacked Laocoon and wrapped their silvery coils round him and strangled him.

'It is a sign,' said King Priam. 'The gods are angry with Laocoon for doubting and turning away the gift the Greeks left. Drag the horse into the city.'

So the wooden horse was dragged into the city and a celebration was held to mark the end of the fighting. Late that same night while the soldiers and people of Troy were asleep, the Greek commanders crept out of the wooden horse and flung open the gates of the city. Sinon had lit the beacon to recall the Greek ships and so the Greek army swarmed into the city and took it.

Menelaus regained his beautiful Helen and forgave her, for he realized that she had been bewitched by Aphrodite. Paris was slain, for no one would defend him. As for the city of Troy, it was razed to the ground, never to be built again. The destruction of this once proud city was so complete that for many years no one knew exactly where Troy had stood. But the tales of the soldiers and kings who fought in the Trojan wars have never been forgotten and are still told today.

PHILEMON AND BAUCIS

The Romans worshipped many gods. Like the Greeks they believed that the gods lived at Olympus, but they called them by different names. The father of the gods, called Zeus by the Greeks, was known as Jupiter to the Romans. Mercury, the Roman messenger of the gods, was known as Hermes to the Greeks. This story tells of two simple peasants and how one day they were visited by the gods.

It was the custom in Roman times to offer hospitality, shelter and food to any passing strangers. Any traveller who found himself away from home at night could be sure of a welcome at any house if he knocked at the door and asked for shelter. And so it was with the gods. They expected the same hospitality when they visited the earth. One day Jupiter and Mercury decided that they would leave the splendid palace at the top of Mount Olympus and come down to earth to mix with mortal men and women. Jupiter, the father of all the gods, liked to make sure that all was well with the men and women he had created. So he and Mercury disguised themselves as men and made their way to Phrygia. Night was falling and so they knocked at the door of the first house they came to. It was a splendid marble house with fountains in the gardens and statues on each side of the door. There was no response to their knock, so they tried again. They knew that there were people in the house, for they could see candles burning at the windows and could hear music coming from the courtyard. Still there was no answer to their knock and as they waited in the gathering darkness they realized that no one was going to let them in.

'Strange,' said Mercury. 'Surely it is the custom of these people to offer shelter for the night. Let us try the next house.'

The next house was much more splendid; there were large gardens, and even a lake. The windows of the house were brightly lit and sounds of revelry and merriment floated up from them. Jupiter knocked loudly at the door and stood back to wait for an answer.

A man poked his head out of an upper window.

'What do you want?' he asked in a surly voice.

'We are strangers to this country,' answered Jupiter pleasantly, 'and we have no lodgings for the night. Will you offer us your hospitality?'

'Be off with you,' shouted the man, banging the wooden shutters, 'we have no room for strangers.'

Jupiter was very angry, but Mercury persuaded him to try again at the next house, but there, much the same thing happened. And so it was with all the splendid houses in the town.

By now Jupiter and Mercury were becoming tired as well as angry. 'We will try once more,' Jupiter told Mercury, 'and if no hospitality is offered to us we will return to Olympus and think how we can punish these selfish humans.'

The last house in the town was very unlike any of the others they had visited. There were no gardens or statues or fountains or lakes, only a bare patch of earth where a goose was pecking at a few grains of corn. The house was wooden and the roof needed mending.

'These people are too poor to offer any hospitality,' said Mercury, 'they have hardly enough for themselves. We shall not find shelter or food here.'

'We shall see,' said Jupiter, and he rapped on the door.

The door was opened almost immediately by an old, but smiling woman.

'Good sirs,' she said, looking up at them, 'pray enter, it is a cold night and you look tired and hungry. We do not have any rich food, but you are welcome to share what we have, and the house is warm and a bed can be found for you.'

Jupiter and Mercury entered the humble cottage and looked around them. An old man sat at a wooden table and a small fire burned brightly in the hearth. He rose and bowed.

'Welcome to our little home.' he said to the two gods, 'A glass of wine will warm you while my wife Baucis prepares food.'

The old woman brought a flagon of wine and four glasses to the table and the gods sat down. The old man poured a glass of wine for each of them and they drank a toast.

'It is a wild night to be in the open,' he said. 'You are very welcome to stay with us.'

'Thank you,' said Jupiter, 'we shall stay, but may I have a little more of this excellent wine?'

'Indeed you may,' said the old man, looking a little worried. 'You may drink as much as we have, but I fear that there is only that flagon left.'

'It is still full,' said Mercury, and to the old man's surprise he saw that it was, even though they had already drunk four glasses from it.

'This is a strange thing,' he said to his wife, 'no matter how much wine I pour from the flagon, it is always full. These strangers must be powerful magicians. Wife, go and kill our goose, for we must prepare a feast for them.'

Baucis curtseyed to Jupiter and Mercury and turned to go out.

'Stay!' commanded Jupiter. 'Your hospitality shall be rewarded. We are not mortals but gods, and we shall provide the feast.'

At once the table was covered with bowls and dishes of meat and fruit. Silver and gold plates shone in the firelight and finest crystal glasses twinkled to the brim with fine wine.

Baucis and her husband Philemon were amazed. They fell to their knees.

'Of all the people in this town you were the only two who offered food and shelter, even though you were the poorest. For this you shall be rewarded and the others shall be punished,' said Jupiter.

From outside the sound of a great tempest rose. Floods washed over the countryside sweeping away all the houses until only the little wooden house of Philemon and Baucis was left, and this Jupiter changed into a beautiful marble temple.

'We will grant any wish you desire,' Jupiter told the old couple.

'We do not need riches,' Philemon told him, 'We only wish to live together in happiness and tend the temple you have created, but there is one wish that you could grant to us — I do not wish to live after Baucis is dead and she does not wish to die after me. May we both die at the same time?'

'It shall be so,' said Jupiter, 'but not for many years yet.'

So for the rest of their lives, Philemon and Baucis lived happily at the temple and when the time came for them to die, they both died at the same instant and Jupiter turned them into two trees, their branches entwined together. And the trees are still there, as is the temple to Jupiter.

DEMETER AND PERSEPHONE

Do you remember the story of Tantalus and how he killed and cooked his own son Pelops? Do you remember that Pelops was brought back to life by Clotho, who made him almost as good as new, except for his shoulder, which had been nibbled by Demeter? This is the story of Demeter and her daughter Persephone, and it explains why Demeter was so upset that she did not notice that the food that Tantalus had brought for the gods was, in fact, his own son Pelops.

Demeter was the goddess of the Earth. It was she who made sure that the corn of the earth grew in abundance. She looked after the fruit and flowers and sent the rain to swell the crops.

Demeter had one beautiful daughter called Persephone, whom she loved more than anything, and when she was not busy with her duties she would talk and sing to her daughter and look after her.

One day Persephone went down to earth to gather some wild flowers for her mother. She was sitting in the grass plaiting columbine and wild hyacinths together to make a necklace when Pluto, the dark god of the Underworld, saw her. Pluto was the loneliest of the gods. It was his duty to guard the souls of the dead. Although he was rich and powerful, his kingdom was dreary and sombre. No sun ever shone there and no laughter rang through the dim halls of his palace. Day in and day out, Pluto would sit on his throne, alone and silent or stride to the gateway of the underworld and stroke the three heads of his watchdog, Cerberus. No one ever came gladly to see him and he had never found a wife. Even when he came up from the underworld to visit the other gods they would shun him and turn away from his grim face. For many years Pluto had been in love with Persephone. He dreamed about her golden hair and laughing eyes, he looked longingly at her slender form and dancing feet. He had even asked Demeter if he might marry her lovely daughter, but Demeter had laughed scornfully and told him that she would never allow her daughter to speak to him, let alone marry him.

From a cave in the hillside Pluto watched Persephone. She was so lovely, so golden and young. He could bear it no longer. He burst from the cave, snatched Persephone up in his arms and fled back to the underworld with her.

That night, when Persephone did not return, Demeter was frantic. She wandered round Olympus asking all the gods if they had seen her daughter, but none of them had. The next morning Demeter began to search all over the earth for her daughter, wandering across Greece and the islands off its coast. She disguised herself as an old woman and asked everyone she met if they had seen a beautiful young maiden with golden hair and shining eyes, but no one could help her. At last Demeter came to Eleusis, a little village about fourteen miles from Athens. There she lived like a beggar, eating nothing but barley meal, water and wild mint. She never smiled, but grieved and mourned ceaselessly for Persephone.

Meanwhile Persephone was living in the dark underworld with Pluto, who had made her his queen. She missed the sunlight and the green grass and many a night she would sob and beg her husband to let her return to Olympus.

'I cannot let you go,' Pluto told her. 'You would never return and I would be alone again,' and he would call Cerberus to play with her, but she would put her hands over her face and weep for her mother.

All the time that Persephone was in the underworld, Demeter neglected her duties. The crops did not grow and the fruit did not ripen on the trees. Zeus saw that a famine was overtaking the land and he sent his messenger, Hermes, to find out where Persephone

was. Hermes searched high and low and could find no trace of Persephone on the earth. He knew that she was not on Olympus and he knew that she was not on earth. That left only one other place — Hades, the kingdom of the dead.

Hermes flew to the entrance of Hades and stroked the head of Cerberus. The dog could not speak, but recognizing that Hermes was a god, let him pass. Inside the entrance of Hades the river of Lethe flowed. It was wide and cold and the only way to the other side was in a little wooden ferryboat which was rowed by Charon, the guardian of the souls who passed over the river of Lethe into the forgetfulness of the underworld.

Charon was a tall and gloomy spirit who never answered any questions. Hermes did not need the ferryboat; he flew over Lethe and into the palace of Pluto. There he saw Persephone.

'You must return with me to Olympus,' Hermes told her. 'Your mother grieves for you so much that she will not tend the earth. Famine is sweeping the land and the corn and barley is dying.'

'But my husband will never let me go,' Persephone replied. 'Only Zeus is powerful enough to make him release me.'

'I shall return to Zeus and tell him where you are,' said Hermes. 'You must stay here for a little while but be sure that you eat nothing that Pluto offers you, particularly the golden pomegranates.'

'It is too late,' she said, 'I have already done so.'

Hermes was horrified. Anyone who had eaten the sacred pomegranates belonged to Pluto for ever.

'How many did you eat?' he asked Persephone.

'Only one, but I was so hungry and thirsty,' she answered.

Hermes sped back to Olympia to tell Zeus that he had found Persephone and what had happened.

Zeus sent for Demeter and told her that her daughter would be returned to her and he ordered Pluto to bring Persephone to the world of the living. Pluto was forced to obey.

'But she is still my wife,' he told Zeus, 'and what is more, she has eaten the sacred pomegranate and belongs to me.'

'But she only ate one, and so she shall only return to you for one third of the year.'

And so it is that for two thirds of the year, Persephone lives with Demeter and her mother is happy and cares for the world. But when the dark months come and Persephone goes to live with her husband, Demeter grieves and pines for her daughter. She allows the crops to die, only reviving them in the spring when Persephone returns again from Hades.

THE TWELVE LABOURS
OF HERCULES

When someone is very strong, he is sometimes described as being like Hercules. He was a great hero who was honoured throughout all of Greece for his exploits of immense strength. This is the story of how he came to be born, and how he came to perform the twelve deeds that he was best known for: The Twelve Labours of Hercules.

Zeus, the king of all the gods, decided that he would like a son who would be a powerful protector of both the gods and the mortals. To achieve this he came down from the lofty Mount Olympus to the city of Thebes and, disguised as Amphitryon, the husband of Alcmene, fathered a son. Alcmene, whose name means woman of might, was herself the daughter of Perseus. On the day that Hercules should have been born, Zeus swore a solemn oath that the descendant of Perseus, about to be born, would one day rule Greece. Unfortunately, his wife Hera, who was a jealous goddess, immediately caused the wife of Sthenelus, himself a son of Perseus, to give birth early to Eurystheus. At the same time she caused the birth of Hercules to be delayed. Having given a solemn oath Zeus was obliged to recognize Eurystheus as ruler of all Greece, and it was this rival who was to impose all the hardest tasks on Hercules throughout his life. Unfortunately, Hera was still not satisfied and sent two serpents to attack the infant Hercules. Hercules was already very strong, and grasping one monster in each hand, wrung their necks.

By the age of eighteen he had been instructed in wisdom, virtue and music, and had developed his strength to such an extent that he was able to kill a ferocious lion that was eating his mortal father's herds.

Shortly afterwards, Hercules defended Thebes against Orchomenus, and although he was successful, Amphitryon, his mortal father, was killed. Creon became king of Orchomenus and gave his daughter Megara to Hercules as a wife. Still Hera had not finished with Hercules and drove him mad. While suffering in this way he mistook his children to be those of his rival Eurystheus (which shows that he was rather jealous too) and massacred both them and their mother. He fled the country, and consulted the Oracle of Delphi to find out how to remove the stain of his crime. Unfortunately for Hercules, the oracle told him to go to Eurystheus and labour for him for twelve years. Hence the Twelve Labours of Hercules.

Hercules' first labour was to kill the Nemean Lion and bring the skin back to Eurystheus. First of all Hercules tried with arrows, but nothing would pierce the skin of the beast. So eventually he had to fight with his hands and finally strangled it. Hercules, however, did not give the skin to Eurystheus. He kept it for himself and made a garment of it, which made him invincible. Although the reactions of Eurystheus to this theft are lost in the mists of time, one can only assume that Hercules' garment protected him from his anger, since he was soon to embark on his next labour.

In a marsh near Lerna lived a hideous monster called the Learnaean Hydra. This enormous serpent had nine heads, and only left the marsh to eat the herds and crops. The breath of this monster was so poisonous that anybody it breathed on died.

Accompanied by his nephew, Hercules drove the monster from the marshes by using flaming arrows, and attacked it with his massive club. Unfortunately, the hydra exhibited the unnerving habit (apparently quite common to hydra) of growing two heads back in place of each one that was chopped off. Hercules told his nephew to set the neighbouring forest on fire and with the help of red hot brands burnt the serpent's heads. Hercules cut off the last head and buried it. He then dipped his arrows in the blood of the hydra, which made them deadly.

Hercules' next labour was to rid the territory of Psophis from the Wild Boar of Erymanthus. The beast devastated the land until Hercules managed to capture it and took it back to Eurystheus. Eurystheus, although he was very powerful seems to have lacked courage, since as soon as he saw the terrifying beast he was so frightened that he ran away and hid in a bronze jar. An addition to this story is that while on the way to capture the beast, Hercules was entertained by the Centaur Pholus, who opened a barrel of special wine. When the other centaurs smelt this wine, they attacked the house of Pholus. They were, however, no match for Hercules and his poisoned arrows and many were destroyed.

Eurystheus then sent Hercules to rid the marshes of Stymphalus of the terrible birds whose beaks, wings and claws were made of iron. There were so many of these birds that when they flew the light of the sun was blotted out. Their most unattractive feature was that they fed on human flesh, and obviously Eurystheus was hoping that they would eat Hercules. He was out of luck again, as Hercules, protected by his clothing made from the skin of the Nemean Lion, frightened the birds with great cymbals made of bronze, and then destroyed them with his poisoned arrows.

Eurystheus then decided on a change in campaign. If Hercules could not be destroyed, perhaps he could be set a task that was so impossible that he would fail. He therefore sent Hercules to bring back alive the hind who lived on Mount Ceryneia. Her main attractions were that she had hooves of bronze, and horns of gold. Hercules almost failed in this, since she was very swift and must not be killed. Sustained by his great strength he chased her for a year before he caught her on the banks of the river Ladon.

The next labour that Hercules performed is perhaps the best known — the cleansing of the stables of Augeias. He was the King of Elis and he owned many herds of cattle including twelve white bulls, sacred to Helios. One bull was called Phaethon and he shone like a star. These magnificent animals had, however, to live in a stable that was heaped with the manure of many years. Hercules promised to clean the stables in one day provided that Augeias would give him one tenth of the herd. When Augeias agreed, Hercules made holes in the walls of the building and diverted the rivers Alpheus and Peneius so that they rushed through the stables. Augeias was not a man of honour, and when the job was done, he went back on his bargain, giving as a reason the fact that Hercules was working for Eurystheus. Hercules was in his own way as unforgiving as Hera and eventually made Augeias pay for this dishonesty.

Hercules was on the island of Crete when the king, Minos, asked him to capture a bull which was terrorising the country. This bull had been given to Minos by Poseidon so that he could sacrifice it to him. Minos was too impressed with the bull and didn't sacrifice it, so Poseidon drove it mad. Hercules captured the bull and carried it on his back, as he was so strong, across the sea to Argolis.

In Thrace at this time lived Diomedes, King of the Bistones. He owned mares that he fed on human flesh. Together with a few volunteers, Hercules captured the mares, having killed their keepers. There was a fierce battle, but eventually the Bistones were defeated and, in a very bloodthirsty fashion, Diomedes was given to his own mares to eat. At the same time, as is generally believed, Hercules saved Alcestis from death. Admetus, her husband, had obtained from the Fates an undertaking that he would not die if some one would consent to die in his place. Hercules was passing by when he saw the unfortunate Alcestis about to be buried. He rescued her from death by defeating Thanatos, death itself, in a fierce struggle and so restored Alcestis to her husband.

Admete, daughter of Eurystheus, very much wanted to have the Girdle of Hippolyte, the Queen of the Amazons, for her very own. To this end Hercules was sent to fetch it. He set off with a number of other famous heroes and had a rather eventful journey, fighting the sons of Minos, and helping King Lycus to conquer the Bebryces. Eventually he reached the country of the Amazons, and at first it appeared that he would have no difficulty, as Hippolyte agreed to give him the girdle, even though it was the mark of her sovereignty.

However, Hera again decided to put a spoke in Hercules' wheel. She disguised herself as an Amazon and spread the rumour that Hercules was going to abduct Hippolyte. The Amazons attacked Hercules, and believing that they had betrayed him, he slaughtered them and their queen, and took the girdle.

Geryon was a triple headed monster who owned a herd of red oxen which were guarded by the herdsman Eurytion and the dog Orthrus. Eurystheus commanded Hercules to capture these oxen, which he did, having first killed Eurytion, Orthrus and eventually Geryon. Unfortunately the journey back was full of danger. Firstly Hercules had to kill the sons of Poseidon, who tried to steal the oxen and then he had to wrestle with Eryx, the king of the Elymans, to obtain the release of one of the oxen who had escaped and been put in the stables of Eryx. While in the hills of Thrace, Hera sent a gad-fly to frighten the oxen and it was only with great difficulty that Hercules managed to herd them together. When he finally brought them to Eurystheus, the king sacrificed them to Hera.

Never one to give up, Eurystheus commanded Hercules to bring back the golden apples that the Hesperides, daughters of Atlas and Hesperus, guarded in their garden on the western edges of the world. To obtain information on how to reach the garden Hercules was lucky enough to capture the prophetic god Nereus, who told him how to reach it.

While crossing Libya, Hercules had to fight with Antaeus, who was the son of Gaea, Mother Earth. He was an enormous bandit who forced all travellers to fight with him. He had the useful power of being able to regain his strength by simply touching the ground with his feet. To overcome this Hercules held him up in the air with his arms and choked him.

Next, Hercules was attacked by the Pygmies. He overcame them by sewing them up in his lion skin.

In Egypt at that time the king was Busiris, who sacrificed a foreigner every year to put an end to a terrible famine. Hercules was unlucky enough to be selected as that year's victim and put in chains and taken to the temple. With his great strength he burst the chains, and slew Busiris and his son.

Continuing on his journey across Ethiopia he killed Emathion and replaced him with Memnon. The Sun gave him a golden boat which shone almost as brightly as the sun, and this he used to cross the sea, and finally arrived at the garden of the Hesperides. This garden was well guarded by the dragon Ladon. He killed this dragon and entered the garden. He persuaded Atlas, whose duty it was to hold the world up, to pick up the apples while he, Hercules, held the world on his shoulders.

When Atlas returned with the apples he was unwilling to take up his burden again and Hercules realized that unless he was careful he would be left with it. Therefore he pretended to agree that he would now perform this duty, but that to make himself more comfortable, he would need to rearrange his lion skin so that his shoulders would be protected. To this end he persuaded Atlas to again support the world while he adjusted the skin. However, as soon as Atlas did this Hercules scooped up the apples and ran away. This was perhaps rather dishonest, but totally understandable.

Finally, Eurystheus, feeling that he would never get the better of Hercules sent him off to fetch the guardian of the infernal gates of Hades, Cerberus. Firstly Hercules went to Eleusis, the most holy place in all Greece. Here he was initiated into the infernal mysteries. Guided by Hermes he took the passage which descends from Cape Taenarum through the earth to the underworld.

Eventually he came upon Theseus and Peirithous, who had unwisely ventured into the underworld. They implored Hercules to help them, which he attempted to do. Unfortunately a massive earthquake stopped him from rescuing Peirithous. Hercules had a busy time in Hades as the legends say that he removed the boulder that was crushing Ascalaphus, overthrew Menoetes, the herdsman of Hades and even wounded Hades himself. Hades agreed to allow Hercules to take the monster Cerberus, provided he could conquer him using only his bare hands. Such was Hercules' strength that this was accomplished and he dragged the animal back to show Eurystheus, who doubtless again hid himself in his bronze pot. Hercules then released the beast and sent it back to Hades.

So at last Hercules was freed, but do not think that he settled down and lived out his remaining years in peace and quiet. He had many more adventures while he lived and his death was the strangest of them all. He had put on a tunic which his new earthly wife sent him. It was soaked in the blood of a centaur that he had killed. She believed that it would ensure his lasting devotion, but it was an act of revenge on the part of the centaur. Hercules was devoured by inner pain, and pulling up trees he made his own funeral pyre. After some difficulty he persuaded Peoas to set light to the pyre and was rewarded with Hercules' bow and arrows. The flames crackled and burned but when they reached his body there was a tremendous crash of thunder and lightning and the son of Zeus disappeared from men's eyes. He was admitted to Olympus and was so reconciled with Hera that he married her daughter Hebe and thereafter lived the magnificent and blissful life of the gods.

ROMULUS AND REMUS

It was dark and windy that night; the River Tiber rushed down from the hills, swollen and dark with soil and mud from the mountains. A slender figure, buffeted by the wind, clambered down towards the banks of the river, clutching in her arms a wriggling bundle. Above the howl of the wind and the thunder of the river a cry could be heard, then another — two tiny voices raised in protest against the cold and the dark. Sobbing, the woman knelt down and gently placed the two babies in a crudely hollowed-out log boat, hardly bigger than the babes. Her tears fell on their faces. She tucked the bundle of shawls tightly round the children and then, with a sudden push, the little boat swirled out into the mainstream of the swiftly flowing river, spinning and turning until it was swallowed up by the darkness; and still above the roar of the wind and the water could be heard the cries of the two infants until that sound, too, faded away into the night.

Who was this woman who could condemn her babies to such a terrible death? What kind of mother could abandon her children to the cruel waters of the Tiber?

Rhea Silvia was no monster. She had been forced to do this dreadful thing. Even the waters of the flooded Tiber were better than the fate that would have befallen her children had they not been cast away in that frail little boat. Only two weeks before, when the twins had been born, their mother had known that their lives would be threatened; for Rhea Silvia was a royal princess, the daughter of the once proud King of Alba Longa. Her father, Numitor, had been stripped of his crown by his own son and Rhea had been impelled to become a Vestal Virgin, one of the priestesses of the temple of Vesta who were forbidden ever to marry. Amulius, her own brother, had urged upon her to abandon her father, to leave public life and join the silent throng of maidens condemned forever to live in the cold marble temple.

Amulius was cruel and ambitious. He knew that because he had taken the throne of Alba Longa by force, the people of that sunny land did not want him to be their king. They loved old Numitor, who had ruled them well, and they resented the usurper-son. He knew that the only way he could keep the power he had snatched from his father was by force, and he also knew that if ever his sister should marry, her children would have a better claim to the throne of Alba

Longa. For this reason he hid Rhea Silvia in the temple and imprisoned his father in a remote villa far away from his court.

And now Rhea Silvia had given birth to twin boys! Amulius was terribly angry. Not only had Rhea defied him, but she claimed that the father of her twin boys was none other than the great god Mars himself. Amulius felt threatened and frightened.

The very evening of the twins' birth Amulius had stormed into the temple of Vesta with two guards. He had dragged his sister out while the two guards carried the crying babies.

'I shall put the babies to the sword,' he told the weeping Rhea. 'They must die, they are too dangerous to me. If I let them live they may grow up to rise against me as I rose against my father.'

In vain had Rhea begged for the lives of her babies, but the only promise she could wring out of her brother was that she herself must destroy the children. That was why she had crept out at dead of night and placed the children in the little wooden boat and sent them swirling away down-river.

'Perhaps someone will see them and save them,' she thought. 'Perhaps the gods will watch over them and guard them — anything is better than a cruel death by the sword.'

So Rhea stood sobbing on the banks of the Tiber while her twin babies were carried away on the foaming waters.

The boat floated on for the rest of the night, the wild spray splashing the twins and the waves tossing the boat to and fro. Then, as dawn filled the sky a sudden eddy caught the boat and pushed it into a little creek. There it came to rest at the foot of a huge fig tree. Perhaps the gods had been watching over the babes, for this fig tree was sacred to them, and now the boat rested safely among its gnarled roots.

The babies were hungry and thirsty and their crying grew louder, so loud that it could be heard deep in the nearby wood.

A great grey she-wolf heard the cries and lifted her pointed muzzle towards the sound. Rising to her feet she loped through the wood towards the fig tree. The she-wolf had given birth to cubs the week before, but hunters had killed them. The cries of the twin babies reminded her of the mewing sounds that her little cubs had made and she padded forward to find out what was making the noise. When she reached the boat she stretched out her neck and pushed aside the shawls with her nose. The twins redoubled their screams. They were not afraid of the wolf, for they were too young to know that wolves were to be feared, but they knew that they were hungry and cold. The wolf looked down at the two tiny children

because she was hungry and still grieving for her lost cubs. She sniffed cautiously at the twins and then did a surprising thing. Instead of devouring the babies she gently picked them up in her mouth and carried them back to her den, and there she suckled them and cared for them.

The years passed and the twins began to grow up. At first they ran about on all fours like little wolf cubs, but they soon learned that their legs were too long and their arms too short to be comfortable like this and they began to walk like normal children. Gradually and with difficulty they learned to speak by listening to the shepherds and farmers who lived around the forest, but although they watched and listened they never showed themselves, hiding in the undergrowth and ferns like young wild animals.

As they grew taller and stronger they became bolder. Their wolf-mother had taught them how to hunt and they knew the lore of the forest better than any ordinary child could. At first they had thought that they were wolves, but they noticed that they were more like the shepherds that they watched in the meadows. They still loved their wolf-mother dearly, but now they stood taller than she and could do things that no wolf could.

Before they had reached their teens they were fearless and strong, and nothing frightened them. They had learned all that their wolf-mother could teach them and they decided that it was time to go out into the wide world. They came down from the woods to the surrounding villages and there they met a herdsman and his wife. Faustulus and Acca Larentia had never had any children and they welcomed the two boys into their home. They named them Romulus and Remus and loved them as if they were their own sons.

So Romulus and Remus grew up, and in time began to forget that the first mother they had known had been a great she-wolf.

Acca Larentia became mother to them and Faustulus became their father. They were sent to school as were all the young men of the village and there they learned about the history of the country where they lived. They heard about the cruel King Amulius, who ruled their land, and they learned that all who disobeyed him were punished by his troops.

Because the boys were so brave they soon became the leaders of all the youths of the district. Little knowing that Amulius, King of Alba Longa, was really their uncle they banded together with other young men to fight against his tyranny. Amulius soon heard of Romulus and Remus and sent an army against them. It was then, in the fields and valleys beside the wood where they had grown up, that Romulus and Remus fought with the King's troops and defeated them. Amulius was overthrown and Romulus and Remus released old Numitor and restored him to power.

As soon as Numitor met the twins he realized that they looked strangely like his daughter Rhea Silvia; he called her to him in secret and showed her the two young men and asked her if she noticed the resemblance. At last Rhea could tell her father of the secret that she had carried in her heart for all these years. She told him the story of how she had cast her twin babies away on that dreadful night twenty years before.

Inquiries were made and when it was discovered that Faustulus and his wife were only foster-parents to the twins, Numitor himself asked the twins what they could remember of their babyhood.

'I remember the forest and the valleys,' said Romulus.

'I sometimes dream of a dark cave . . .' said Remus.

'We often had nightmares about stormy rivers and rushing water,' said Romulus. 'Even now we do not really like the river when it is in flood . . .' and then it all came back to them.

'I remember a great grey she-wolf,' said Romulus. 'She was taller than we were, and she taught us to hunt and prowl through the darkness . . .'

They pieced the puzzle together and realized that they were indeed the grandsons of Numitor, saved from death by a she-wolf.

Numitor was delighted and took them to the temple of Vesta where they met their real mother.

'These are indeed your sons,' said Numitor. 'You little thought that you would ever see them again and now they have restored me to power and overthrown the very man who first threatened their lives.'

Romulus and Remus became the king's most trusted friends. They built a great city which spread across the seven hills and valleys beside the wood where they had grown up.

When they began to build the city the brothers could not decide what it was to be named. They resolved that they would each climb to the top of a hill and the one who saw the most birds would name the city. Romulus saw a flock of twelve birds and his brother saw only six, so the city was named after Romulus and was to become the greatest of all the cities of the ancient world. Romulus and Remus governed the city together, but as so often happens, they became jealous of each other and began to quarrel. Romulus believed that Rome could be made safer by building a wall around it but Remus disagreed.

'The power of Rome and its reputation is enough to guard the city,' he told his brother. 'You will only waste time and money by building such a wall.'

Romulus would not listen and one summer, while his brother was away, he ordered the wall to be built. When Remus returned he laughed at Romulus.

'This is a puny wall,' he sneered, 'it would not keep out a flock of sheep,' and to prove his point he leaped over the wall with one bound.

Romulus was so angry that he completely lost his temper. He drew his sword and killed his twin brother.

'Thus perish any other who leaps over my walls,' he proclaimed, but he also ordered the walls to be built higher.

Romulus grieved greatly that he had killed Remus in a fit of temper and resolved never to draw his sword in anger again. He welcomed strangers to Rome and encouraged people from foreign lands to come and live there. Rome prospered and became rich and powerful. So many men and soldiers came to live there that soon there were too few women and it became very difficult to find a wife.

Romulus thought of a plan. The neighbouring people were the Sabines and the Sabine women were said to be the most beautiful of all the women in Italy. The Sabine men guarded their women jealously and would not allow them to meet the Romans. Romulus declared that he would hold a fantastic festival and that all should be invited. Rome was famous for its festivals and the Sabine men relented and agreed to attend. They came in their hundreds, bringing their wives and daughters with them.

The festival was truly magnificent. Thousands of oxen and sheep were roasted over open fires, enormous pies and loaves were baked, hundreds of vats of wine were made, grapes and figs and peaches from the surrounding countryside were brought into Rome and the whole city was decorated with branches of sweet-smelling myrtle and laurel. Silken banners hung from the houses and the trees, and at night flaming torches made the darkness seem like noonday. Plays and concerts were performed, and magnificent games were held in the amphitheatres and squares where gladiators fought with wild animals, and contests of swordmanship and archery entertained the crowds for hours.

For seven days the Romans and the Sabines feasted. As you can imagine a great deal of wine was imbibed and soon many of the Sabine men became very drunk. On the last night they started to fall asleep, exhausted by the wine and the merriment; even a splendid display of fireworks failed to rouse them and so, when they were sure that the Sabines could not stop them, the Roman men kidnapped the Sabine women and hid them away.

When the Sabine men awoke they discovered that their womenfolk were missing. They searched for them for days and when at last they found them, most of the women said that they would rather stay in Rome. The Sabine men were forced to make a pact with the Romans and their King, Titus Tatius, became joint ruler with Romulus.

Still Rome prospered and grew. The first wooden houses were pulled down and marble and stone villas were built. The city spread all over the seven hills and even as far as the wood where Romulus and Remus had grown up. This part of Rome became known as the Lupercal, which means 'wolf's den' in Latin. Romulus gave offerings to the gods at the foot of the fig tree where he and his brother had been cast up in their little wooden boat; the fig tree remained but now it was surrounded by a vast marble temple and standing by the altar was a bronze statue of a she-wolf suckling two baby boys. A statue like this can still be seen in Rome today.

54

The years passed and Titus Tatius died, leaving Romulus to be the sole ruler of the mighty city. Romulus ruled wisely and well, always taking care that his laws were just and that everyone was treated fairly. He was loved by the Romans and when one day he disappeared his people were greatly grieved. He never appeared again and his body was never found; because of this no-one ever knew what had happened to him and the Romans began to say that the gods must have taken him to live with them. They remembered that Romulus and his twin were said to have been the sons of Rhea Silvia and the great God Mars and so they made Romulus into a god. They called him Quirinus and worshipped him as the founder of their city. One of the seven hills of Rome was named after him and a great festival was held each year where sacrifices were dedicated to the man who had made the city of Rome so powerful.

TARQUIN

For many years Rome had been ruled fairly and by laws that made each Roman citizen free and unfettered. And then came the reign of Tarquin. Tarquin the Tyrant was a man who saw Rome as his plaything and the people of Rome as his slaves. True, the people of Rome had elected Tarquin themselves, but this was a costly mistake. Soon all those who opposed the rule of this haughty man found themselves imprisoned. Their goods and chattels, houses and servants were taken from them and brought to swell the wealth of Tarquin.

The Senate, the ruling body of Rome, which once had the power to overthrow any tyrant, was weakened. Tarquin murdered or deposed any senators who opposed him and put in their place his chosen friends who he knew would obey him without question. No longer were the streets of Rome filled with merriment. At night the Romans hid in their houses afraid to venture out into the streets for fear of the roving bands of soldiers paid by Tarquin.

Not only did Tarquin rule Rome with an iron fist, he was also the ruler of all the Roman states. Before many years he had subdued all the rebel kings of the surrounding lands and made their kingdoms into slave states answerable only to him. All that is except for one. This was the state of Aricia, governed by Turnus Herdonius. This king would not give it to the Roman dictator and refused to pay the taxes that cruelly impoverished the other states.

Tarquin heard about this and laid a plan. He called a meeting at a temple to the goddess Ferentia, where he was to meet with the other princes of the region. When they were all assembled Tarquin was nowhere to be seen. Turnus saw his advantage and began to address the other princes.

'We have suffered greatly from the tyranny of this Roman Tarquin,' he told them. 'We always give in because while we are stronger than Tarquin and his armies when we are all together, while we are separate we cannot defeat him. Why do we not join together and free ourselves from his cruel enslavement?'

As Turnus spoke he saw the expressions on the princes' faces change and turning round, he discovered that Tarquin was standing behind him. Furious that he had been tricked into showing his hand Turnus left the meeting.

Tarquin called another meeting for the following day. There he bullied the other princes into attacking Aricia, and Turnus was assassinated, leaving Tarquin in full control. So once again, Tarquin was sole controller of all the Roman states.

The years passed and the people of Gabia decided that they had had enough of the cruel taxes that they were forced to pay. They rebelled and refused to pay any more taxes. Tarquin sent a great army against them, but he did not succeed in conquering them, for Gabia was surrounded by a high and impregnable wall and no one could breach it. After the battle a badly wounded man staggered to the gates of Gabia and begged to be let in. The commander of the Gabian army recognized him as Sextus, the son of the King of Rome. Sextus seemed to have been terribly tortured.

The prince of the Gabians took him in and cared for him. Sextus insinuated himself into the king's favour and soon the king ordered all his soldiers to obey Sextus. In reality Sextus was a spy for Tarquin and when he had gained the trust of the Gabians, he betrayed

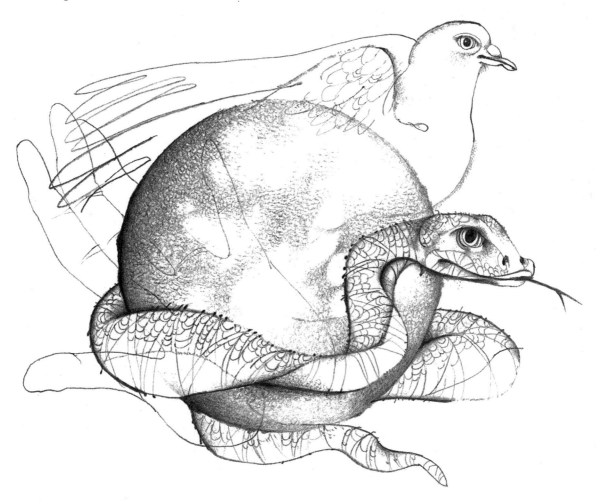

them. Having gained the confidence of the prince, he ruled in his absence and beheaded the best advisors and commanders. When the prince returned, Sextus pretended that he had uncovered a plot against the prince. Gradually Sextus took control of Gabia and delivered it into his father's hands and so Tarquin's rule continued.

In Rome, Tarquin began to build a great temple to the god Jupiter. Men were brought from all over the Latin States to work on this temple, and if they would not come willingly they were dragged there in chains and forced to work as slaves.

One day the skull of a man was found in the earth while the foundations of this temple were being constructed. Tarquin let it be known that this skull was the head of an ancient soothsayer and that the ruler of land on which it was found would rule the world. From that day to this the hill on which the temple was built was called the Capitol, which means 'the head' in Latin.

Until now, the people of Rome had believed that the reason that Tarquin had never been overthrown was that he was favoured by the gods, but now sombre omens began to occur. A great plague swept through Rome and Tarquin, fearing that this was a sign from the gods that he had angered them went to consult the Oracle at Delphi. He took with him his three sons, Titus, Arruns and Sextus (the man who had betrayed the Gabians and had received their kingdom in exchange). He also took his nephew, Lucius Junus. This nephew knew how much his cousins hated him and how jealous his uncle was of anyone who threatened him, so he had pretended to be stupid. He had been so successful at this that his nickname was Brutus the Dunce. Tarquin consulted the oracle and asked who would rule after him. The oracle replied:

'Whichever man first kisses his mother will be the power in Rome.'

The three sons of Tarquin took this to mean their mortal mother and hastened back to Rome, but Brutus pretended to trip and fall and while he was on the ground he pressed his lips to the earth, the mother earth that all Romans worshipped. So it was Brutus who became the ruler of Rome after Tarquin.

It was the treachery of Sextus that brought about the downfall of Tarquin and his sons. One day, while Tarquin, Sextus, Titus and Arruns were resting in their tent during a battle campaign against the Ardians, they fell to talking about the beauty of their wives. Collatinus, one of the most loyal of Tarquin's commanders, told them of the beauty of his wife Lucrecia. This so fired the imagination of Sextus that he sought out Lucrecia and carried her off by force, not caring that Collatinus had fought bravely and well for him

and his father. Lucrecia escaped and told Collatinus what had happened and then, overcome with the shame and disgrace, stabbed herself. At this Collatinus swore revenge against Sextus and his father. Brutus, hearing this, revealed what had occurred at the Oracle of Delphi.

'If Tarquin is overthrown, I shall be the next ruler of Rome,' he told Collatinus, 'I and shall rule fairly and well.'

Brutus and Collatinus returned to Rome and told the citizens what had happened. The Romans, angered at Sextus' treachery and tired of the tyranny of Tarquin, hailed Brutus as their new ruler. And so, when Tarquin returned to the city he found the gates of Rome barred against him. For the first time, all the people of Rome joined together and Tarquin and his sons were driven out into Etruria. Sextus was sent to Gabia where the Gabians executed him.

So ended the rule of Tarquin the Tyrant and for the first time for many years the Romans knew what it was to be free.

HOW THE WORLD WAS MADE

This is the story of how the world was made. It is a German story and has been told to German children for centuries.

Before the earth was born the universe was dark and terrible. It consisted of one huge, deep, steep-sided valley — an enormous ravine called Ginnungagap. There was only one spirit in the universe and that was Fimbultyr, who had never been born and would never die. Fimbultyr divided Ginnungagap into two halves. The northernmost half he called Niflheim and the southern half Muspelheim. Niflheim was cold and foggy, great cliffs of ice fell steeply down to where the river Hvergelmir burst out of the ice and flowed in twelve separate icy streams along Ginnungagap.

Muspelheim was as hot as Niflheim was cold. Sheets of flame flared upwards and the rocks melted in the heat. In the kingdom of Muspelheim lived the god of that place, Surtur. He was the only one capable of bearing the heat and fire of that blazing furnace. He would sit on a rock and watch the tongues of fire streaming away towards Niflheim.

Where the fire and the icy water met, a huge cloud of steam rose up and it was out of this steam that Ymir was born. He was a terrifying giant whose groans echoed up and down Ginnungagap. An enormous cow was also born from the steam. She was called Audhumbla and fed Ymir with her milk. Some time later, while Ymir was sleeping two giant children appeared from his arms. From the left arm sprang a boy and from the right arm, a girl. The children and grandchildren of these giants became a race of people called the Hrimthurses, dark, moody giants who inhabited Niflheim.

Later still, the great Audhumbla freed another god from one of the blocks of ice in that cold and desolate place. This god was Bure, and his son Bor had three further sons, Wotan, Hoenir and Loki. Wotan became the father of all the gods. After Wotan, Hoenir and Loki were born there were two races of gods and they fought over who should reign. Battle raged over Ginnungagap and finally the gigantic Ymir was slain. His wounds poured with rivers of blood and from these were born the children and grandchildren of Ymir. Wotan, Hoenir and Loki made the body of Ymir into the earth. They took his skull and made it into the heavens and placed a dwarf at each corner to guard it. The dwarf of the north was called Norder, the dwarf of the south was called Suder. The dwarf of the west was called Wester and the dwarf of the east was called Oster. The three gods then sprinkled the heavens with sparks from Muspelheim and made the stars. Now they could tell day from night and so the days, weeks, months and years were created.

The earth they called Midgard, but it was a dreadful place with great seas of blood from Ymir's wounds and although trees and grass grew there, there were no men. The three gods then created a man and a woman from two trees that grew along one of the beaches. Wotan turned them into humans and blew life into them, Hoenir gave them their sense and reason, and Loki gave them their shape, hearing, sight and speech. The man was called Ask and the woman was called Embla and from these two the whole German people are descended. Wotan took Ask and Embla and showed them Midgard. 'This is your land,' he told them. 'Here you will lack for nothing, you will find all you need to eat and drink, be happy and prosper.'

The centuries passed and the children of Ask and Embla multiplied throughout the land of Midgard. The gods, too, had married, and Wotan, the father of them all, had taken Freyja, the daughter of the god Fjyorgynn as a wife. Freyja and Wotan had many children and their first-born son Thor ruled as king. The gods dwelt in Asgard at the centre of the universe in a magnificent palace called Valhalla.

Wotan looked down on the earth; it had changed greatly since he and his brothers had made it. The seas were now clear, the land was rich and the children, grandchildren, great-grandchildren and great-great-grandchildren of Ask and Embla looked after it faithfully.

'These humans that we have created have done well,' he told the other gods. 'I should like to build a bridge between Asgard and Midgard. Some of the humans are as courageous as gods, they fight bravely. When they fall in battle the Valkyries shall bring them to Asgard where the earth's heroes can share Valhalla with us.'

The Valkyries were a race of warrior maidens who lived with the gods. They rode magnificent horses which could fly through the air. They wore silver armour and watched over the soldiers of Midgard.

All the gods agreed and a great arching bridge was created that stretched from Asgard to Midgard. It was called the Bifrost and shimmered with colour. Only on certain days could it be seen, and then only when the Valkyrie maidens were carrying one of the heroes of Midgard to an eternal life in Valhalla.

Now that Asgard and Midgard were joined, a grave problem arose. There were races of giants living on the earth and they were jealous of the gods.

'If men can reach Asgard by climbing the Bifrost bridge, then the giants will try to invade Valhalla,' Wotan decided. 'We shall build a fortress at the foot of the bridge and Heimdall, our most faithful son, shall guard it.'

The fortress was called Himinbjorg and faithful Heimdall never slept. If danger approached he would summon the gods by blowing a golden trumpet that made the heavens shake and the stars shiver.

Wotan also protected the earth. He planted a giant ash tree called Yggdrasil, which was so enormous that the tips of its branches touched the top of the sky. Its trunk stretched through the heavens and its roots plunged deep into the earth. There were three roots. Underneath the first was Midgard, the land given to men by Wotan. Under the second root was Nastrand, the gloomy kingdom ruled by the dragon Nidhogg. He guarded the souls of men and women who had died — all except the souls of the heroes who had been taken to Valhalla by the Valkyries. Under the third root lived the giants.

Three rivers flowed under Yggdrasil, and close to the second river lived three maidens, Urd, Verdandi and Skuld. These maidens held the key to the future. They tended the tree of the world and watered it, for they knew that the safety of the world depended upon it. And since they were also the controllers of destiny they knew full well how important their task was. Their greatest enemy was Nidhogg the dragon, who continually gnawed at the roots of Yggdrasil, hoping to kill the life-giving tree and claim the souls of all the men and women who lived under its protection. From the third root flowed the river Mimir, which protected all the wisdom and knowledge of the world.

In the topmost branches of Yggdrasil lived a gigantic eagle, the deadly enemy of the dragon Nidhogg, watching with sharp eyes for any chance to kill the cruel guardian of Nastrand. And in the trunk of the mighty ash tree lived Ratasok the squirrel. This sly creature told Nidhogg everything that the eagle said and reported all Nidhogg's words to the eagle. As he ran up and down the trunk of Yggdrasil he stirred up rumours and trouble and kept the earth in turmoil.

The giants and Nidhogg hated the gods with a consuming and terrible hatred. They continually plotted to overthrow Asgard and would do anything they could to harm Wotan and his family. In the dark and sombre kingdom of Nastrand, as well as Nidhogg, lived three other monsters: Fenrir, who was an enormous wolf, Midgard the serpent and Hel, the goddess of death. These monsters were the children of Loki, the brother of Wotan, and Angrboda, one of the giantesses. They had been raised by their mother and her gigantic

64

family and from the day they were born they had been taught to hate the gods of Asgard. Loki, who knew how awful his children were, tried to keep them a secret from his brother, but while they were still young, Wotan found out about the serpent Midgard. Realizing that such a creature was dangerous to Asgard he took the serpent up to Asgard and threw him down as hard as he could into the sea. What Wotan did not know was that the serpent, Midgard, like all Loki's children, was half a god and could not be killed so easily. Instead of being destroyed, the serpent grew and grew until it circled the earth and began to squeeze tighter and tighter. It was so huge that when it was irritated it would lash its tail and cause storms and whirlpools. At last it grew so large that all feared it, and only Thor, the eldest son of Wotan and Freyja, was brave enough to be able to calm it. From that day to this the serpent Midgard twines round the earth, controlled only by the strength of Thor.

Fenrir, too, was growing as fast as his terrible brother. When he opened his mouth his jaws spanned the heavens. Naturally the gods found out about Fenrir and realized that he must be controlled, but who could govern such a creature? Even his giantess mother was afraid of him and no one but Thor dared to try to capture him.

Wotan called a meeting of all the gods. Everyone came except Loki, who hid in Nidhogg's kingdom.

'What are we to do?' Wotan asked the gods. 'This mighty monster will destroy everything and we are powerless against him. 'He is half a god and cannot be killed.'

Thor stood up. He was the handsomest of all of them with fair hair and broad shoulders; his arms were muscular and strong and he carried a great iron hammer.

'We must trick the monster,' he said, 'and I have a plan.'

Thor shouted down from Asgard so that Fenrir could hear him.

'You may think that you are stronger than the men of earth, and it is true,' he bellowed, 'but you are not as strong as the gods of Asgard.'

Fenrir heard Thor and began to laugh. The mountains trembled and the rivers stopped flowing at the sound of Fenrir's voice.

'Nonsense,' replied the wolf, 'nothing is stronger than me!'

'We do not believe you,' shouted Thor. 'Prove it to us. If we can bind you with chains that you cannot break, will you admit defeat?'

'Certainly,' replied Fenrir, 'no chain could ever hold me.'

So Thor, who was an excellent blacksmith, went to his anvil and, using his mighty hammer, forged the strongest chain he had ever made. Each link was as large as the trunk of an oak tree. Thor took it down to Fenrir and bound the wolf up.

Fenrir smiled evilly and took a deep breath, then another and another and each time he breathed in he swelled up until at last, with a cracking and rending sound the chain snapped.

The gods were appalled, for the strength of Fenrir was greater than they had ever dreamed.

'We will try once more,' announced Thor, and Fenrir, who was feeling very smug about his success, agreed. This time Thor did not make the chain, but went secretly to the three maidens who held the key to the future — Urd, Verdandi and Skuld. He asked them to make a chain that would keep the earth and Asgard safe from the terrible Fenrir. The three maidens worked fast and when their chain was completed they dipped it into the river Mimir which held all the wisdom of the world. Then they took it to Thor.

Thor looked at it in amazement. 'This is no use,' he said, holding it in one hand, 'this would not hold a kitten, let alone a wolf as strong as Fenrir.'

'Try to break it, mighty Thor,' said the three sisters. 'It is not only a chain of iron that can hold strength enough to bind Fenrir.'

Thor took the chain and tugged at it as hard as he could. The veins stood out on his forehead and his shoulders creaked with the strain and yet, for all his strength he could not break it.

Once again Thor went to Fenrir.

'One last try,' he said to the wolf, 'and then we will admit that you are the greatest of all the gods.'

But Fenrir was wary; the chain that Thor held out seemed slender and fragile, and he suspected trickery. 'How do I know what sorcery you have used in this chain?' he asked.

Thor looked innocent. 'I have used no sorcery,' he said; and this was true, for Thor himself had not made the chain.

'I do not trust you,' snarled Fenrir. 'To prove good faith I shall ask for a sign of trust. One of you must put his right arm in my jaws, and keep it there while you bind me; if no one will do this then I shall know that you are trying to trick me.'

The gods looked at each other in horror. It seemed as if Fenrir had outwitted them, and then Tyr, the god of war, stepped forward and thrust his right arm between the sharp teeth of the monster wolf.

Quickly Thor bound Fenrir with the chain the three wise maidens had made. Then he stood back.

The great grey wolf again breathed in as he had before but the chain held. He strained all his muscles but the chain still held. He squirmed and wriggled and struggled but it was to no avail — the chain was unbreakable. In fury he snapped down on the arm of Tyr and severed it at the elbow. Tyr shuddered but smiled bravely.

'What is the loss of an arm compared to the end of the world,' he said, and that is why Tyr, the god of war, has only one arm.

The gods had conquered and Asgard and Midgard were safe. They took the bound body of Fenrir and tied his tail to a huge boulder at one end of the Bifrost bridge and pinned the jaws of Fenrir to the other end with a silver sword. Where the sword pierced Fenrir's jaw a river was born, poisonous and yellow, called the river Wan. And so Fenrir was enslaved, stretched across the Bifrost bridge until the end of eternity, guarded by the gods of Asgard, for should he ever free himself his anger would be terrible to behold.

THE SIDH OF IRELAND

The Sidh are the spirits of Ireland; their name is pronounced 'shee'.

Wonderful tales are told of them and Irish songs recount the history of these magical people. Here are just a few of these stories.

The king of all the Sidh was called Dagda. He had many, many sons and to each of them he gave a kingdom and taught them how to rule it. These kingdoms lay around the hill of Brug na Boinna and inside the top of the hill stood the castle of Dagda himself. Unfortunately, when Dagda had divided his kingdom up amongst his sons, the oldest son, Angus, had not been there and Dagda, in the hustle and bustle of the occasion, had forgotten all about him. When Angus returned he heard what had happened and went to his father.

'Oh, father,' he said sorrowfully, 'have I done anything to displease you? All my other brothers have received a kingdom and now there is nothing left for me.'

Dagda was horrified. 'My son,' he said 'you have never displeased me, you are the wisest and bravest of all my sons. I must be growing old, for I had forgotten all about you. I do not know what to do. I will give you anything you ask for, but I cannot take away a kingdom from any of your brothers.'

'So be it,' said Angus. 'I only ask that you allow me to govern Brug na Boinna itself for a day and a night.'

Dagda kept his promise and from that day onwards Angus became the king of all Ireland, for after all, eternity is made up only from days and nights.

Before the Sidh ruled Ireland it was a miserable land, cold, poor and barren, ruled by a race of monster-spirits called the Fomorians. The Sidh had seized the land from the Fomorians and had brought beauty and peace to it. First Brigit and Cairpre brought poetry and song and music. Then Diancecht brought health and well-being, planting herbs and berries that could be used to cure illnesses and pains. The magical blacksmith Gribnoum and his brothers Creidne and Luichne, both skilled in working with wood and ivory, brought the arts of carving, furniture making and forging and the land blossomed and flourished, and that is why Ireland is so beautiful today.

From time to time, all the Sidh gathered together at Brug na Boinna to reminisce about the old days.

At these gatherings each Sidh had to tell a tale and here are some of them. The first is the story of the lovely Deirdre.

'I remember the old days well,' said Deirdre, one of the most beautiful of the Sidh maidens. 'I was young then, and even more beautiful than I am now. I was walking along a valley in County Leinster when I came across two young men playing at hurling. The taller of the men was so beautiful that I fell in love with him at once and knew that I should pine away if I could not stay with him for ever. But he was a mortal and could not see me, and I knew that unless he came into my fairy palace of his own free will I could never show myself to him. I went down to the lake and found the jawbone of a great pike that was washed up on the shore. This I strung with my own golden hair to make it into a harp and then I returned to where the young men were still playing. I began to pluck the strings of my harp and sing magical songs. The young man, whose name was Aedh, followed the sound of my music until he reached the entrance to my fairy hill wherein my palace lay. I entered, still playing the harp and Aedh followed me. Once inside I ceased to be invisible and he saw me and in turn fell in love with me. What happy days we had then. I showed him all the delights of our fairy kingdom, taught him to ride the Tuatha de Danann, our fairy horses who can fly on the wind, and to hunt with Bran and Sceolan, the hunting dogs. We bathed in the inland seas of Ireland and for three years we were happy. But Aedh was only mortal and at last began to long for his own people. I tried in vain to hold him to me with spells and enchantments, but one day he slipped away from me and sought the help of Saint Patrick, who took him back to his father, who was King of Leinster. Ah, I still remember him and how happy we were, if only he had stayed with me and had never grown old.'

So Deirdre's tale ended and another of the Sidh took her place.

'Speaking of hurling,' said Finvara, the king of the Sidh people of Connaught, 'do you remember the match we played against the Sidh people of Munster? It was like this. As you know, when the Sidh play at hurling there must always be two humans present. We had chosen Paudyeen O'Kelly and little Donal to go with us and we set off for a place called Moytura. There the Sidh of Munster were waiting for us and the hurling match began straight away. The people of Munster soon began to get the better of us, and then, Paudyeen O'Kelly joined in. To be sure he was strong for a mortal and soon the Sidh of Connaught were winning again. And what did the people of Munster do then but turn themselves into a swarm of flying beetles and begin to gobble up every growing thing between Moytura and the sea. Of course you all know what the Sidh of Connaught did to stop that. We turned ourselves into a flock of doves and began to gobble up the beetles in turn. That is why to this day the scene of the great hurling match is called Pul-Na-Gullum, the 'place of the doves'.' Finvara sat down to loud applause and Brigit, the wisest of the Sidh, stood up. It was Brigit who had brought poetry and learning to Ireland. Her name meant 'fiery arrow' and the left side of her face was stern and frightening while the right side was beautiful to behold.

'I tell the tale of how the Sidh came to live under the green hills of Ireland,' she began, and the host of Sidh sat back with a sigh, for this was one of their favourite stories.

'After I and my sisters and brothers had brought our gifts to Ireland, the fame of this lovely land of ours spread across the world. It came to the ears of the Milesians who at that time were living in Spain. These were the descendants of Mil and were led by his son Ith. The Milesians were the first men to reach our land. At first we fought them fiercely, for we did not want to share our land with anyone, but they were almost as powerful as we were and in the end we were forced to ask Ith to decide how the land should be divided. Ith told us that we were all brothers and should live together peacefully. At first we tried, but our people felt cheated and at last several of them banded together and killed Ith. The Milesians were cast into confusion by this and returned to Spain, carrying with them the skin of Ith. There they gathered together a great fleet of ships and set out again to regain the land that Ith had told them to share.

'Our people waited at the seashore to try to defeat this fleet with enchantments and at first this worked. Three times the Mils tried to land and three times the fleet was driven back. We had sent our most powerful sorcerers, Banba, Fodla and Eriou to fight the people of Mil and it was they who guarded the coast with spells.

'But the Milesians had a powerful sorcerer on their side too. His name was Amargen, and he managed to find out the secret names of our sorcerers and so broke the enchantment. The Mils landed and made camp. They sent messengers to bargain with us, but we would not give in and prepared to go into battle. Strangely the Milesians would not fight. We heard later that Amargen had told them that his magic showed that the time was not yet right. So they returned to their ships and sailed a little way out to sea. At once our sorcerers called up a great storm and the winds drove the ships of the Milesians far round the coast, but here the magic of Amargen conquered, and the Milesians discovered a landing place that was not guarded. They landed and at once the Sidh hurried to do battle. This took place at Tailtiu and the people of the Sidh conquered. Our king

made a treaty with them because they had fought so bravely and at last peace returned to Ireland. The years passed and the men of Mil and the people of the Sidh lived happily together.'

Brigit looked round at the people of the Sidh. 'Do you remember some of the marvellous magic we had in those days?' she asked. 'Do you remember the spear that the great fighter Lug carried? It was tipped with gold and hafted with ivory. Its aim was true and it flew straight to its mark, but the most magical thing of all was that it made its bearer invisible. And do you remember that cauldron you once had, Dagda?' she asked, turning to the king of all the Sidh.

'I do indeed,' answered Dagda, 'and a wonderful thing it was too and most useful to me with so many sons. It never emptied and no matter how many people ate from it it always held more. There was nothing that the cauldron could not provide,' King Dagda sighed. 'I also remember the magic stone Lia Fail. Whoever stood upon it became the king of Ireland.'

'Yes,' said Brigit, 'I remember too the gift I gave to the people of the southern part of our land. That too was a stone, and anyone who kissed it gained the power of poetry and the ability to tell wonderful stories. That stone I gave to one of the Milesian kings.'

'There is one gift we have never lost,' said Dagda, 'and that is the gift of music. The gift that you brought to us all.'

At that the Sidh took up their instruments and began to play. The music of the Sidh was like no other music in the world; it could do many things. It could fill the heart of the listener with joy and happiness. It could bring back memories of childhood and youth so that the old felt young again. It could charm the birds from the sky and soothe the fishes. It could conjure up gentle rainstorms that would water the ground and cause the crops to grow. It could make the sun shine down so that the fruit ripened on the trees and the corn grew golden in the fields and it could soothe the hearts and minds of men so that when their last dark journey drew near they fell into a gentle slumber and did not fear the approach of death.

As the strains of the music died away, the last storyteller rose to his feet. His name was Froech.

'I will tell the last tale,' he said. 'It is to do with the power of our music and how through this I gained the hand of my wife. When I was young I fell in love with the daughter of the Milesian king of Connacht. I went to ask for her hand in marriage, but her father had promised her to a nearby prince. I begged and pleaded as did his daughter, but the king would not give in. I went to see the prince who had been promised her hand and begged him to release her from her father's promise, but even though he knew that she would never be happy with him, he still refused. At that I took out my harp and began to play. I played a song of war and battle that put fear into the heart of the prince and then I played a song of peace and tranquility that showed him how much better it was not to fight. Then I played a song of love, so that all who heard it could under-

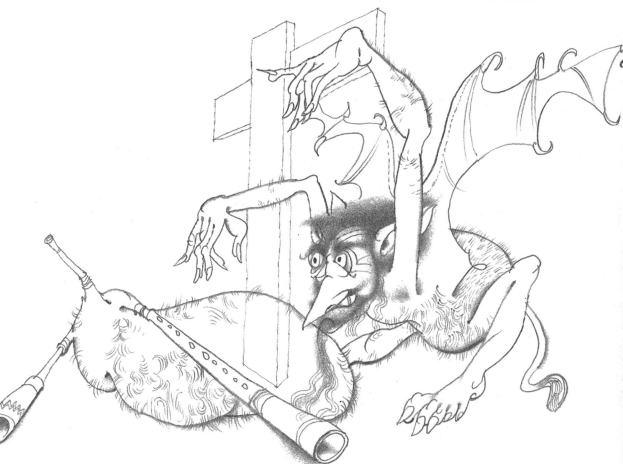

stand how much I loved the king of Connacht's daughter. At last I played a song of sleep so that all who heard it became drowsy and while they slumbered I crept away with my true love and returned to my castle under the green hills of my kingdom. All their life the people of Connacht remembered my music and they never tried to regain their princess.'

Froech sat down and played the same song of love again, and all the Sidh heard how much he loved his mortal bride and understood then why she had never wished to return to the land of men, as did so many of the mortals who came to live in their fairy kingdom.

VAINAMOINEN

Once upon a time in a far off land called Kalevala, there lived two brothers. The oldest was called Vainamoinen and the youngest Ilmarinen. They were both handsome men, tall and strong with broad shoulders and wide smiles, but Vainamoinen earned his living as a musician, whereas Ilmarinen had taught himself to be the best blacksmith in Kalevala. It was said that there were no instruments that Vainamoinen could not play and that there was nothing that Ilmarinen could not make. Besides being a great musician, Vainamoinen was also wise in the ways of healing. He could make medicines from the herbs and fruit which grew in his native land, he could set broken bones and heal wounds, advise mothers on how to help their children to grow up strong and healthy, and even cure the animals that came to harm in the forests and on the plains of Kalevala. The two brothers lived together in perfect harmony, each helping the other and spending their days in happiness and usefulness.

At last the two brothers decided that it was time that they each found a bride.

'I have heard of the beauty of the daughter of Queen Louhi of Pohjola,' Ilmarinen told his brother. 'They say that the Aino is the loveliest of all the princesses of the north.'

Vainamoinen had also heard of Aino, but had heard other things about the dismal and harsh land of Pohjola.

'They also say that Queen Louhi is a cruel and greedy queen,' he replied. 'You must take care when you visit her kingdom.'

'You are only jealous,' Ilmarinen retorted. 'I know that you too wish to marry the beautiful Aino. You are only trying to put me off so that you can win her.'

It was true that Vainamoinen wanted to marry the princess and when he saw that he could not dissuade his brother they each decided to journey to Pohjola and see which of them the lovely Aino would choose.

The next morning Ilmarinen harnessed his horses to his sleigh and set off across the snowy lands which lay between Kalevala and Pohjola.

Vainamoinen wandered down to the seashore and looked out across the grey waves. As he stood there he heard a sad voice wailing and crying. He hunted for the source of this mournful sound and discovered a little boat lying on its side in the sand dunes. The boat's

sails were ragged and torn and the paint that covered the wooden hull was faded and peeling.

'Here I lie, useless and tattered,' the little boat sobbed. 'Once I sailed across the wide seas to distant lands, journeyed through storms and sunshine to golden shores and strange islands; but now I lie rotting in the sand dunes, with no one to sail in me, and no one to care for me.'

'All your troubles are over,' Vainamoinen told the little boat. 'I shall care for you and mend your sails. Together we will sail across the sea to Pohjola.'

Quickly Vainamoinen pulled away the torn sails and made a new set from an old red cloak. He repainted the sides of the boat with bright blue paint and polished up the little boat's anchor. Then he pulled the little boat down to the edge of the sea where the waves danced and chuckled.

'I will serve you faithfully, Vainamoinen,' said the little boat, 'and if I can help you in any way you may be sure that I will.'

Together they sailed away across the sea to Pohjola and when they arrived they met Ilmarinen.

'Well met, brother,' called Vainamoinen. 'Together we shall try for the hand of the lovely Aino, and may the best man win.'

Pohjola was a terrible place. The houses were small and mean, and even the castle of Queen Louhi was made of wood. The land was poor because very few crops grew there and the animals were thin and weak.

The queen and her daughter sat in the highest room of the castle round a small fire that smoked and crackled. They were guarded by two fierce wolfhounds, Lukki and Halli. These dogs never slept and if any stranger entered the kingdom they growled and barked to warn their mistress. The two dogs were growling now.

'We have visitors,' said Queen Louhi. 'I shall ask the fire what they want of us.' The queen picked up one of the logs lying beside the smoking fire and threw it into the feeble flames.

'If the log weeps blood it means war, and if the log weeps water it means peace.'

The log hissed and crackled and a clear, amber liquid flowed out.

'It weeps honey, mother!' said Princess Aino. 'What does this mean?'

'It means that suitors come to seek your hand,' answered Queen Louhi, 'suitors from the far off land of Kalevala.'

Vainamoinen and Ilmarinen entered the chamber and bowed low before the queen and her daughter.

'All hail, Queen Louhi,' said Ilmarinen. 'I have heard of the fabled beauty of your daughter and I come to woo her.'

'All hail, Queen Louhi,' said Vainamoinen. 'I too have come to woo your daughter.'

Queen Louhi looked sharply at the two young men and then at her daughter. Aino's eyes were modestly cast down and a faint blush stained her cheeks.

Queen Louhi saw how she could turn the situation to her advantage.

'Sit down, young sirs,' she told them. 'This is a most important choice for my only daughter. Tonight we will eat together and perhaps you, Vainamoinen, would play for us on the Kantele you carry.'

Vainamoinen played for them on the stringed Kantele, and the sound of his voice and the sweet music of the strings floated round the chamber and up to the roof with the smoke from the fire. As he played he looked at Aino, but her eyes never met his. She looked only at Ilmarinen or at the floor, and she said nothing. Her mother was silent too, but Queen Louhi was silent because she was plotting, whereas Aino was silent from shyness.

In the morning, Queen Louhi called the two brothers to her. She had spoken with her daughter and knew full well that Aino preferred Ilmarinen, but she did not let the brothers know that Aino had already made her choice.

'My daughter cannot decide which of you she wishes to marry,' she said, 'and so I shall set each of you a task. The one who completes the task first shall gain the hand of Aino.'

She handed a wooden spindle from her spinning wheel to Vainamoinen.

'You must take this spindle and turn it into a ship; but this must be no ordinary ship. It must be a magnificent ship as long as a fir tree is tall, a ship which will sail by itself, with no sailors to guide her and no wind to blow her along.'

She turned to Ilmarinen and handed him a small golden ring.

'You, Ilmarinen, must take this ring and turn it into a grinding mill; but this must be no ordinary mill. It must have three sets of grindstones; the first must grind flour, the second must grind salt and the third must grind fine gold.'

The brothers prepared themselves for their tasks. Ilmarinen went to his sleigh and took out his tools. His task was difficult to be sure, but he, Ilmarinen, the greatest blacksmith in all Kalevala, would surely be able to undertake it.

Vainamoinen was worried. He was a wonderful healer and

a splendid musician, but what did he know about ships? He wandered down to the seashore and sat down in his little boat.

'Why do you look so sad, Vainamoinen?' asked the little boat. 'Is there any way I can help you?'

'I fear not,' replied Vainamoinen. 'I must take this spindle and turn it into a fine ship which will sail with neither wind nor crew, or I shall never marry the lovely Aino.'

'I cannot do this for you,' said the little boat, 'but I know of a giant who could help you. The only way you can fulfill your task is by using three magic words and the only person in the whole world who knows those words is the giant Antero Vipunen. He sleeps some way from here, and the way there is hard and dangerous. To reach him you must endure three torments. The first is a path covered with hundreds and hundreds of sharp needles, each needle pointing upwards to pierce the feet of the bold traveller who would dare to walk there. The second is a path covered with thousands and thousands of sharp swords, each sword pointing upwards to pierce and cut the feet of the brave traveller who would dare to walk there. The third is also a path, this time strewn with the blades of hundreds of thousands of axes, each blade sharpened like a razor, and each one pointing upwards to cut and slash the feet of any daring traveller who tries to walk there. Only when you have walked along these three paths will you reach the meadow where Antero Vipunen lies slumbering.'

Vainamoinen shuddered when he thought of those three paths. He went to his brother and asked him to make him a pair of steel boots that would protect his feet from the needles, the swords and the axes.

'Please help me, brother,' begged Vainamoinen. 'I also need a tiny golden box to keep the three magic words in.'

'I shall make no boots for you, and no golden boxes,' Ilmarinen told his brother. 'I am far too busy to waste time helping you. I must finish the mill before nightfall.'

Vainamoinen set off. When he reached the first path he wrapped his cloak round his feet and so avoided the sharp points of the needles. When he reached the second path he made rough shoes from the branches of a fallen tree and so avoided most of the sharp sword points, but when he reached the third path the blades of the axes cut through the wooden shoes he had made and cut into his feet. Vainamoinen struggled on and at last reached the meadow. There he paused and made a salve from the sweet herbs that grew among the rich green grass of the meadow, spread this on his feet and the cuts healed.

There ahead of him in the long waving grass was the sleeping giant Antero Vipunen. This giant was as tall as the tallest pine tree, as broad as a long-boat and as hairy as a grizzly bear. He snored and grunted in the sunshine. Antero Vipunen had been asleep for three hundred years, but this was no more than a nap to him.

Vainamoinen walked bravely up to him and drove his sword into the giant's hand. Antero Vipunen twitched his fingers as if no more than a gnat had stung him.

Vainamoinen stood by the giant's ear and shouted as loudly as he could.

'Wake up! Wake up!' but the giant did not stir.

Vainamoinen went back to the axe-path and pulled up one of the axe heads. Quickly he tied it to a long stick and walked back to the giant. Antero Vipunen lay with his mouth open and Vainamoinen crawled into the giant's mouth, down the long red throat and into Antero Vipunen's stomach. There he began to hack at the inside of the giant with his axe.

This time Antero Vipunen awoke.

'Ooh! Oh! Ouch!' he roared. 'How my stomach hurts. I must have eaten something which disagreed with me.'

Vainamoinen chopped away inside the giant's stomach.

'Aargh! Ooooh!' yelled the giant.

'Can you hear me?' Vainamoinen shouted.

'Who is there? groaned the giant. 'It sounds as if you are inside me.'

'Indeed I am,' answered Vainamoinen, 'and I shall chop away at your stomach unless you tell me the three magic words.'

'Never!' roared the giant.

'Oh yes, you will!' shouted Vainamoinen and swung the axe as hard as he could.

'Stop, stop, please stop!' yelled the giant.

'Only if you tell me the words,' shouted Vainamoinen.

'Very well,' said the giant.

So Vainamoinen crawled out of the giant's stomach and the giant whispered the words to him.

'Remember,' said the giant, settling himself down to sleep again, 'you may use the words only once. After that they lose their magic, so use them wisely.'

The giant lay back, but just before he fell asleep he sneezed and the sneeze was so strong that it carried Vainamoinen over the path covered with axes, over the path covered with swords and over the path covered with needles and back to the wooden castle.

Evening was falling and Ilmarinen was still working away at the mill.

Vainamoinen smiled to himself and prepared to chop the spindle into three pieces so that he could use the three magic words on them. As he swung his axe he felt an odd trembling in the earth and the axe seemed to twist in his hand. Instead of cutting the spindle, the axe embedded itself in Vainamoinen's leg, just below the knee. It was a terrible wound and blood began to pour from Vainamoinen's leg onto the ground.

'Help me, help me,' he called to Ilmarinen. 'I cannot stop the blood, even I cannot heal this wound. The axe must be enchanted. Only you, my brother, who are the master of all the axes in the world can help me now.'

Ilmarinen was horrified to see the wound in his brother's leg. He began to chant a spell, a spell that should heal the wound.

'Axe, axe, heal this cut,
Stop the blood from flowing.
Axe, axe, heal this wound,
While the wind is blowing.
Axe, axe, heal this hurt,
Before the moon is glowing.
Axe, axe, heal this wound,
Before the stars are showing.'

But the wound went on bleeding and the axe did not heal it. 'You are right,' said Ilmarinen, 'the axe is enchanted. Only Queen Louhi could have made such a spell, but I can undo it.'

'Come iron, come steel,
Come steel, come iron,
By the fire that made you,
By the hand that forged you,
Heal this wound.'

Ilmarinen chanted these words and stretched out his hand towards the axe. The axe twisted again on the ground and then sprang upright and the dreadful wound on Vainamoinen's leg was healed.

'Thank you, my brother,' said Vainamoinen. 'Without you I should be dead. In gratitude I shall give you the three magic words of Antero Vipunen. It is obvious that Queen Louhi wishes you to marry her daughter and I shall not stand in your way.'

Vainamoinen told Ilmarinen the three words. Ilmarinen swung his great hammer and shouted the first word. As the hammer struck the completed mill the first set of millstones started to grind out fine white flour.

Ilmarinen swung his hammer again and shouted the second word. The mill began to grind out fine white salt from the second set of millstones.

Ilmarinen swung the hammer the third time and shouted the third magic word, and the mill began to grind out fine gold from the third set of millstones.

So Ilmarinen gave the magic mill to Queen Louhi and won the hand of the fair Aino. The two brothers and Aino returned to Kalevala.

Sadly the very next year the beautiful Aino fell ill. For many days she lay quiet and still, the roses in her cheeks faded and her lovely eyes closed. Vainamoinen tried as hard as he could to heal her, but none of his medicines worked, and then, one cold night, just as the moon rose in the sky, Aino died, leaving Ilmarinen and Vainamoinen to grieve for her.

The years passed and the brothers grew older. Neither of them married, they were happy with each other's company, but they were very poor. One evening a traveller came to their door, and, as was the custom in Kalevala, they invited him in and offered him food and drink.

'We only have a little,' they told the traveller, 'but you are welcome to share it.'

After they had eaten and listened to Vainamoinen play wonderful tunes on his Kantele, the traveller told them of his voyages.

'... and the richest land I ever visited was Pohjola,' he related to them. 'There they have a magic mill which they call the "Sampo". It is a marvellous machine that grinds not only fine white flour, but fine white salt and pure gold. It has made the queen so rich that she can buy anything. But she still cannot buy happiness or a kind heart. She is the cruelest queen in the north.'

Vainamoinen and Ilmarinen listened in amazement.

'Just think ...' murmured Ilmarinen, 'that is our mill. We have made Pohjola rich.'

'Yes,' said Vainamoinen, 'and your beautiful Aino has been dead all these years and yet still her greedy mother has the mill. The mill is rightfully ours.'

When the traveller had gone, the two brothers put on their cloaks and walked to the seashore. There Vainamoinen's little boat was moored, with its blue paintwork still bright and its red sail untorn.

'Take us to Pohjola, little boat,' said Vainamoinen. 'We go to claim our magic mill, the Sampo, which has ground out riches for the queen for all these years.'

The little boat set sail with the two brothers, across the oceans to Pohjola. They had not gone very far when ahead of them they saw a smooth grey island.

'How strange that an island should have no grass or trees,' said Vainamoinen.

'That is no island,' said the little boat. 'That is a huge fish. Chop off its head.'

Vainamoinen did as he was told and they carried the head of the great fish with them all the way to Pohjola. When they landed they walked to the nearest village. Although Queen Louhi was rich, her people were still poor, and so the brothers cooked the great fish-head and shared out the meat amongst the villagers.

'We see that you are a musician,' said the villagers. 'The jawbone of that fish would make a wonderful Kantele.' They picked all the meat from the jawbone of the fish and from the spines in the fins they made strings. Vainamoinen strung the Kantele and began to play. As he drew his fingers across the strings the music that poured forth was truly magical.

The brothers journeyed on until they came to the castle of Queen Louhi. The old wooden castle had gone and in its place stood a magnificent castle made from ivory, with a roof of pure gold and golden trees and flowers in the garden round it.

Queen Louhi knew that they were coming, for her two hounds, Halli and Lukki, had been growling and barking. As she had done before the first visit of the two brothers, she threw a log onto the fire.

'If the log weeps blood it means war, and if it weeps water it means peace,' she said. The log wept tears of blood.

'War is coming to Pohjola,' she said. 'I must guard the magic mill very carefully.' She commanded one thousand soldiers to guard the mill day and night and she unleashed her two fierce hounds and allowed them to roam round the castle so that they could chase and catch anyone who tried to steal the mill. When the brothers entered her throne room she told them,

'You need not think that you can steal my mill, it is well guarded. Even though Aino is dead, the mill is mine and I shall never let it go.'

But Vainamoinen was crafty. 'Oh, Queen Louhi,' he said, 'we have not come to steal your mill, but merely to play and sing to you. To be sure, Ilmarinen would love to see the mill he made so many years ago. May we look at it?'

Queen Louhi could not resist the chance to gloat over the mill and she commanded the soldiers to bring it to the chamber.

'Guard it well,' she said. 'The brothers are only to look at it.'

The mill was brought and Queen Louhi showed the brothers how it still ground out flour, salt and gold.

'I shall sing a song in praise of the magic mill,' announced Vainamoinen and he took up his Kantele and began to sing.

The music that Vainamoinen played was so beautiful and magical that soon all the soldiers fell into a deep slumber. The queen slept and even her two great wolfhounds slept. Quietly Vainamoinen and Ilmarinen took up the mill and crept away to their little boat and sailed away with it across the sea towards Kalevala.

They had not been gone long when Queen Louhi awoke. She saw that the mill was gone and in a terrible fury she called upon the powerful god Ukko, who controlled the wind, storms and sea.

'Avenge me, O Ukko,' she demanded. 'Vainamoinen and Ilmarinen have stolen the magic Sampo, the mill which grinds flour, salt and gold.'

Immediately Ukko caused a great storm to arise. The storm rushed across the sea and tore at the red sails of the little boat.

'Throw the mill overboard,' begged the little boat, 'for I cannot sail in this storm with the mill on board.'

The brothers would not and the boat rocked about madly. The boat heeled over to the right and the millstones which ground out flour were smashed. Then the boat heeled to the left and the mill-stones that ground out gold were smashed. At this the brothers tossed the broken mill over the side and the little boat made its way safely to the shores of Kalevala.

From that day to this, the magic Sampo has remained at the bottom of the sea. It grinds no more flour and no more gold, for only the wheels that grind salt are left. Day and night they grind away, never ceasing and never slowing. And that is why the sea is so salty.

KING ARTHUR

Long ago, when the green land of Britain was covered with great forests, and wolves and bears roamed wild in the countryside, there lived a powerful king. His name was Uther Pendragon and he was the bravest of all the kings of Britain. His closest friend and advisor was an old man called Merlin.

Now Merlin was no ordinary man. In the days when the old magic had not died there were many great wizards and Merlin was the greatest wizard who had ever lived. Because he knew so many magical spells and was so very wise in the ways of the world, King Uther Pendragon always asked Merlin for advice and help. King Uther's wife was the beautiful Ingerne, Duchess of Tintagel, and when they had been married for about two years, Ingerne gave birth to a baby boy. They named him Arthur and Merlin was present at his christening.

'Sire,' said Merlin, holding the baby in his arms. 'This child will grow up to be the greatest king that Britain has ever known. Would you allow me to bring him up to be a good and wise king?'

'We can bring him up ourselves,' said Ingerne, for she did not want to lose her baby.

'To be raised in a royal household is not always the best training for kingship,' Merlin told them. 'What will your child know of the people he will one day reign over if all he sees are castles and palaces? How will he know how ordinary people live, what they need and what they lack if he always has everything he wants? Let me take him and put him where he will learn all he needs.'

So Uther Pendragon and Ingerne agreed, for they knew that Merlin was the best person to help their son to learn to rule wisely and well. Thus Merlin took the baby away and for many years no more was heard of little Prince Arthur.

In those days, the country of Britain was made up of many different kingdoms, each ruled by a different king. Uther Pendragon was the most powerful of all the kings, but his lands were often threatened by the people of the North who were greedy for Uther's lands and possessions. When Uther fell ill the men of the North formed a huge army and sailed southwards round the coast of Britain to overthrow the dying monarch.

Merlin went to Uther and advised him.

'Sire, only you can lead your armies into battle,' he told Uther.

'The soldiers trust you and will fight fiercely if you are there, but if you are not, then they will surely be overthrown.'

Uther left his sickbed and rallied his men round him. He knew that he had only a few weeks to live but even so he was determined that his men should not know how near he was to death. The two great armies met at a place just outside St Albans, a town close to London. The Northmen believing that Uther's army had lost heart without their king to lead them were amazed when they were met with fierce opposition. The battle was short but decisive — the Northmen were soundly beaten and fled back to the north. Almost the last thing that Uther heard was the cheering of his soldiers and the joyful sound of victory trumpets.

The king was dying. He sent for Merlin and made his last wishes clear. His son Arthur was to become king and Merlin was to be chief advisor to the crown. But where was Arthur? He was a young man by now and almost old enough to rule, yet no one knew where he was, and Merlin would tell no one what had become of the heir to the throne. When he was asked he would answer,

'All will be made clear in time,' and he would say no more.

The winter after the death of Uther Pendragon a strange stone appeared outside one of the largest churches in London. Buried in this stone, so that only the richly carved hilt could be seen, was a great broad sword, and carved round the stone in clear letters was the legend: WHOSOEVER PULLS THE SWORD FROM THE STONE IS THE RIGHTFUL KING OF BRITAIN.

'But Arthur is the rightful king of Britain,' the people said. 'Why does he not pull the sword from the stone?'

Months passed and still Arthur did not appear. People began to believe that like his father, he was dead.

Many knights came to London to try to take the sword from the stone, but none succeeded and strife began to break out in the land. There was no one to rule and some of the knights tried to take the crown by force, but they failed.

The following summer, a great tournament was held in London and knights and soldiers came from all over Britain to take part. One of these knights was Sir Hector, who brought his two sons with him. Sir Hector's elder son was Kay, a young man of eighteen. The younger son, who was only just sixteen, was not yet allowed to carry arms, although he was fully trained in the arts of horsemanship and combat. Because he was not allowed to join in, the younger son was acting as squire to Kay and Sir Hector. He looked after their horses and took care of their armour and weapons. Sir Hector and Kay took

part in many of the tournaments, particularly the single combat contests where two men fought each other on foot with swords and shields. During the first contest, Kay's sword broke and Kay sent his brother to fetch his other sword.

The young lad darted away as fast as he could, for the place where they were staying was a long way away from the tournament ground, and he did not want his brother to miss any of the contests. As he ran through the streets he passed the churchyard where the magic stone stood. The young man did not stop to read the inscription; all he saw was a sword that no one seemed to want. He vaulted over the churchyard wall and took hold of the hilt of the sword. With one smooth pull he drew the sword from the stone.

It was a beautiful sword, as sharp as a razor and well balanced. Kay's brother ran back to the tournament as fast as he could, pleased that he could return so quickly. He was in such a hurry that he did not notice the amazed look on the faces of the people who had seen what he had done.

'He must be the rightful king . . .' said one man.

'But he seemed not to know what the stone said . . .' said another.

'The inscription said that only the rightful king could take the sword,' said another.

The news spread through London and people began to make their way to the tournament ground to see the boy who had pulled the sword from the stone and proclaim him their king.

Sir Hector and Kay were just as amazed when they saw the sword.

'Where did you find this?' they asked. 'Don't you know what this sword is?'

Sir Hector fell to his knees before his younger son.

'Sire . . .' he said.

'Oh get up, father,' said his son, 'don't be silly . . .'

'Arthur,' said Sir Hector, for that was the boy's name, 'the time has come for me to tell you the secret that I have kept in my heart for nearly sixteen years. Although you have always thought that I was your father, you are not, in fact, my real son. When you were a tiny baby, the wizard Merlin brought you to me. He would not tell me who your real parents were, but he asked me to bring you up as if you were my own child. He told me that you must be taught all the arts of a knight as well as honesty and duty. He said that you must be treated as any other boy even though you had a high destiny to fulfil. I see now that Merlin knew all along that you were the rightful heir to the throne of Britain.'

'And so I did,' said a deep voice.

88

Turning round, Arthur saw a tall, white-haired man. It was the wizard Merlin.

'Your real parents were Uther Pendragon and Ingerne, King and Queen of Britain,' said Merlin. 'You are truly the rightful king. It was only in this way that I could ensure that you would gain the throne. If the people of Britain did not believe you to be the king, they would not allow you to rule them. Now all can see that you, and only you, could draw the sword from the stone. Other men have tried and failed; other men have tried to take the crown and have failed. You will not fail, for you are the true son of your father.'

A great cheer rose up above the tournament ground, and the people there fell to their knees and hailed Arthur as king.

And so Arthur took the crown and led his people into battle. He had ruled for several years when the sword vanished. It had gone as mysteriously as it had arrived.

That evening Merlin took Arthur to a quiet and secret lake, high up in the Welsh mountains. A small rowing boat was moored at its edge but there were no oars.

'Get into the boat,' Merlin told King Arthur, 'and do not be afraid of anything that may happen to you.'

Arthur did as he was told and as he seated himself, the boat began to move smoothly out into the lake. When it reached the centre of the lake it stopped. All around Arthur the lake shimmered in the moonlight, as still as a mirror. Then, without a sound, and without causing a ripple, a slender white hand rose from the waters. The hand held a sword.

'Take the sword,' Merlin's voice whispered.

Arthur reached down and took the sword. Faintly through the water he thought he could see the face of a beautiful woman, but as he grasped the sword the hand sank back under the lake again and the face disappeared. The little boat moved back to the shore bearing Arthur and his precious gift.

'This is the sword Excalibur,' Merlin told the king. 'It is a magical sword and may only be carried by you. It will protect you in battle and while you wear it you will never be wounded.'

'Who was the beautiful woman I saw under the water?' asked Arthur.

'That was the Lady of the Lake,' answered Merlin.

All his life Arthur carried the sword Excalibur, and as Merlin had said, he was never wounded.

Some years later, Arthur married the beautiful daughter of King Laodegan. Guinevere was said to be the loveliest lady in Britain and for many years she and Arthur were happy together. When the wedding was celebrated, knights and kings came from all over the kingdom bearing rich gifts for the happy couple. Of all the wedding presents that Arthur and Guinevere received, the most wonderful was a huge wooden table, richly carved and painted. The table was completely round and could seat one hundred and fifty knights. It was a present from Queen Guinevere's father Laodegan, and with it came one hundred knights, all sworn to the service of King Arthur.

This table became famous as the round table of legend. Only the bravest and noblest knight was allowed to sit there and because the table had no top or bottom, no knight could claim that he was more important than the others. When Arthur had decided who was to be allowed to sit at the round table, he held a great feast and for the first time the knights were all seated together. Suddenly, during the feast, the room became dark and on the back of the chairs where each knight was sitting, their names appeared in golden letters. Sir Lancelot of the Lake, Sir Gawain, Sir Bors, Sir Hector, Sir Perceval, Sir Galahad, Sir Pinel, Sir Kay, Sir Bedivere: these and all the other knights saw their names written in glowing letters and knew then that many adventures awaited them.

ROLAND

Roland was the nephew of Charlemagne, the king of France who had conquered all of Spain apart from Saragossa. He was a great favourite of the king, who prized valour and courage in battle above all things, for Roland had already proved himself to be both heroic and noble.

Oliver was Roland's closest friend and companion-in-arms; in fact they were soon to become brothers, for Roland was engaged to be married to the beautiful Aude, Oliver's sister. Roland's only enemy at this time was in fact the Count Ganelon, his own stepfather, who was jealous of Charlemagne's high opinion of Roland, and had sworn he would bring about the downfall of his stepson.

Nobody suspected Ganelon of treachery. Charlemagne was deeply worried about the bad tidings he had received from Spain. The Saracen king, Marsilion, had sworn an oath of allegiance to Charlemagne and had promised to follow the Christian faith. But, little by little, Marsilion had become less humble, enlarging his kingdom and acquiring greater riches and possessions, whilst setting fire to the Christian churches one by one and having mosques erected in their place. This news was a thorn in the side of Charlemagne. In the meantime those Spaniards who had remained devoted to the Christian faith were begging Charlemagne to come to their aid. He answered their pleas, leading his army even as far as Saragossa itself where crosses were replaced on the roofs of the houses. Marsilion wept to see the downfall of his domain.

He sent messengers to Charlemagne bringing valuable gifts to try to stop the fighting. But Charlemagne's advisers were divided as to the meaning behind these symbols of peace; Roland and Oliver wished to continue the war as they felt that Marsilion was a cruel man and was likely to betray them at the first opportunity. The archbishop Turpin and the Count Otto shared their views, but Ganelon and his friends thought that they should be reasonable.

'Why could the Christians and Muslims not come to some peaceful agreement?' he asked. 'Surely Marsilion as such a great leader is a man of his word and we should therefore take this peace offering.'

He was thinking of the fabulous jewels and riches belonging to Marsilion.

Roland was annoyed at his stepfather, for he was sure that Marsilion would deceive his uncle yet again. He suggested that if an ambassador were to be sent, then who better than Ganelon himself since he was so sure of Marsilion's good faith. Now this made Ganelon extremely angry but at the same time fear grew in his mind. It was common knowledge that Marsilion had executed previous ambassadors and he was determined that this time he would be revenged upon Roland. An evil plan grew in his mind.

He was certain that Roland had only made the suggestion so that he would inherit his stepfather's property if he were to be murdered. Ganelon did not understand Roland and thought he was as grasping and mean as Ganelon himself. He laid his plans.

He visited Marsilion and was treated with great kindness and hospitality, for Marsilion could see through him and realized that Ganelon could be very useful against the Emperor to whom he was so close. On his return Ganelon informed Charlemagne that Marsilion was an honest man and would not betray them. He was prepared to promote the Christian faith as well as making yearly payments of gold as a mark of his trust, if Charlemagne would withdraw most of his troops except for those in occupation. Charlemagne saw no reason to disbelieve this story. The plot was laid perfectly; Charlemagne even appointed Roland to command the rearguard as Ganelon wished.

Retreating back to France over the plains of Roncevaux, Roland was carrying as ever his famous sword 'Durandal' and his horn 'Oliphant', which was so loud and piercing that it always drove terror into the hearts of his enemies. It was a clear day and as Roland was riding along he perceived a cloud in the distance on the horizon behind them. He wondered at first what it could be and then finally it dawned on him that it was a vast army of Saracen horsemen galloping very swiftly in their wake. It was by now obvious that they were intent on battle and that Marsilion's promises were as empty as the winds rattling across the plains. Charlemagne was very far away from them, moving ahead back to France, but he could even now be summoned by the earshattering blasts from Roland's horn Oliphant. Oliver, the ever faithful and wise comrade, urged Roland to call for help before it was too late, for they were outnumbered ten to one. But Roland was a warrior brave and valiant and the lust for battle was flowing through his veins as he heard their cries. He wished to punish Marsilion for his lies and deceit, though nobody as yet realized the hand that Ganelon had played.

The sun rising over the flat, featureless landscape glinted on the glowing, golden helmets of the Saracen hordes, making their tall spears flash and sparkle in the early morning light. Their black hair flowed in the wind of their passage as they rushed ever nearer to start the assault. Roland grouped his men as best as he could to face the onslaught and they waited to meet the enemy, for escape in those empty lands was impossible.

Leading the Saracens was the nephew of Marsilion, Aldarot, charging forward bearing the flag of Marsilion. The cry of 'Allah! Allah!' echoed down the plain as the two armies clashed together. The air was thick with lances and spears which flew to meet their mark. As the men fought one against the other their horses stumbled and fell, some ending their masters' lives as they rolled over and crushed them. The luckier soldiers were able to scramble to their feet and snatch a sword or even a dagger out of a sheath to slash at any part of the enemy that was not protected by armour. The cries of war and death soon filled the surrounding area as men stricken with many terrible wounds staggered and fell on to the bare, dry plain which was to be their final resting place on this earth. Lances were broken in two and the flags and standards which had been borne so proudly over the land were ripped to shreds by swords and torn by

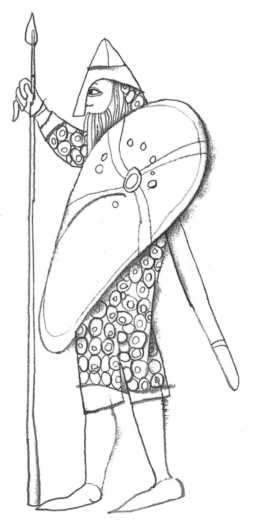

battling men lurching this way and that. Soon they had all fluttered to the ground to be trampled underfoot. Roland skilfully parried any blow that came his way and found that he was soon very close to Aldarot, who was battling with a fervour that overcame almost all. But not Roland. Roland raised his sword above his head. It had been blessed by the Archbishop Turpin so that it would never fail him against the pagans, and brought it down with all his strength against Aldarot's sword which shivered and finally shattered into two pieces on the ground. Roland raised Durandal again and pierced his enemy's neck so that Aldarot swayed for a long moment, staring at Roland with rapidly glazing eyes, he finally fell heavily, shuddered once and died.

Marsilion was both furious and despairing when news was brought to him of the death of his nephew; furious that Roland had outwitted them again and despairing because Aldarot had been very close to him. He screamed for revenge against his enemy, threatening his commanders with a horrible death if they failed in their duty to slaughter Roland. He then despatched into the fray his own son, trusting that he would succeed where all the others had hitherto failed. His son was never seen again, his head hewn bloodily from his shoulders by the mighty sword of Oliver.

Roland stood there, his sword and hands covered with the blood of his enemies, and surveyed the battle scene. Things were going badly for him and his friends. They were now encircled by the murderous Saracens. Marsilion himself had launched into the attack, having spent even his own son in the feud against Roland, and was now forging ever closer through the sea of black and gold Saracen heads to the small knot of fighting men that surrounded Roland. By now even Roland could see that battle was overcoming them. Mortally injured or murdered Frenchmen outnumbered the living at this stage. He decided to sound his horn Oliphant to summon Charlemagne to avenge them at least, if not to rescue them. However now it was Oliver who was against the sounding of the horn.

'How may we sound the horn when help will come too late?' he gasped. It was the Archbishop Turpin who finally decided the matter. And so Roland at last sounded a tremendous blast from his horn that could be heard thirty leagues away within Charlemagne's earshot. However, so hard had he blown that the effort burst a blood vessel in his temple. The battle continued, but the French were fading fast. Oliver was pierced by so many wounds that the blood running into his eyes blinded him. Such was his anguish and terror that he was lashing out at anyone who approached him, whether friend or foe. And so it was that the faithful Oliver delivered a fatal wound to his friend Roland, whom no-one else had been able to touch.

Horns were blowing wildly in the distance. Charlemagne was charging back to the battle, and on hearing their horns and wild cries the Saracens lost heart and turned tail after a final attempt to kill Roland. Archbishop Turpin was dying on the battlefield, his body dismembered and barely recognizable. Roland was left alone, for no pagan hand was able to destroy him. Knowing that death was near he attempted to smash Durandal against a rock, rather than have it fall into enemy hands. And it was while he was doing this that his soul finally passed away.

Charlemagne wept when he saw the bloodshed that had been wreaked on his men and he became distraught when he found the remains of Roland and Oliver, swearing revenge would be taken against Marsilion.

At last the bodies were returned to Aix-la-Chapelle where the dreadful news was broken to the lovely Aude, Roland's fiancée. On hearing of her lover's and brother's death she fell down and died of a shock and a broken heart.

So ended the tragic tale of Roland and Oliver, two of the bravest knights to fight for Charlemagne.

LUG THE WARRIOR HERO

In the old days, when Ireland was ruled by the people of the goddess Danu, there were many great hero gods. The greatest of all these was Lug, for he was not only a mighty warrior but also the wisest man in the world. The Tuatha De Danann, as the people of the goddess Danu were called, were a peaceful people. They would fight fiercely to protect their lovely island if anyone tried to come there and invade them. This tale tells how the Tuatha De Danann, helped by Lug, defended Ireland against the Fomiori.

The King of the Tuatha was called Nuada of the Silver arm, because he had one arm entirely made of silver. His real arm had been chopped off at the Battle of Mag Tuired and his silver arm had been made for him by Dian Cecht the healer.

Nuada was holding a great feast at Tara for all his warriors and advisors. The entrance to the castle was guarded by a door-keeper who had been told that only people who were skilled at some craft or other should be allowed to enter. On the night of the feast a handsome young warrior followed by a troop of soldiers strode up to the door-keeper and demanded entrance.

'And who might you be?' asked the door-keeper.

'I am Lug Samildanach, son of Cian and Ethne and grandson of Balar of the Fomiori, and I wish to join the army of Nuada of the Silver Arm,' replied the young man proudly.

'What skill can you offer in the service of Nuada of the Silver Arm?' asked the door-keeper. 'Only those who are skilled may enter.'

'I am a blacksmith,' replied Lug.

'Then you may not enter,' said the door-keeper. 'We already have a blacksmith called Colum Cualleinech.'

'But I am also a wheelwright,' the young man responded.

'Still you may not enter, for we have a wheelwright called Luchta mac Luachada,' answered the door-keeper.

'I am also a harper and a champion,' said Lug.

'Still you may not enter, for we have a harper called Abcan mac Bicelmois and a champion called Ogma mac Elathan.'

'I am also a hero,' persevered Lug.

'Still you may not enter, for we have a hero called Bresal.'

'I am a soldier and a fighter,' Lug went on.

'Still you may not enter. In Dagda is our fighter. We have no need of you,' replied the door-keeper.

'I am a magician and a sorcerer,' continued Lug.

'Still you may not enter, we have magicians and sorcerers,' answered the door-keeper.

'I am a doctor and a poet.'

'Still you may not enter, we have a doctor and a poet in Tara already.'

'And do you have one man in Tara who can do all these things?' asked Lug.

'I will ask the king,' replied the door-keeper and he went into the hall and told Nuada about the young man who wished to enter.

'This is indeed a clever man,' Nuada said. 'Take all the chessboards of Tara out to him and we shall see if he is as wise as he claims.'

The chessboards were brought out and Lug played a hundred games of chess and won them all.

'Let him enter,' commanded Nuada of the Silver Arm. 'For never has so wise, strong and brave a man come to my court.'

And so Lug joined the band of soldiers and heroes who were to fight against the Fomiori.

Nuada then held a council of war to decide who should lead the Tuatha De Danann into battle. Lug was chosen because he was the wisest and cleverest of them all.

The following morning, In Dagda, the greatest of the Danann fighters, went early to Connacht to meet the war goddess Morrigan. She was a terrible creature with iron fingernails and teeth and hands that were so strong that she could splinter a tree trunk as easily as you could wring out a cloth. She was washing herself at a ford by the river and In Dagda came and stood beside her.

In Dagda was Morrigan's favourite warrior and they fell to talking about the coming battle. In Dagda cunningly flattered Morrigan, telling her that she was the most beautiful of all the goddesses and that he loved her more than the sun and moon. Morrigan asked him to kiss her, for she knew full well that she was hideous and that everybody recoiled from her. In Dagda swept her into his arms and kissed her soundly, even though her iron teeth cut his lips badly and her iron fingernails scratched him through his chain-mail armour. In return for the kiss, Morrigan told In Dagda how the battle could be won.

At noon, the battle began. The two enormous armies faced each other across a gentle valley and the sun gleamed on their lances and spears. At the back of the army of the Danann waited Dian Secht the healer. He would take the slain from the field of battle and bathe them in an enchanted spring which would bring them back to life, although they would never speak again. The king, Nuada, had decided that Lug was far too important to be allowed to fight and had told him to stay at the top of the hill and watch and advise.

A horn gave the signal for the battle to start and the two armies surged together. The valley rang with battle cries and the clashing of steel against steel. In Dagda was in the thick of it, swinging his enormous battle club, while Nuada's silver arm flashed above the struggling bodies. Lug, watching the battle, became so enraged that he forgot his orders and charged down to the fighting.

The armies struggled back and forth; first the Tuatha De Danann seemed to be winning and then the Fomiori seemed to gain the upper hand.

The leader of the Fomiori was none other than Lug's grandfather, Balar the Dreadful. This chieftain's right eye was covered with an iron eyelid that was only raised during battles because his eye was so horrible that it killed anyone it looked at. Four Fomiori warriors raised the eyelid and Balar began to gaze about him. The destruction was terrible: soldiers from the people of Danann began to fall in their hundreds as Balar slowly turned his head from side to side. Then Lug loaded his sling with a smooth granite stone and whirled the sling round his head. The air hummed and whistled as the sling turned and at its furthermost point Lug let the stone fly — straight into Balar's eye. It struck Balar with such force that his eye was driven right through his head and looked backwards on the army of the Fomiorians.

And this was how the Fomiori were beaten. Thousands of them were slain by the gaze of Balar and the others were driven into the sea. Balar's head was buried so that his terrible eye would never again look on the living; for even though Balar was dead, his eye still stared blindly up at the sky and threatened to kill the stars.

After the battle, Morrigan declared peace throughout Ireland and for one hundred years after this there was no more fighting.

THE TWILIGHT OF THE GODS

Nearly all the myths from the northern lands tell of the ending of the rule of the gods. In Iceland this is called Ragnarok, which means 'The destiny of the gods' and in Norway and Sweden it is called 'Ragna Rokkr,' which means 'The twilight of the gods.' You have heard many myths about the strength of Odin and Thor, of Loki's cunning and cleverness and of the giant's ceaseless struggle to overthrow the gods of Asgard. But the gods were not always fair and it was their treachery in betraying their word that eventually brought about their downfall. This is how it came about.

The beautiful land of Asgard had been protected by a series of impregnable walls which had been built by a giant who had demanded as payment the hand of Freyja. The gods had promised the giant that he would marry Freyja when the walls were finished but had broken that promise. Because the gods could not keep their word, strife began to break out all over the world and in all the lower regions of Niflheim treachery and malice became commonplace. This terrible state of affairs was made worse by Loki, who betrayed Baldur, one of the best loved of all the gods. Baldur, who spread happiness and peace wherever he went, began to be troubled by strange dreams. He went to Thor and begged that the other gods should protect him and they agreed. The gods made everything in the earth promise never to betray or harm Baldur. All the animals, trees, plants and men of the earth agreed. All that is, except one, the little mistletoe plant which had been thought too young to take the oath. Only Loki knew this. One day, when the gods were laughing and joking and playing a game of hurling everything they could at Baldur to test his invincibility, Loki secretly collected a branch of mistletoe and persuaded Hod, a blind god, to throw the mistletoe branch. This pierced Baldur through the heart and killed him. This enraged the gods and, knowing that it was Loki, with his love of malice that had caused this thing to happen, chained Loki up. Loki escaped, and, filled with bitterness against the gods, joined forces with the demons and giants of earth to fight against the gods. One of Loki's children was the terrible wolf Fenrir, who the gods had chained up many years before in order that Fenrir should not destroy the universe. Now the children of Fenrir were growing and one of them became so strong and powerful that it chased after the sun and ate it up, leaving nothing but a dull red glow in the sky. Worse

100

was still to come. Heimdall, the god who guarded the Bifrost bridge, the pathway from the earth to Asgard, had his sword stolen by Loki and was tricked into allowing the giants to begin to march on Asgard without sounding his great battle horn. Fenrir finally escaped and began to chew at the roots of Yggdrasil, the sacred ash tree which guarded the universe. Two monstrous boats appeared, driven forward by the waves created by the writhing body of the serpent Midgard. On one, the giant Hrym rode and on the other sat Loki, accompanied by his gigantic son Fenrir. The fire giant, Surt, attacked from the south and when they all reached the Bifrost bridge and marched over it the heat from the fires that Surt caused made the Bifrost bridge crack and splinter in two.

The two armies faced each other, the giants and Fenrir on one side and the gods, led by Odin on the other. As the battle began, Odin charged at Fenrir, his sword upraised, but Fenrir opened his huge mouth and swallowed Odin. Vidar, one of Odin's sons, soon avenged his father by standing on the wolf's lower jaw and holding the beast's muzzle open with his right hand, stabbed Fenrir in the heart, through the throat.

Midgard the serpent, who had wound itself round the earth all those years ago, now rose out of the ocean and threatened Thor. He crushed its head with the magic hammer Mjöllnir, but alas, the poisonous breath of the serpent Midgard overcame the god of thunder and Thor, too, fell dying. Loki and Heimdall fought hand to hand and each killed the other. Only Tyr, one of the bravest gods, who had lost his right arm when the gods had first chained Fenrir, was left on the battlefield. It was to the dog of the underworld that Tyr lost his life, but not before he had mortally wounded Garm.

The battle was over. No gods were left to protect the earth. The giants were victorious and swarmed over the lands, destroying them and setting them on fire. After the fire the seas rose up and flooded everything. The old universe was gone and in its place was a wasteland, with no living thing moving in it.

And was this the end? No. Out of the destruction of the old world grew a new one, one that was ruled by gods who kept their word, gods who preferred peace to war and gentleness to battle. But that is another story.

THOR'S HAMMER

Thor was the favourite son of the great god Odin. Even when he was young he showed such strength that his mother had had to make him a teething ring of iron because he chewed through his silver one as soon as it was put into his mouth — and that was before his teeth had even started to grow! When Thor reached full adulthood his power was legendary, as was his most famous possession, a magical stone hammer. This hammer was called Mjöllnir and never missed anything that it was hurled at. What was even stranger, it always returned to the hand of Thor and then shrank until it was tiny enough to hide in Thor's sleeve. Yet the moment Thor drew it out, it grew to its full size immediately, ready to be hurled at the next god or mortal who angered Thor. Not that many gods or mortals dared to anger this god of thunder, since his temper was as legendary as his strength.

Thor had a brother called Loki and hardly ever have two brothers been born who were so different. Where Thor was burly and tall, Loki was slender and of middle height. Where Thor was open-faced and ruddy-cheeked, Loki's face had a closed and secretive look and his cheeks were pale. Where Thor's voice was loud and jolly, Loki always spoke softly and hissed like a snake when he said words with an 's' in them. Where Thor was fast to act but sometimes slow to think, Loki had a quicksilver mind and weighed up everything he did before he acted. Nevertheless, the two brothers were fond of each other, and often, when Thor needed advice, it was to Loki that he turned. And when Loki needed the help of his brother's huge strength, he turned to Thor.

One day a dreadful thing happened in Asgard, the kingdom of the northern gods. Thor strode out of his castle Bilskirnir, and shouted in a voice that made the roofs and mountains of Asgard shake,

'Where is my hammer — Mjöllnir? Who has stolen my hammer?'

The gods were horrified. They had been feasting and carousing the night before and had gone to their homes in a very jolly mood indeed. Thor had been the jolliest of all, and had stumbled several times on the way back to Bilskirnir. His snores had rumbled through the night until even the gentle Freyja, the best loved and most peaceable goddess in Asgard, had finally complained. Even Odin could not wake his snoring son, so the gods had returned to their beds and pulled their wolfskin blankets up round their ears.

'The dragon Fafnir would not have woken Thor last night,' said Loki. 'Let alone a sneak thief who must have crept into Bilskirnir while Thor slept. But who would dare to do such a thing?'

Thor, of course, had no idea. He strode about, shaking his fists and roaring until the trees of the forest that grew at the edge of Asgard trembled so much that all their pine needles fell to the ground, leaving the branches spindly and bare.

'Enough of this roaring and fuming,' said Loki. 'This will do no good, we must think what to do. No mortal could have entered Bilskirnir, so some giant from the realms of Niflheim must be the culprit. Leave this to me, my brother, I shall seek him out.'

Loki went to the goddess Freyja. She was sitting by her spinning wheel, spinning fine wool into cloaks for the Valkyrie maidens and humming one of the more gentle war songs to herself.

'O, lovely Freyja,' Loki began, 'most beautiful of all the goddesses, would you lend me your magic cloak of eagle's feathers, that I might fly to the realm of giants to seek the hammer of Thor?'

'Of course, dear cousin,' replied Freyja in her sweet voice, 'and all success to your venture.'

Loki donned the cloak and sped on the winds to the dreary kingdom of Niflheim. There he met the giant Hymir.

'Tell me, dear Hymir of the wise head,' said Loki flatteringly, 'have you heard anyone speak of the great hammer of Thor lately?'

'Er ... no ... er ... er ... the hammer of who?' asked Hymir, who could never remember names.

'Then tell me if any of your number have seemed particularly happy today,' Loki went on.

Hymir scratched his head with his club which had an iron spike sticking out of it and rolled his eyes round in his head,

'I heard tell that er ... er ... Thrumm ... no, Thremm .. no, that's wrong ... Thrymm, that's it! that's it ... Thrymm was singing this morning and he hasn't been heard to sing for four thousand years or so. He's your man,' and Hymir wandered off, still scratching his head and murmuring 'Threem ... Throom, no that's not it ... Thrymm! That's your man!'

Hymir was right. Thrymm had indeed stolen the hammer and had hidden it eighty leagues below the ocean, under the coils of the serpent Midgard, which was why the hammer could not return to Thor's hand as it usually did when it was away from its master.

Now Thrymm was one of the ugliest of all the giants. He never cut or combed his hair or beard so he looked like a great mountain covered with dried bracken. His teeth were long and yellow and his

104

fingernails curved and black. He only ever wore one suit of clothes which was so dirty that when he took it off it stood up by itself. But in spite of all this he had a romantic nature and longed for a beautiful bride. He was passionately in love with the lovely Freyja and pined for her day and night. He knew that in the normal way of things there was no chance that Freyja would accept him and this was why he had stolen Thor's magic hammer. He hoped that the gods would persuade Freyja to accept him as a husband in return for the hammer.

'I shall return the hammer to Freyja on our wedding day,' he told Loki, 'as is the custom at our weddings. After that she may do with it as she chooses.'

It was the custom in those lands for the new husband to give the bride his most precious possession before they were married and Thrymm's most precious possession was the hammer he had stolen from Thor.

Loki returned to Asgard with the news and went straight to Odin, the father of the gods.

'Thrymm is quite serious about this,' he told Odin. 'Unless Freyja promises to marry him we shall never regain the magic hammer, and that would be a terrible thing. You must speak to Freyja.'

With a trembling heart Odin went to see Freyja, the gentlest of all the goddesses. She was sweeping the floor of the great hall of Valhalla with an ebony broom and singing her favourite battle song. She stopped when she saw Odin.

'Welcome, dear brother,' she said, 'and what can I do for you today?'

Odin twisted his beard round and round in his fingers and shuffled his feet in his battle boots.

'Sister Freyja,' Odin began, 'you know how important Thor's magic hammer is to all of us . . .'

'I do indeed,' said Freyja. 'Without it we should all have been defeated many times.'

'Well,' Odin went on, 'it's like this — the giant Thrymm had stolen it and will only give it back on one condition.' Here Odin paused and looked at the peaceful face of Freyja.

'And what might that be, dear brother?' asked Freyja, polishing one of the great cast-iron candelabra that stood at the side of the hall.

'I don't think you are going to like this, dear sister,' said Odin. 'Thrymm says he will only return the hammer if you consent to marry him.'

A dreadful silence fell on the hall as Freyja looked at Odin in disbelief. 'What!' she said. 'What did you say?' and the sound of her voice blew out half the candles in the hall.

'If you consent to marry him,' muttered Odin, glancing behind him and working out the distance to the door.

'Marry him!' said Freyja. 'Marry Thrymm! That ugly, unwashed, ignorant giant ... me, the gentlest of all the goddesses to marry Thrymm!' She picked up the nearest candelabra and broke it over her knee.

'Me! The goddess of beauty and motherhood to marry that horrible creature who never scrubs his teeth or his fingernails!' And she picked up the broom and began to hit Odin about the head and shoulders. 'Me! The goddess of learning and gentleness to marry that ...' here Freyja ran out of breath and words and shook her fists over her head. Her neck swelled up with rage so much that the heavy gold necklace that she always wore snapped and clanged to the floor.

'Well, don't think, don't do anything except go back to Thor and tell him that he might as well marry Thrymm himself because I won't.' And with that Freyja swept out of the hall and slammed the door behind her so hard that the rest of the candelabra fell down with a crash and all the battleaxes and shields and battle pennants that hung from the roof hurtled to the floor.

Odin picked himself up, disentangled his horned helmet from three battle pennants and a candelabra and went back to see Thor.

'She says no,' he told his favourite son. 'She says that if you want your hammer back you'll have to marry Thrymm yourself.'

'Just a moment,' interrupted Loki, who had been trying to calm his brother, 'that's a marvellous idea!'

'What do you mean?' growled Thor. 'Are you trying to make fun of me?'

'Certainly not,' said Loki, putting a prudent distance between himself and his brother. 'Think about it for a moment. You know that a bride is always veiled until the marriage is over, and you know that Thrymm is not the cleverest of giants. You also know that the bride must receive as a wedding present the most precious thing that the groom possesses. Now what is the most precious thing that Thrymm possesses?'

'My magic hammer,' replied Thor, grinding his teeth.

'Well then,' said Loki, 'why don't you pretend to be Freyja? You can dress up in her long blue cloak and grey veil and borrow her golden necklace. As long as you say nothing, how will Thrymm know that it is you and not Freyja? And once you have the hammer, there will be no question of a wedding anyway.'

'That's not a bad idea,' said Odin, 'but you'll have to go with Thor, for who knows whether he'll control his temper or not...'

So it was decided that Loki should send a message to Thrymm to say that Freyja had consented to be his wife and that she would soon be arriving for the wedding feast. Freyja willingly gave Thor her blue cloak and grey veil and golden necklace and Loki dressed Thor up and took him down to Niflheim where Thrymm was waiting.

All the giants were there. There was Hymir the thick-witted, and Surt, the giant of fire who wore a blazing crown and sat by himself for fear of scorching the other guests. There was Suttung, who knew the secret of the marvellous wine that the gods and giants loved, but who was always drunk because of this. There was the giantess Grid, who carried a girdle, gloves and magic wand that made her the strongest of all the giants; and there were many many more, most of them very merry from the wine that Suttung had brought with him.

Fortunately the hall where the wedding feast was to be held was dark and gloomy, as were most of the giant's dwelling places and Thor's disguise hid him well. Loki and his disguised brother were seated at the places of honour, next to Thrymm, who had plaited greasy red ribbons into his hair and beard and looked even more horrible than usual.

'Here is your bride,' announced Loki as they entered.

Thrymm took the hand of his supposed bride eagerly, but was surprised to find it gnarled and rough.

'What is this?' he asked Loki. 'My bride's hand feels strangely rough!'

'Ah! Well . . .' said the quick-witted Loki, 'er . . . yes, that is because she has been sewing her bridal clothes for the last three days without ceasing and the needle has pricked her fingers so much that they have become roughened.'

The feast began and rich food was placed before the guests. To Thrymm's surprise his bride ate more than all the other giants, and not only at eating did the bride prove to be the greediest but at drinking too! Flagon after flagon was drained and plate after plate of food disappeared beneath the veil of the bride.

'This is surely a strong appetite for a bride,' Thrymm remarked, looking suspiciously at Loki.

'Ah! Well . . .' replied Loki, 'it is, um . . . not surprising to me, er . . . um . . . after all, she has been so busy preparing herself for the wedding that she has had no time to eat for three days.'

The feast continued and Thrymm became more and more curious to see his bride. At last he could bear it no more and attempted to lift the grey veil. He only caught a glimpse of the face beneath and reeled back, amazed at the ruddy complexion and blazing eyes that he saw.

'Is this the face of the gentlest of all goddesses?' he asked Loki.

'Ah! Well . . .' replied Loki, 'er . . . yes . . . it is no wonder that she seems flushed and bright-eyed. For the last three days she has had no sleep because she was so excited by the idea of her forthcoming marriage, she was so overcome that it has given her a fever.'

At this Thrymm decided to delay no longer.

'Let us be married,' he roared.

'First the Bride-Gift,' insisted Loki. 'At so important a wedding all the customs must be obeyed.'

'Very well,' Thrymm agreed, and he commanded that the hammer should be brought from a side chamber where he had hidden it after bringing it from beneath the oceans.

Two servants carried it in and the other giants withdrew to a respectful distance, as did Loki, who knew exactly what was about to happen.

Ceremonially the hammer was laid across the knees of the bride.

'Now will you be mine?' demanded Thrymm of his bride.

'No,' replied the bride, 'but you shall be mine!' And casting off the veil and the cloak Thor swung the mighty Mjöllnir round his head and struck Thrymm as hard as he could.

At the first blow, all the greasy, red ribbons fell from Thrymm's hair and beard.

At the second blow, all Thrymm's yellow teeth fell out.

At the third blow, all Thrymm's black fingernails fell off.

And at the fourth blow, Thrymm was driven deep into the earth never to be seen again. Not that any of the giants saw this happen, for they had all fled from the hall after the second blow.

So Thor regained his hammer and Freyja remained free; and it is said that Thor carried the red ribbons and yellow teeth and black fingernails back to Freyja as a present — but it is also said that Freyja was not very pleased about it.

THOR, LOKI
AND THE ENCHANTER

Here is another adventure of Thor and his brother Loki. It shows how even the gods themselves may sometimes be deceived.

One day, Thor felt the need for adventure. He and his brother Loki left Asgard and came down the Bifrost bridge to earth. There they met two young peasants.

'We are off to seek an adventure,' Thor told the young men in his jolly booming voice, 'would you like to come with us?'

The two young men, who had no idea that Thor and Loki were gods, agreed and the four of them set off for Niflheim and the land of the giants. They marched along at a good pace and soon came to an enormous forest. This forest was so huge that even after three days of travelling they had still not come through it. On the third night Thor decided that they should rest and the two peasants were delighted, for they were amazed at the strength of their companions and had not liked to complain of tiredness.

'We must find shelter,' said Thor, 'for we shall be cold when we stop marching.'

He looked around and saw a house just ahead of them in a large clearing. A very strange house to be sure, but it seemed empty and would give them shelter.

They entered the house through its enormous doorway and found that there were five long narrow rooms leading off the central chamber.

'This will be fine,' boomed Thor. 'There is a room for each of us and one for our sacks of food.' Each of them made themselves comfortable and settled down to sleep. But sleep was difficult that night, for all through the hours of darkness they heard rumblings and groaning and the earth shook and quivered.

'How did you sleep?' Thor asked the others in the morning. 'I had a most disturbed night. Perhaps we should go on and find somewhere quieter to rest.'

They picked up their sacks of food and set off through the forest again. They had not gone very far when they came across the biggest giant any of them had ever seen. Although all of them had seen many giants in their time they were each amazed that anyone so big could live on the earth.

The giant was lying on his back snoring and wheezing and they understood now where the strange sounds that had kept them awake the night before had come from. They walked all round the giant and marvelled. Just as Thor was about to tap the giant lightly with his hammer to wake him up the giant stirred and stretched and stood up. He towered over them.

'Good morning,' he said, and his voice made the trees shake and the grass flatten as if in a gale. 'I am the giant Skrymir. I recognize you,' he said, pointing at Thor. 'You are Thor, the god of thunder.'

The two peasants were as amazed by this as they had been by the giant.

'No wonder they needed no rest in three days' marching,' one whispered to the other. 'We have been journeying with the gods!'

Skrymir stretched again and then looked around him.

'Where is my glove?' he asked. 'I must have dropped it.'

The four travellers then realized that they had spent the night inside the giant's glove. They led him to it and Skrymir asked if he might join them on their journey.

'Indeed you may,' answered Thor. 'But we shall stop early tonight, for we are all tired. You may carry our food sacks.'

They marched on and on and when night came Skrymir immediately lay down and fell asleep. Thor and his companions tried to open the sack of food, but Skrymir had tied it so tightly that even Thor could not loosen the drawstring that held the neck of the sack closed. This irritated Thor so much that he picked up his hammer and hit the sleeping giant on the head as hard as he could. Skrymir stirred in his sleep. 'The flies round here are very irritating,' he said and fell asleep again. This made Thor even angrier and again he swung his hammer at the giant's head, almost snapping the handle with the force of his blow.

'Mmmmm . . .' mumbled the giant. 'The night moths seem to be alighting on me.'

Again Thor swung his hammer and this time the hammer sank into Skrymir's head.

'Mngngngng . . .' muttered the giant, 'bird's eggs must be dropping out of the trees. I think I shall never get any sleep here.'

The giant rose and said to Thor and his companions, 'I shall be off now but if you go on to the castle over there, you will find giants far stronger than me. I am but a babe compared to them.'

The giant left and Thor, Loki and the two peasants journeyed on to the castle. The castle gateway towered over them and by the side of the gate was a vast iron bell. Thor rang it and demanded entrance.

A great voice boomed out at them.

'Whoever enters here must first prove his strength,' the voice roared. 'We will have no weaklings here.'

The voice belonged to Utgardaloki, the master of the castle and one of the most powerful magicians of that place.

'It is Thor. The god of thunder, and Loki, his brother, who rings,' Thor bellowed back. 'We will match our strength with any of you.'

Loki stepped forward. 'Throughout Asgard I am known as the mightiest eater of the gods,' he announced. 'I challenge any one of you to an eating match.'

At that a thin, red-headed giant called Logi stepped out and behind him two giants each carrying an enormous plate heaped high with joints of meat. There must have been meat from at least sixteen oxen on each plate. Loki sat down and started to eat and in no time had emptied the plate, leaving only the clean bones. Imagine his surprise when he looked at his opponent's plate and found that the thin red-haired man had eaten not only the meat but the bones and plate as well.

'I am the fastest runner on earth,' announced one of the peasants who had been journeying with Thor and Loki. 'I am Thjalfi the swift. Match me with one of your clumsy giants.'

At this another giant stepped out. His name was Hugi and he looked so weak and frail that Thor began to laugh. Utgardaloki gave the signal and Thjalfi and Hugi began to race. Although the peasant ran as fast as the wind he could not catch up with Hugi.

'And now it is my turn,' announced Thor. 'First I challenge anyone to outdrink me.' For Thor could drink more than any god or human.

An enormous drinking horn was brought out of the castle and Thor took a deep breath and raised it to his lips. He took three great gulps from the horn but to his amazement, when he put it down the level in the horn was only a little lower than before.

'I am also the strongest of all the gods,' he boasted, 'give me another test.'

'If you can lift my cat up, then I shall believe that you are the strongest,' said Utgardaloki. He whistled and a small grey cat slunk out of the castle. Thor grinned and bent down to lift the little animal, but no matter how hard he tried he could only lift one paw of the cat from the ground.

'One last test,' Thor demanded, 'and then I shall admit defeat.'

'Very well,' said Utgardaloki. 'You must wrestle with my old nurse Elli and we shall see who wins.'

An old, wrinkled woman came slowly out of the castle and stood before Thor.

112

'Are you afraid to wrestle with an old woman?' she demanded. 'No, by the Bifrost Bridge!' retorted Thor, and rushed at her. They grappled together and slowly but surely, Elli forced Thor to his knees.

Thor and Loki were ashamed and amazed.

'Never have I been beaten before,' said Thor. 'These are indeed mighty giants.' They turned to go when Utgardaloki stopped them.

'Stay a moment,' he said. 'I will explain why you were defeated. I would never dare to let you in, for you are truly the strongest gods of all. When you met Skrymir in the forest it was none other than myself. When I lay down I covered my head with mountains to protect myself. You may see what damage you did.'

Thor looked at the mountain range in the distance and saw huge trenches and valleys had been gouged out of it.

'When Loki tried to outeat Logi, he failed because Logi is none other than fire, and fire consumes everything. Thjalfi has been beaten by Hugi because Hugi is thought, which runs faster than anything. The drinking horn that Thor could not empty is always full because the other end is dipped into the sea, and by lowering the level of the horn, Thor has caused the first tides to appear. The cat is none other than the serpent Midgard, which is coiled round the centre of the earth and by lifting one paw, Thor has caused gigantic earthquakes. Finally the old nurse, Elli, is really old age, and no one can defeat age. So you see, your strength is amazing.'

Thor was furious when he found out that he had been tricked. With a mighty war cry he rushed at Utgardaloki and raised his hammer to smash him into the ground. But the magician was too quick for him and in a twinkling the castle and the giants disappeared, leaving only the sighing trees of the forest and the rushing winds of the plain.

MARGOT THE BLACK

This is the tale of a terrible queen. A woman so evil that she willingly made a pact with the Devil. A woman so wicked that she was prepared to give away another life to gain what she wanted.

Margot, daughter of Sambor, Duke of Pomerania, was said to be so beautiful that few men could look at her without being overcome by her loveliness. Certainly King Christopher of Denmark fell in love with her and married her without knowing that her beauty hid a heart as hard and cruel as winter.

Soon the people of Denmark began to hear tales of her cruelty, tales of her greed and wicked ways. It was even said that she could call up the Devil. She was never known as Queen Margot, only as Margot the Black.

In the reign of King Christopher, Denmark was often at war. The frontiers could not be defended well and fighting constantly broke out along the borders of the land. King Christopher asked his queen for help. She agreed, but warned the king that she must be allowed to do whatever she wanted or she could not help him. Weakly the king agreed.

That night Margot the Black conjured up the Devil. She made a bargain with him.

'If you build a wall for me,' she told Satan, 'I will give you anything you want. The wall must be high and strong, with iron gates — it must stretch across the borders of our land and keep out any enemies of Denmark.'

'If I do this for you,' said Satan, 'what will you give me in return?'

Margot the Black was wise in the ways of evil and knew that the Devil liked nothing better than the souls of innocent people.

'I will give you the soul of the first living thing to pass through the iron gates,' she said. She pricked her finger and signed her name in her own blood and so the pact was sealed.

That night was the blackest night ever known in Denmark. People locked themselves in their houses and peered timorously through the shutters. Strange noises filled the land and terrible figures were seen against the clouds. The smell of sulphur crept into the houses and a dull red glow was noticed over the borders of Denmark. In the morning a huge wall with just one iron gate stood stern and harsh against the sky. The Devil had fulfilled his part of the bargain and now waited for Margot to pay the dreadful price.

Margot the Black stood on the ramparts of the terrible wall and watched for the first unwary traveller. About midday a travelling merchant came into sight, and Margot chuckled. Here was her hostage. Here was the innocent soul she had promised to the Devil.

'Open the gates,' she called down to the guards, 'welcome the poor traveller in.' The guards obeyed, although they were surprised that their wicked queen should show such hospitality. As the great iron gates creaked open the weary merchant spurred his horse on. But before he could pass through, his little dog, who had been running beside his horse, darted ahead and so passed through the gates first. The Devil was furious, but the bargain had to be kept. He had been promised the first living thing to pass through the gates and so he had to be content with the dog and not the merchant. He vowed then never to deal with Margot the Black again. Margot, too, was furious, for she knew that she could never call on Satan again and her power would from that day never be so strong.

But that is not the end of the story. When Margot the Black died her ghost came back to haunt the ramparts of the great wall. Every night she could be seen, dressed in a great black cloak, riding on a white charger with her raven hair blowing in the wind and a crown on fire round her head. The wicked spirit of the woman who made a pact with the Devil has no rest and it is said that even today her ghost still haunts the ruins of the wall.

BIG KAMINIK

This story comes from the frozen lands of the north. Eskimo mothers have told it to their children for many years, and in Greenland, where this tale comes from, the children often skip to the words of the song that was once sung about Kaminik.

Once upon a time there lived a fisherman and his wife. They lived in the village of Norssit which in those days was near to the sea. Today, the same village is found high up in the mountains. Now, you may say that a village cannot possibly change its position, but this is just what happened and this is how it came about.

The fisherman and his wife had one child, a boy that they called Kaminik. The years passed and while the other children of the village grew tall and strong, little Kaminik never grew any taller than he had been when he was three, even though he was nearly twenty years old.

Because he was so small he was afraid of almost everything and spent a great deal of his time hiding away from the fierce husky dogs that pulled the villagers' sledges over the icy lands round the village. When he did creep out from his hiding place, the village children would dance round him and sing this song:

Poor Little Kaminik

You don't grow so quick

We are growing tall

You stay very small,

and they would make snowballs and throw them at him and chase him back to his mother and father's house where he would hide again.

His father, too, used to say to Kaminik,

'You are so small; all the other village boys help their fathers when they can. They go out with them fishing and hunting for seals and whales, but you cannot help me. You're far too small and not even as strong as the kitten that plays by your mother's hearth. You will never grow up into a man.'

This made Kaminik very sad and he decided that he would leave the village and go out into the world where no one knew him and no one would tease him. His mother made a kayak for him out of sealskins and sadly waved goodbye as her son set out across the icy seas.

Kaminik steadily paddled his kayak through the waves and as he looked back he could see the shore and the village growing smaller and smaller until they disappeared into the mist. All that day and night he paddled on, through seas that grew colder and colder. Enormous icebergs towered above him and on one of them he saw a gigantic seagull, four or five times bigger than himself. Kaminik was very frightened.

'This is a strange part of the world,' he thought to himself. 'Even back at the village, where everything seemed bigger than me, I never saw a seagull as big as that!' He paddled on as fast as he could. He was growing very tired by now, and then, ahead of the prow of his little boat, he saw an island.

'I shall rest here,' he said to himself, but before he had reached the shore of the island, it began to move. Kaminik looked in amazement as first an enormous head and then an enormous body rose up out of the middle of the island! It was the Giant Akitinek. The giant stretched and yawned, and his yawn caused huge waves that very nearly upset Kaminik's little kayak. Kaminik cried out in fear and the giant heard him. Reaching down, the giant took up Kaminik and his kayak in one huge hand.

'What have we here?' boomed the giant, peering down at Kaminik. 'A little man I declare! I shall take you home to show my wife,' he said and began to wade through the sea, carrying Kaminik carefully. When the giant reached the mainland of Greenland where he lived, he walked ashore and strode over the mountains, until he came to his house.

'Here you are, my dear,' he said to his wife, placing Kaminik and his kayak on the table, 'I have brought you a present.'

Akitinek's wife was almost as large as her husband, but even though she was so much bigger than he was, Kaminik could see that she had a kind face.

'Oh,' said the giantess, clasping her hands together, 'he is so sweet. I have always wanted a little boy of my own. We shall bring him up as our son. What do you think of that, little man?' she asked, but Kaminik did not reply, he had fallen sound asleep in his kayak.

So Kaminik stayed with the giant Akitinek and his wife and was very happy with them. The giants were always very gentle with him, but at first Kaminik was often frightened, for in the land of the giants everything is big and the houseflies seemed like big birds, and the spiders like large dogs. Soon though, Kaminik noticed a strange thing. The spiders and the flies seemed to be getting smaller, and so did Akitinek and his wife. Kaminik could not understand it and then one day, Akitinek said to him,

'Well well, my little adopted son, you seem to be growing up at last.'

It was true. Kaminik grew in leaps and bounds, and soon he was as tall as Akitinek and just as strong. He could catch seals and whales with his hands and once, he even wrestled with a huge polar bear and overcame it. Akitinek and his wife watched all this with pride. One day, Akitinek said to Kaminik,

'It is many years since you have seen your real parents. Would you like to journey to Norssit to see them again?'

'I would, adopted father,' answered Kaminik.

Together they made an enormous kayak for Kaminik. It was so large that it took the skins of a hundred seals to cover it. Each blade of the paddle that Kaminik used was as big as a double bed, and its handle was as long as a fir tree is tall. Akitinek's wife loaded the kayak with food, for Kaminik's appetite was now so huge that he would eat a whole ovenful of loaves at one sitting and still be hungry for more. She also put many presents in the kayak for Kaminik's parents.

'Promise that you will come back,' begged the giantess. 'We have come to love you so much and you are now so huge that you will not be comfortable living with ordinary people.'

'I promise to return,' said Kaminik, 'for I am happy here, but I wish to see my village again and surprise all those who once laughed at me for being so small.'

Kaminik set off. What had seemed such a long journey when he was small now took only half a day. He arrived at Norssit just as the men had returned from a fishing expedition. Kaminik could see his father unloading the fish from the boats and his mother standing at the doorway of their house. Kaminik stood up in his kayak and called out a greeting to them. You can imagine how amazed the villagers of Norssit were to see such a giant.

'Do you not remember me?' called Kaminik, and he sang the song that they had taunted him with so many years ago.

'Poor little Kaminik
You don't grow so quick
We are growing tall
You stay very small.'

And then he laughed and laughed until the houses shook and all the husky dogs that had once frightened him so much ran away and hid under the sledges. Kaminik took the presents to his parents and told them all that had happened to him. That night they feasted and made merry and in the morning Kaminik said farewell to them all.

Before he left he did a strange thing. He carefully lifted up all the houses of the village of Norssit and placed them on the top of the mountain.

'Why are you doing this?' the villagers asked him.

'It is to keep you safe,' he told them, 'for when I launch my kayak, the waves that it makes would drown the whole village if it was not high up and away from the sea.'

Then Kaminik launched his kayak and it was just as he said. The waves rose up and up until they covered the place where Norssit had once stood.

And that is why the village of Norssit is now found high up in the mountains instead of by the sea, and that is the end of the tale of Big Kaminik who was once the smallest man in Greenland.

THE LIVING DEAD

This is a strange and mysterious tale about two graveyards, a rich merchant and the spirits of the dead. It all begins on the borders of Lithuania and Germany at a little village called Ragnit. This village was known as 'Ragnit of the two Cemeteries', for close together to the west of the village lay two graveyards; one was the German cemetery and the other was the Lithuanian cemetery.

Ragnit was a happy village, surrounded by beautiful countryside and close to the swiftly flowing river Niemen. Why then, during the stormy months of the autumn did the people of Ragnit hide inside their houses and bolt the doors and bar the windows? Why did they lock up their dogs and cats and tie their horses up in the stalls in the barns and stables? Why did the cattle in the fields and the pigs in the sties crouch low into the straw while the chickens clucked and fussed and hid their heads under their wings and didn't look out until morning? Because on those dark and stormy nights the spirits of the dead travelled between the two graveyards to visit each other.

For the rest of the year the people of Ragnit went about their business in the normal way, no one minded being out after dark at all, but when the winter months came, up would go the shutters and locks would be put on all the doors. One day, a rich merchant came to live in Ragnit. There was no house splendid enough for him so he decided to build one himself. He chose a plot of land that lay directly between the two graveyards for, he thought to himself,

'Here I have space all round me, no one can look into my windows, no one will cross my land or walk over my flowerbeds.'

The villagers looked at each other and nodded wisely, but they said nothing to the rich merchant because he was still a stranger to them, and they took many years to accept strangers into their midst.

Soon the splendid house was finished and the merchant moved in and furnished it richly. The summer months passed and all was well and then, autumn came and with it the first night of the storms!

The merchant heard the wind howling round the house and went outside to see that his horses were safely in the stable. As he stepped out of the house a great gust of wind rushed across the land and his house fell in a heap at his feet. The merchant was amazed and angered.

'That was a fierce wind,' he thought, 'but even so my house should not have fallen down.'

He rebuilt the house, but it was no use. The next stormy night came and down fell his house again. This happened three times and at last the merchant decided that he must go and ask the wise man of the village why it was that only his house fell down during the stormy nights while all the other houses of Ragnit stood firmly through the strongest gales.

The wise man of the village had been born between the first two strokes of midnight on the night of All Hallows, and all people born at that moment have 'second sight' and can see things that ordinary men and women cannot.

'Come with me,' said the wise man to the merchant, 'I will show you why your house falls down on stormy nights.' They walked to the heap of rubble that had once been the merchant's house.

'You see, over there, and over there,' said the wise man pointing first to the German Cemetery and then to the Lithuanian Cemetery. 'Those are the resting places of the dead of our village. But they do not always rest, on stormy nights they fly up from their graves and visit each other, just as they used to do when they were alive. Now look around you and see if you can see any other houses.'

'Why, I cannot,' said the merchant. 'Only that old barn over there.'

'That is because the people of the village know very well that they must not build anything that would stop the dead from visiting each other. Farmer Hans built that barn, but the corner stuck out into the pathway of the dead and look what they did to it.'

The merchant looked, and could see that the corner of the barn had been cut off as if an enormous pair of shears had cut it away.

'If you wish your house to stand, you must build it away from the pathway of the dead,' the wise man told the merchant. 'Only then will it stand in peace.' And that is just what the merchant did. He built his house right away from the two cemeteries, as did all the other villagers of Ragnit, and for all I know, are doing so still.

TILL EULENSPIEGEL

Till Eulenspiegel was a most mysterious character: he was said to have been born in Germany about 1300. He was thought to be the son of a peasant and many amusing stories were told about him. He was rather like Simple Simon of the nursery rhyme, silly and seemingly stupid but very cunning when he wanted to get his own way. Stories of how he had tricked noblemen, innkeepers, tradesmen and clergymen were written down in a book that was published in 1519 which was later translated into English under the name of 'The Marvellous Tales of Master Tyll Owlglass'. Even before this he became so famous that as far away as England, in the fourteenth century, the English poet Chaucer retold one of Till's adventures as part of the Summoner's Tale, one of the Canterbury Tales.

Hundreds of songs and plays were written about him and paintings of some of his most famous exploits were made, and can still be seen today.

No one really knows for sure whether Till actually existed, but there is museum to Till Eulenspiegel at Schoppenstedt in Germany and a tomb at Molln where he is supposed to be buried. This is probably the most peculiar tomb in the whole of Germany. The strange thing about it is that instead of being buried lying down as everybody was in those days, Till is supposed to be buried upright, and what is even more peculiar, no one knows whether he is buried standing on his feet or on his head, a fitting memorial to a man who spent his life fooling people. The gravestone above the tomb is carved with these words:

In 1350 these words were written,
When Till Eulenspiegel was sheltered here.
All you who pass here
Always think,
That what has happened to me,
Will one day happen to you!

And on the top of the tombstone on the left is a carving of a wise owl, and on the top at the right is a mirror. This is a pun on the meaning of his name, 'Eulen,' which means owl and 'spiegel,' which means mirror.

WISE LIBUSE

Today, Prague is one of the greatest cities of Europe, but it was not always so. In the olden days when Prince Krok ruled Bohemia, the city of Prague did not exist. There was only a small town called Vysehrad near to where Prague is now. This is the story of Princess Libuse of Vysehrad, and how the city of Prague was founded.

Krok of Bohemia had three daughters. The oldest was called Kazi and had long blond hair and green eyes. She was tall and graceful and could play the harp like an angel. The second daughter was called Teta and was round and plump with a lovely smile. She could embroider so well that butterflies would alight on the flowers that she had made from silken threads because they thought the flowers were real. The youngest daughter was called Libuse. She was the merriest of the sisters and could call the birds of the air down to her where they would flutter about her head and sing to her. All the sisters were beautiful and very clever and all of them knew a great deal about magic. This was not the sort of magic which brought harm to people, but the sort which helps the crops to grow and cures illness and brings happiness and laughter to the land. The three sisters gave advice freely and helped everyone they could. Libuse was the sweetest of the sisters and the people loved her. They flocked to the great castle of Vysehrad to ask for her help and listen to her wise words.

When Krok died the people of Bohemia chose Libuse to be their princess and in a magnificent ceremony at the biggest church in Vysehrad she was crowned and declared to be the ruler of all Bohemia.

For several years Libuse ruled her people wisely and well. Bohemia was a happy land and everything prospered because it was guided by such a clever ruler; but after several years people began to murmur and mutter.

'Libuse is very beautiful,' they said, 'and still not married. It is time she chose a husband.'

They went to the princess and asked her why she had not married.

'I have never found any man I can love,' she told them. 'My country is my first love.'

So the years passed and although many suitors came to court Libuse, none of them gained her hand.

At that time there were several noblemen in Bohemia who were quarrelling about who owned the lands round Vysehrad. They simply could not agree and so they went to Princess Libuse to ask her to decide. The princess thought about the matter carefully and then gave her judgement; she awarded the land to the poorest of the noblemen. This led to a great uproar.

'Now see what becomes of us when we are ruled by a woman,' said the noblemen who had lost their lands. 'It is time we had a man on the throne. He would not be so soft.'

When Libuse heard this she was very angry, but she hid her anger. 'Are you sure that you wish to be ruled by a man?' she asked them. 'Do I really care for you so badly? You think that I am too gentle. Very well, come to the castle tomorrow morning and I will tell you the name of the man I will marry.' That night Libuse went to the temple of the pagan god that she worshipped.

'Great Perun!' she prayed. 'Tell me what I must do. '

For many hours she prayed, but no answer came to her. Then, just as dawn was breaking, the voice of the god Perun spoke. Libuse listened and bowed her head.

'It shall be so,' she said, and returned to the castle where her people were waiting.

Once again she asked them if they really wanted to be ruled by a king.

'It is easy to choose a king, but what will you do if he is cruel and wicked. He holds the power of life and death over you. Your lands and houses will belong to him and not to you. Now you are free, but how do you know that the man who I marry will not be stern and harsh? Once you have chosen the king you cannot put him away easily. Think again, my people, are you not content as you are?'

But the Bohemian people would not listen to their princess.

'Tell us the name of our king,' they demanded. 'Tell us the name of the man you will marry.'

'Very well,' sighed Libuse. 'He is called Premysl. He lives in a village called Stadice, which lies by the River Belina.' 'How will we recognize him?' they asked.

'He is a tall man, with golden eyes. He works in the fields and his plough is pulled by two white bulls and he eats from a table of iron. Go and ask him to be your king. Take royal robes with you so that he may be royally dressed when he comes to take the crown.'

'How shall we find the way?' they asked.

'Take my two white horses and ride to the south from here. When you reach the valley of the River Belina you will see Stadice at the foot of the mountains.'

126

What wise Libuse did not tell them was that Premysl had been chosen by the god Perun, and that her magic had shown her that he would become a great ruler and king, the founder of a line of kings and queens of Bohemia.

The messengers set out and soon reached Stadice. In a huge field outside the village they found Premysl ploughing the land with a great plough pulled by two white bulls.

The messengers fell to their knees before him and told him that he had been chosen to be the king of Bohemia.

'Very well,' said Premysl, 'but before I come with you we will all eat together.' Premysl unyoked the two bulls and turned them loose.

'Go back to where you came from,' he ordered, and the messengers watched in amazement as the two bulls rose into the air and disappeared.

From his pocket Premysl took a long loaf of bread and broke it in half. One half he thrust into the ground and the other half he put back into his pocket. With a mighty heave he turned his enormous plough over so that the blade was uppermost making a rough iron table and on this he put the half loaf and some cheese from his pocket. He walked over to a nearby spring and brought back water and then the messengers and Premysl ate a hearty meal. After they had finished, Premysl dressed himself in his new robes.

'I am nearly ready,' Premysl told the messengers. 'Let me see what the future holds.'

He turned to where he had planted the half loaf and there, in its place, grew a strange tree. It had three branches covered with leaves and fruit, but two of the branches were withered while the tallest one was laden with heavy fruit.

'This means that I shall be the founder of many royal dynasties, but only one will prosper,' Premysl said.

Before they left for Vysehrad Premysl put his old pair of wooden shoes into his pocket.

'This will remind me and my children and my grandchildren that we are all descended from humble peasants; even though we will be rulers from now on, we must never become vain or haughty,' he said.

So Premysl married Libuse and ruled the country justly. It was Premysl who founded the city of Prague and made it rich — so rich that it became known as the Golden City. He never forgot that he was once a humble peasant and even today, the coat of arms of Vysehrad bear a picture of the wooden shoes that Premysl carried with him.

ALBERT
THE GREAT MAGICIAN

In the year 1193, in the little town of Lauingen in Germany, a boy was born who was one day to be known as one of the wisest men who had ever lived. He was born the son of the Count of Bollstädt and was christened Albert. When he grew up he became a monk of the Dominican order and studied at Paris and Cologne. He wrote thirty-nine books and was famous all over Europe for his learning and scholarship. When he gave a sermon, people would come from miles around to hear the great man speak and listen to his wisdom. Famous men, such as Thomas Aquinas, studied with him and learned from him. History books speak of him as Albert the Great, Count of Bollstädt.

Albert was not only learned in academic subjects, but knew a great deal about the occult sciences. It is said that he could predict the future, could conjure up bodiless heads who would speak to bystanders and tell them what would happen to them in life. It was believed that he could speak strange incantations and change icy winter into warm summer in less than a second.

Even more miraculous than this, he once held a splendid feast for King William of the Low Countries. When the royal guest arrived he was startled to find that the table, although laid with wonderful crystal glasses and silver and gold plates and cutlery, had not a scrap of food or wine on it.

'I see that we shall go hungry tonight,' the king remarked.

'Not at all, sire,' replied Albert the Great, 'I have a marvel to show your majesty.' He turned to his servants. 'Draw the tapestries over the windows,' he commanded, 'light the sconces and throw herbs into the fire.'

The servants obeyed and the room was lit only by the flickering light from the sconces set round the walls. The sweet smell of herbs rose from the fire and Albert's guest watched in amazed silence as the magician took out a long ebony wand. He drew a huge circle round the table and made sinuous movements in the air with his arms. The fire flared up and there, on the table, a marvellous meal appeared. Haunches of venison on silver salvers, roast meats and chickens, and salmon surrounded by succulent vegetables, fresh peaches and cherries — a meal truly fit for a king.

One of the strangest tales told about Albert the Great is how he humbled a king. This is what happened: One summer, a young man made the acquaintance of Albert the Great. This young man was an idle fellow who had wasted his father's fortune. He flattered Albert and pretended friendship with him. One evening the two were drinking together when the young man lifted his glass and said to Albert,

'My dear friend, today I am poor, but if ever I should become rich and powerful, I shall never forget you.'

Now soon after this the young man came into a fortune, and what was more, became first a Count, then a Duke and finally a King. Everything he touched prospered and he became immensely wealthy with several large palaces, hundreds of acres of land and servants by the thousand. News of this came to Albert the Great.

At this time, Albert had fallen on hard times. Although he still kept his house, he had very little money and at times was forced to beg through the streets for a living. He remembered the promise that the young man had made to him and decided to visit this king who had once sworn never to forget his old friend.

The journey was hard and long and when Albert arrived and asked for an audience he was kept waiting for many hours. At last he was ushered into the throne room.

'Sire,' he said, bowing before the splendidly dressed monarch, 'you are wealthy and well fed, while I am poor and hungry — can you spare alms for an unfortunate brother?'

'Certainly not,' the haughty king replied. 'A fine thing it would be if I had to concern myself with all the poor of the world. If I gave alms to every beggar I might just as well give up my throne.'

'So be it then,' said Albert, 'as surely as you are holding that glass.'

The king looked at the poor beggar in horror and the glass slipped from his grasp and shattered on the marble floor.

'Now perhaps you remember me,' Albert the Great said sternly. 'Do your promises mean so little to you, and is your heart so proud that you have no room in it for kindness and charity?' In a twinkling the grand palace was gone and the king found himself sitting on a crude wooden bench in the house of Albert the Magician.

'What has happened?' asked the bewildered king. 'Where am I?'

'Brought down by your pride and haughtiness,' Albert told him. 'You think that you have been king for three years, but it has all passed away in three seconds. Your ingratitude has cost you your kingdom.'

This was only one of the wonderful stories told about Albert the Great. He lived to a ripe old age and when he died the townspeople of Lauingen built a monument in honour of their most famous citizen.

THE DRAGON GUELRE

In France, between the rivers Rhine and Meuse, there is an area called the Gueldre. You may say that this is a strange name for a region and so it is, but the reason for the name is even stranger.

Long ago this part of France was plagued by the most awful dragon. To be sure there were many dragons in those parts, but this one was particularly horrible. It was covered in slimy scales and had glaring red eyes. Its teeth were as long as barbers' poles and the spike on its tail was so sharp that it mowed the grass in the meadows when the dragon swished it about. But what was particularly frightful about this dragon was the noise that it made. When it heard anybody coming it would roar, "GUELRE, GUELRE". This may not look frightening when it is written down, but you try saying it aloud in a gruff voice and then imagine that sound magnified sixteen thousand times! The dragon frightened the people so much that no one ever dared to try and kill it. Indeed, they were so terrified of it that they would not go anywhere near its lair in case they heard the dreadful noise it made.

Since the dragon's lair was near the best grazing land for miles about, the cows could not graze and became thinner and thinner and the people became poorer and poorer. This state of affairs would have lasted for ever had not one brave man decided that the time had come to do something about it. This man was called Leopold von Pond and he was the son of the local landowner.

'I am going to fight the dragon!' he told his father. 'I have read a story where a tiny mouse defeated a great lion because it was not afraid. I shall do the same.'

Leopold von Pond buckled on his armour and sharpened up his lance until it was so sharp that it could cut the breeze into little pieces. Then he set off on foot because it was not too far to the dragon's lair and anyway his horse refused to come out of the stable. As he neared the lair the noise of his armour clanking woke the dragon up.

'GUELRE, GUELRE, GUELRE!' roared the dragon, and the sound was so horrible that even the brave Leopold shook and shivered inside his chain mail.

'GUELRE, GUELRE!' roared the dragon again, puffing out clouds of evil-smelling smoke and sulphur. Soon the air was so full of smoke that the dragon could not see what Leopold was doing, which was just as well, because Leopold had crept up behind the dragon and was about to stab him with his razor-sharp lance.

One thrust and it was done.

'GUELRE ... GUEL ... GU ..' moaned the dragon and then no more was heard. Brave Leopold von Pond had killed the dragon and the people could live happily ever after. In thanksgiving the people of the region built a splendid castle for Leopold on the very spot where he had killed the dragon. The king knighted him and gave him the title of Count of Guelre and ever after the region was known as the Gueldre in honour of the brave knight who had delivered the countryside from terror.

THE PIED PIPER
OF HAMELIN

The town of Hamelin was in an uproar: there were mice and rats everywhere! Rats in the houses, rats in the barns, rats in the streets, rats in the palace and the Mayor's office. Mice ran about all over the place. They hid in the pantries and kitchens, eating everything they could find. They hid in the wardrobes and made nests among the clothes, they scampered about in the Council Chamber and their squeaking made it difficult for the Mayor to be heard.

'Something has got to be done!' announced the Mayor, brushing a cheeky mouse from his hat where it was eating the feather. 'This state of affairs simply cannot be allowed. I haven't had a wink of sleep for three weeks and my wife tells me that as soon as she bakes any bread the mice and rats queue up outside the kitchen and when her back is turned, they rush in and devour it all.'

'That's right, that's right,' said Adolphus the Corn Merchant. 'I have put padlocks on all my storeroom doors but it's no use, the rats chew their way through the walls and raid the corn and barley. If this goes on we shall starve in a few weeks.'

'Look at my cloak,' said Bartholomew the Tailor, 'the mice have nibbled away all the fur from the edge and last night began to eat the silk lining. We shall have nothing to wear if no one rids us of these pests.'

'Worst of all,' said the Town Clerk solemnly, 'several rats have eaten three books of the laws passed by the Council and unless we stop them no-one will know what to do or how to behave.'

'We will offer a reward to whoever can rid us of these creatures,' said the Mayor. 'How much do you think would be suitable?'

'Not too much,' said the Town Clerk.

'One hundred crowns and not a penny more!' said the Mayor.

A large notice was nailed to the Town Hall door and the people of Hamelin waited to see who would come and save them. Not a single person arrived and in desperation the Mayor and the Council raised the reward to five hundred golden crowns, and sent the Town Crier of Hamelin out into the countryside to tell everyone about it.

And then, in May, a strange man arrived at the Town Hall.

'Well,' said the Mayor, looking scornfully at the man's tattered clothes. 'What do you want?'

'I am the Pied Piper,' responded the tattered man. 'I can rid you of

the plague of rats and mice. Is it true that there is a reward of five hundred golden crowns?'

'It is,' said the Mayor, 'but I don't believe that you can do it.'

'Oh, but I can,' said the tattered man, 'but you must promise that I shall receive the reward if I succeed.'

'Of course, of course,' said the Mayor, but already his crafty mind was working out how to cheat the Pied Piper.

The Pied Piper strode out of the Town Hall and took a thin reed pipe from his pocket. Putting it to his lips he began to play a strange tune. The sound of the flute curled round the houses like wisps of smoke. To the amazement of the citizens of Hamelin, the rats and mice began to pour out into the streets. As the Pied Piper walked along, still playing his pipe, the horde of rats and mice followed him, out of the town, across the countryside and away from Hamelin.

The next day the Pied Piper came back to Hamelin, but not a single rat or mouse followed him. He marched up to the Town Hall and demanded his reward.

'The reward was offered to the person who would rid Hamelin of all the rats and mice,' said the Mayor. 'It will not be given if one single rat or mouse remains.'

'That is so,' said the Pied Piper. 'The reward is mine.'

'Then what is this?' asked the Mayor, taking from his pocket a tiny, terrified mouse (a mouse that he had caught the day before and hidden away so that he could cheat the Pied Piper).

'No reward for you,' said the Mayor. 'This little mouse proves that you have not done what you claimed.'

The Pied Piper looked steadily at the Mayor. 'I will give you one month to reconsider,' he told him, 'and if, when I return, you do not deal with me fairly, then I shall take my own reward, and it will be something that you cannot afford to lose,' and he turned on his heel and left.

'Ha!' said the Mayor, 'what can a ragamuffin like that do?'

The month passed and the Pied Piper returned.

'Will you give me my reward?' he asked.

'No,' replied the Mayor.

'Very well then,' said the Pied Piper.

Once again he took out his pipe and began to play the haunting tune. This time it was not the rats or mice who followed him, but all the children of Hamelin. They followed the Pied Piper away from Hamelin and not one of them ever returned. So the town of Hamelin paid a far greater price than they expected, and all because of the greed of the Mayor.

THE FAITHFUL WIVES
OF WEINSBERG

There is a town in Germany called Weinsberg, dominated by the ruins of a large castle which is called The Castle of the Faithful Wives. Here is the story of how it got its name.

In the middle of the twelfth century King Conrad III laid siege to the castle because his life-long enemy, Duke Welf of Bavaria, had sought refuge there. The siege went on for month after month.

Every day a messenger of the King would ride up to the foot of the castle wall and call out, 'Duke Welf! Your King demands that you surrender to him.'

And each morning the messenger received the same reply; 'Tell your King to go to the Devil.'

The Duke knew that winter would soon be upon them and that his supplies would not be able to last until spring, but still he refused to surrender, until one morning when his commander came to him and said, 'Sire, we have two days' food left. The well is running dry. We must surrender'.

'Never!' cried the brave Duke, but he knew that what had been said was true.

With sorrow in his heart he awaited the King's messenger the next morning, and when he heard the cry, 'Duke Welf! Your King demands that you surrender,' the Duke replied, 'Very well, but I ask for safe conduct for my men and their wives and myself and my wife back to our own castle in Bavaria. If this assurance is given, I will surrender.'

The messenger rode back to the King and repeated Welf's message. 'I agree,' the King said, 'that the womenfolk may return to Bavaria in safety. And with them they may take anything that they can carry on their backs. But the men, I will put to the sword.'

The message was duly presented to Duke Welf. The Duke listened horrified and was about to shout his refusal when his wife, who was at his side, stopped him, and whispered something to him.

'But, my dear!' he gasped with surprise. 'To accept these terms means certain death for me and my men.'

'Accept the terms and I will never again ask you for anything.'

'If I accept them, I will not be here for you to ask,' the Duke replied.

But the Duchess was so insistent that, with a heavy heart, the

Duke shouted to the messenger below. 'Very well. Tell your master that I accept. The women will leave at dawn tomorrow. Tell your King that I trust him, and that they will be allowed to return to Bavaria with all that they can carry on their backs.'

Word spread around the castle that at dawn, all the women were to leave with whatever they could carry on their backs. The night was spent in frenzied preparations and tearful farewells. Many of the wives declared that they would rather remain and die with their husbands, but the Duchess was adamant.

And so, at dawn the following morning, the courtyard was filled with weeping women carrying bundles and baskets on their backs. They stood waiting for the Duchess to lead them from the castle.

But when she appeared from her chambers, a puzzled gasp went up from the women and their husbands, for she was carrying nothing. And the Duke, who was at her side, was wearing, not his heavy armour, but a light doublet and hose.

As the sun's rays crept into the courtyard the Duchess cried to the women, 'Put down your possessions and do as I do.'

And to the men she cried, 'Take off your armour!'

The men and women, mystified, did as they were bid.

'Page,' the Duchess commanded, 'open the door. And, brave women, do as I now do and prepare to carry your most precious possession out of this place.' Having said that she bent down and her husband gently climbed upon her back. She almost stumbled under his weight, but somehow she managed to straighten herself and carry him through the open gates. The other wives did likewise.

Within minutes a very strange procession was to be seen winding its way out of the castle gates and past the astonished eyes of the King and his army.

When the King saw the faithful wives struggling to keep straight under the weights they were carrying, he was impressed. He turned to his brother and said, 'Would that our womenfolk would be so faithful. They could have carried fine cloths, precious jewels, gold and silver. But, no. They carry their menfolk.'

'But these are your enemies,' his brother protested. 'You must kill them or you will live to regret it.'

'But I gave my word. I said that the women could have safe conduct back to Bavaria along with whatever they could carry. I did not specify what that should be. If a King's word cannot be kept, then it is a sorry world we live in.' And he sent his messenger to tell the women that their faithfulness had so impressed him that they could put their men down and continue their journey home in safety.

ONDIN AND THE SALT

In Austria, many hundreds of years ago, there lived an old fisherman called Friedl. He lived in a large house on the banks of a large lake, with his daughter, Gunde. Friedl was very old and could not handle his fishing tack very well, so it was left to Gunde to do most of the fishing. Every morning, she would row out into the middle of the lake and spend the hours hard at work. When she returned home, her father would inspect the morning's catch and no matter how many fish she had caught, he was never satisfied.

Friedl was much too mean to pay for a servant, so poor Gunde spent the rest of the day cleaning and cooking, but she did not really mind because she loved her father dearly.

As well as being hard working, Gunde was also extremely beautiful, and many men from far and near had asked Friedl for her hand in marriage. But each time Friedl refused. Who else would do his fishing, clean his house and cook his meals? If Friedl allowed Gunde to marry he would have to pay three servants to do her work.

Gunde was not upset. Although she had liked all the men who had asked her to marry them, she had not yet been in love.

One day, however, a handsome young hunter came to live in the forest. His name was Antoine and as soon as Gunde saw him she fell head over heels in love with him. And as soon as he set eyes on Gunde, he fell hopelessly in love with her. The happy couple spent hour after hour walking through the forest and along the shores of the lake, talking about the future and how happy they would be when they were married.

Gunde and Antoine decided on a day when Antoine should come to the cottage and ask Friedl for Gunde's hand. On the appointed day, Antoine duly turned up, his heart beating wildly.

Now, Antoine was as brave as any man and better-looking than most, but he was poor — as poor as poor could be. So when Friedl asked him if he would be willing to pay for the servants that he would need to replace Gunde, Antoine could only shake his head. 'Then go,' said Friedl. 'Come back when you are rich enough and then you may marry Gunde, but until then I forbid you to see her.'

Gunde was an obedient child and did mean to stop seeing Antoine, but her love for him was so strong that occasionally she would slip out of the house to meet her lover. 'One day you will be rich,' she would say comfortingly to him, 'and Papa will have to let us marry, then.'

But Antoine knew that no matter how hard he worked in the forest, he would never be able to afford to pay for three servants. And he grew sadder and sadder.

One night after one of their meetings when the two lovers had talked and talked about what life would be like when they were married, Antoine was unable to sleep, so he decided to go fishing. The day had been very cold and the moon shone down from the cloudless sky. Stars twinkled and glittered from the velvet blackness and as Antoine walked to the lakeside he could not help but be filled with wonder by the beauty of the night. When he arrived at the water's edge, he cast his line and sat under an old oak tree and began to think of his dear Gunde.

After a few minutes, the line tightened and the rod was almost snatched from his hands. Antoine stood up and began to pull in the line. But the fish was not going to give in easily. 'It must be enormous,' thought Antoine as he struggled to land the monster. It took a long time and every ounce of his strength, but at last he managed it. He gave a huge tug and suddenly the monstrous fish came from the water.

Only it was not a fish. It was unlike anything Antoine had ever seen before. It was like a little green man with long hair. It had arms and legs, but where its hands and feet should have been, there was webbing, just like a frog.

'Who are you?' asked Antoine, more afraid than he showed.

The little creature muttered something incomprehensible, and as he spoke two great tears rolled down his cheeks. 'I meant you no harm,' said Antoine. 'Are you hungry?'

The little fellow nodded.

'Then come with me back to my house and I will give you something to eat.'

Antoine held out his hand and the little thing took it in his webbed hand and the two made their way through the forest to Antoine's cottage. They ate a little fish and drank a little wine and soon the little man was smiling and happy. Antoine was now feeling sleepy and he said to the little fellow, 'Go, sit by the fire and sleep.' But the little man was afraid of the flames. Antoine had to coax him into a chair. When he held out his hands to the heat, the little man did the same, and the look of fear vanished and a smile spread across his strange little face. Within a few minutes he was sleeping peacefully and Antoine left him and went to bed.

The next morning, Antoine expected the little man to be gone. But no, there he was sitting by the embers of the fire. 'Do you have a name?' asked Antoine for the umpteenth time. The little green creature nodded.

'Then do tell me what it is. If you are going to stay here, I must know what to call you.'

The little man croaked something that Antoine could not make out. It sounded like 'Ondin'.

'Ondin?' he enquired and the little man nodded.

From then on, Ondin followed Antoine like a dog. When they went hunting, he would run hither and thither through the undergrowth and fetch the game that Antoine had caught. He was a very inquisitive little creature and loved to look at everything in sight. When the two went near the lake, the little man jumped up and down with great joy. Water was obviously his element, but when Antoine asked him if he wanted to return to his beloved water, Ondin shook his head and jumped up into Antoine's arms.

One day, about a week later, as the two were crossing the forest a herd of deer passed by. Ondin became very agitated and ran into the undergrowth to hide from them.

'Poor thing,' thought Antoine, 'he is obviously afraid of the fine stag,' and followed him to try to comfort him. He found Ondin sitting by a small stream, shivering with fear.

'It's all right,' said Antoine. 'No one is going to harm you,' and he stooped down to pick Ondin up. But as he did so he lost his footing and slipped on a patch of smooth rock. In his panic to right himself he dropped Ondin into the water. A few seconds later, the little green creature came to the surface with such an expression of distaste on his face, and with such a spluttering and spitting that Antoine thought he was having some kind of fit.

Ondin managed to clamber back onto the bank, still spitting and shaking.

'What on earth is the matter?' asked Antoine.

The little man pointed at the water and spat again.

Antoine knelt down with a puzzled expression on his face and scooped up some of the water from the stream into his cupped hands. When he sipped the water an even more puzzled expression came over his face. For the water was salty and they were many miles from the sea.

In those days, salt was one of the most valuable things that there was, and people who were lucky enough to own salt mines were very rich indeed. Antoine ran home as fast as he could and picked up

a spade. He returned to where Ondin was still sitting, and began to dig as quickly as his muscles would allow him. He had only gone down a few inches when the spade hit something hard. He threw it to one side and began to clear the loose earth away with his hands. Within a few instants he was looking at a beautiful white vein of pure salt. As he dug wider he could see that the salt vein stretched for a great distance and went as deep as he could imagine.

He hugged Ondin and said, 'Now I will be rich and Friedl will have to let me marry Gunde.'

The man and the strange creature made their way back to the hut where Antoine washed and put on his best clothes. He cleaned Ondin, too, and together they went into town to register their claim on the salt vein.

Word of Antoine's good fortune soon spread around the town, and wherever he went, people crowded round him to congratulate him.

'It is all his doing,' Antoine would say pointing at Ondin. 'If he had not fallen into the stream, I would still be a poor hunter.'

Antoine bought himself a suit of fine cloth and a pair of beautiful leather boots. The next morning he was up bright and early and put on his new clothes. With Ondin at his side, he rowed across the lake to Friedl's house. Gunde saw him from her window and rushed to meet him.

'I have come to ask for your hand in marriage again,' said Antoine as the two embraced.

'But you know what Father said. You must pay for three servants to do my work, if he is to allow me to marry you.'

'That is no problem now,' said Antoine. 'Thanks to this little fellow here, I am now a rich man and could afford thirty servants.'

'What is it?' asked Gunde, nervously recoiling from the little green man.

'My dearest friend, my faithful companion,' said Antoine and explained how he had caught Ondin when he had been fishing after their last moonlight meeting.

'Then I hope that you will be my friend, too,' said Gunde and bent down to kiss the little creature. 'For if Father allows us to marry, I shall owe all my happiness to you.'

Ondin had never been kissed before and he drew back from Gunde's lips.

Antoine laughed and coaxed him to allow Gunde to kiss him.

The happy lovers went inside the cottage and, of course, Friedl had no alternative but to give his permission for the wedding.

Two weeks later the forest echoed to the sounds of laughter and merrymaking. The churchbells pealed joyfully across the lake and everyone agreed that the bride was the most beautiful they had ever seen. Antoine looked so handsome in his fine new clothes that all the women were envious of Gunde. And even Ondin looked smart. Gunde had made him a beautiful suit of green silk which he wore, with tremendous pride. And this time when Gunde bent down to kiss him after the wedding, he did not recoil. He decided that he quite liked being kissed by such a pretty lady, and every night from then on when Antoine and Ondin returned from their salt mine, Gunde would kiss, first, her handsome husband, and then, her favourite little green man.

And the three of them lived happily ever after.

And today, in the Austrian mountains salt is still mined. But it could have lain there undiscovered, if not for an unhappy lover who went fishing one night when he was unable to sleep.

WILLIAM TELL

At the beginning of the fourteenth century, the country that is known today as Switzerland was ruled by the Archduke of Austria, Albert I. Albert was also the overlord of Germany, and, not content with ruling Switzerland, Germany and Austria, he wanted to extend his empire as far as possible. His greedy eyes looked towards Bohemia and he would also have loved to extend his rule to Italy in the south. He wanted his empire to stretch from the Mediterranean to the North Sea and from the Caspian Sea to the Atlantic.

As his empire grew, he found it almost impossible to rule single-handedly, so he appointed governors to rule in his place. Being a greedy, cruel man himself, his friends tended to be as greedy and cruel as he was and it was these friends whom he appointed to positions of power throughout his empire.

But throughout the empire there was much discontent. Troops of Austrian soldiers were often ambushed in mountainous areas by nationalist patriots who resented the Austrian rule. And for each ambush, the emperor would imprison, without trial, as many men, women and children as there had been soldiers.

Also, expanding an empire is a very expensive business. Soldiers have to be paid. Supplies have to be paid for, too. Horses are required, boots and uniforms must be purchased. And even bribes must be funded somehow. As Albert enlarged his empire, he needed more and more money and so taxes were raised higher and higher.

In one area of Switzerland there lived a hunter called William Tell. He hated the Austrians passionately, and tried to have as little to do with them as possible. He was proud of being Swiss and looked forward to the day when the Austrians would be forced to retreat and hand back the country to the Swiss.

At this time the area in which William Tell lived was ruled by an Austrian baron called Gessler. Gessler was as cruel as the emperor, he was proud to serve, and much more cruel than most of the other governors. Not only was he cruel, but he was as ambitious as his emperor. Just as Albert wanted to rule all of Europe, Gessler wanted to rule all of Switzerland, and Gessler would go to any ends to please his master. If twenty Austrians were ambushed, then Gessler would imprison twenty men, women and children. If the emperor demanded one thousand extra schillings in taxes, then Gessler would go and collect two thousand five hundred — two thousand for the emperor and five hundred for himself.

The people hated Gessler.

One day Gessler decided on a new way of pleasing his emperor. There was, after all, a limit to the number of people his prisons would hold and it was not possible to collect taxes once all the peasants' money had been taken. So he erected large poles in the market squares of each village in his domain, and on each pole he set an Austrian cap.

He then ordered that every Swiss subject who passed the hats had to salute them. It was, he declared, the Austrian emperor that they were really saluting. There would be a large fine imposed on anyone who failed to salute, but as the peasants had no money and could not pay the fine, they all did as they were ordered and saluted the token 'emperor'.

Now William Tell, being a hunter, did not come into the town very often, and when he did he made his visits as short as possible so as to avoid any contact with his Austrian overlords.

One day, however, his wife had to go to market to buy salt and William and his son went with her to protect her on her trip. They arrived at the market place at exactly the same time that Gessler arrived in the village on his annual tour of inspection.

Tell walked past the pole without even noticing it. 'Guards!' roared Gessler. 'Arrest that man.'

Six burly soldiers surrounded Tell and forced him down onto the ground.

Gessler then ordered that Tell be brought before him, and the soldiers obeyed.

'Why do you not salute your emperor?' demanded Gessler.

'I see no one I recognize as emperor here,' replied Tell from the ground where he had been thrown.

'The pole and hat represent your emperor.'

'Sir,' replied Tell with a grin on his face, 'the emperor must be fatter than that, considering the money that he gathers from us poor people in taxes.'

'Impudent wretch!' yelled Gessler, his plump face turning a deep shade of angry red. He lashed out with his foot and kicked Tell on the side. 'As you are obviously a fool, I will give you one last chance. Rise to your feet and salute your emperor.'

'I repeat, Sir,' said Tell, 'I see no one here that I recognize as emperor.'

By this time, Gessler's fury was boiling over.

146

'Guards,' he commanded. 'Bring that boy over to me. The one who is crying for his father, for he must be this man's son.'

'Leave my son alone,' shouted Tell. 'He has done nothing.'

'The father's crime is enough to justify punishing the son,' sneered Gessler. 'But *I* shall not harm him. I shall be merciful.'

The guards brought the child before the Governor.

'Do not cry, child,' smiled Gessler. 'I shall not harm you ... But perhaps your father will.'

'I shall never harm so much as a hair on my son's head,' shouted Tell.

'No?' The smile on Gessler's lips grew wider. 'You are obviously a hunter, Sir,' he said. 'And as a hunter you must be a good archer. Let us see just how good. Guards! Tie the child's hands behind his back and bring me an apple.'

The crowd who had gathered around murmured to each other as the soldiers did as they were told. An apple was brought to Gessler, who stepped forward and placed it on top of the boy's head. Turning to Tell he shouted. 'Let us now judge for ourselves just how good a shot you are, Sir. Come, with one arrow you must shoot the apple off your child's head.'

The crowd gasped with horror.

'If you fail,' continued Gessler, 'you and your wife and your son will never see the sun shine again, for I shall have you cast into the deepest dungeon in my castle.'

'And if I succeed?'

'If you succeed, then this time you shall go free. You see,' he said, turning to the crowd, 'I am a merciful man, am I not?' And he laughed at their silence.

Very carefully, Tell put an arrow into his crossbow. For what seemed like several minutes he carefully aimed. The crowd stood in hushed silence. A bell pealed from far away across the valley, and that was the only sound heard.

There was a loud swish as the arrow left the bow and flew through the air. The crowd gasped as the apple on the child's head split neatly into two halves and the arrow thudded into the tree behind.

Gessler was furious. The crowd was jubilant and cheered and cheered and cheered.

'Silence,' boomed Gessler. 'Silence. I demand silence.'

Eventually, the tumult lessened and Gessler called to Tell, 'Very well, you win this time,' and turning to the guards he ordered them to release the terrified child.

'Hold,' shouted Gessler as father and son ran towards each other.

'You drew two arrows and yet I said you only had one chance. What was the other for?'

'Had I missed, and so much as shaved a hair from my child's head, the second arrow would have found your heart, as sure as one day Switzerland will be free.'

On hearing these words, the crowd broke into a tumultuous cheer.

'Silence,' roared Gessler. 'Guards, arrest that man. Send the people back to their houses. Order a curfew.'

The guards pulled William Tell to the ground and dragged him towards the lake. 'Take him across the lake to my castle,' yelled Gessler. 'I will come too.'

Tell was bundled aboard a rowing boat. Six soldiers took the oars and Gessler sat in the bows calling the strokes. The boat headed out to the centre of the lake. Half way across, a sudden storm blew up. The mighty waves crashed around the little boat. It tossed upwards and downwards in the heavy waters. It almost overturned, righted itself and then almost overturned again. The soldiers panicked and Gessler's face turned purple, then red, then blue. 'Help!' he screamed at the top of his voice, the spray crashing into his panic-stricken face.

'Stay still,' shouted William Tell, who knew the lake and its behaviour as well as he knew his own hand. 'Give me an oar.'

'Do as he says,' pleaded Gessler.

Tell's hands were hurriedly untied and an oar was thrust into them. Seeing his chance, Tell stood up and spun round, swinging the oar round his head. The soldiers tumbled to the bottom of the boat and in the melee, Tell leaped overboard.

He dived downwards and downwards, for he knew that if he could hold his breath long enough, the underwater currents would carry him to safety. With a tremendous effort, he managed to do this and a few minutes later, his lungs nearly bursting, he was washed up on the shore near to the jetty where they had set off. He hid until nightfall, and then made his way deep into the forest.

From that time onwards Swiss resistance to Austrian rule intensified and today, Switzerland is a free country where the name of William Tell is still spoken of wherever people who love freedom are gathered together.

FAITHFUL FLORENTINE

There was once a ruler of the principality of Metz in Germany called Alexander. He was a deeply religious man and he decided to go on pilgrimage to the Holy Sepulchre in far-off Jerusalem.

His betrothed, Florentine, could not accompany him so she made him a pure white shirt to wear on his journey.

'Wear this always,' she said to him as he was about to set off. 'No matter what happens it will remain as pure and white as my love for you. I will remain faithful to you no matter how long you are away. And when you return, the shirt will still be as fresh as it is now.'

She kissed her dear love tenderly and Alexander set off.

But things did not go well for him, for when he crossed the border into Turkey, he was taken prisoner by the Saracen. He was put to work in the palace gardens, forced to dig the soil, and pull the hoe and the plough. The work he did was dirty, but no matter how dirty his hands and face became, his shirt remained as white and fresh as it was on the day that his beloved had given it to him.

Naturally this did not go unnoticed and Alexander was hauled before the Saracen to explain the mystery.

'There is no mystery,' he said. 'My faithful betrothed sewed this shirt for me and it will remain as pure as this as long as she is faithful to me.'

'No woman could remain so faithful for so long,' replied the Saracen, refusing to believe Alexander's story, but Alexander was so adamant that at last the Saracen was convinced.

He sent for his most handsome guard and commanded him to journey to Metz to search for Florentine. The guard did as he was commanded and several weeks later, he arrived in Germany.

He went straight to the Castle of Alexander and sought an audience with Florentine. As soon as he saw her he fell in love with her, for she was as beautiful as she was pure.

'Your grace,' he said to her, 'I come from the mighty Saracen to tell you that Alexander is his captive.'

Now Florentine was a very brave woman and she refused to show any emotion in front of the soldier.

'You will never see him again,' said the soldier, who was as handsome as Florentine was beautiful. 'Come, marry me and together we will rule Metz.'

'Never,' replied Florentine. 'As long as my dear Alexander lives, I shall never be unfaithful to him.'

The soldier stayed for several weeks and every day he asked Florentine to be his wife, and each time he received the same reply.

He saw how hopeless his suit was, so he set off early one morning to return to his native land.

Florentine watched him leave from her window and as soon as he was out of sight she summoned her maid. 'Bring my harp, and bring me the pageboy's best clothes.'

The startled maid did as she was told. A few minutes later Florentine rode out of the castle disguised as a minstrel. Her long hair was tucked into a silken cap and her pageboy's best clothes fitted her to perfection. Day after day she followed the soldier, keeping out of his sight at all times.

As he neared the Turkish border one night, the soldier stopped at an inn to spend the last night before he returned to the Saracen.

Florentine, too, stopped at the inn a few minutes later and asked for a room.

After supper, Florentine took out her harp and began to play a sad tune. The soldier was so moved by it that he demanded that the harpist he brought before him. When Florentine stood in front of him, he did not recognize her; so good was her disguise. 'Play, minstrel,' the soldier said and Florentine did as she was commanded.

'Tomorrow we will journey together,' the soldier said. 'You will play before my master, the Saracen. Be ready to leave at dawn.'

And so, at first light, Florentine and the soldier set off to cross the border into Turkey.

A few hours later Florentine was standing before the mighty Saracen, her heart aching. For, in the garden beyond the throne, she could see her dear Alexander toiling in the hot sun. His hair was long and filthy. His hands were rough and red, but his shirt was as pure as it had been so long ago.

Florentine began to play songs of forgotten love and parted sweethearts. So sweetly did she play that the Saracen felt a lump swell in his throat. She continued with her haunting songs until the Saracen could stand it no longer. 'Bring the German to me.'

When the servants brought Alexander into the throne room, he looked at the pageboy and did not recognize her as his beloved Florentine.

'Alexander,' said the Saracen, 'the songs of this youth have so moved me that I am giving you your freedom. Return to your own land and your faithful betrothed.'

With a happy heart Alexander set out on his journey. He had not gone far when he was overtaken by the pageboy with the harp. 'Sir,' said the lad, 'may we journey together, our paths lie in the same direction.'

And so the faithful Florentine and the unsuspecting Alexander

journeyed across Europe. As they neared Metz, the page stopped and said, 'Sir, here our paths separate. Give me something to remind me of our journey.'

'Anything you desire,' said Alexander, 'for it is to you that I owe my freedom.'

'A corner of your shirt is all I want,' replied the page.

'Anything but that,' said the surprised Alexander. 'Gold, jewels, land, but not that.'

But the boy insisted and eventually Alexander agreed with a heavy heart. The boy took a knife from his bad and cut a band of cloth from the hem of the shirt. 'Thank you, Sir,' he said. 'And now we part.'

Alexander rode on and arrived at the castle before Florentine. 'Bring my betrothed to me,' he ordered.

'Sir, she has not been here for many a week,' said the servant. 'A soldier came and she left the same day as he. He was so handsome.'

With a heavy heart Alexander retired to his chambers.

But a few moments later, Florentine came into his rooms. She had changed out of the pageboy's clothes and was wearing her most beautiful dress.

'My love,' she said and moved across the room to embrace her betrothed, but he turned from her and shouted, 'Oh, unfaithful wretch. A servant told me that you went off with a handsome soldier. Have you only just returned?'

'My Lord,' said Florentine softly. 'It is true that I followed a handsome soldier from here. I followed him because he led me to you.'

'Liar,' he said, still in an angry voice.

'My Lord, I speak the truth. I followed the soldier and he took me to the Saracen. There I sang for him and he was so moved that he released you. And together you and I journeyed home, parting only a few minutes ago.'

'But I journeyed with the pageboy who sang for the Saracen,' exclaimed Alexander.

'It was I,' said Florentine. And as she spoke, she took the band of white cloth from around her girdle and gave it to the astonished Alexander.

'Why did you not reveal yourself to me as you journeyed with me?' he asked.

'To test you. Had I revealed myself to you, you could only have behaved properly in my company. But as I was in disguise, you had every chance to be unfaithful with any maiden you met on your journey. I had to be sure that you still loved me as much as I love you. We have been separated for so long, your heart could have changed.'

'My darling. I loved you when I set out on my journey and every day of our separation my love for you grew tenfold. Now I love you more than life itself.'

'And I love you with equal strength,' replied Florentine.

And from that day, Florentine and Alexander were never parted.

GYULA AND EMELKA

The River Vah flows through southern Slovakia; and three hundred years ago there was a large castle at Lowenstein that stood on a high cliff overlooking the river.

The castle was owned by a rich landowner who had one daughter. She was called Emelka and she was the most beautiful girl in the whole region. She could have married any one of a hundred rich suitors, but she fell in love with a handsome young servant called Gyula.

When her father found out about it he was furious. 'You want to marry Gyula?' he roared. 'Impossible. Why, he's nothing but a servant.'

'I will marry no one else,' cried Emelka, with tears streaming down her pretty face. 'As long as he lives, I shall be his.'

Her angry father paced up and down the vast library, and suddenly came up with a way of getting rid of Gyula.

His brother in the north of the country owed him a large sum of money, so he sat down and wrote to him. 'Brother, the bearer of this letter is a thief and a cheat. Unfortunately, he is popular in the district so I am unable to punish him. Throw him into your deepest dungeon and keep him there for all time. If you do this, your debt is cancelled.' He signed and sealed the letter, and summoned Gyula. When the handsome youth came before him he said, 'Take this letter to my brother and wait for a reply.'

Gyula set off that very day and rode hard and long to reach his master's brother within two days. The brother took the letter from Gyula and read it in astonishment. 'This letter claims that you are a thief and a cheat, yet you look like an honest lad to me. I am commanded to cast you into my deepest dungeon, yet I cannot believe that you are deserving of such a fate.'

Gyula thought for a moment and then explained to the brother that his master wanted to rid of him as he had fallen in love with Emelka.

'Obviously you cannot return to Lowenstein, but I will not imprison you. You must volunteer for the army and go and fight the Turks. I will tell my brother that you drowned while trying to cross the Vah.'

And so Gyula went off to join the army and a messenger was sent to his master saying that he was dead.

Poor Emelka. When she heard the tragic news she was distraught and for week after week, and month after month she stayed in her room weeping until she had no more tears to shed.

The months turned to years, and Emelka's father made plans for her to marry his wealthy neighbour. The preparations were made and Emelka unsmilingly watched as her wedding dress was stitched and the castle was decorated with spring flowers.

On the morning of her wedding, her handmaiden went to awaken Emelka and was horrified to find her mistress dead, an empty phial of poison clasped in her hand.

Emelka's father was heartbroken. For weeks he did nothing but sit in the sun-filled garden calling out his daughter's name.

Meanwhile, Gyula had proved to be a brave soldier. He was quickly promoted to officer rank and after several fierce battles he was made colonel and then general. He was a good officer and much loved by his men. When peace came he had become very rich and he knew that Emelka's father could not refuse to allow him to marry his daughter.

He rode back to Lowenstein, hardly stopping to rest and after several days' journey he arrived late one night at the river Vah. The moon was full, and Gyula could see the vast castle towering above him on the opposite side. He forded the river and rode towards the castle. Suddenly his horse stopped dead and refused to move forward one inch.

Puzzled, Gyula dismounted and prepared to make the rest of his journey on foot. As he walked through the small wood at the bottom of the castle cliff, he stopped as surely as his horse had done. What he saw in front of him terrified him so much that his heart almost stopped beating. For in a moonlit clearing the shadowy figures of ghostly maidens were dancing. They all wore thin wedding dresses and carried posies of flowers. Their hair was decorated with small blossoms. 'The Wilis!' exclaimed Gyula. He had heard of them from his old grandmother. They were the ghosts of girls who had killed themselves rather than marry someone they did not love. And they were doomed to dance until they found their true loves.

A soft breeze sprang up and the maidens stopped dancing. They glanced around and saw Gyula looking at them. One by one they floated past him, murmuring, 'You are not my love'. Until the very last one floated by and stopped in front of him. 'You are my love, my Gyula,' she said.

Gyula looked into her face and saw that it was his beloved Emelka who stood before him. Even in death, she was very beautiful. Her face was white and her lips were the palest pink. Her eyes shone as she whispered Gyula's name over and over again. She laid down her posy and slowly took a chain from around her neck which she gently slipped over Gyula's head.

'Dance with me,' she whispered.

And Gyula danced. She was ice cold to touch and no matter how fast they danced she remained ice cold. Gyula grew more and more tired, but Emelka had so enchanted him that he could not stop.

For dance after dance they moved across the clearing until Gyula could go on no longer. He slumped down on the dewy grass.

They found him there the following morning. He was dead.

His body was carried into the castle and Emelka's father was called for. He immediately recognized Gyula and when he saw the chain around his neck he knew it instantly, for he had given it to his daughter many years before. He sank to his knees, sobbing bitterly. 'Forgive me,' he murmured. 'Please forgive me.' And he ordered his servants to bury Gyula beside Emelka. 'I parted them in this life,' he whispered. 'Please bring them together in the next life.'

And so Gyula and Emelka, who had been denied happiness in this world, were buried side-by-side to be together for ever.

KING SVATOPLUK

It was the feast day of Saint Peter and Saint Paul, and in the cathedral at Velehrad the townspeople were about to celebrate mass. The Archbishop himself was at the altar waiting. The choirboys were singing sweetly, and the heads of most of the congregation were bowed in silent prayer. The crimson robes of the priests shone in the morning sunshine that streamed through the beautiful stained-glass windows. It was a scene of great beauty and of heavenly peace.

The congregation finished their prayers and sat up straight to await the Mass. The Archbishop stood silently in his place and waited. He waited and waited.

Suddenly the peace was broken by the voice of a small child. 'What are we waiting for?' he asked his mother.

'I don't know, child,' his mother replied. 'Hush.'

'But I am getting hungry,' the child persisted. 'Mass should have been over by now.'

The man directly behind tapped the woman on the shoulder and whispered to her. 'King Svatopluk commanded the Archbishop to wait until he arrived, before celebrating the Mass.'

'But the King is out hunting,' said the child. 'I saw him ride out of the castle this morning.'

The child had spoken so loudly that the Archbishop could not help but overhear. He signalled to the choir to begin the Mass and began to read the great words of the beautiful service.

Just as he was about to beckon the worshippers forward to take the wine and the bread there was a mighty commotion as the great wooden doors swung open and the king stormed in. He was dressed in his hunting clothes and his sword was in his hand. 'How dare you start without me, Holy Man!' he shouted at the Archbishop.

'And how dare you enter the house of God with your sword drawn?' retorted the Archbishop, purple with rage. 'Get out of here!'

'You tell me to get out?' roared Svatopluk. 'I am your king.'

'God is my king,' the Archbishop roared back. 'Now leave His house.'

'I leave this house and I curse you and your God,' said Svatopluk.

The townsfolk were horrified to hear such blasphemy.

'And you,' continued the furious king, pointing at the Archbishop, 'you have until dawn to leave my lands.'

The Archbishop stepped forward. 'Mark my words, Svatopluk. Until now you have been a good ruler. Good fortune has smiled upon you. You have been fortunate in battle. Peace now rules the land. But now your fortune has ended.'

Svatopluk stormed from the cathedral and the Archbishop continued with the service.

The very next morning at dawn, the Archbishop left Svatopluk's kingdom and as he crossed the border he noticed the armies of Schlesweig march into Svatopluk's land, clearly ready to battle.

From that day on, for year after year, Svatopluk's land was under constant attack from the armies of Germany in the south and Hungary in the east. The French armies in the west marched against him

as soon as he had repulsed the Hungarians, and when after a long, hard battle the French retreated, Turkish invaders stormed across his south-eastern border.

Svatopluk was so busy planning and plotting with his generals that he forgot all about the Archbishop and his curse; until one day he was walking through the camp and overheard two soldiers talking.

'My family is starving, for there is no food, now that we are constantly at war!' said the first.

'Mine too,' said the second. 'It is all the King's fault. He should never have cursed God.'

Svatopluk went back to his tent and spent the night in deep thought. The next morning before anyone awoke, he rode out of the camp. He rode for three days and three nights until he came to the monastery on the Mount of the Holy Virgin. In the shade of a beautiful elm tree he took his sword from its sheath and plunged it into the ground. He knelt down and kissed it, just where the blade crossed the handle. He made the sign of the cross and vowed never to make war again and to spend the rest of his days serving God and man.

He went inside the monastery and begged to see the Abbot.

When the Abbot saw the king, he knelt down before him, much afraid, for he knew Svatopluk to be a cruel man.

'Father,' said Svatopluk. 'It is I who should kneel before you. Pray rise, I come to seek God.'

And from that day on, Svatopluk spent all of his time in prayer, travelling over the kingdom preaching God's word. Nobody recognized him, for his appearance was greatly changed.

And once, when he stood outside the cathedral where he had cursed God, so long ago, an old woman came up to him and said, 'You have something of the look of the old king about you.'

'What happened to him?' asked Svatopluk.

'He disappeared,' replied the old woman. 'Strange, but from the day he disappeared things began to get better. Maybe he sacrificed himself as a penance. If he did, I bless him for it.'

And Svatopluk was happy.

ILYA MUROMETS

Once upon a time in a small village in Russia, there lived a humble peasant and his wife and their son, who was called Ilya Muromets. Ilya was thirty years old and he was crippled. He could not use his legs to walk and his arms and hands hung uselessly by his side.

Each morning his mother and father would carry him from his bed, wash him and feed him, and sit him by the fire. There he would remain all day until his poor parents returned from their labours in the fields.

One day, while his parents were out, there was a loud knock upon the door. 'Come in,' cried Ilya from his place by the fire. 'The door is on the latch.'

The door opened and three men entered the poor cottage. Ilya could see from their clothes that they were pilgrims, on their way to the holy shrine of St Andrew.

'Rise from your chair, Sir, and bring us some water,' said the first pilgrim, who was older than the other two.

'Alas, good pilgrim, I am unable to rise, for I was born crippled and can neither walk nor use my arms,' replied Ilya.

The old man stepped forward and laid his hands on Ilya's brow. The other two knelt beside him and the three prayed quietly. Suddenly Ilya felt a rush of power flow to his legs. Without thinking he moved his arms to touch his legs. He jumped up and cried, 'I have never been able to move my arms before. I have never been able to stand before. You are indeed holy men that can give me strength. Sit, holy fathers, warm yourselves by the fire and I will bring you wine and not water.'

With that, Ilya rushed down to the cellar and brought them the best wine that his poor father could afford. The three men drank thankfully and then the eldest handed the jug of wine to Ilya. 'Drink the rest of this,' he said, 'and you will have the strength of ten heroes.'

Ilya did as he was bid and as he drank he could feel the strength of ten heroes flow through his limbs. 'Thank you,' he cried joyfully. 'How can I ever repay you?'

'You must serve Mother Russia and protect her from her enemies. For this you will need the strength of one hundred and ten heroes. We have done our best. You must journey forth and seek out the giant Svatogor. Befriend him and he will give you all the strength you require for your task.' With that the three holy men bade Ilya farewell and returned to their pilgrimage.

Ilya rushed out to where his parents were toiling in the fields. When he got there, they were sound asleep, tired out by their exhaustion. Ilya looked at the work they had done. For hour after hour they had toiled, but all that they had managed to do was to clear a small patch of their field. Ilya smiled lovingly at his sleeping parents and set to work. With the strength of ten heroes running through him, it was only a matter of a few minutes before he had cleared the entire field. When he had finished, he awoke his parents, who were amazed to see what had happened. Ilya explained that the Holy Men had given him the strength of ten heroes, but that he needed the strength of one hundred and ten to defend Mother Russia from her invaders. His father then said, 'You must take my old horse, for the giant Svatogor lives many miles from here.'

But Ilya had grown so strong that the old horse could not carry his weight, so the kind parents spent every penny that they had, and bought Ilya a fine young horse. Ilya fed it lovingly every day and soon the horse was strong enough to carry him to meet Svatogor.

Svatogor lived near the Holy Mountain many miles from Ilya's home. For three days and three nights Ilya journeyed until, at last, he came to the mountain. Hanging from a huge fir tree, Ilya spotted a hunting horn. On it was inscribed: 'Let him who seeks Svatogor blow three times.'

Breathing the breath of ten heroes Ilya put the horn to his lips and blew hard. The air was rent with three loud blasts. A few seconds later the very ground began to shudder as though an earthquake was about to rip the world apart. Ilya stood firm and heard a voice from far above call 'Who seeks Svatogor?' Ilya looked up, as far as he could see. There towering above him, astride a vast horse, was Svatogor. He was so tall that his head seemed to touch the sky. When he raised his hand, he almost touched the sun.

'Ilya Muromets,' replied the peasant's son.

'And what do you want of me?' demanded Svatogor.

'The strength of one hundred heroes.'

'Humph,' retorted the giant and with that he bent down and swept poor Ilya, horse and all into his saddle-bag.

Svatogor commanded his horse to move on, but the poor beast stumbled.

'How do you expect me to move, with all that weight in the bag?' asked the horse.

Svatogor took Ilya and his horse out of the bag and set them down

again. 'You must be strong to make my horse stumble,' he said. 'Come, we will ride to my Holy Mountain and be friends.'

And so Ilya and Svatogor rode off to the Holy Mountain. Svatogor was so impressed by Ilya that together they set out to protect Russia from her enemies. But Ilya always remembered that somehow he had to get Svatogor to give him his extra strength so that he could fulfil his destiny.

One day, the two were riding out together when they came upon a high pine tree. In its shade there lay a large coffin bearing a strange inscription. 'Let the one whom this coffin fits lie in it.'

Ilya dismounted and lay in the coffin, but it was far too large for him.

'It's more likely to fit me, Ilya,' said Svatogor. He dismounted and clambered into the coffin. No sooner had he done so, than the lid slammed shut.

'Ilya,' cried Svatogor, 'take my sword, cut through the locks and release me.'

Ilya did as his friend asked, but the sword was too heavy for him even to lift.

'Lean over the coffin,' came the muffled voice of Svatogor from within the coffin, 'and I will breathe more strength into you.'

Again Ilya did as he was bid. Svatogor took a deep breath and blew as hard as he could. Ilya felt the power seep through the lock of the coffin and into his blood. He tried to pick up the sword and was surprised at how light it now felt in his hands. With a mighty blow, he brought the sword down on the coffin. But before it touched the wood, a band of iron appeared just where the blade fell.

'Lean over the coffin and I will breathe more strength into you,' cried Svatogor.

Ilya did so, and again he felt the power surge through him. He brought the sword down and with a mighty clang the iron band smashed through and the lid sprang open. There lay poor Svatogor, dying from his efforts. His face was as white as a blizzard and his breathing was as soft as a zephyr.

'Ilya,' he whispered, 'you now have all my strength. Go and fulfil your destiny. Free our beloved Russia from the invader. But first sit with me until I die and then bury me in the shade of this tree.'

With tears in his eyes, Ilya did as Svatogor asked. When nightfall came, the giant breathed his last breath and died. Ilya toiled all night and dug the giant's grave. As dawn broke and the sun began to bring colour to the landscape, Ilya laid his friend in the earth and prayed for his soul. He rode off with a heavy heart vowing that never would he forget Svatogor. Every battle he fought and every victory he won would be dedicated to the giant's memory.

After several days' journey, Ilya drew close to the town of Chernigov where he intended to rest for a few days. As he rode over the summit of the hill that shaded Chernigov, Ilya saw that the city was under siege. Around the city walls were the tents of the Tartar armies. Three standards flew from each of the tents and Ilya immediately knew that the army was led by three Tartar tsarevitches and that each Tsarevitch had forty thousand men at his command. The poor townsfolk of Chernigov stood no chance against such an army. The only sound that Ilya could hear was the wailing of the townsfolk. This saddened him. But soon his sadness turned to anger. And as his anger rose, so too did the wind. 'Ilya,' it seemed to be saying, 'remember that you have the strength of Svatogor as well as the strength of ten heroes.'

With a great roar, Ilya drew Svatogor's mighty sword and spurred his horse into a gallop. Faster and faster they rode down the hillside and into the Tartar camp. With the strength of one hundred and ten heroes flowing through him, Ilya was invincible. Wave after wave of attacking Tartars tried to dismount him and each one met the same bloody reply. The three tsarevitches soon realized that nothing they could throw against him would defeat Ilya Muromets and those who still lived withdrew back over the hill into their own lands. Word soon spread amongst Russia's enemies that the country was no longer weak and defenceless, but was protected by a mighty warrior called Ilya Muromets.

The townspeople of Chernigov begged Ilya to stay with them and rule over them, but Ilya could not. 'Are there not still foreign armies in the north around Kiev? I must do for the citizens of Kiev what I did for you.'

The townsfolk protested. Did Ilya not know that to go to Kiev meant crossing the mighty Blacklands which were damned by the wicked Nightingale, whose whistle made the earth tremble, blackened the sky and scorched the land. 'He whistles his terrible whistle if anyone tries to cross the Blacklands,' warned the townsfolk.

But Ilya was determined.

'At least let us give you something to protect you,' said the mayor and handed Ilya a golden crossbow.

In the morning, Ilya set off with the good wishes of Chernigov's people ringing in his ears.

As he came near to the Blacklands, Ilya's heart sank. The land was bleak and flat. The sun was covered by huge black clouds. The only thing growing was a clump of oak trees right in the middle of the dreadful heath. Summoning every ounce of courage, Ilya rode forwards and neared the oak trees.

'Who dares ride across my Blacklands?' demanded a voice from far above Ilya. He looked up and saw an enormous bird circling above him. It was nothing like the nightingales that Ilya knew. It was as big as an eagle and as cruel as a vulture.

'Ilya Muromets,' shouted the brave hero.

The bird landed on top of an oak tree and opened its beak, about to release its terrible whistle. As it lifted its head back, Ilya drew an arrow from his quiver and fired it from his golden bow. The arrow was accurately fired, for before the bird could make any sound the arrow pierced its throat and it slumped to the ground. Ilya dismounted and picked up the dying bird. 'You are indeed as mighty as I have heard,' croaked the bird. 'I curse you and yet I hail you as the mightiest warrior in all of Russia.' With these words, the bird let out its dreadful whistle for the last time and died. Ilya tied a rope around its neck and strapped it to his saddle. He rode on across the Blacklands. But they were no longer black. The sun was bathing them in a golden glow. Flowers were springing to life. Trees were budding and birds were singing.

Before long Ilya arrived at Kiev. He made his way to the royal palace and begged for an audience with the Prince. When he explained what it was he wanted, his wish was granted.

As he entered the throne room, the dead bird in his hands, the whole court rose and cheered.

'Sire,' Ilya said as he knelt before the throne, 'I bring you the enchanted ruler of the Blacklands. Dead.'

The Prince was incredulous. But on examining the bird, he saw that what Ilya had said was true. 'You may have anything that you want,' he said in deep gratitude.

'Sire, to rid the north of the invaders is all I want. Give me command of your armies and together we will ride out to meet the enemy in battle.'

The Prince happily agreed and a few days later the two men rode through the city gates of Kiev at the head of the most splendid army ever assembled by a Prince of Kiev. When word had spread of Ilya's gift to the Prince, every man and boy in the city had rushed to join up, and every woman and girl had stitched them the most splendid uniforms.

The battle was long and bloody. At one point the Prince began to fear that even with Ilya against them the invaders were invincible.

His men were being well beaten on the right and left flanks, and in the centre they were only holding their own. Suddenly at noon, when the sun should have been at its highest, the clouds gathered and blackened the sky. A strong wind began to blow from behind the Kiev army, forcing their soldiers forwards and the invaders' armies backwards. The wind blew stronger and stronger forcing the invaders further and further back, until they were overtaken by the Kiev soldiers, who, seeing the Tartars running before them, were given fresh spirit. By nightfall the last Tartar was either dead or had been driven out of Russia for ever.

Of Ilya Muromets there was no sign.

Some say that he rode off when he saw that the battle had been won and continued to fight tyranny and injustice whenever he found it. But one soldier knew differently. When the tide of the battle had turned and the Kiev armies were winning, he had looked around him to see what was happening behind him. He hardly believed what he saw. For just as the wind was blowing its strongest, a gap appeared in the heavy clouds and a hand swept down to earth and gathered Ilya Muromets upwards as easily as if he had been a feather.

And there was a wonderful expression of pure joy on Ilya's face as the clouds closed behind him.

ISIS AND OSIRIS

Egypt was once ruled over by the god Osiris. He was a wise and much-loved ruler. He taught his subjects how to plough their fields, how to build houses, to make pots and to fashion pots on wheels. He taught them to sing songs, to read and to count. The people loved him greatly.

Their happiness was complete when Osiris took a wife. She was the lovely Isis and she was so good-natured and kind that she was soon as popular as her husband with the people of Egypt. A son was born to the happy pair, which made their joy absolute. They called him Horus.

There was only one thing that marred Osiris' happiness. His brother Typhon was an ill-tempered youth, who was as quarrelsome as he could possibly be. He never had a kind word for anyone and if he had the slightest chance to do an evil deed, he would grasp it eagerly.

Typhon loathed his brother. He was jealous of his popularity with the people. He envied him his beautiful wife and lovely son. He believed that he would make a much better ruler than his brother.

'If I were king,' he would say to himself, 'I would make the people work much harder to make me richer. I would force the men into my army and make war to extend my empire. My brother has no idea how to use his power.'

Now, as well as being ruthless and ambitious, Typhon was not the sort of man to sit around and do nothing to realize his dreams. So he made a secret pact with the queen of neighbouring Ethiopia and with several discontented Egyptian princes. In exchange for their support, he would give them huge amounts of money when he grabbed the throne.

One day, when Isis and Osiris were swimming in the warm sea, Typhon crept out from behind a tree and carefully measured the mark that Osiris' body had made as he lay in the sand. With stealth he tiptoed away and went to his jeweller.

'Make me a chest to these measurements, exactly. Decorate it with the most precious jewels in your possession and bring it to my palace as soon as it is ready.'

For many a week the jeweller toiled at his work and eventually it was finished. When Typhon saw it he was greatly pleased and rewarded the craftsman well.

That evening Typhon invited Isis and Osiris to a great banquet.
He also asked his princely allies. The feasting went on well into the
night and when at last everyone had eaten their fill, Typhon clapped
his hands. The great doors of his room swung open and his servants
carried in the jewelled chest. There were gasps of astonishment from
all in the room. Isis and Osiris were genuine in their appreciation of
the magnificent chest. Typhon's allies were laying a carefully re-
hearsed trap.

Typhon announced that whoever the chest fitted the best, should
have it. Immediately all the allies rushed to try to lie in the chest, but,
of course, it fitted no one. Typhon turned to his brother and said,
'Osiris, why don't you try?'

Osiris stepped forward and lay in the chest. It fitted him perfectly,
but before he could stand up again, Typhon's allies rushed forward
and slammed the lid down. They locked it tightly and carried it from
the room.

Poor Isis watched in horror as she saw the men take the chest to
the highest tower in the palace and cast it into the river below. She
ran from the room and made her way down to the river banks. There

she saw the chest float down to the sea. For day after day she followed it in a fragile papyrus boat. Each time she almost caught up with it, a gust of wind would blow it further ahead.

Eventually, the chest was blown ashore in the kingdom of Byblos. It came to land in the shade of a magnificent tamarind tree and no sooner had it reached the shade, than the tree's branches stooped down and wound themselves around the chest. Isis screamed as the bejewelled chest disappeared into the very trunk of the tree.

She ran to the spot and collapsed, weeping dreadfully.

For three days and three nights she lay there until, on the fourth morning, the King of Byblos passed. As soon as he saw the tree which had grown to superb maturity he commanded that it be cut down and taken to his palace there to be used as a pillar. He took pity on the weeping woman at the base of the tree and ordered that she come to the palace. The weeping Isis mournfully followed the small procession into the city.

Isis was sent to the servants' quarters where she taught the slaves the feminine wiles that she had learned when she had ruled Egypt. She made them skilful in the art of decorating their faces in the Egyptian way, and helped them oil their hair with scented oils.

Word of her ways soon spread to the ears of the Queen and she commanded that Isis be brought before her. Isis charmed the Queen with her beauty and wisdom and soon she was made nurse to her child.

As time passed, the baby began to remind Isis of her own child in far-off Egypt and she came to love it as strongly as if it were her own. She was no longer a rich queen, so there was only one gift left to her with which she could endow the child. As a goddess, she was immortal and she decided to make her charge immortal, too.

One night as the Queen slept Isis began to bathe the child's body in the flames of immortality. Each night thereafter as the Queen slept, Isis made another part of his body immortal. And as the flames of immortality bathed the child, Isis would change herself into a beautiful dove and circle the pillar which contained the sleeping body of Osiris.

One night when Isis was flying round the pillar and the Queen's chamber was enveloped in the warm glow of the flames of immortality, there was a dreadful storm which awoke the Queen.

When she saw her child's body bathed in fire, she screamed.

Isis flew down to the foot of her bed and transformed herself back to human shape.

The poor Queen was terrified. 'Please do not be alarmed,' said Isis,

stepping forward, and she explained who she was and how she came to be there. 'Your child is so like mine that I wanted to give him my gift of immortality. That is why he is bathed in flames.'

'But, the bird . . . you were a bird . . .'

'My husband, Osiris, is locked in a jewelled chest, imprisoned in that tamarind pillar. I fly round him so that he knows I am near.'

'My poor Isis,' said the Queen. 'Had I but known who you were we could have released Osiris. But now my husband loves the tamarind pillar so much. And when he learns of our son's immortality, he will be jealous and banish him from the land.'

'In that case,' said Isis, 'we must plan . . .'

For the next few days Isis continued to play the part of handmaiden to the Queen. One night when she was serving the Queen and the King, she nodded silently to the Queen.

'My love,' said the Queen. 'Would that we were immortal, then we could live as happily as we are now, forever.'

'Immortality is only for the gods,' said the King.

'Excuse me, Majesty,' said Isis. 'But in my land it is said that the mighty tamarind tree has the gift of immortality.'

'The tamarind tree?' exclaimed the King.

'Yes, Sire. It is said that he who is not afraid to stand in the burning wood of the tamarind tree will be granted eternal life.'

Isis was so convincing that the King believed her. But he was very afraid.

'Would I become immortal if I did so?' he begged Isis.

'Sire, it is said that the child who is heir should be one to gain immortality. For the parents are pleased to know that their heir will ensure that their names last as long as his immortality.'

'Bring my son,' the King commanded.

'But husband,' the Queen said in great alarm. 'What if what has been said is untrue.'

'If it is untrue and our child dies, then fear not, for we will have another. But if it is true and our son becomes immortal, then our names will live as long as his immortality.'

The child was brought before the King, who commanded that the tamarind pillar be cut down and burned.

His orders were obeyed and soon the huge pillar was burning fiercely with the child in the middle of the flames. The courtiers were amazed when the child appeared to be quite unconcerned and slept peacefully as the flames grew higher and higher.

'It is true,' cried the King, hugging his wife. 'Our dear son is becoming immortal.'

Suddenly all the courtiers gasped as with a mighty crash a bejewelled chest fell from the flames. The crash was so colossal that the lock smashed open. Isis rushed forward and embraced her beloved husband. Before anyone could move she turned herself back into a dove and Osiris into a mighty eagle.

Together the two flew back to Egypt, but when they arrived they were grieved at what they saw. They had left behind a happy land, and now it was a sorrowful sight. The people who had once gone smilingly about their business now were in chains.

Isis and Osiris flew on until they reached their palace. Osiris knew enough about his brother to realize that although he would never dare kill their son, he would never let him be free, so they flew to the topmost room in the topmost tower, and sure enough, there was their beloved son, who had now grown tall and strong.

The couple flew into the chamber and immediately transformed themselves back to the human form. 'My son,' said Isis and ran forward to embrace him. The boy was startled, but he knew instantly that the woman was his mother.

'We must get away from here,' said the boy. 'There are many escaped slaves in Babylon who will march against Typhon to free Egypt once more. All they await is a leader.'

Isis and Osiris regained their bird shapes and changed Horus into a steely hawk. The three flew off to Babylon where they recruited a large army.

They trained hard for many months and, eventually, Osiris decided that they were ready to march against Egypt. The march was long and hard, but the soldiers were pleased to be returning home and they marched in high spirits. When they crossed the border they met with little resistance, for the attack was completely unexpected. And as they freed more and more slaves, their numbers swelled tenfold.

After several days' marching and several skirmishes, the slave army found itself facing the combined might of the forces of Typhon, the Abyssinian Queen and the Egyptian princes.

The battle was long and hard. It lasted for several days and the balance swung backwards and forwards. First the slaves took ascendancy and then they were driven back by the forces of Typhon; then the slaves would find fresh heart and push forward again. And so the battle continued, until eventually the knowledge that if they were beaten they were doomed to a life of continual slavery, gave the slaves the final amount of heart needed to win and they managed to beat off the last attack of Typhon's forces.

Isis and Osiris demanded that Typhon and his princes be brought before them.

'Brother,' said Osiris, 'show repentance and I will forgive you.'

'Never,' cried Typhon and spat on the ground before him.

'In that case . . .'

And Osiris waved his hands in the air, and instantly Typhon and all his princes were transformed into tamarind trees, which they remain to this very day.

ISHTAR IN HELL

In Egypt, Ishtar was the goddess of love and faithfulness. She also brought happiness to those who worshipped her, and she liked nothing more than looking down on earth and watching the people enjoy themselves. If anything threatened to destroy the joy that she created, she would do her utmost to put it to rights. She would calm the seas if a storm went on for too long. If gales threatened to bring danger, she would blow in the opposite direction and cause the gales to lessen.

Ishtar had a sister called Ereshkigal and one day, she said to her lover, Tammuz, 'I am going to go and visit my sister.'

Tammuz was horrified, for Ereshkigal was the goddess of Hell. Whoever saw her was cast into Hell and never seen again.

'You cannot,' he cried. 'I will never see you again if you do, and I love you too much to bear that.'

But Ishtar was insistent. 'She is my sister, she will not harm me. When we were children, we laughed and loved together. She will remember that and not let me come to harm.'

And so, despite Tammuz's constant pleadings, Ishtar set off on her journey.

Tammuz was sad, for he did not believe that he would ever see his beloved again.

After a long and tiring journey, Ishtar arrived at the gates of her sister's palace, in Hell. It was a gloomy, forbidding place and Ishtar was afraid. But she remembered the love that she had felt for her sister and refused to believe that any harm would come to her, so she knocked loudly at the heavy wooden door.

After what seemed like hours of waiting she heard the sound of shuffling footsteps at the other side of the door. 'Who is there?' a creaky voice demanded.

'The goddess Ishtar comes to visit her sister Ereshkigal.'

'Go away,' the voice replied. 'The goddess of Hell only sees those who come to visit her for eternity.'

'Go and tell my sister that Ishtar is here. She will see me.'

The footsteps slowly shuffled away.

'Ishtar!' said the surprised Ereshkigal. 'Why has she come? I must see her, for I remember the love that we had for each other. Bring her to me.'

'But mistress,' said the little hunch-backed man who had talked to

175

Ishtar from the other side of the door, 'if she comes in, I must do to her what I do to all men and women who enter your palace.'

'I know,' said the goddess, 'but I must see her. Bring her to me.'

And so, the little man returned to the outside door.

'You may enter,' he said to Ishtar when he had opened the door, 'but first you must give me your shawl.'

Ishtar did as he asked and entered the palace of Hell.

He led her through a long passage with a door at the end of it. As they passed through the door, he suddenly wrenched the golden ear-rings from her ears.

'Why did you do that?' the angry Ishtar demanded.

'It is the law of Hell. No one can see Ereshkigal unless they are naked of all precious things.' And the two proceeded deeper into the castle.

They came to another door and as they passed through it, the little man ripped the golden necklace from around Ishtar's neck. Again she angrily asked him why he had done it and again she was told that it was the law of Hell. At the third door, Ishtar was robbed of her beautiful rings and at the fourth of her golden belt. At the fifth her bracelets were ripped from her wrists and at the sixth the golden chains from around her ankles. As they went through the seventh door there was not a single precious thing around Ishtar's body and in the chamber beyond, there stood Ereshkigal waiting for her sister. The two women embraced and wept, Ishtar because she was so happy at seeing her sister, Ereshkigal because she, too, was happy to see her beloved sister, but also because she knew what she must do.

After they had stopped crying and had begun to laugh, as they remembered the happiness of their childhood days, Ereshkigal said to her sister, 'Have you left anything precious behind you? Did my slave remove all your precious things?'

Ishtar was surprised at the question, but nodded. 'Yes,' she said. 'I have nothing precious left.'

'Then,' cried Ereshkigal, 'you must stay here for eternity. For it is the law that only those who stand in my presence with something precious may return.' With that, she swept out of the room leaving the horrified Ishtar alone. The little hunchback entered the room chuckling to himself. 'Come, Ishtar. A chamber has been prepared for you. I hope you find it comfortable, for it is yours for all time.'

He grabbed her by the wrists and pulled her roughly into a luxurious chamber. He threw her onto the silken bed and then left her alone, locking the door behind him with the key of timelessness.

Ishtar wept. And as she wept, rainclouds gathered in the skies

above the land and the rain began to fall. She wept for days and days and it rained on Earth for days and days. And then she became very angry and banged on the door with all her might. She banged for day after day, and the thunderbolts clashed for day after day in the skies above the Earth.

From his place above the Earth, Tammuz could see what was happening. He had tried to warn Ishtar and she had ignored him. But his love for her was as strong as ever and he had no choice but to set out for Hell to try to rescue her.

He travelled for day after day, until he stood before the gates of the Palace of Hell. He knocked at the heavy door and after a long wait a voice from the other side said, 'Who stands before the gates of the Palace of Hell?'

'Tammuz,' he replied. 'Let me in.'

'Why are you so eager to enter Hell? Most men spend their lives trying to avoid it.'

'I come to see my beloved Ishtar. Let me in.'

The hunchback opened the door and with a wicked smile on his face, bade him enter. He led him along the long passage and as they passed through the door at the end of it, he ripped the golden crown from Tammuz's head.

'Why did you do that?' Tammuz demanded angrily.

'It is the law of Hell,' explained the hunchback. 'No one can see Ereshkigal unless they are naked of all precious things.'

At the second door he plucked the golden lyre from off Tammuz's shoulder, and at the third the rings from his fingers. At the fourth, the red ruby on his tunic was taken from him and at the fifth his beautiful golden belt. The sixth door cost Tammuz his quiver of golden arrows and the seventh his golden bow.

'Who stands before Ereshkigal?' she demanded as Tammuz was taken into the chamber behind the seventh door.

'Tammuz,' he declared. 'I come for my love.'

'And who is your love?'

'Ishtar, your sister.'

'Ishtar is here and here she must stay. She stood before me with nothing precious and only those who stand in my presence with something precious may return.'

'But you trick them. Your hideous servant robs everyone of all precious things.'

'As he has done to you,' said Ereshkigal. 'You have nothing precious, so you must stay here, locked in your chamber by the key of timelessness.'

At that the hunchback grabbed Tammuz by the wrists and began to pull him from the presence of the goddess of Hell.

'Wait,' cried Tammuz. 'I still have the most precious thing in the world!'

'Nonsense,' shouted the hunchback. 'I took your golden crown and your golden lyre. Your rings and your fine rubies are all gone, along with your belt and your arrows and your bow. You have nothing precious.'

'I still have my love for Ishtar. That is the most precious thing I possess and nothing you can do can steal that from me.'

'Let him go,' Ereshkigal's voice was soft and thoughtful. 'And bring Ishtar to me.'

The hunchback did as his mistress commanded and a few minutes later Ishtar was shown into the room. When she saw Tammuz she smiled and ran towards him, and in the sky, the sun shone for the first time since Ishtar had been locked in by the key of timelessness.

'My love, my precious love,' she wept as she embraced Tammuz.

'Your *precious* love,' said Ereshkigal. 'Then when you stood before me you were bearing something precious.'

'Of course,' said Ishtar. 'My love for Tammuz is much more precious than the things I lost on my way to your presence.'

'Oh, dear sister,' smiled Ereshkigal. 'Why did you not say that? Did I not tell you that those who stood in my presence with something precious might return? Here you both stand with your love for each other, your most precious possession. You may return. Do not think badly of me for what I did. I had to, for it is the law and it has to be applied to all, regardless of who they are. Now go. Be happy. Be together always.'

And so, Ishtar and Tammuz made their way out of the Palace of Hell to their own palace where they still live happily to this day.

THE VOYAGES
OF SINBAD THE SAILOR

There was once a rich merchant who had a son called Sinbad. When the merchant died, he left Sinbad a vast amount of money and precious jewels. Sinbad was lazy and spent all his day with undesirable friends, squandering his wealth. Within a few years he had spent most of his inheritance.

One day he happened to pick up an old book and his eyes fell upon these words:

'Three things are more important than any other: the day of death is more important than the day of birth, the living dog is more important than the dead lion, and poverty is less important than the grave.'

He thought about these words for some time and realized how silly he had been. So he sold what was left of his possessions and decided to invest the money he raised in a journey overseas to buy precious things which he could resell at a profit when he returned. He would spend what he had raised on hiring a ship and crew and with anything left over, he would buy goods to sell overseas to pay for his purchases.

So that is what he did. He went to the bazaar and spent some money on goods for trading. Then he hired a few porters and ship and crew, and then they set sail. They crossed the Persian Gulf and sailed into the Sea of Levant.

One day, the ship approached a beautiful island and the captain cast anchor. The merchants were enchanted by the loveliness of the place and were eager to set their feet upon land. So they went directly ashore. There some lit cooking fires, others washed in the island's clear streams and still others, Sinbad amongst them, walked about enjoying the sight of the trees and greenery.

They had spent many hours in these pleasant pursuits when all at once the ship's lookout called to them from the gunwale,

'Run for your lives. Return to the ship. That is not a real island, but a great sea monster stranded in the sea on whom the sand has settled and trees have sprung up so that he looks like an island. When you started your fires it felt the heat and moved. In a moment it will sink with you into the sea and you will all be drowned. Run! Run!'

All who left, left their gear and goods and swam in terror back to the ship. But Sinbad had walked too far to get away in time. Suddenly the island shuddered and sank into the depths of the sea; the waters surged over Sinbad and the waves crashed down upon him. He had nearly drowned when a wooden tub in which the crew had been bathing floated his way. He jumped into it and began to paddle with his arms towards the ship. The captain, however, was in such a fright that he set sail immediately with those who had reached the ship, heeding not the cries of the drowning.

Darkness closed in around Sinbad and he lay in the tub, certain that death was at hand. But after drifting for an entire night and a day, the tides brought him to the harbour of a lofty island. He caught hold of one of the branches and managed to clamber up onto the beach. Alas, he could walk no farther, for his legs were cramped and numb, and his feet swollen. So he crawled on his knees until he came upon a grove of fruit-laden trees amidst springs of sweet water. Sinbad ate and drank and his body and spirit began to revive.

After several days, Sinbad set out to explore the island. As he walked along the shore he caught sight of a noble mare tethered on the beach. He went up to her and she let out a great cry. Sinbad trembled in fear and turned to leave.

Before he had gone very far, a man came out of a cave, followed him and asked, 'Who are you?'

'Sinbad,' the surprised merchant replied.

'Where have you come from?' asked the man.

'I am a stranger who was left to drown in the sea, but good fortune led me to this island.'

When the man heard Sinbad's tale, he took his hand and led him to the entrance to the cave. They entered, descended a flight of steps and he found himself in a huge underground chamber as spacious as a ballroom.

Sinbad looked around and said, 'Now that I have told you of my accident, pray tell me who you are, why you live under the earth and why that mare is tethered on the beach?'

And so the man began his story:

'I am one of many who are stationed in different parts of the island. We are grooms of King Mirjan who guard and protect all of his horses. The mare you saw was one of a magical breed that eats not hay, but is nourished by the light of the moon.

'Every month when the moon is at its fullest, we bring the mares to the beach and then hide ourselves in these caves. In the morning when the moon has worked its spell, we return with the mares to our master. And now I shall take you, too, to the king.'

181

The rest of the grooms soon arrived, each leading a mare and the grooms set out, journeying to the capital of King Mirjan. The groom introduced the king to Sinbad, wherupon Mirjan gave him a cordial welcome and asked to hear his tale. So Sinbad related all that had happened. When he had finished the king said, 'Your rescue is indeed miraculous. You must be a blessed man destined for great things.' And the king promptly made Sinbad his harbour master, showered him with gifts and all manner of costly presents.

Sinbad lived in this way for a long while. And whenever he went to the port, he questioned the merchants and travellers for news of his home, Baghdad, for he was weary of living among strangers and

hoped to find some way to return home. But he met no one who knew of his beloved city, so he despaired.

One day a large ship came sailing into the harbour. When it had docked, the crew began to unload the cargo while Sinbad stood by and recorded the contents. 'Is there anything left in your ship?' Sinbad asked when the crew seemed to have finished.

'There remains in the hold only assorted bales of merchandise whose owner was drowned near one of the islands on our course. We are going to sell the goods and deliver the proceeds to his people in Baghdad.' When Sinbad asked for the drowned merchant's name, the captain replied, 'Sinbad the Sailor'.

On hearing this, Sinbad let out a great cry.

'O captain, I am that Sinbad who travelled with you. I was saved by a wooden tub that carried me to this island where the servants of King Mirjan found me and brought me here. These bales are mine and I pray you to release them to me.'

But the captain did not believe Sinbad.

'O captain,' Sinbad exclaimed, 'listen to my words. I will tell you more about my voyage than you have told me, then you will believe me.'

So Sinbad began to relate to the captain the whole history of the journey, up to the tragedy of the island. The captain then realized the truth of Sinbad's story and rejoiced at his deliverance saying, 'We were sure that you had drowned. Praise be to the power that gave you new life.'

The captain gave the bales to Sinbad, who opened them up and made a parcel of the finest and costliest of the contents as a present to King Mirjan.

Having done so and honoured with even costlier presents from King Mirjan, Sinbad returned to Baghdad with the crew of the ship.

With all the presents that the King had given him, Sinbad was rich and settled down again in Baghdad.

Sinbad was leading a most pleasurable life until one day he took it into his head to travel around the world. So he brought a large supply of merchandise, went down to the harbour and booked passage on a brand new ship. At last, fate brought him to an island, fair and green filled with fruit-bearing trees, fragrant flowers and singing birds. Sinbad landed and walked about, enjoying the shade of the trees and the song of the birds. So sweet was the wind and so fragrant were the flowers that he soon fell into a deep sleep. When he awoke he was horrified to find that the ship had left without him.

Giving himself up for lost he lamented, 'Last time I was saved by fate, but fate cannot be so kind twice. I am alone and there is no hope for me.'

He was so upset that he could not sit in one place for long. He climbed a tall tree and, looking in all directions, saw nothing but sky and sea and trees and birds and sand. But after a while his eager glance fell upon some great thing in the middle of the island. So he climbed down from the tree and walked to it. Behold, it was a huge white dome rising high into the air.

Sinbad circled around it but could find no door. As he stood wondering how to enter the dome, the skies darkened. Sinbad thought that a cloud had hidden the sun, but when he looked up he saw an enormous bird of such gigantic breadth that it veiled the sun.

Then Sinbad recalled a story he had heard long ago from some travellers. It told of a certain island where lived a huge bird called the roc, which fed its young on elephants. As Sinbad marvelled at the strange ways of nature, the roc alighted on the dome, covered it with its wings, and stretched its legs out on the ground. In this strange posture the roc fell asleep. When Sinbad saw this he arose, unwound his turban and twisted it into a rope with which he tied himself to the roc's legs.

'Perhaps,' he thought, 'this bird will carry me to inhabited lands. That will be better than living on this deserted island.'

In the morning the roc rose of its egg, for that is what the dome was, and spreading its wings with a great cry, soared into the air dragging Sinbad along, but never noticing him. When the roc finally alighted on the top of a high hill, Sinbad, quaking in his fear, wasted no time in untieing himself and running off. Presently he saw the roc catch something in its huge claws and rise aloft with it. Looking as closely as he dared Sinbad realized it was a serpent as gigantic as had ever roamed the earth; yet it seemed puny compared to the roc.

Looking further around, Sinbad found that he was on a hill over-looking a deep valley, which was surrounded by mountains so high that their summits disappeared into the clouds. At the sight of the wild and impassable country Sinbad moaned, 'Woe is me: I was better off on the island. There I had fruit to eat and water to drink, but here there are neither trees nor fruits nor streams and I will surely starve.'

Then Sinbad took courage and went down into the valley. Imagine how amazed he was to find that the soil was made of diamonds and it swarmed with snakes and vipers as big as palm trees. Sinbad ran for his life. Again he lamented at his misfortune.

As Sinbad walked along the valley, a roc flew overhead and dropped a slaughtered beast at his feet. Looking at the beast he had an idea. He took his knife from his belt and cut the meat into large, sticky pieces. When he had done this he threw the chunks into the valley. Suddenly the air was filled with huge eagles who swooped down into the diamond-filled valley and picked up the meat. Because the meat was so sticky, the precious stones stuck to it. Sinbad ran

after them and shooed them away, picking up the diamonds as he did so.

When he had gathered all the diamonds, he unwound his turban and lay all the meat on it. He tied it around himself and lay on his back and waited. A few minutes later, one of the huge eagles flew overhead and seeing the juicy meat, swooped down. He picked the meat up in his might talons, the turban and Sinbad with it. They flew for many miles, until Sinbad saw that they were passing over a huge, blue lake. He let out a loud cry and the startled bird dropped him, diamonds and all.

Sinbad landed in the lake with a large plop. Fortunately he was a good swimmer and swam as fast as he could for the shore. He walked along the sandy beach until he came to a small village. He asked one of the men there, how he could get to the nearest port. The man scratched his head and said, 'The nearest port is many miles from here, much too far to walk. We only have one horse in the village, so we could not sell it to you, no matter how much you offered.'

Sinbad showed the man his diamonds. 'Sir,' he said, 'if your horse is strong enough to carry two, I will give you ten diamonds for a lift. You and I can both ride on its back, and with the money you get for the diamonds you can buy ten hundred horses.'

So the man agreed to do this and the two set off. It was a long and tiring journey, but eventually they reached the port. There Sinbad sold some of the diamonds and bought beautiful silks and golden ornaments with the money he received. He hired a boat to take him back to Baghdad, and when he arrived he sold all his goods for a huge profit and settled down in the town again, living a most pleasurable life.

But as time passed he once again grew weary of his idle life of ease and comfort. So once more he laid in a considerable supply of merchandise to trade, and set sail in a fine ship with a company of merchants. For weeks they travelled on calm seas, stopping at many ports and gaining great profits through their trade. But one day, when they were far out at sea a mighty storm arose. The waves lashed the ship and the gales drove them they knew not where. The next morning when the storm had calmed, the captain climbed up to the gunwale and scanned the ocean in all directions. Suddenly he let out a great cry and tore his garments in despair.

'O my fellow travellers,' he cried, 'the wind has driven us far off course and we have run aground at the Mountain of the Hairy Apes. No man has ever left this place alive. We are doomed.'

186

Hardly had he finished speaking when thousands of apes were upon them, surrounding the ship on all sides, swarming about like locusts. They were the most fearsome creatures, only two feet tall, but covered with black hair, evil-smelling, black-faced and yellow-eyed. They gnawed at the ship's ropes and cables, tearing them in two, so that the sails fell into the sea and the powerless ship was stranded on the mountainous coast. Then the apes chased all the men off the ship, stole the cargo and disappeared.

Sinbad and his companions were left on the mountain island where they fortunately found fruit and water. They ate and drank and then decided to explore the island.

They had walked for a mile or two when they came across what looked like an uninhabited house. As they came close to it they could see that it was a tall castle and the gate was open. They went in and found themselves in a large courtyard which was completely empty. They lay down and fell asleep, hoping that the castle's owner would return before nightfall.

All at once the earth trembled under them and the air rumbled with a terrible noise. The owner had returned and he was a gigantic creature shaped like a man but as tall as tree, with eyes like fiery coals and teeth like elephant's tusks. His mouth was like a well, his lips hung loose onto his chest and his nails were as long and sharp as lion's claws.

The merchants almost fainted with terror at the sight of him. Then the giant seized Sinbad, who was but a tiny plaything in his hands, and began to run his mighty hands all over him, prodding him here and there. But Sinbad was too thin for the giant's huge appetite, so he put him down and picked up another. Finding him too thin as well, the giant tried another and another until he came to the captain of the ship, who was a fat, broad-shouldered man. The giant found him tempting enough to eat and promptly did so. That done he lay down and fell asleep. In the morning he got up and left the castle.

The next night the giant returned and again the earth trembled, and again he went through all the men until he found one tasty enough for his supper.

When the giant departed the next morning the terrified men decided that they could not sit by and watch the giant eat them all.

'Let us try to slay him,' they said. 'We will build a raft of firewood and planks and keep it ready at the shore.' As soon as the giant came home, he grabbed one of the men and ate him for his dinner. He lay down and fell asleep shortly afterwards.

When the men were quite sure that the giant was sound asleep, they took two iron spits and heated the ends in a fire, until they were as red-hot as the coals themselves. They crept up to the sleeping giant and thrust the glowing spits into his eyes.

His scream rent the air and he jumped up fumbling for the men. But he was quite blind and he could not prevent the men rushing to the raft.

But even when they had passed beyond the giant's reach, they could find no respite from danger, for the sea was stormy and the waves swollen. One by one the men died until there were only three men and Sinbad left. Finally the winds cast them upon an island where they found fruit to eat and water to drink. Exhausted by their hazardous voyage, they lay down on the beach and went to sleep.

They had barely closed their eyes when they were aroused by a hissing sound and saw that a monstrous dragon with a huge belly was spread in a circle around them. Suddenly it reared its head, seized one of Sinbad's companions, and swallowed him whole. Then the beast left and Sinbad said, 'Woe to us. Each kind of death that threatens us is more terrible than the last. We rejoiced at our deliverance from the sea and apes and the giant, but we are now at the mercy of something even more evil.'

The frightened men climbed into a high tree and went to sleep there. Sinbad rested on the top branch. When night fell, the dragon returned. He looked to right and left and finally discovered the men in the tree. He stood up on his hind legs and swallowed Sinbad's companions. Again, the dragon left satisfied with his dinner. Then Sinbad climbed down and resolved to find some way to save his life. So he took pieces of wood, broad and long, and made a cage with them. He crept into the cage and when the dragon returned he saw Sinbad sitting in the cage. He immediately tried to eat him, but he could not get his jaws round the cage.

All through the night, the dragon circled around Sinbad's cage, hissing in anger. But when the dawn came and the sun began to shine, the dragon left in fury and disappointment.

Sinbad ran to the beach where he spied a ship on the horizon. He broke a branch off a tree, unwound his turban from his head and tied it to the branch. He began to wave it like a flag and at last, one of the sailors spotted him and the ship turned to shore. They cast anchor and took the grateful Sinbad aboard, and carried him back to Baghdad.

One day, several months later, Sinbad was visited at home by a company of merchants who talked to him about foreign travel and

trade, until the old wanderlust came back to Sinbad, and he yearned
to enjoy the sight of foreign lands once more. So Sinbad resolved to
join them on their voyage and they purchased a great store of precious goods, more than ever before. They set out and sailed from
island to island.

After several months of travelling and trading they sailed into
a furious storm which tore the sails to tatters. Then the ship founder-
ed, casting all on board into the sea.

Sinbad swam for half a day, certain that his fate was sealed, when
one of the planks of the ship floated up to him and he climbed on it,
along with some of the other merchants.

They took turns paddling and soon the current drove them to an
island. Sinbad and his companions threw themselves onto the beach,
ate some of the fruit that they found there and then each man fell
into a troubled sleep. The next morning they began to explore the
island. Coming across a house, they were about to knock at the door
when a host of half-naked savages ran out, surrounded them and
forced them inside where the king awaited. The king extended

a most cordial welcome and invited them to dinner. Gratefully they sat down and were immediately served such food as they had never tasted in their lives.

Sinbad, however, was not hungry and he refused all the food that was offered to him. He was soon glad that he had done so, for as the men tasted the food they lost all their senses and began to devour it like madmen possessed of an evil spirit. Then the savages gave them coconut oil to drink, whereupon their eyes turned around in their heads and they continued to eat even more ravenously than before.

Seeing all this, Sinbad grew anxious for his safety. He watched carefully and it was not long before he realized that he was amidst a certain tribe of savages of whom he had once heard a traveller tell. Every man who came to the savages' country was given food and oil which made their stomachs expand and at the same time to lose their reason and turn into idiots. In this way, the unfortunate victims never stopped eating. Every day they were led out to pasture like cattle and grew fatter and fatter. When they were judged fat enough, the savages slaughtered them and sent them off to market.

So Sinbad understood the evil folk that he had fallen among and watched sadly as his friends ate and drank. The savages paid no attention to Sinbad, for as the days passed he grew thinner.

One day he slipped away and walked to a distant beach. There he saw the old man who was the herdsman, charged with guarding his friends. As soon as the herdsman saw Sinbad, so gaunt and bony, he realized that this was not one of the madmen and wanted to help him escape.

'If you take the road to the right,' the herdsman said, 'it will lead you away from the house of the savages.'

Sinbad followed the kind old man's advice and did not cease travelling for seven days and seven nights. He stopped only to eat and drink, for the path was strewn with roots and herbs and water was plentiful. On the eighth day he caught sight of a group of men gathering peppercorns.

'I am a poor stranger,' he said to them. 'May I have a peppercorn?'

One of the men threw him a handful and Sinbad told them the story of the hardships and dangers that he had suffered.

The men marvelled at Sinbad's tale and brought him to their king, to whom he repeated his tale. The king instantly liked Sinbad and invited him to stay in his sumptuous palace.

One day the king invited Sinbad out to ride with the hunt. Now Sinbad had noticed that neither the king nor his citizens had saddles on their beautiful steeds.

'Why, O Lord, do you not have saddles? Riding is much easier with them.'

'What is a saddle?' the king asked, for he had never heard of such a thing before.

Sinbad offered to make one for him, so that he could ride in greater comfort. In a few days, Sinbad had fashioned a magnificent saddle of polished leather with silk fringes and presented it to the king. The king tried it and was delighted. The next week his Vizier asked Sinbad to make a saddle for him as well. In a short time, everyone wanted a saddle, so Sinbad went into business and became a prosperous saddle maker.

Then one day the king said, 'Sinbad, I have such affection for you that I cannot permit you ever to leave. I must therefore insist that you marry one of our women so that you will remain here for the rest of your days.'

So Sinbad married a beautiful and rich lady of noble ancestry and lived with her in peace and contentment.

One sad day, however, Sinbad's wife took ill and died within a week. The mournful Sinbad was about to make arrangements for a funeral in accordance with the customs of his own country when a messenger arrived from the king.

'My lord offers you deep condolences and asks that the funeral be conducted according to the customs of our land,' the messenger said.

Sinbad agreed, for he wished only to honour his wife.

Now it happened that the customs of the country were very strange. When a woman died she was buried in a deep cave and her husband, still alive, was buried with her so that she might have companionship in the afterlife.

On the day of the funeral, the whole town arrived in front of Sinbad's house and they walked in procession to the burial cave — a vast underground cavern that ran beneath a mountain. The body of Sinbad's wife was lowered down. Then the townsfolk lowered him down on a rope ladder.

Sinbad found himself in a cave filled with rotting bodies and skeletons, for it had served as a burial site since time immemorial. It was a horrible, foul-smelling place and Sinbad again lamented that the greed that had made him leave Baghdad had ended in such a way. There was no escape from the cave of death.

The day after the funeral, Sinbad noticed a mountain goat at the far end of the cave. Seeing that the beast was fat and healthy, Sinbad realized that there must be another opening in the cave, one unknown to the townspeople. So he followed the beast and after

a while saw a shaft of light. Indeed, it was another opening. Sinbad joyfully climbed out and found himself high over the sea on a steep cliff which only an animal so agile as the goat could climb. Although he felt sure that he was to die there, he was thankful that he would not die in the cavern of death.

When Sinbad was near to death, a ship passed by and spotted him. The ship cast anchor and with the help of strong ropes, the sailors scaled the cliff and rescued Sinbad.

When he arrived back in Baghdad, Sinbad promised his friends and relations that he would never leave them again. This time he kept that promise.

ALADDIN

In far-off China there once lived a magician who was as ugly as he was wicked. His magic was tremendously powerful, but he was not satisfied with it. He wanted to be the most powerful and the richest magician in the whole of the world, for he knew that there were others who could equal him.

One day as he was walking in the market place his eyes fell upon a ring that was brighter than any ring that he possessed. It glittered in the bright sunshine and threw off dazzling patterns of red and blue on the canopy of the jewel-seller's stall. The magician had to have it and after long bargaining with the jewel-seller, a price was agreed which satisfied both men.

The magician rushed home with his new treasure and as soon as he was inside, he hurriedly pulled off all the rings that he was wearing and slipped the new one on. He moved his hand hither and thither, and marvelled at the glorious colours that the ring cast off. With greed and lust in his eyes, the magician watched the beautiful patterns until he could bear it no longer and he lovingly stroked the ring. Suddenly, the room darkened and was filled with smoke. The magician was terrified and began to shake with fear. He shook even more when a voice boomed out, 'Who calls the Genie of the Ring?'

'The what?' asked the magician, his voice trembling as much as his knees.

'Who calls the Genie of the Ring?' the voice repeated.

'I did, I suppose,' said the magician.

'And what do you want, oh Master?' the Genie of the Ring asked.

'What can you give me?' asked the magician.

'Money, jewellery, precious metals, rich cloth, enough to satisfy most men.'

'I am not most men,' said the magician. 'I want power. I want to be the richest and most powerful man in the world.'

'For that you need the Genie of the Lamp, not the Genie of the Ring.'

'Where can I find this Genie of the Lamp?'

'Come, I will show you,' said the Genie and with a rush of wind and a blaze of sparks the two were suddenly transported to an oasis far from anywhere. In the centre of the oasis there was a trapdoor.

'There you will find the Genie of the Lamp. Under the trapdoor,' said the Genie of the Ring.

The magician rushed forward and pulled at the trapdoor. But it refused to move, even by as much as an inch.

'Foolish man,' scoffed the Genie of the Ring. 'I offered you enough to satisfy most men and you wanted more. Only one person in the whole world can open the door.'

'Who?' demanded the magician. 'Who can open the trapdoor?'

'Aladdin. Aladdin, the washerwoman's son. Anyone else who enters the garden will die instantly,' laughed the Genie and with a rush of wind and a blaze of sparks he was gone.

The magician rubbed his eyes in disbelief and suddenly found himself back in his own home.

He immediately summoned all his servants and commanded them to find out where Aladdin, the washerwoman's son, lived. One by one his servants went out and searched, and one by one they returned with no information. The magician angrily sent them out again and eventually one of the servants came back with the news that Aladdin lived in the poorest district of the town, some distance from the magician's palace.

The very next morning the magician set out to see Aladdin, and even his own servants did not recognize him. His long, dirty fingernails had been cleaned and cut. His straggly hair and greasy beard had been washed and trimmed and he was dressed in fresh, newly-laundered clothes. He quickly made his way to where Aladdin lived and when he saw the boy he rushed up to him and put his arms around him.

'Aladdin. My dear nephew. We have never met, but I am your poor father's brother. I have been travelling for many years, visiting holy places.'

'My father's brother?' said Aladdin. 'No one has ever mentioned that my father had a brother.'

'No matter, child. It is the truth. Take me to your mother. My poor brother's wife.'

The boy did as he was told and the two went into the steamy laundry where Aladdin and his mother lived.

'Sister-in-law,' cried the magician as soon as he saw Aladdin's mother.

'Sister-in-law? My poor husband had no brother,' said the woman.

'He did. Indeed he did. But we quarrelled many years ago and I have been on pilgrimage ever since.'

The woman did not believe him at first, but when the magician took ten gold coins and gave them to her, saying 'Take this. Buy some clothes for the child,' she was happy to believe him.

For several days the magician stayed with Aladdin and his mother, insisting on paying for everything.

One day, about a week after his arrival the magician asked the woman if he could take Aladdin on a journey for a few days. By this time the widow was convinced that the magician was her brother-in-law and gave her consent.

The man and boy travelled together for several days until they came to an oasis. 'Aladdin,' said the magician. 'Raise the trapdoor, child, and bring me the lamp that you will find down there.'

Aladdin did as he was told and lifted the trapdoor. There was a flight of stairs and the magician then told Aladdin to go down them and bring him the lamp. Aladdin went down the steps and found himself in the most beautiful garden that he could ever have imagined. The trees were laden with precious jewels that dazzled Aladdin's eyes with their magnificent colours — there were pearls, diamonds, rubies and many, many more. At the end of a golden path, Aladdin could see the lamp. He made his way towards it and tried to lift it, but it would not budge. 'Uncle,' the boy cried. 'I cannot lift it on my own. Come and help me.' But the magician was afraid and called back, 'Try harder, nephew, for I cannot come into the enchant-ed garden.'

The boy tried and tried, but it was no good. He kept calling for his uncle and still his uncle refused to come down. After many hours the poor child was exhausted and made his way back to the steps. But the magician was furious. 'Ungrateful wretch!' he screamed. 'You shall stay there for ever. If I cannot have the lamp, then no one will.' And with that he slammed the trapdoor down, leaving Aladdin in the enchanted garden.

Poor Aladdin. He ran back through the garden looking for a way out, but there was none. Eventually he made his way back to where the lamp was and unthinkingly tried to lift it. He was amazed when he did so quite easily. He ran back to the trapdoor and shouted, 'Uncle, I have it. I have it.' But the magician was miles away and no one heard Aladdin's cries. Aladdin sat down and wept. As he did so his hands rubbed the lamp, and suddenly there was an enormous puff of smoke and with a blaze of sparks, the most enormous Genie appeared before Aladdin.

'You called me, Master. What is your command?'

'M ... M ... M ... Master! C ... C ... Command,' stuttered Aladdin.

'Yes, Master! I am the Genie of the Lamp. Anything you wish shall be granted.'

'Then take me home,' cried the astonished boy and in an instant

Aladdin was outside his own home. 'Mother,' he cried and rushed inside to tell her everything that had happened to him.

'We need never be poor again,' he said and rubbed the lamp. When the Genie appeared Aladdin asked him to bring gold and silver and fine clothes; and in an instant the Genie did as Aladdin had commanded. For many days, whenever Aladdin or his mother

wanted anything they summoned the Genie, who did as he was asked.

One day, Aladdin was in the market when soldiers of the Sultan's army appeared and began to push the crowds roughly to one side. 'Stand back,' they cried. 'The Sultan's daughter is coming and she must not be seen. Turn around.' Everyone did as they were command-ed and the Princess passed through the market place. Now Aladdin had obeyed the soldiers, but found himself looking into a large mir-ror. As the Princess passed by, Aladdin saw her reflection in the glass and instantly fell in love with her. He ran home as fast as he could and burst into the house. 'Mother,' he gasped. 'I have seen the Sul-tan's daughter.'

His mother was horrified. 'But it is instant death for anyone who casts eyes on the Princess. It is the law.'

'I saw her in a looking glass,' said Aladdin. 'Mother. I must marry her!'

'Marry her!' exclaimed his mother. 'Aladdin, child, we are poor people. You cannot marry the Princess.'

'But the lamp,' said Aladdin. 'With the Genie we can become as rich as the Sultan.'

And so, despite his mother's doubts, Aladdin summoned the Genie. He commanded him to build a vast palace and to fill it with jewels and precious things.

Before the mother and son could blink, they found themselves in a sumptuous room furnished with gold and silver. Their clothes were made of the finest silks and jewels sparkled from their fingers.

The next morning the Sultan awoke as usual and went to his window to look out over his capital. He blinked once, then twice, then three times. For where there had been a vast park, the night before, there now stood the most beautiful palace that the Sultan had ever seen.

The astonished Sultan immediately summoned his Vizier and demanded an explanation. The Vizier hurried from the palace and into Aladdin's splendid new home.

When Aladdin saw the Vizier approach, he went to meet him. 'Tell your master that the palace and all the precious things are for the Princess if he will give me permission to marry her.'

The Vizier ran back to the Sultan and told him what Aladdin wanted. The Sultan ordered that his daughter be brought to him, dressed in her most beautiful clothes. 'Go and bring this Aladdin to me,' he called to the harassed Vizier.

As soon as the Princess saw Aladdin she fell as deeply in love with him as he had with her.

'How did you come to build such a magnificent palace overnight? How is it that you are obviously so rich, yet I have never heard of you?' demanded the bewildered Sultan.

'Sire, my fortune I made in a far-off land. By trade,' said Aladdin, who did not want anyone else to know of the Genie of the Lamp. 'I had one million servants toil silently the night to build the palace.'

'And why do you want to marry my daughter?'

'Because, sire, I had heard of her beauty, and now that I see her for myself I see that I was told wrongly, for no words can describe such beauty. Sire, allow me to marry her. I will make her happy. She will want for nothing.'

The Sultan thought for a few seconds. He loved his daughter very much and did not really want to lose her. But he loved riches, too.

'Very well, I consent,' he said, 'but only on condition that you take her to the palace across from mine, and that you both live there for ever.'

Aladdin was overjoyed and promised to bring the Princess back.

The wedding was the grandest that had ever been seen, and the couple were as happy as happy could be to live in their splendid palace. Everyone who saw them was astonished at how completely happy they were together and expected them to live there for ever and ever. And that is exactly what the lovers planned to do; but they had made these plans without considering the wicked magician.

Thousands of miles away, the magician was wondering what had happened to Aladdin. One day, about three weeks after Aladdin and the Princess had been married, he went into a great book-lined room and from the back of a secret drawer he took out his crystal ball. Murmuring some strange incantations, he rubbed his hands over the ball. Imagine his horror when he saw Aladdin and the Princess in their splendid palace. His voice got louder and louder and soon he was screaming a strange spell at the top of his voice. He turned three times and vanished into thin air.

He reappeared at nightfall outside Aladdin's palace. He walked around the walls and saw that it was heavily guarded. He wanted the lamp more than ever and as the night passed, he made his plans to get revenge.

The next morning, he watched as Aladdin set out on a fine horse, obviously going hunting. He then made his way to the market where he bought several beautiful new lamps.

Soon he was back outside Aladdin's palace, shouting, 'New lamps for old! New lamps for old!' From deep inside the palace, the Princess heard the strange call, and suddenly remembered the old lamp that her husband kept in a cupboard. 'How well pleased he will be to have a fine new lamp,' she thought to herself and ran to fetch it.

'Lampseller,' she called from a window. 'Wait. Here is an old lamp for a new one.'

The magician's greedy hands grabbed the lamp and his eyes lit up with joy. He had the lamp. 'Thank you, Lady,' he called up to the Princess. 'Here is your new lamp,' and with that he was off.

He rounded a corner out of sight of anyone and rubbed the lamp. Instantly the Genie appeared. 'What do you require, oh Master?'

'Take Aladdin's palace and the Princess to my home in Africa.'

No sooner had he spoken than there was a loud gust of wind. The palace was being hammered by a violent dust storm, and when the dust cleared, the palace had vanished.

When the Sultan awoke from his afternoon nap, he went to his window as he now always did to admire his son-in-law's magnificent palace. Imagine his horror when all that he saw was the park that had been there before. He immediately summoned his Vizier and demanded that Aladdin be brought before him. It took a few hours to find the young man, but eventually he was brought before the furious Sultan.

'What have you done with my daughter? Where is the palace?' the Sultan demanded.

Aladdin could only shake his head in astonishment as he had no idea what had happened.

'Take him away,' roared the Sultan. 'Throw him into the deepest dungeon and let him remain there until my daughter is returned to me.'

Poor Aladdin was dragged away and cast into the deepest, darkest dungeon in the palace.

Meanwhile, thousands of miles away in the depths of darkest Africa the poor Princess was weeping and begging the magician to take her back.

'Keep the palace, but let me return,' she begged.

'Never,' replied the magician. 'Now you are here, here you will stay. Not as a princess, but as my wife. Prepare yourself, my dear, for tomorrow we will be wed. Tonight we will feast.' With that, the magician departed and left the poor girl to her thoughts. She thought long and deep, and after many hours she came up with a plan.

That evening, she dressed herself in her most beautiful robes, rubbed the most expensive perfumes on her soft skin and waited for the magician. She ordered her servants to bring her the most succulent meats and the sweetest fruits. To drink, she ordered the most potent of all the wines in the cellar. When the magician appeared later, she greeted him with a deep curtsey.

'At last you have come, my master,' she said.

'Ah,' sighed the magician. 'I can see that you have thought over my proposal and are going to be sensible.'

'Come, drink with me,' the Princess said softly.

She poured two glasses of wine and watched as the magician drank deeply. She quickly filled his glass and beckoned him to the table. All through the meal she laughed and smiled and kept the magician's glass full, while she hardly drank at all.

'You are without doubt the most powerful man in the world. That weakling Aladdin is nothing compared to you,' she said after they

had eaten. 'Where does your power come from?' Before he could answer, she filled his glass yet again. 'Let us drink a toast to your power,' she said and watched with great satisfaction as the magician emptied his glass.

'My power,' the magician said, 'comes from this old lamp.' As he spoke, he took the lamp from under his cloak. 'I only need to rub it gently...' He never finished his sentence. The Princess had filled him so full of wine, that he slipped to the floor, completely drunk.

The Princess picked up the lamp and rubbed it gently. Immediately the Genie appeared. 'What do you command, oh Mistress?'

'Take this man and set him in a place from which he can never escape.'

The Genie stooped down and picked up the sleeping magician as easily as if he had been a piece of fluff. He disappeared for the flick of an eye, and was back. 'What else, oh Mistress, do you command?'

'Take me and my palace back to where we belong,' said the Princess.

There was a sudden rush of wind and in an instant the palace was back in its proper place.

The next morning, the Sultan awoke from his troubled sleep and went to the window to look sadly at the park where the palace had once stood. He blinked once, and then twice, and then three times.

'Vizier!' he shouted. 'Come quickly. Look!'

Within a few minutes, Aladdin had been released from his deep dungeon and was reunited with his beloved wife.

'You are indeed a powerful magician, Aladdin, who can make palaces appear and disappear. But do not do it again. Next time I will not be so merciful!'

Aladdin was quick to agree, and he and his Princess lived happily together for many, many years.

And the lamp? It was locked away in the deepest dungeon in Aladdin's palace, and it is probably still there to this day.

RAMA AND SITA

In distant India the lands around the city of Ayodhya on the banks of the river Saragu were once ruled by the wise King, Dasaratha. He had three wives. The first was called Kausalya and they had a splendid son, Rama, who was heir to Dasaratha's throne. His second wife, Kaikeya, was the mother of his son, Bharata, and his third wife, Sumitra, bore him fine twins, Lakshmana and Satrughna.

The king, his three queens and their four sons were all very happy. Only Kaikeya was occasionally jealous that Rama would one day rule over the kingdom rather than her own beloved Bharata.

Rama grew up as tall and handsome as his father, and one day Dasaratha announced, 'Rama, you have now grown to manhood. It is time that you took a wife and had children of your own. I have chosen for your bride the lovely Sita.'

Rama had never met Sita, but it was the custom at that time for fathers to choose their sons' brides. It was also the custom that the sons never saw their brides until the wedding day.

The marriage was duly announced, and preparations for the great occasion were soon underway. On the day before the ceremony, Rama looked out of his window and saw the bridal procession enter the city gates. There were mighty elephants and beautiful horses. Graceful cheetahs strained at their leashes, adding excitement to the magnificent procession. In the centre, a huge white elephant decorated with gold carried a curtained box on its back, and Rama knew that in it sat his future bride.

That night he was unable to sleep. He was worried in case Sita's beauty proved to be an exaggeration, and by morning he had convinced himself that his bride would be old and fat and probably toothless, too.

Imagine his delight when Sita was revealed to be as beautiful as had been rumoured. She was tall and graceful and her dark eyes shone with happiness when she looked at her handsome husband for the first time. At once she fell in love with Rama, and he too fell in love with her.

The marriage ceremony was long and impressive. The music was enchanting and afterwards all the courtiers were invited by Dasaratha to a splendid banquet. There was much jollity and laughter and clapping as the sumptuous feast was carried in. Suddenly, when the merriment was at its height, Dasaratha slumped forward, his hand on his chest. The guests were silent as the court physician quickly examined the king and then whispered to the three queens. 'He is dead,' the physician said in a sad voice, and the guests watched, horrified, as the king's body was carried from the room.

A little later, Kaikeya left the palace and went into the hills beyond. She made her way to a small clearing and gathered some curious-looking herbs. She quickly returned to the palace and made an infusion of them. When it was prepared she went to the chamber where the king's body was lying and said to the other two widows and all their children who were there,

'Stand aside. Let me draw near.'

They all did as they were told, and the woman raised her husband's head gently off the pillow. She parted his white lips and poured a little of the liquid into his dead mouth. She then laid his head back on the pillow and rubbed more of the herb infusion all over his body.

A few seconds later, Kausalya screamed, 'He's breathing! He's breathing! Kaikeya has brought him back to life.' And sure enough, Dasaratha's chest was moving up and down, drawing air into his lungs. A moment later, his eyelids flickered open and soon he stirred, as if awakening from a deep slumber. The astonished onlookers knelt before him as he held out his hand to Kaikeya. 'You have brought me back to this life. You may have any two wishes and if it is in my power to grant them, I shall do so.'

Kaikeya did not hesitate. 'Declare my son Bharata your heir instead of Rama, and banish Rama from here for fourteen years.'

'But mother,' cried Bharata. 'I do not wish to be king. Rama is the rightful heir.'

'Quiet,' commanded Dasaratha. 'I gave my word. Bharata, you are now my heir. Rama, I command you to leave here and live in the jungle as a penitent.'

'I will obey,' said Bharata. 'But when the fourteen years are up and Rama is free to return, I will hand over the reins of power to him.'

'I must go where my husband goes,' declared Sita. 'If he leaves for fourteen years, then I, too, will go.'

'You cannot,' said Rama. 'The jungle is a dangerous place. It is no place for you.'

'I WILL go,' repeated Sita.

'And I too,' said Lakshmana.

And so, the very next morning, Rama, his newly-wedded wife and his half-brother prepared to leave the palace.

Rama's mother stepped forward. 'I have but one gift for you,' she said handing a sword to Rama. 'It is an enchanted sword. Wherever it is aimed it will fall.' And she kissed her son and her stepson tenderly.

Lakshmana's mother stepped forward. 'I too have a gift,' she said, and gave him a bow and a quiver of arrows. 'This quiver will never run empty. The arrows will always find their targets.'

Then Satrughna, Lakshmana's twin brother, stepped forward. 'Take this,' he said and thrust an alabaster pot into Sita's hand. 'It is the infusion that brought the king back to life.'

And so bearing only the sword, the quiver and bow, and the pot, the three made their way out of the palace. Dasaratha watched from his chamber, his heart heavy with sadness, for he knew that he would not live another fourteen years to see them return.

The three travelled long and far and eventually came to Mountain Chitrakutu where the Holy Hermits lived. Valkimi, the leader of the hermits, came forward to greet them. 'Prince Rama,' he declared, 'I had heard that you and your brother were to come here. And this lovely creature must be Sita. I wish you all happiness.'

Rama and Sita thanked him.

'You must build yourselves a hermitage before the rains start. You will be helped.' And he bowed and left the three of them to search for a suitable spot.

The news soon spread to the other hermits that Rama and his bride and half-brother had arrived and all of them helped to build a fine hermitage.

Hermits live a simple life and are quiet and gentle people. After a short time, the three found that the tranquillity of the Holy Mountain was as beautiful and peaceful as the jungle around it and they began to be very happy. Their happiness grew deeper every day and for year after year they lived in great contentment. Sita became more and more beautiful as the years passed, and Rama's love for her grew with each setting of the sun.

In the jungle all around the Holy Mountain, there lived demons. They did not bother the hermits because they knew they were able to resist any of the temptations they could offer, but those unwise enough to travel in the jungle at night were often scared by the shining eyes and eerie laughter of the demons as they roamed the jungle.

One day, as Rama and Sita knelt quietly in prayer at the altar outside their hermitage an ugly old woman passed. She was Shurpanakha, sister of the master demon. She fell in love with Rama as soon as she looked at him. She was used to getting anything that she wanted and when she called out to Rama, 'Come, oh beautiful warrior. Come and be my husband,' she was astonished when he replied, 'Woman, I am married already.'

Just then Lakshmana came out of the hermitage. He had grown more handsome than Rama and Shurpanakha fell in love with him, too.

'Come both of you. We will live in my brother's palace in the jungle. I will make you both rich and we will be happy, the three of us,' she said.

'And leave our beloved Sita,' laughed Rama. 'Go, old hag. Leave us alone.'

No one had ever called Shurpanakha an old hag before and she became furious.

She ran towards Sita and grabbed her around the neck. Her scrawny hands tightened around the poor girl's throat squeezing the life out of her.

Rama pulled his enchanted sword from its sheath, where it had lain untouched for years, and brought it down on Shurpanakha's nose. The old hag screamed terribly as her hands flew up to stop the ghastly flow of blood gushing from the hole where her nose had been.

'I will have my revenge for this,' she shouted as she ran off into the jungle.

When her brother saw the ghastly mess that Rama had made of Shurpanakha's face, his fury matched Shurpanakha's. He immediately sent fourteen thousand evil demons to kill Rama and his wife and half-brother.

The battle was long and horrible; fourteen thousand against two. But Lakshmana's magic quiver never ran out of arrows and each arrow fired killed every demon in its path.

Shurpanakha watched in astonishment as wave after wave of demons were slaughtered by the magic arrows. She looked in terror as she saw an arrow fly straight towards her brother and bring him down, along with one thousand demons. Terrified and angry, she ran from the hermitage and fled through the jungle to the palace of Ravana, king of all demons. When she told him her story, Ravana wanted to send even more demons after Rama, but his son, Manan, said, 'Wait, father. If we send ten million demons after Rama, it will be no use. He and his brother are clearly invincible. But Sita is not. We must lure her away from Rama and Lakshmana. They will surely die of grief.'

And so Ravana and Manan made their way to the hermitage and waited for their chance. It came a few days later. Rama went out hunting, leaving Lakshmana to guard Sita.

Disguising his voice as that of Valkimi, the leader of the hermits, Manan, called out, 'Help! Somebody help me!' Lakshmana rushed out of the hermitage into the undergrowth to search for Valkimi. Further and further away from the hermitage, Manan lured him, and as he was still searching, Ravana ran into the house and grabbed the terrified Sita from her chair. Although she struggled fiercely, the demon was far too strong for her and he dragged her into the jungle.

When Rama came home, he listened, horrified, to his brother's tale. The two men sadly went to Valkimi's hermitage and told them their story.

'I cannot help you,' said Valkimi. 'Only Sugriva and his councillor Hanuman would know where Sita has been taken. You must go to them at Mount Rshyamuku and ask for their help.'

So Rama and Lakshmana went and collected the sword, the bow and arrow and the alabaster pot and made their way to Mount Rshyamuku.

Sugriva and Hanuman listened to the two brothers. Hanuman

stroked his long beard and said, 'Go into the clearing and light a fire of sandalwood. As the smoke rises, a bird will appear. Ask it where Sita has been taken and it will help.'

Rama did as Hanuman had said. He collected sandalwood and made a big fire. As the smoke whirled into the air, a magnificent bird flew down and asked, 'What do you want of me, oh Rama?'

'How do you know who I am?' asked Rama.

'I know everything,' answered the bird.

'Where is Sita, my wife?' begged Rama.

'She is being held by Ravana at his palace on the island of Lanka.'

'How can I get her out? Please tell me!' pleaded Rama.

'You alone cannot,' said the bird. 'You need the aid of Louhi, leader of the monkeys.'

'Monkey! How can monkeys help me?'

'Monkeys are as intelligent as humans. I can fly to Lanka, but you cannot fly with me. Louhi can lead you to the shores across from Lanka.'

'How can I find Louhi?' asked Rama.

'Wait here,' said the bird and flew off.

An hour passed. Two. Rama was about to make his way back to Lakshmana when there was the sound of footsteps approaching the clearing. Rama watched in astonishment as an enormous monkey approached him and said,

'I am Louhi. I have come to lead you to Lanka. Go and collect your brother and be back here at dawn.'

'But monkeys cannot talk. I must be dreaming,' said Rama.

'Rama! The gods are pleased with the devotions you have offered them since your exile. With them, anything is possible. They give us the gift of communication to help you. Now go.'

At dawn the next morning, Rama and Lakshmana returned to the clearing where Louhi was waiting for them. He beckoned them to follow and the two brothers went into the jungle behind the monkey. For three days and nights they went deeper and deeper into the thick undergrowth, until they came to a lake that was so large that the other side was not visible from the shore. In the middle of the lake, Rama and Lakshmana could just make out an island. 'There,' said Louhi, 'is where Sita is being held.'

'But how are we to rescue her? If we sail out, we will be spotted and destroyed,' said Rama. 'We must somehow get them to leave the island and bring Sita to the shore.'

Louhi beckoned to some birds. 'Fly over to the island and tell the Princess Sita that help is at hand,' he ordered and the birds flew off.

Meanwhile Sita was miserable and frightened. She was being held prisoner in the most beautiful palace she had ever seen. Every room was more sumptuously furnished than the next. The furniture was all made of pure gold and studded with precious jewels. The carpets were of finest silk and rich fabrics hung on every wall. The gardens were a glorious sight. There were the greenest of green lawns and flower-beds containing orchids and roses and gardenias, as well as sweet-smelling herbs that filled the air with a wonderful aroma. Fountains played everywhere sending sparkling streams into the blue, blue sky above. Yet all that Sita wanted was to be reunited with her beloved Rama. Every day, Ravana asked her to be his wife and every day she refused.

'I would,' she said, 'rather die.'

Sita was walking in the gardens when a bird landed in the pathway in front of her. She was astonished when she heard it speak.

'Princess,' the bird said, 'Rama and his brother are on the shore waiting to rescue you. You need be patient for only a few more hours. Be not afraid of anything that happens and do what Ravana tells you to do.'

Before the astounded Sita could say anything, the bird flew off . . .

It alighted on the shore where Louhi and the others were waiting. 'She is safe but sorrowing,' said the bird. 'I told her that help was at hand.'

'Good,' said Louhi. 'Now go into the jungle and tell all the monkeys to come here tomorrow morning.'

The next morning every monkey in the jungle obeyed Louhi and by the time the sun was high in the sky, there were more than one million monkeys on the shores of the lake.

'Now,' said Louhi to the bird, 'return to the jungle and tell every stinging insect to come here.' The bird immediately flew off.

'Go and cut down branches and fashion clubs from them,' said Louhi to the monkeys and they set about doing that.

Just when the sun was at its highest, the sky grew darker and darker. Every stinging insect had followed the bird. There were millions of them.

'Attack the island,' commanded Louhi.

Within minutes there was panic on the island. The demons raced hither and thither trying to escape the vicious stings of the insects, but it was useless.

'Leave this island,' thundered Ravana. 'You,' he shouted at Sita, 'come with me.' He grabbed poor Sita, pulling her to the shore and onto a boat. They were almost the last to leave. In front of them,

210

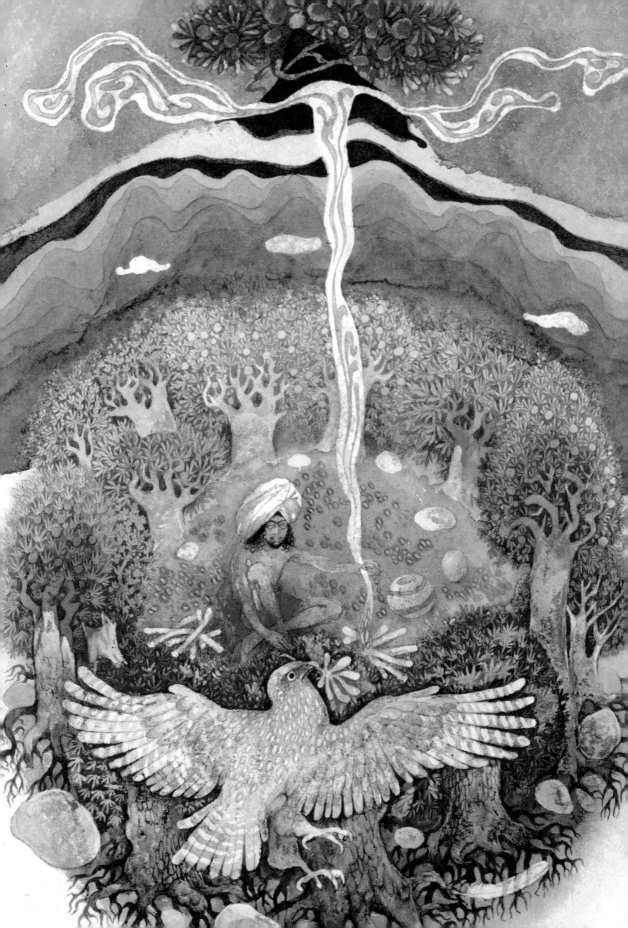

hundreds of thousands of demons were rowing as hard as they could to reach the shore and escape the insects.

Louhi and all the other monkeys were hiding in the undergrowth around the lake. Louhi waited until he saw that Ravana and Sita had landed and then he shouted, 'Attack!'

The demons watched horrified as wave after wave of monkeys rushed out of the undergrowth bearing clubs. The battle lasted until night fell without either side gaining victory. When it was dark, the monkeys retreated to the undergrowth and the demons sought refuge in their boats. Ravana had not let go of Sita, so she had no chance of escape. She had seen her beloved Rama in the midst of the fighting, his enchanted sword killing demon after demon. Lakshmana had fired arrow upon arrow, and each one had killed every demon in its path, but there were still many more demons on the banks of the lake than there had been at the hermitage a few days before.

As soon as it was light the next day the battle began again. Despite the courage of the monkeys and the enchanted weapons of Rama and Lakshmana the demons began to gain ascendancy. The monkeys began to retreat, and Sita watched in horror as she saw twelve demons come upon Rama from behind. Rama's sword was flashing to right and left, but by the time he realized what had happened it was too late. The demons felled him to the ground and in an instant Rama was dead.

Sita screamed and lurched back horrified as Ravana, seeing what had happened, turned to her and said, 'Now Sita. Rama is dead. Marry me.'

'I would rather die first,' replied Sita, tears of sorrow streaming down her face.

Night fell and it was obvious that the monkeys were being beaten. They had seen the brave Rama fall to the ground and they had lost their fighting spirit.

Lakshmana carried his dead brother from the battlefield into a clearing in the undergrowth. With his eyes misty from tears, he began to dig a grave for Rama. The soil was soft and it was not long before he had completed his sad task.

He lifted his brother gently and laid him in the grave. He knelt down beside it and said softly, 'Oh Rama. If only things had been different, you would be ruling in our father's kingdom. But now, you are dead. If only our father had not died at your wedding . . .'

Suddenly Lakshmana remembered that although their father had died he had been brought back to life by their step-mother's magic infusion. He then recalled that their step-brother had given them what was left before they set off on their long exile. He knew where it was, so he ran as fast as he could to the battlefield.

The monkeys were sitting around dejectedly. Lakshmana could see Louhi talking excitedly to a group of them, and he ran over to where they were. 'They want to go back to the jungle now that Rama is dead. They see no way that the battle can now be won,' said Louhi . . .

'If Rama came back, would that put new spirit in them?' asked Lakshmana.

'Of course, but that is not possible,' said Louhi.

But Lakshmana smiled. 'Remember what you said to my brother. The gods can do anything. Gather as many of your troops who are left and meet here at dawn tomorrow.' With that, Lakshmana ran to collect the alabaster pot. It was exactly where he remembered it should be. He picked it up and ran back to his brother's grave. •

Rama lay in the shallow grave, the moon shining on his dead face. His eyes were closed and his lips were blue.

His heart beating quickly, Lakshmana cradled Rama's head in his arms and he poured some of the infusion into his mouth. The rest he spread over Rama's body and rubbed it into his skin.

Nothing happened. Rama remained as dead as he had been. Lakshmana waited and waited for what seemed like forever. He knelt down and wept, and as he cried one of his tears fell into Rama's open mouth. Lakshmana looked down at his brother for one last time before he would cover him with earth. His heart nearly stopped beating as he suddenly saw Rama's eyelids flicker, and he wept even more as Rama stirred as if awakening from a deep sleep.

'Brother,' he cried as Rama stood up, 'you are alive!'

'Yes,' whispered Rama softly. 'And only you could have brought me back.'

Then he stepped out of the grave and the two half-brothers embraced. Together they walked arm-in-arm back to the camp. The monkeys stared in amazement as Rama appeared.

As the sun rose the demons reappeared to finish off the battle.

They had expected to face an already-defeated army that would take only a few minutes to beat into submission.

Instead, they were met by almost as many monkeys as before, for word had spread back to the jungle and every monkey who had not come at first, now appeared — determined to win.

With their new fighting spirit and with surprise on the demons' side, the new battle was short. Within one hour the demons were in retreat.

Ravana watched, horrified, from his boat in the lake, Sita at his side. When he saw that all was lost, he commanded his oarsmen to row him to the other side of the lake. Rama saw what was happening, grabbed Lakshmana's quiver and arrows and quickly ran to the shore. His aim was steady and the arrow was true. Ravana fell, dead, into the water and Rama swam towards the boat.

With their leader slain, the remaining demons fled in all directions. Rama clambered onto the boat and embraced Sita — his beloved wife.

The reunited husband and wife rowed back to the shore where Lakshmana was waiting for them. Louhi stood slightly aside while the three rejoiced at being together again. After a few minutes he shyly approached them.

'I must now return,' he said. 'The monkeys have gone back. Remember that with the gods all things are possible.' And with that Louhi lumbered off into the undergrowth.

Rama, Sita and Lakshmana looked towards the island for the last time and started off on their journey back to the hermitage.

When they arrived Valkimi and the other hermits on the Holy Mountain were overjoyed. 'Rama. Sita. Lakshmana. You have returned. The gods have been good, let us give them thanks.'

The four made their way to Valkimi's temple and gave thanks to the gods for the safe return. When they had finished their devotions Valkimi said, 'It is now fourteen years since you came here. You may now return to Ayodhya.'

The following morning Rama, his brother and his wife set off to return to Ayodhya. They arrived a few days later and went straight to the palace. As they approached, a guard saw them and ran to tell Bharata that Rama, the true king, was on his way.

Bharata ran out to welcome them. 'Brothers,' he shouted. 'Sita. You have all returned. I am thankful, for we heard of the events at Lanka.'

'I suppose,' said Lakshmana, 'that you are now so used to ruling that you have no intentions of giving up your throne.'

'On the contrary,' laughed Bharata. 'I could not be happier. My mother acted as she did because she was jealous. I never wanted to rule. The throne is Rama's by right. Our father died many years ago and our mothers followed him to the grave shortly after. Brothers. Sister-in-law, I rejoice at your return. I have never called myself king; only Regent, ruling in your absence. Come, let us be friends.'

And the three brothers and Sita went into the palace where Lakshmana's brother, Satrughna, was waiting for them.

214

There were great celebrations throughout the country when Rama took his rightful place as ruler of Ayodhya with Sita as his queen. He appointed Lakshmana as ruler of the northern province, Bharata as ruler of the southern province and Satrughna as ruler of the eastern province. He gave the western province to the hermits of Mount Chitrakutu as a way of thanking the gods for Sita's safe return from the demons.

And unlike his father, he did not take more than one wife. He was happy with Sita and he knew that their children would never have to go through the tortures that they had endured, because of another wife's jealousy.

ORION

If you look up into the sky on a clear, dark night, you may be able to see a group of stars called Pegasus. There are hundreds of stars in Pegasus, and one of them is called Pelai.

Pelai lived in a magnificent palace with his lovely wife and their beautiful daughter. One day the daughter looked down to the Earth and saw a young hunter called Orion. Orion was as tall and handsome as any of the gods in the sky and the girl fell in love with him immediately.

Orion was out hunting one day shortly after the girl had first seen him, and as he turned into a clearing in the forest, he came upon the most beautiful girl he had ever seen. It was the daughter of Pelai, who, as soon as light had come to the sky, had slipped out of her night palace and come down to earth. Orion fell in love with her as deeply as she had fallen in love with him. The happy couple spent the day hunting and laughing and walking hand-in-hand through the forest, as lovers do. When night approached, the girl said, 'I must leave now. I must return to my father's palace in the night sky. We can never meet again. For I am allowed but one trip to your world. If I try to come back, my heavenly light will be put out forever.'

Orion was heartbroken. 'Then I must come to you,' he whispered.

'Your love will have to be the strongest of all if you are to ascend to the sky and live with me,' the girl said gently, and disappeared.

Poor Orion. His love was the strongest of all. But how could he find a way to the heavens?

Day after day, Orion would climb to the highest cliffs, scale the tallest trees, and even, in utter despair, reach out as far as he could. But it was of little use. The night sky was as far away as ever. Orion sat down and wept. As he shed his tears, an old woman walked by. 'My son,' she said as she passed, 'why do you cry? You are young. You are handsome. What has made you so sad?'

'Oh woman,' wailed Orion. 'Love has made me weep so,' and he explained his plight to the old woman.

She listened silently and when he had finished she said, 'There is only one way for you to ascend to the heavens. You must gather your most precious possession and offer it to the night gods tomorrow when the moon is high. If they are pleased with your offering, they will take you to live amongst them.'

Orion was overjoyed and rushed home to find his most treasured possession. As a hunter, his bow and arrow were of great value to him, so he gathered them up. He was about to leave his humble hut and return to the clearing when he remembered the belt that his parents had given him when he had reached manhood. It was studded with precious stones and his parents had sacrificed much to afford it.

With his bow and arrow and his belt he ran back to the clearing and waited until the sun was at its highest. There was a thin veil of cloud covering the stars, but exactly when the moon should be at its highest, the sky cleared and Orion could see the shining stars.

Suddenly, a soft voice whispered in the breeze, 'Orion, what is your most precious possession that you can offer?'

'My bow and arrow, by which I make my living,' said Orion.

The breeze wrenched the bow and arrow from his hands and Orion watched it disappear upwards and upwards.

A few seconds later the breeze whispered, 'It is indeed a precious gift, but we want your *most* precious possession.'

So Orion took the belt from around his waist and held it up to the stars. Again the breeze wrenched it from his hands and Orion watched as it disappeared heavenward.

'It is indeed a precious gift, but there is something else that you have that is even more precious,' whispered the breeze.

'I have nothing else of value,' cried Orion.

'There is one thing so precious that if you offer it to the gods they will grant you your wish.'

'Nothing. There is nothing more,' sobbed Orion.

'Then I leave,' breathed the wind.

'No. Wait!' cried Orion. 'My most treasured possession, I cannot give away, for it is not mine to give. It was entrusted to me and in return I gave a similar gift.'

'What is it?' demanded the breeze.

'It is the love that my sweetheart gave to me. That is my most treasured possession.'

As soon as he had said the words, the breeze became stronger and wrapped itself around Orion pulling him upwards and upwards and upwards, until at last he was in the sky looking down at the world.

'My love,' a voice behind him whispered. Orion turned round and there was his beloved. 'You had to know that my love was your most treasured possession before you could come here. I am so happy that you knew it.'

The happy couple embraced and have been together in the sky ever since.

THE LITTLE PRINCE
OF THE SUN

The islands of Tonga lie in the South Seas, and many hundreds of years ago they were ruled by a very powerful king. He had one daughter who was said to be the most beautiful girl in the world, and he was very proud of her. But the king was so jealous of her beauty that he refused to let anyone, other than her handmaiden, see her.

The handmaiden felt sorry for her beautiful mistress and one day she said to her, 'It is so sad that you are always shut up within the palace walls. Why, you cannot even swim.'

'I have heard of swimming, but although I know I would like it, my father would never allow me to go to the seashore,' said the princess.

'It is your birthday tomorrow,' said the maid. 'Why do you not ask your father if you can go out as a special treat.'

So, the princess went to the king and asked if, just this once, she could leave the palace and go swimming.

The king thought for a minute and said, 'I hate to see you sad, so I will arrange something as a surprise.'

The next morning, the king escorted his daughter down to the seashore. All his subjects had been commanded to stay indoors so that they could not see her. During the night, the king had had a shaded causeway built out to the nearest island.

'There, my daughter,' he said. 'You may walk out to the island and there you may spend the day swimming, out of sight of any of my people.'

So the princess went out to the island and happily splashed about in the warm, deep green water. After an hour or two she lay down on the sand to rest. While she lay there, the god of the Sun passed over the island and shone down on the princess. As his rays warmed her she smiled up at him and her smile was so beautiful that he immediately fell in love with her.

The next day the princess asked her father if she could return to the island and she looked so beautiful, kissed by the sun, that her father willingly gave his permission.

And so, every day from then on the princess swam in the warm seas around the island and would then lay down and allow the sun to kiss her, for she grew to love the sun as much as he loved her. The two lovers were blissfully happy and eventually the princess gave

birth to a handsome baby boy whom she called 'Little Prince of the Sun'.

As the child grew, he became the most handsome boy in the islands. He could run faster than anyone else, throw the javelin further and swim long after the others had tired. He was also very proud and would boast to his friends, 'The king is my grandfather, and my mother is the most beautiful woman in the world. I am the best among you all.' And because he was so strong and proud, the others always agreed with him.

One day he went too far. He picked a quarrel with the smallest boy in the village and forced him to the ground. As he sat astride him, the little prince forced him to say, 'You are the best in all the islands, because your grandfather is king, and your mother is a beautiful princess.'

One of the other boys watching suddenly shouted, 'Your grandfather may be king and your mother a beautiful princess, but who is your father? At least we all have fathers and you do not.'

And all the other boys began to taunt him, calling, 'Who's got no father? Who's got no father?'

The little prince was enraged and began to chase the others away, but their taunts rang in his ears. 'Who's got no father? Who's got no father?' And he began to cry. Huge salt tears rolled down his cheeks as he ran back to his house. 'Mother,' he called and threw himself into her arms. 'The boys in the village said I do not have a father. Tell me, who is my father?' And he cried so hard that his whole body became racked with pain.

The princess felt so sorry for her son that she said to him, 'My child, do not cry. Your father is a great king. No one in the whole world has a father as powerful as yours.'

'But who is he?' demanded the child.

'Other children have ordinary mortals as their fathers. But you, my son, are the child of the god of the Sun. He is your father!'

The boy stopped crying immediately. 'If my grandfather is king, and you, my mother, are his daughter, and my father is the sun, then I am much too grand to live on this island. How can I talk to the other boys if the sun is my father?'

The princess was horrified at these words, but before she could ask anything the boy continued, 'I must leave here and go and visit my father.' He stood up and kissed his mother tenderly. 'I will come back when I have spoken to him.'

And with these words he left the house despite his mother's pleadings. She ran towards the door to call after him, but the boy had disappeared into the forest and she never saw him again.

The Little Prince of the Sun crossed the forest and went to the cove where his boat was anchored. He hoisted the sail and when the tide was high enough he pushed his boat into the water. The wind blew him towards the east and at mid-day the sun was right overhead. The Little Prince cried out to him, 'Father! Father! Stop, it is me, your son.' But the sun did not hear him and continued his journey to the west. The Little Prince tried to follow him, but the wind blew him in the wrong direction. He watched sadly as his father raced across the skies and slipped out of sight over the western horizon.

That night the Little Prince was all alone in the dark, dark ocean. When it was at its darkest, the Little Prince remembered that the sun rose in the east, so he raised his sail and sailed to the point where his father would rise from the sea in the morning.

When the first rays of light spread over the ocean the next morning, the Little Prince called out, 'Father! Wait for me.'

'Who calls me?' asked the sun.

'Me. Your son,' said the Little Prince. 'You must know me. I am the son of the Princess of the Islands of Tonga and of you, god of the Sun.'

'You are my son?' asked the sun.

'Yes, I am. Oh please stop and talk to me.'

'My son, I cannot. What would the people say if I did not shine in the sky? I must go or I shall be late.'

'Please stay. Hide behind a cloud and come down and talk to me,' pleaded the Little Prince. 'If you are behind a cloud, the people will not know that you have come down to talk to me.'

The sun admired the boy's intelligence and wit, so he called on a cloud and under its cover he slid down to the surface of the water. There the father and son talked. 'Tell me of your life on the islands,' said the sun.

So the boy told his father of his mother and of his grandfather; about his friends and how he was the best swimmer and the fastest runner in all the islands. And the sun told the Little Prince many of the secrets of the sky. Eventually the sun told the child that he must continue his journey across the sky or else men and women would begin to get alarmed. 'Stay here till night comes and my sister, the moon, appears. When she leaves the water to begin her journey across the sky, call to her and tell her that you are her nephew, my son. She will offer you a choice of two gifts.'

'And which one should I take?' asked the boy.

'One is called Melaia and the other Monuia. Ask her for Melaia and you will have eternal happiness. If you disobey and take Monuia, then great misfortune will come your way. Goodbye, my son.'

And the sun went back behind the cloud and began to race across the sky. The people looked up and said, 'Look. The sun is late and is now rushing across the sky much faster than usual.'

The Little Prince took down his sail and stayed where he was until nightfall. When the night came he raised his sail and skimmed across the ocean to where the moon would rise. The moon saw the boat and the handsome young boy sailing in it.

'Boy,' she called out. 'Why do you sail like the wind across the seas to look into my face?'

The Little Prince stopped his boat right in front of the moon and said, 'I am the child of your brother, the sun, and the princess of the Islands of Tonga. My name is the Little Prince of the Sun and you, Moon, are my aunt.'

The moon was astonished and said, 'How wonderful to have a human nephew. But move your boat, for I must begin my journey. Look, the stars are already in the sky.'

'If I do, Aunt, you must give me the gift that my father said you would offer me.'

'I have two gifts in my possession,' laughed the moon knowingly, 'which one did the sun tell you to ask for?'

Now the Little Prince was a devious child. When he was told to do one thing he always did the other. Always! So he said to the moon 'My father told me to ask for Monuia. So may I have it, please?'

The moon was horrified. 'He said Monuia! Are you sure that he did not say Melaia?'

'No, Aunt. He said that you were to keep Melaia and that you were to give me Monuia.'

'I cannot give him Monuia,' said the moon to herself. 'Surely my brother would not want to harm his son.'

So she took Melaia from her purse and handed it to the boy. 'Here,' she said, 'here it is. But you must not open it until you are safe on your own island.'

Unbeknown to both the moon and the boy, the sun had been watching all this from the opposite horizon. He had delayed his setting until the moon had talked to her nephew. When he saw what had happened, he was furious, and with the last ray of light he stretched out across the sky unseen by either his son or the moon. He removed Melaia from the boat and put Monuia in its place. He returned Melaia to his sister's pocket.

As the boy sailed away, the moon began to rise in the sky and to hurry across it to make up for lost time.

The people below looked up and said, 'How strange. The moon was late and now she is running through the stars.'

The boy sailed on and across the ocean until he was in sight of his own island. 'I cannot wait to open my present until I am home, surely it will not matter if I open it before.'

So he picked up Monuia from where it lay and took it out of its covering. His eyes lit up with joy when he saw the most beautiful oyster shining in the dying light of the moon.

'Such an oyster must contain a magnificent pearl,' and he took his knife and opened the oyster. Inside there was such a pearl as no man had ever seen before. The Little Prince was about to take it from the shell when, as if by command, a storm began to blow. The little boat was tossed around on the waves, but the boy was oblivious to the danger. He could not keep his eyes away from the pearl. Suddenly from out of the stormy seas every type of fish began to rise to the surface and to swim towards the little boat. There were dolphins, sharks, tuna fish, eels, and even whales. But still the Little Prince was unaware of anything but the pearl.

The storm continued and more and more fish were swimming towards the boat. Just before they came close to the boat, they submerged and swam under it. As if by magic they all surfaced at once, tossing the boat high out of the water.

Poor child. He was tossed out of the boat and he landed deep in the ocean. He stood no chance of saving himself. He was dead before he knew what was happening. As he splashed through the surface, the oyster snapped tightly shut and nipped the top of his little finger off.

The Little Prince's body was never found. It lies deep down in the South Seas. The oyster, however, was washed ashore on his island a few days later. Inside it there was the most magnificent black pearl shaped like the top of a finger. No other pearl like it has ever been found before or after.

You see, Monuia was the goddess of the tide, which the moon controls and which can bring danger to those who disregard her.

HAMISH
AND THE GOLDEN FISH

Long, long ago in the misty valley of northern Scotland, there lived a boy called Hamish. He had two brothers, and the three boys lived in a small whitewashed cottage with their widowed mother.

The widow worked hard to make ends meet. Hamish did his best to help her, but his two brothers were as lazy as lazy could be. When Hamish went fishing to catch something for the family to eat, his two brothers would still be in their beds. As Hamish stood patiently helping his mother to wind wool and to spin, his two brothers would be roaming the hills or carousing in the village.

The widow loved her children equally, but she hoped that when she died the two brothers would see sense and work as hard as Hamish.

The sad day came when the widow died and with a heavy heart Hamish dug her simple grave. When night came he carved a cross and the next day the three brothers mourned deeply at their mother's graveside.

But the following morning, they lay in their beds and shouted to Hamish, 'Where is our breakfast?' and Hamish set to and cooked breakfast. 'Hamish, the hens need feeding,' they called from beds, and Hamish went to feed the hens. 'Don't forget to milk the cow,' they yelled, and Hamish did as he was told.

This went on day after day. One day, about a month after the widow had died, the brothers cried, 'Hamish, there is no salt fish left. Go and gather your line and catch some fish to salt.' And Hamish did as he was told.

He set off, up the mountain to where the bubbling stream widened to a deep pool. Hamish had often had good luck there and this particular morning was no different. Within an hour, he had caught enough fish to keep the three of them for one month. He was ready to go home when he decided to cast his line one last time. Imagine his surprise when he pulled the line up and there, on his hook, was a golden fish! Not only was it golden, but it was wearing a golden crown on its head. Hamish was rooted to the spot.

'What do you think you're up to?' the fish suddenly said.

'What!' Hamish cried out in amazement. 'Who spoke?'

'Who do you think spoke? Me, of course. There's no one else here, is there?' the fish said angrily.

'But fish don't speak,' said Hamish.

'Of course we speak,' the fish mocked. 'How else do you think we communicate with each other. But I am the only one that can speak your language.'

'You must be a very important fish,' said Hamish, 'if you can speak to humans.'

'Well, I was important. In fact I was king of the pool. But not now,' said the fish sadly. 'Now that you have caught me, I expect that I'll end up smoked and brown like a kipper. Unless you throw me back.'

Now the fish was very big, and looked very tasty, but Hamish was quite sorry for it. After all, he was obviously a very important fish.

'I'll tell you what,' said the fish. 'If you throw me back, I'll grant you three wishes. I am a magic fish.'

'Very well,' said Hamish. 'I wish that my brothers would work as hard as I do. I wish that the hens would lay ten times more eggs than they do, and that the cow would give ten times more milk.'

'Very well,' said the fish. 'Now throw me back.' And Hamish did.

By the time Hamish got home, his brothers were in bed, for it was very late. The next morning Hamish got up early as usual but did not begin to prepare breakfast. After all, his brothers should now be as hardworking as he. But half an hour later his brothers shouted from their beds,

'Hamish, where is our breakfast? Come on lazy. We're hungry. And then you can collect the eggs and milk the cow.'

'Perhaps the magic will start tomorrow,' thought Hamish as he cooked his brothers' breakfast. He went out to collect the eggs and was sorry to see that there were no more than usual. And the cow gave her normal amount of milk.

'Oh well,' thought Hamish, 'it must start tomorrow.'

But the next morning, his brothers stayed in bed and the hens laid as usual, and there was no extra milk. And Hamish worked as hard as ever before.

One day a month later, his brothers called, 'Hamish, there is no more fish left. Collect your line and go fishing.' And Hamish did as he was told.

He set off up the mountain to the pool and cast his line. There were many fish and Hamish caught almost more than he could carry. He decided to cast his line just once more before going home, and sure enough, he caught the same golden fish with the golden crown.

'Put me back, and I'll make you rich,' said the fish.

'You told me last time that you would grant me three wishes if I put you back,' said Hamish.

'Silly,' said the fish. 'Whoever heard of a fish that could grant wishes.' Hamish grabbed his mallet and quickly killed the cruel fish. He took it home and prepared to cook it. His brothers were out in the village. When Hamish cut the fish open, imagine his surprise when a purse of gold fell from the fish's stomach. 'Someone must have dropped it in the pool, and the fish must have swallowed it.'

With all the gold in the purse, Hamish knew that he was rich, so before his brothers returned, he packed his bags and left. They never saw him again, and when they came home, all they found was a half-cut fish lying on the kitchen table.

CONFUCIUS

More than fifteen hundred years ago, in China, one of the five ruling spirits, the Lord of the Night, looked down on his people and was saddened by what he saw. Everyone had forgotten the old ways: wars were being fought for no other reason than territorial gains; neighbour cheated neighbour, and son cheated father. Bribery was common and corruption was rife.

He decided to send among the people a man of such perfect goodness that all would come to love and respect him and follow his example of peace and understanding. He would stop wars and restore happiness to family life.

He searched the country for a good woman who would bear this child, and after many months he found her in the town of Lou, in the province of Shan-Tung. He watched her for many days and when he was satisfied that she was the perfect mother to bring up the child, he appeared to her in dream one night and said to her, 'Woman, you are going to have a child who will become a king without a crown.'

Sure enough, nine months later, the woman gave birth to a son which she called K'ong-tseu. When he was born, there was a piece of red thread around his left foot. Today, fifteen hundred years later, we still know about this child, for he became Confucius, the great Chinese prophet.

He was a very odd-looking little boy and as he grew to manhood he became even odder. He was exceedingly tall and his face, unlike the yellow colour of other Chinese, was very dark — almost black. His mouth was enormous, stretching almost from ear to ear, and his lower lip never quite met his top one, so that his perfectly white teeth could always be seen. His voice was deep and beautiful to listen to. He seemed almost to hypnotise all who listened to him.

He had a disciple called Yan-Hui. One day Confucius and Yan-Hui climbed a mountain known as Tai-schan which was sacred to the people of the province of Shan-Tung. Confucius pointed his finger towards the south and said to Yan-Hui, 'Do you see that river over there?'

'Yes,' replied his companion.

'Follow its course with your eye.'

Yan-Hui did as he was told.

'What do you see?' asked Confucius.

'The river flows past the gate of the town of Wu.'

'Is there anything in front of the door?'

'I can see something white but I cannot make out what it is. It is like a piece of paper billowing in the wind,' said Yan-Hui.

'It is not a piece of paper, it is a white horse,' replied Confucius.

'Come now, Confucius,' said Yan-Hui. 'Even you could not make out what it is at this distance. It is many miles to Wu.'

'We will go and see,' said Confucius, and the two men climbed down the hill and set off along the dusty track to Wu. As they went Yan-Hui told everyone who passed that his friend claimed to have been able to see a white horse outside the gates of Wu from the top of Tai-shan. The people were incredulous and many of them followed ready to mock the odd-looking man when he realized his mistake.

By the time they got to Wu, there were many hundreds of people following Confucius and Yan-Hui. There, in front of the gates was the most magnificent white charger anyone had seen. Its coat glistened and shone in the sun. Its mane and its tail were the colour of newly-minted gold, and its body and legs were perfectly shaped. The people were stunned and excited at the same time.

'How could anyone have seen this from so far away?' they said to one another.

'Who is this man?' they asked.

Soon there was a loud babble of conversation among the people that grew louder and louder as each second passed.

It stopped suddenly when Confucius held up his hand and fixed the crowd with his dazzling eye.

He began to preach to them and his voice was so beautiful and his message was so simple and honest that the people listened for hour after hour.

Eventually word of Confucius spread right across the province and into every corner of the country. People flocked to hear Confucius's message and many who heard it were so impressed that they put their bad ways behind them and began to live good lives.

One day, many years later the Prince of Wu was out hunting with some of his friends. He fell some way behind them and was galloping to catch up when a small deer appeared in his path. He reined in his horse quickly, for the deer showed no signs of moving. The Prince dismounted and went to 'shoo' the deer off. To his surprise, he noticed that the deer had a piece of red thread wound around his left foot. The deer looked up at the Prince and moved away in such a way as if he was deliberately trying to draw the Prince's attention to the red thread.

When the hunt was over, the Prince returned to Wu and told Confucius about the strange happening.

Huge tears welled up in Confucius's eyes. 'It is a sign from my father, the Lord of the Night, that I must prepare myself for death. I have not done well enough. I have changed some people, but not enough to please my father.'

The Prince was saddened and said, 'But Confucius, no one could convert the whole world. Everyone has changed who has heard you speak, and although there are still wars, and dishonour amongst families, the world is a much better place now than it was before you began your mission.'

'No matter,' cried Confucius, 'it is not enough. I must follow my father's wishes.'

That very night Confucius died and his body was placed in a tomb, outside the city walls. The people mourned him greatly and he became known as Confucius the Omniscient. Within a few years the whole of China began to follow his doctrine and his religion became the official religion of the land.

Many hundreds of years passed, kings died and new kings took their place. The land came to be ruled by the Emperor Tsin-Shi-Huang. He was cruel and mean. He ruled his subjects with an iron hand and whatever he said had to be obeyed on pain of certain death.

Everything that he did was contrary to the ways of Confucius.

One day he rode into the city of Wu and asked his minister,

'Is this the place where that old fool Confucius has his tomb?'

'Yes master,' replied the minister. 'His tomb is outside the city walls, about a mile from here.'

'Take me to it,' commanded the King.

The King and his retinue rode out to the tomb. When they reached it Tsin-Shi-Huang ordered that it be opened. The people were thunderstruck.

'But Sir,' they protested. 'That would be sacrilege.'

'To disobey me is sacrilege,' shouted the King, purple with rage. 'Open it.'

Reluctantly, his orders were obeyed, and the stone that guarded the entrance of the tomb was rolled back. The King entered the cavern, astonished to find that the air inside it was not at all musty, but quite fresh.

As his eyes grew accustomed to the darkness, he was astonished to see that there was a couch that looked new and on the ground underneath it there was a pair of beautiful red silk slippers.

The King sat down on the couch and kicked his own shoes off. He slipped his feet into the silk slippers and was delighted to find that they were unusually comfortable. He looked around the tomb. It looked more like the office of a working man, than the tomb of a dead one. He noticed a desk in one corner and went over to it. On the leather top there was a pot of ink and a quill pen. Alongside was a sheet of paper with fresh writing on it. The puzzled King picked up the paper and was horrified when he saw what was written on it.

'Tsin-Shi-Huang, you live the life of a degenerate,
You enter my tomb and rest on my couch.
You wear my slippers. You are not fit to do so.
You will die at Schakiu.'
The frightened King ran from the tomb and ordered that it be closed at once. He mounted his horse and rode away as quickly as he could.

From that time on the King refused to go anywhere near Schakiu. No matter what the occasion was he would not go.

One day, about a year later, he was out riding. His horse stumbled over a rock and Tsin-Shi-Huang was knocked off the horse's back. His head hit the rock and he was rendered unconscious. For many days he lay in a deep coma. Nothing would bring him round. Eventually the court physician said that only one man had the power to revive the King — the wise Doctor of Schakiu.

The almost lifeless body was put into a carriage and taken to that town. There, the Doctor made an infusion of many herbs and held the steaming bowl under the unconscious King's nose. Within a few minutes the King's eyes opened and a few minutes later he was sitting up on his bed.

'Where am I?' he asked his physician.

'Sir. We had to bring you to Schakiu, for only the Doctor here knew how to revive you.'

At that the King burst out laughing. 'Why,' he roared, tears of laughter running down his cheeks, 'that old fool Confucius prophesied that I would die here. But I have been given life here. Ha.'

No sooner had he spoken, than his eyes opened wide. They almost popped out of his head. His face went red, then blue, then purple. It was as if invisible hands were squeezing the life out of him, for he could not breathe. A few seconds later, he slumped back dead. The horrified courtiers rushed up to him, but it was too late. The prophecy of Confucius had come true.

Tsin-Shi-Huang had died at Schakiu.

THE STRANGER
WITH THE CURLY BEARD

Many hundreds of years ago in China, the area that is now Peking was covered by a mighty lake. It was as deep as the Pacific Ocean and when the winds blew huge waves would crash onto the shores. In the lake there lived the Dragon King and his ugly old wife.

As the population grew, the people needed more land to build houses on and to create fields to grow crops to feed themselves. A wonderful plan was drawn up, canals were dug all around the lake and the waters were drained away leaving a magnificent plain where the city of Peking was build.

The Dragon King and his wife were furious at being driven from their home. They swam up the canals and into the river and made their home in a much smaller lake hundreds of miles from their old home. There, night after night they plotted to have their revenge and vowed to destroy the city of Peking and the people who lived in it.

They waited for year after year until the time was ready.

Their chance came when they heard that all the men in Peking were out of the city building a huge wall to keep China's enemies out of their land. They swam down the rivers and along the canals until they were standing on a small hill overlooking the city. The Dragon King weaved a spell and turned himself and his wife into a ragged, poor old man and woman. He snapped his fingers and a large hand-cart appeared. On it were two magic vats, that could never be filled, no matter how much water was put in them.

When night came, they went round every well in the city and pumped the waters into their unquenchable vats. Just as dawn was breaking, they had emptied the last one, and they slipped out of the city before anyone was awake.

When the women rose from their beds and went to the wells to draw water for the day, they were horrified to find there was no water in any of the wells. Not even a drop.

They sent a messenger to tell their husbands, who were busy at their building. General Liou Po-Ho was thunderstruck when he heard the news, for he alone realized what had happened. He knew that there was only one solution.

Only one man could save the city, so he called all the men toge-ther and said to them.

'Men of Peking, you have heard what has befallen our city. One of you and only one of you can save Peking. Which one is it?'

At that, all the men rushed forward shouting and begging to help. The General heard each one and shook his head, until a strange little man said, 'General. It is me. I know how to save our city.'

Everyone laughed, for the man was very small and strange-looking. The strangest thing about him was that his beard, unlike everyone else's, which were straggly and straight, was a mass of thick curls.

'How do you know it is you?' asked the General kindly.

'Sir,' said the stranger with the curly beard. 'Only one person is powerful enough to have emptied all our wells.'

'The Dragon King,' said the General. 'And if you know that then you must know how to foil him, for you must be . . .'

'His half-brother,' said the stranger.

The General said to his assembled men, 'Many years ago when I was a boy I was standing by the canal banks when the great sluice were opened for the first time to empty the lake. I saw the Dragon King and his wife swim by, vowing to have their revenge, and chuckling that the only man who could stop them would be his half-brother, who had long since left the land to travel abroad. This man with the curly beard is that half-brother. Only he knows how to save our city.'

'Sir,' said the stranger with the curly beard. 'I need the services of your bravest soldier and your fastest horse. The soldier will need the sharpest lance he can have.'

Immediately all the men rushed forward to volunteer. The old man looked them all up and down and eventually pointed to one and said, 'You are Kao-Liang. You are the bravest soldier. You will save our city.'

'What must I do?' asked Kao-Liang.

'Follow the marks of the wheels of the water cart and you will come upon the Dragon King and his wife. They will be changed into a sad and helpless couple toiling to pull their water cart and you may feel sorry for them. Do not. Gallop at full speed towards them and pierce the vats with your lance. All the water will run along the tracks back to the wells.'

'That sounds the simplest of things,' said Kao-Liang.

'The difficult part is still to come. Although the water will run back to the wells, for you to escape you will need every ounce of your courage. Once you have pierced the vats you must turn and gallop away. You must not look back until your horse has taken one hundred paces. No matter what you see you must not look back.'

234

Kao-Liang agreed and one hour later rode out on the fastest horse, carrying the sharpest lance.

He soon picked up the tracks of the cart and rode off in their direction. Soon in the dust of the road he saw an old couple bent double, pulling the water cart. They were so frail and shrunken that, just as the stranger with the curly beard had said, he felt sorry for them. But mindful of his words he put the kindness out of his mind and galloped at the cart, his lance at the ready. As fast as lightning he galloped, and with a mighty crash he pierced the vats with his lance. They burst open with mighty explosions, just as Kao-Liang turned his horse and galloped away.

The sky went black and the sound of horrible laughter filled the air. Kao-Liang rode as fast as he could and behind him he could hear the sounds of hundreds of horses chasing after him. He felt as if a whole army was at his heels and he wanted to look back to see. But his courage did not fail him and he rode on and on. The ground trembled under the thudding of the horses' hooves. Sweat fell from his brow and his heart beat faster and faster. He felt his horse slow down as though something was pulling his tail, but still he did not look back. And all the time he was counting . . . eighty-nine, ninety, ninety-one, ninety-two . . .

When he got to one hundred he looked round.

But he had made a mistake. In his excitement he had miscounted and taken one pace too few. He had only gone ninety-nine paces and not one hundred.

As he looked round he saw a huge wall of water rush towards him. He spurred his horse on, but the water foamed and roared after him. Poor Kao-Liang. Within ten steps the water had overtaken him and he was lost forever under its frothing surface.

Immediately, the water calmed down and flowed gently along the cart tracks and back into the wells of the city of Peking. The citizens were happy but their happiness was tinged with sadness, for Kao-Liang had been the most popular young man in the city. Soon their sadness turned to anger.

'Why had Kao-Liang died? Why could the stranger with the curly beard not have ridden out after his half-brother, the Dragon King?' they asked themselves. An angry mob gathered and marched to the palace of General Liou Po-Ho, demanding the blood of the stranger with the curly beard.

The General looked furious as he appeared on his balcony to calm the mob down. 'How dare you,' he thundered at them. 'Instead of demanding his blood, you should be grateful to the man with the

curly beard. He alone knew how to save our city from certain death. He knew that Kao-Liang may have to sacrifice his life, but Kao-Liang was aware of the risk he was taking, and went gladly to save us. I am ashamed of you and if Kao-Liang is looking down on you from the Palace of the Eternal Heavens then I hope that he is ashamed of you too. Return to your homes. Remember, things become more appreciated if sacrifice has been made for them. We used to take our water for granted, but now that Kao-Liang has given his life that we may have water, we know how precious it is. We must always remember the lesson taught to us by the stranger with the curly beard.'

QUETZALCOATL

Long, long ago in the continent of South America, a large part of the land was ruled by the Serpent of the Snow. The Serpent of the Snow was a fierce warrior who, whenever his domain was threatened by invading armies, would lead his men into battle and inspire his soldiers with his brave leadership and incredible courage. His men loved him so much that they followed his example and the army became invincible.

He was also a wise ruler and all the people in the land loved him dearly.

One day the armies of neighbouring Golhoucan marched against him and invaded the northern part of his kingdom.

The Serpent of the Snow rallied his soldiers and marched off to meet the invaders. They were led by the wicked Chilalman, who was as mean as the Serpent of the Snow was generous, and as cowardly as he was brave. Chilalman did not lead his armies, but directed them from behind. If the tide of battle turned against him, Chilalman was the first to turn and flee.

The Serpent of the Snow knew this, so he was very surprised when he saw that Chilalman was sitting on a fine white horse at the head of his armies.

When Chilalman saw the Serpent of the Snow ride toward him, he called out, 'This time, Serpent, you have met your match, my power is greater than yours.' And saying this he drew an arrow from his quiver, fixed it into his bow and aimed straight at the Serpent's heart.

But the Serpent of the Snow managed to swerve to avoid the arrow.

Chilalman was furious, for the arrows had been given to him by the witch Uitznuac, who had promised him that whoever the arrow was aimed at would fall dead. Chilalman drew another arrow and fired it, but the Serpent was too quick for it. Again and again Chilalman fired at the Serpent, but each time the same thing happened.

Eventually the quiver was empty and the Serpent led his armies into the middle of Chilalman's. The battle did not last long, for Chilalman's men were as cowardly as he was, and seeing the fear in their master's face, they lost any heart they had had before they saw the way in which the Serpent had ducked Chilalman's arrows.

When the battle was over, the Serpent of the Snow rode back to where the arrows had found their mark. He picked them all up and ordered them to be burned.

When the flames of the fire were at their highest, they suddenly parted and from them flew the most beautiful bird that the Serpent or his men had ever seen. Its breast was the brightest green and its wings were the most dazzling red; its eyes were deep blue and its beak and talons were as bright as purest gold.

The Serpent of the Snow was so moved by the bird's beauty that he knelt down before it. Seeing this, his soldiers did the same, and the bird flew low over them and came to land at the Serpent of the Snow's feet.

'Thank you, for you have released me from the curse of the witch Uitznuac. She captured me and imprisoned me in the arrows. Only one as great as you, Serpent of the Snow, could have escaped from my path, and only one as true as you could have released me from Uitznuac's curse. Rule well and wisely in your land, and if you ever need my help you will find me at the Palace of the White Gold in the mountains of Guatemala.'

With that the bird flew off and from that day the people of the Serpent's kingdom worshipped him as a god. They named him Quetzalcoatl.

Whenever they needed his assistance, which was not very often, they went to his palace and he gave what they asked. And if Quetzalcoatl heard of anyone in need, he would bring relief. If he saw, as he flew about the countryside, anyone in pain, he would bring consolation. If he saw hunger, he would bring food and wine. The people came to love him as dearly as they loved the Serpent of the Snow, and they built temples to him and dedicated themselves to him.

The Serpent had twin sons, and he passed a law that when he died, the kingdom was to be divided between the two. One of them was to rule the land north of the Great River all the way up to the mountains of Guatemala and the other was to rule south, down to the mountains of Mexico.

The sad day came when the Serpent died and his kingdom was divided as he had wished.

The son who ruled in the south was called Cintoetl and he was as brave and wise as his father. He ruled his part of the kingdom wisely and well and the people loved him.

The son who ruled in the north was called Tollan. He was weak and foolish. He loved being flattered and spent all of his time hunting, or seeking pleasure. He handed over the government of his land to whoever flattered him most. These flatterers were greedy and selfish men. They cared nothing for the people. All that mattered to them was to gather riches for themselves, and power for their families. They raised taxes and made the people work for them for little reward.

As Quetzalcoatl flew around the countryside he was sad at what he saw, and he did his best to bring some relief to the poor peasants, but their misery was such that there was little that he could do.

One day when Tollan was out hunting, he saw Quetzalcoatl sitting sadly in the branches of a tree. He was envious of the love that his people had for the beautiful bird, so he quietly dismounted from his horse and crept towards the tree. When he was close to the bird he drew his bow and taking careful aim, he fired an arrow at him. The arrow pierced Quetzalcoatl's wing making it impossible for him to fly away. Tollan took a large bag from his belt and unceremoniously dumped the bird in it.

With a greedy smile on his face, he rode back to his palace and proudly showed his courtiers his prize. At first they were horrified, but soon they gathered round and mocked Quetzalcoatl.

'Where is your power now?' asked one.

'There is nothing you can do to help the people,' mocked another.

Tollan ordered that a cage be built for the bird, so that when his courtiers came to see him, they would always be reminded that it was he, Tollan, who had captured the bird.

'Just think,' said Tollan. 'If I can capture Quetzalcoatl as easily as I did, I must be much mightier than he. The people should worship me as their god, and not this silly bird.'

And so all the temples that had been built in Quetzalcoatl's honour were pulled down and new ones built. The people were ordered that on no account was Quetzalcoatl to be worshipped, and that Tollan, the most powerful king on the face of the earth, was to be their new god.

Everyone were horrified at this, but such was the power that Tollan and his favourites held over them that they had no option but to obey.

When Cintoetl in the south heard of his brother's doings he was furious. He immediately sent messengers to his brother to demand that Quetzalcoatl be released and that the temples to him now be rebuilt.

'Tell my brother,' sneered Tollan, when he had heard what the messengers wanted, 'that Quetzalcoatl is now mine. I am more powerful than him and that if Cintoetl wishes to rebuild Quetzalcoatl's temples he will have to beat my armies first.'

When this message was repeated to Cintoetl he sent his brother an ultimatum.

'Unless my ambassador reports to me within one week that the temples that have been built in your honour have been raised to the ground and those dedicated to Quetzalcoatl have been rebuilt, my armies shall march against you in battle.'

Tollan read the message and laughed out loud. He went up to the cage where Quetzalcoatl now spent all his days and plucked a feather from his tail. He ordered his court painter to paint his face on the feather.

When this was done, he said, 'Take this to my brother. He whose face is shown on the feather is mightier than the bird from whence it was plucked.'

At these words all the courtiers applauded and mocked the poor bird once again.

Cintoetl's ambassador rode from Tollan's palace and journeyed all through the night to deliver the sacrilegious feather to his master.

As soon as he saw it, Cintoetl ordered that his armies get ready for war. A week later all was ready and Cintoetl rode out at the head of a mighty column of warriors. On the tunic of each soldier there was an image of Quetzalcoatl on their hearts.

When they approached the border, Cintoetl stopped and turned to speak to his men.

'I would do anything rather than fight my own brother and his armies. We fight, not for gain, or reward, but for what we believe in. Had it not been for Quetzalcoatl's help in the past, many of our people would have died or starved. Whenever he saw anyone in need, he helped, and now that he is in distress we must fight to the last man to release him from his misery.'

The army crossed the border into Tollan's kingdom. A few miles further on they crossed a small range of foothills and there, in the valley below, they could see Tollan and his army waiting to meet them.

All of Tollan's soldiers bore an image of him on their tunics. Tollan himself was sitting astride a magnificent black charger. On his wrist he held Quetzalcoatl. The bird was hooded and chained to Tollan's wrist like a falcon waiting to be released and flown.

'Brother,' cried Cintoetl. 'I give you one last chance. Release Quetzalcoatl and return to your palace. Tear down your temples and build new ones in honour of the mighty bird.'

'I am more powerful than Quetzalcoatl,' shouted Tollan. 'It is right that my people worship me as a god.'

No sooner had the words been spoken than an arrow whizzed past Cintoetl's ear and thudded into the tree behind him. The feathers in the arrow were the bright green ones from Quetzalcoatl's breast. Cintoetl drew his sword and spurred his horse into action. His men did the same and soon his army was galloping across the plain to meet Tollan's soldiers.

The battle was long and bloody. By dusk there were many dead on both sides, the grass of the plain was coloured red with the blood of hundreds of soldiers and horses.

As dusk gave way to darkness, the battle continued and it was fought all through the night. Tollan ordered that his archers dip their arrows in burning tar and fire them into Cintoetl's armies. The flaming arrows burned many soldiers horribly, and as a second volley lit up the night sky, Cintoetl's men took flight and ran from the battlefield.

As they rode after them in pursuit, one of Tollan's men stumbled over a body. As he rolled over, he recognized that it was Cintoetl. His face and arms were burned black, and he was bleeding from a wound in his side. He ran across to Tollan and told him what he had found. Tollan galloped to where the soldier pointed and saw his brother lying there.

'He is dead,' he thought to himself and took the hood from off Quetzalcoatl's head so that the bird could see for himself that his would-be saviour lay dead in the field of battle.

As he did so, there was a low groan from beneath him, and Tollan realized that Cintoetl still lived. He ordered that a stretcher be brought to him and that his brother be taken to his palace.

When Cintoetl regained consciousness a few hours later he was horrified to find himself in a cage, at the right-hand side of Tollan's throne. On the other side he could see Quetzalcoatl sitting dejectedly on his perch. Between them Tollan sat on his throne.

'So brother, you have come back to consciousness,' sneered Tollan. 'Welcome to our palace. You see now that I am mightier than you and the bird that you worship. Fool, to question my power.'

All the courtiers took up this cry and soon the chamber echoed with the word 'Fool'.

Cintoetl was horribly burned. His face was black and the flesh on his arms was red and raw. As the courtiers filed past his cage, taunting him with the cry 'Fool,' one girl said to Tollan, 'Sire, this man is your brother and he is in pain. Show him how merciful you are and let me tend his wounds.'

'We are merciful,' said Tollan. 'Do what you will with him. But he

may not leave his cage. Nurse him, so he is well when I have him
executed.'

The girl, who was called Cochtocan, went to her chamber and
collected some soothing oils and towels. She returned to the throne
room and Tollan unlocked the cage. She rubbed the oils into Cintoetl's wounds and dried them with the cool towels.

Every day she came to him to care for him.

At first she could hardly bear to look at him because he was so
deformed by the flames that had burned him, but as her oils began

to do their work, the blackness left his face and the flesh on his arms
became less red and less raw. Soon he was as he had been before. His
handsome face and dark eyes attracted the girl, and his gentle manner was in marked contrast to that of his brother, Tollan.

One day, Cintoetl asked Cochtocan why she had treated him so
kindly, after all, their people were enemies.

'Because you are a human being. I would do the same for anyone,
no matter who or what he was.' And as she spoke, she smiled, and her
smile was so lovely and caring that Cintoetl felt himself warm towards her.

Each evening as he lay in his cage, the taunts of Tollan's courtiers and the plaintive cries of Quetzalcoatl ringing in his ears, he began to think of Cochtocan and to look forward to her visits.

The day came when his wounds were completely healed, but still the girl continued to come to him. When he asked her why, she told him that Tollan had commanded that as soon as he was healed, he was to be put to death, for Tollan was afraid of his brother.

'I tell him that you are still not well,' said Cochtocan, 'and he believes me.'

'For how long will he carry on believing you?'

'Not for much longer. For you are well, and I cannot go telling him lies.'

'Then you must help me escape,' said Cintoetl.

'I cannot. Tollan would kill me if he found out.'

'But you could come with me,' said Cintoetl.

'Why should I want to do that?' asked Cochtocan, her eyes lowered.

'Because ... because ... I love you and would like to make you my wife.'

The girl began to cry. 'Oh Cintoetl, I have loved you since the moment when first I saw you lying, horribly burned in the cage. But Tollan keeps the keys on a chain around his waist. He never lets them out of his sight. He lets me in here, and lets me out.'

'Then here is what you must do,' said Cintoetl, and explained his plan to Cochtocan.

The next evening all the courtiers were gathered in the throne room. Cochtocan approached Tollan's throne and knelt before him. 'Sir,' she said, 'Cintoetl is now completely well and is ready for what you have in mind for him, but first as I nursed him back to health, I crave one favour.'

'Whatever you ask,' said Tollan.

'I wish to carry Quetzalcoatl on my wrist to watch the execution.'

Tollan laughed out loud. 'Why, you are a girl after my own heart. Of course you may.'

The following morning all the court stood in the yard outside the throne room. Tollan and Cochtocan came out and nodded to everyone. They all bowed back. Quetzalcoatl was chained to Cochtocan's wrist. Tollan clapped his hands, and immediately Cintoetl was brought out into the sunshine.

'Brother,' said Tollan as he stopped in front of him, 'I kept you alive and brought you back to health so that all could see you die at my command and know how powerful I am.'

244

With that, Cintoetl was dragged to a pole in the yard in front of a line of archers.

'Each of these archers is an expert and never misses his target,' said Tollan. 'But only one has the order to kill you. You must shout out a number and that archer will fire, but only the right number will kill you. The others will just miss you.'

'And if I refuse,' cried Cintoetl.

'Then Quetzalcoatl will die . . . very, very slowly . . .'

'Then do your work.'

Cintoetl was blindfolded and made to stand against a high wall.

The crowd hushed as they saw him take a deep breath. For a moment all was silent, then Cintoetl cried out 'Seven'.

An arrow whizzed through the air and thudded into the wall behind Cintoetl.

The crowd gasped. They hushed again as they saw Cintoetl ready himself to call out another number, but before he could do so, Cochtocan slipped the chain from around Quetzalcoatl's talons and the bird was free. It made straight for Tollan and before anyone knew what was happening, the bird had gouged his eyes from his face. Tollan screamed as the blood gushed from the space where his eyes had been . . . He was a foul sight.

In the commotion no one was paying any attention to Cintoetl and Cochtocan. She ran towards him and slipped the blindfold from his eyes. They ran to the gate where two horses were waiting.

Soon they were out of sight of the palace, with Quetzalcoatl flying above them. None followed, for Cochtocan had loosened all the shoes from all the horses apart from the two that they were riding.

Soon they were back in Cintoetl's land and the people rejoiced when they saw their king back amongst them.

Within a few days an army was ready to march against Tollan and this time there was hardly any fight. With Tollan unable to command his troops the war was over in an hour.

Cochtocan and Cintoetl were married and lived happily ever after. Quetzalcoatl was restored to his Palace of the White Gold and peace reigned in the land for ever more.

THE MAGIC TREE

One day at the end of the last century, a small white boy was walking across a plain in the middle of Africa. His parents had recently arrived in the continent to try to farm the barren land. The boy was very tired so he sat down in the shade of the only tree that he could see for hundreds of yards around. As he sat in the shade a soft breeze began to blow and stirred the twigs of the old tree.

'So someone has come again. I have no more magic. Go away.'

The boy was frightened. 'Who said that?' he cried in terror.

'I did,' said the breeze in the tree.

'But I . . . I . . . don't understand.'

'You want nothing from me?' asked the breeze in the tree.

'Only the shade of your branches,' said the boy. 'Why do you ask?'

'Child. I have been here for many hundreds of years. I was planted by the god of the Creation to serve the tribes that once lived here.

'When I grew to maturity there were many peoples living all around. They were poor but hardworking. They tilled the soil and planted their crops and they were happy. There were four main tribes and two or three minor ones and they all worked together in harmony. One day the elders came to me and said, "Give us some relief from our poverty. We work in the hot sun from morning until night and we barely scrape a living."

'So I gave them the gift of a wonderful animal. It could survive on only a little grazing and it could breed quickly. The people were very happy, and with the animal they became rich and prosperous. It gave them much milk. Their carcasses were full of fine meat. Clothes could be made from their skins, and their bones could be used to make beautiful ornaments.

'The tribes became so rich that they stopped tilling the land and brought in servants from far away to do the work for them.

'At first, they treated the servants well, but as they became richer, they became greedier and began to be cruel and harsh.

'One night the servants' witch doctor came to me. He had painted his body in bright colours and he wore horns on his head. There were ornaments around his neck and over his shoulders.

'"Oh tree," he said to me. "We have heard that you have magic power. When we came here at first we did not mind working for our masters. They treated us with kindness and consideration. But now they are cruel and treat us badly. They whip us and starve us, no matter how hard we work for them. Give us our freedom".

'I did as they asked. I told the witch doctor that at the next full moon I would make the breeze blow through my branches and call all the villagers to me. I would keep them there until the slaves had made good their escape.

'And when the full moon came, I called the tribes to me. I used my magic to root all the tribesmen to the spot while their servants escaped. I held them there for two days to give them time to get far away, and when I knew they would be safe, I released their masters from my magic.

'But the servants were not only content with their freedom. They took all the herds and left nothing for their old masters.

'I did not think that the tribes would know that it was I who was responsible for the freedom of their servants, but they soon realized what had happened.

'They came back later and said, "Tree. We realize that you gave our servants their freedom and we know, too, why you did so. We treated them so badly. But now we have nothing. Help us."

'And so I gave them a seed that would grow into a rich grass that would feed them and any animals that they had. And they planted it and they grew rich again. But they had learned their lesson. They cultivated their own fields and cared for their own animals. And they were happy.

'But then the white man came. And he was envious of the lush fields and fat livestock. So he took them for himself and made slaves of the tribes. They returned to me and asked yet again for help. I gave them a germ that would cause fever in the white man. "But you must not touch anyone who catches the fever, otherwise you too will die," I said.

'They took the germ and soon many of the white men caught the fever. At first there was no danger to themselves. But one stupid girl had fallen in love with her white master and as he lay in his fever she kissed him, and so she became ill. And then her family. Soon the fever had touched all the people, black and white, and it spread to the animals.

'Within weeks everyone was either dead or had left the area and I was left alone with my magic. So I called to the god of the Creation. "My magic has brought nothing but pain and tyranny and suffering. Take it from me."

'And the god of the Creation replied, "I'll do as you ask, but I leave you one gift."

' "What is it?" I asked him.

248

'"I will not tell you. But from now on you will have one gift to bestow on anyone who comes to you."

'To this day I do not know what it was. But no one comes here any longer, so it does not matter.'

By this time the little white boy was feeling refreshed, so he stood up and left the shade of the tree.

He told no one what he thought had happened.

His parents decided to build their house quite close to the tree. At first it was a simple structure, but they worked hard and they prospered. Soon they could afford to extend it. They built terraces and verandahs and the house became the most important in the area.

One day some builders came and erected a fine seat around the trunk of the tree.

The following day the boy and his mother and sister came to sit on it and enjoy the shade that the tree's branches afforded.

'How wonderful it is to sit in the cool shade on such a hot day as this,' said the boy's mother. 'We are so lucky to have this tree so close to the house.'

'It's almost like a gift from the gods,' laughed the daughter.

And the little boy looked up into the tree's branches and smiled.

NAMA AND THE ELEPHANT

There was once a very beautiful girl called Nama who lived with her parents, her brothers and sisters in the village in the south of Africa. Apart from her beauty, she was also set apart from the other girls in the village by the fact that her mother was the youngest of seven children, and so was Nama. As the seventh child of a seventh child, Nama had been given the gift of magic powers by the gods which her people worshipped.

One day, when Nama had gone to draw water from the well, an elephant happened to pass. He looked at the lovely black girl leaning over the well and immediately fell in love with her.

When she made to return to the village, he followed her and noticed which house she entered. He went into the jungle, picked some beautiful flowers and returned to Nama's house. He stood outside and trumpeted as loud as he could. Nama and her parents and her brothers and sisters rushed out of the house to see what all the noise was about and were naturally surprised to see an elephant standing there, holding a rose in his trunk.

'What do you want?' asked Nama's father.

'I want to marry your daughter,' said the elephant.

The family all began to laugh. 'Imagine,' they said to each other. 'An elephant wants to marry our Nama,' and the more they said it the more they laughed.

'I don't see what's so funny,' said the elephant. 'I am willing to pay quite a lot for her.'

'Willing to pay for her,' said the father and the whole family stopped laughing immediately; after all, business was business, and daughters did have to get married eventually . . . 'How much?'

The elephant said a certain amount and Nama's father replied, 'That's not quite enough. After all, our Nama is the most beautiful girl in the neighbourhood, but it is enough to start bargaining. Come into the house out of the sunshine. Wife, bring us something cool to drink.'

And so the elephant and the father entered the house to discuss the matter further, while Nama's brothers and sisters ran off to tell everyone that Nama was going to marry an elephant. Soon the whole village had heard the news, and when Nama's father and the elephant had reached a bargain and left the house, the villagers were all waiting to hear how much the elephant had paid. When they did hear, they were aghast. It was more money than most of the villagers had ever imagined. The elephant must love Nama a great deal to pay so much. Nama was not even consulted. She was only a woman, and they did not count for much in those days.

No one took any notice of her tears and her wailings. Once the bargain had been made, she was helped up on to the elephant's back and sent on her way to her new home.

As they passed through village after village, everyone came out of their houses to wave, for word had spread quickly of the elephant who had paid a king's ransom for his human bride. Their curiosity was for the elephant, and no one took any notice of poor Nama, weeping on the elephant's back.

Eventually, they came to where the elephant lived. In a large clearing in the jungle there was an enormous palace, and as they stopped outside it the elephant trumpeted as loudly as he could. A few seconds later, an old female elephant came out of the palace.

'Mother,' said the elephant, 'I have brought home a bride.'

'Where?' asked the old elephant, expecting to see a fine young elephant beside her son.

'On my back. Isn't she beautiful?' said the proud elephant.

'Indeed,' said the mother. 'For a human being she is very beautiful, but she is not an elephant's wife. She cannot be.'

'She is my wife. I paid a king's ransom for her.'

The old elephant was very sad. Like all mothers she wanted her son to marry and have youngsters, but this would not be possible with a human bride. But she knew how strong and obstinate her son was, and for his sake she did her best to pretend to be happy. She helped Nama off her son's back and showed her to a splendid room.

News spread round the elephants in the jungle, and soon all the elephants came to call and to look at the elephant's human bride. The old female elephants smiled sympathetically at their friend, for they knew how sad she must be, and the young males were all envious of their friend for having married such a lovely human girl. The young females were not at all friendly, after all; one of them should, by rights, have married the fine young elephant, not this young upstart human.

And poor Nama was miserable.

For weeks she stayed in the palace and would not leave it. One day she could stand no more and said to her husband, 'Please let me go. You are very kind, but I do not love you. How could I? After all you are an elephant and I am a human.'

252

The elephant became angry and said, 'I am an elephant but I love you and you are human. Why cannot you love me?'

'I cannot,' cried Nama and ran from the room.

Every day from then on she asked the elephant for her freedom and the elephant always refused. 'I paid your father a king's ransom for you, why should I give you up! I cannot get it back. So you must stay.'

Many months passed, and Nama remained as beautiful as she always had been, but her sadness had become almost unbearable. Even the elephant was touched by her melancholy.

One day he said to her, 'I will let you go if your father will repay me the money I paid for you.'

So Nama wrote to her father and asked him to do as the elephant had asked, but her father wrote back and told her that he had lost all the money that he had received, as well as everything he had had before. He was as poor as poor could be, and it was impossible for him to repay the money. Nama must stay where she was and be happy.

Nama showed her husband and his mother the letter. The elephant was very happy, but his mother was very upset, for she could see how unhappy Nama was.

'Shortly after you came here, you told me that you were the seventh child of a seventh child and had magic powers,' she said to Nama one day. 'Is there nothing you could do to repay the money?'

'Nothing,' said Nama. 'It is not the kind of magic that can conjure up money. At its most powerful, all it can do is change the form of growing things. There is nothing ...' She stopped suddenly, for she had had an idea.

That night while everyone slept, Nama went into the forest to where she knew a certain flower would be in bloom. She plucked four handfuls of the fullest blooms and returned to the palace where she mixed them with some special herbs and boiled everything together until the dawn came.

The next night she went to another clearing where another flower grew and she gathered four handfuls of the fullest blooms. She returned to the palace and boiled them together with some more herbs.

The next night she mixed the two lots together and boiled and boiled them until the liquid had become a thick smooth cream.

As her husband slept she rubbed the cream into the dull tusks that grew out of his face.

The next morning she said to her husband, 'May I return to my people?'

'How can you, Nama?' said the elephant. 'Your father has no money to buy you back. You must stay here and try to be happy.'

'But I have now repaid the dowry,' said Nama. 'Look at yourself in a glass,' said Nama.

The elephant sent a servant to bring a glass, and when he looked in it he was astonished to see that his dull tusks now gleamed as white as the purest snow.

'What have you done?' he asked Nama.

'I have repaid the dowry,' replied Nama. 'The tusks that used to be made of matted hair are now fashioned in the finest ivory and are worth more than my father paid you.'

The elephant was as good as his word and allowed Nama to return to her village where her family rejoiced to see her. Nothing but ill-luck had befallen them since she had left, but soon after her return their fortunes changed and they became rich again.

Back in the jungle, the old female elephant did her best to console her son. She knew how much he had loved Nama and how broken-hearted he was. But time is a great healer, and it was not long before the elephant had fallen in love again, this time with a beautiful young female elephant. Everyone was very happy and when their first child was born, it too had fine ivory tusks like his father.

And that is why all elephants have ivory tusks. Because an elephant fell in love with a girl called Nama, a long, long time ago.

The Love Affairs

— *of* —

Nathaniel P.

{ a novel }

Adelle Waldman

HENRY HOLT AND COMPANY   NEW YORK

3 1398 00444 7604

Henry Holt and Company, LLC
Publishers since 1866
175 Fifth Avenue
New York, New York 10010
www.henryholt.com

Henry Holt® and 🏛® are registered trademarks of
Henry Holt and Company, LLC.

Copyright © 2013 by Adelle Waldman
All rights reserved.

Library of Congress Cataloging-in-Publication Data
Waldman, Adelle.
   The Love Affairs of Nathaniel P. : A Novel / Adelle Waldman.—First Edition.
     pages   cm
   ISBN 978-0-8050-9745-0
   1. Young men—New York (State)—New York—Fiction.
2. Authors—New York (State)—New York—Fiction.   3. Man-woman
relationships—Fiction.   4. Self-realization—Fiction.   5. Brooklyn
(New York, N.Y.)—Fiction.   I. Title.
   PS3623.A35674L68 2013
   813'.6—dc23
   2012040366

Henry Holt books are available for special promotions and
premiums. For details contact: Director, Special Markets.

First Edition 2013

Designed by Kelly S. Too

Printed in the United States of America
1   3   5   7   9   10   8   6   4   2

This is a work of fiction. All of the characters, organizations, and events portrayed
in this novel either are products of the author's imagination or are used fictitiously.

The Love Affairs *of* Nathaniel P.

To my parents, Edward and Jacqueline Waldman

To give a true account of what passes within us, something else is necessary besides sincerity.

—George Eliot, *Romola*

The Love Affairs *of* Nathaniel P.

It was too late to pretend he hadn't seen her. Juliet was already squinting with recognition. For an instant she looked pleased to make out a familiar face on a crowded street. Then she realized who it was.

"Nate."

"Juliet! *Hi*. How *are* you?"

At the sound of his voice, a tight little grimace passed over Juliet's eyes and mouth. Nate smiled uneasily.

"You look terrific," he said. "How's the *Journal?*"

Juliet shut her eyes briefly. "It's fine, Nate. I'm fine, the *Journal's* fine. Everything's fine."

She crossed her arms in front of her and began gazing meditatively at a point just above and to the left of his forehead. Her dark hair was loose, and she wore a belted blue dress and a black blazer whose sleeves were bunched up near her elbows. Nate glanced from Juliet to a cluster of passersby and back to Juliet.

"Are you headed to the train?" he asked, pointing with his chin to the subway entrance on the corner.

"*Really?*" Juliet's voice became throaty and animated. "Really, Nate? That's all you have to say to me?"

"Jesus, Juliet!" Nate took a small step back. "I just thought you might be in a hurry."

In fact, he was worried about the time. He was already late to Elisa's dinner party. He touched a hand to his hair—it always reassured him a little, the thick abundance of his hair.

"Come on, Juliet," he said. "It doesn't have to be this way."

"Oh?" Juliet's posture grew rigid. "How should it be, Nate?"

"Juliet—" he began. She cut him off.

"You could have at least—" She shook her head. "Oh, never mind. It's not worth it."

Could have at least what? Nate wanted to know. But he pictured Elisa's wounded, withering look if he showed up so late that all her guests had to wait on him to start dinner, heard her slightly nasal voice brushing off his apology with a "whatever," as if she had long since ceased to be surprised by any new bad thing he did.

"Look, Juliet, it was great to see you. And you do look great. But I've really got to go."

Juliet's head jerked back. She seemed almost to wince. Nate could see—it was obvious—that she took his words as a rejection. Immediately, he was sorry. He saw her suddenly not as an adversary but as a vulnerable, unhappy young—youngish—woman. He wanted to do something for her, say something earnest and truthful and kind.

"You're an asshole," she said before he had the chance.

She looked at him for a fraction of a second and then turned away, began walking quickly toward the river and the adjacent strip of restaurants and bars. Nate nearly called after her. He wanted to try, at least, to put things on a better footing. But what would he say? And there was no time.

Juliet's strides, as she receded into the distance, were long and determined, but she moved stiffly, like a person determined not to let on that her shoes hurt her feet. Reluctantly, Nate started walking in the opposite direction. In the deepening twilight, the packed street no longer seemed festive but seedy and carnival-like. He got stuck behind a trio of young women with sunglasses pushed up on their heads and purses flapping against their hips. As he maneuvered around them, the one closest twisted her wavy blonde hair around her neck and spoke to her companions in a Queen Bee–ish twang. Her glance flickered in his direction. He didn't know if the disdain on her face was real or imagined. He felt conspicuous, as if Juliet's insult had marked him.

After a few blocks, the sidewalks became less congested. He began moving faster. And he began to feel irritated with himself for being so rattled. So Juliet didn't like him. So what? It wasn't as if she were being fair.

Could have at least *what*? He had only been out with her three or four times when it happened. *It* was no one's fault. As soon as he realized the condom had broken, he'd pulled out. Not quite in time, it turned out. He knew that because he was not the kind of guy who disappeared after sleeping with a woman—and certainly not after the condom broke. On the contrary: Nathaniel Piven was a product of a postfeminist, 1980s childhood and politically correct, 1990s college education. He had learned all about male privilege. Moreover he was in possession of a functional and frankly rather clamorous conscience.

Consider, though, what it had been for *him*. (Walking briskly now, Nate imagined he was defending himself before an audience.) The party line—he told his listeners—is that she, as the woman, had the worst of it. And she did, of course. But it wasn't a cakewalk for him, either. There he was, thirty years old, his career finally taking off—an outcome that had not seemed at all inevitable, or even particularly likely, in his twenties—when suddenly there erupted the question of whether he would become a father, which would obviously change everything. Yet it *was not in his hands*. It was in the hands of a person he barely knew, a woman whom, yes, he'd slept with, but who was by no means his girl-friend. He felt like he had woken up in one of those after-school specials he watched as a kid on Thursday afternoons, whose moral was not to have sex with a girl unless you were ready to raise a child with her. This had always seemed like bullshit. What self-respecting middle-class teenage girl—soon-to-be college student, future affluent young professional, a person who could go on to do anything at all (run a multinational corporation, win a Nobel Prize, get elected first woman president)—what such young woman would decide to have a baby and thus become, in the vacuous, public service announcement jargon of the day, "a statistic"?

When Juliet broke the news, Nate realized how much had changed in the years since he'd hashed this out. An already affluent, thirty-four-year-old professional like Juliet might view her situation differently than a teenager with nothing before her but possibility. Maybe she was no longer so optimistic about what fate held in store for her (first woman president, for example, probably seemed unlikely). Maybe she had become pessimistic about men and dating. She might view this as her last chance to become a mother.

Nate's future hinged on Juliet's decision, and yet not only was it not his to make, he couldn't even seem to be unduly influencing her. Talking to Juliet, sitting on the blue-and-white-striped sofa in her living room with a cup of tea—*tea!*—in his hand, discussing the "situation," it seemed he'd be branded a monster if he so much as implied that his preference was to abort the baby or fetus or whatever you wanted to call it. (Nate was all for a woman's right to choose and all the lingo that went with it.) He'd sat there, and he'd said the right things—that it was her decision, that whatever she wanted he'd support, et cetera, et cetera. But who could blame him if he felt only relief when she said—in her "I'm a smart-ass, brook-no-bullshit newspaper reporter" tone of voice—that, obviously, abortion was the natural solution? Even then he didn't allow himself to show any emotion. He spoke in a deliberate and measured tone. He said that she should think hard about it. Who could blame him for any of it?

Well, she could. Obviously, she did.

Nate paused on a corner as a livery cab idled past, its driver eying him to see if he was a potential fare. Nate waved the car on.

As he crossed the street, he began to feel certain that what Juliet actually blamed him for was that his reaction, however decent, had made abundantly clear that he didn't want to be her boyfriend, let alone the father of her child. The whole thing was so *personal*. You were deciding whether you wanted to say yes to this potential person, literally a commingling of your two selves, or stamp out all trace of its existence. Of course it made you think about how different it would be if the circumstances were different—especially, he imagined, if you were a woman and on some level you wanted a baby. Sitting in Juliet's living room, Nate had been surprised by just how awful he felt, how sad, how disgusted by the weak, wanton libidinousness (as it seemed to him then) that had brought him to this uncomfortable, dissembling place.

But did any of it make him an asshole? He had never promised her anything. He'd met her at a party, found her attractive, liked her enough to want to get to know her better. He'd been careful not to imply more than that. He'd told her that he wasn't looking for anything serious, that he was focused on his career. She'd nodded, agreed. Yet he felt sure the whole thing would have played out differently if he could have said to her, Look, Juliet, let's not have this baby, but maybe some other, at some future point . . . But while he admired Juliet's sleek, no-nonsense demeanor, that brisk, confident air, he admired it with dispassionate fascination, as a fine example of type, rather than with warmth. In truth he found her a bit dull.

Nevertheless, he had done everything that could have been expected of him. Even though he had less money than she did, he paid for the abortion. He went with her to the clinic and waited while it was being performed, sitting on a stain-resistant, dormitory lounge–style couch with a rotating cast of teenage girls who typed frenetically on their cell phones' tiny keyboards. When it was over, he took her home in a taxi. They spent a pleasant, strangely companionable day together, at her place, watching movies and drinking wine. He left the apartment only to pick up her prescription and bring her a few groceries. When, finally, around nine, he got up to go home, she followed him to the door.

She looked at him intently. "Today was . . . well, it wasn't as bad as it could have been."

He, too, felt particularly tender at that moment. He brushed some hair from her cheek with his thumb and let it linger for a moment. "I'm really sorry for what you had to go through," he said.

A few days later, he called to see how she was feeling.

"A little sore, but okay," she said.

He said he was glad to hear it. There was a long pause. Nate knew he should say something chatty and diverting. He opened his mouth to speak. But a panicky premonition came over him: this phone call would lead to an endless string of others, the day at Juliet's apartment to a regular movie date, all tinged with a sense of obligation and an almost creepy quasi flirtation.

"I've got to run," he said. "I'm glad you're feeling better."

"Oh." Juliet drew in her breath. "Okay . . . Bye, then."

He probably should have followed up after that. As he turned the corner onto Elisa's street, Nate conceded that he should have called or e-mailed a few weeks later. But, at the time, he hadn't known if a call from him would have been welcome. It might have been a painful reminder of something she would rather put behind her. Nor did he know what he would have said. And he'd gotten distracted, caught up in other things—in life. She could have called him.

He'd done more than many guys would have. Was it his fault if he just didn't feel that way about her? *Could have at least what?*

The front door of Elisa's building was propped open with a large rock. Light from the hallway made a yellow arc on the concrete stoop. Nate paused before entering, taking a breath and running a hand through his hair. Inside, the stairs sagged and groaned under his feet. Elisa's landing smelled of sautéed onions. After a moment, the door swung open.

"Natty!" she cried, throwing her arms around him.

Though he and Elisa had broken up more than a year ago, her apartment, on the top floor of a row house in gentrifying Greenpoint, still felt almost as familiar to Nate as his own.

Before she moved in, its brick walls had been plastered over and covered with floral wallpaper. The thick, irregular beams of the wood floor were hidden under carpet. Elisa's landlord, Joe Jr., once showed Nate and Elisa photos. After more than twenty years, its elderly Polish occupant had left to live with a daughter in New Jersey. Joe Jr. had torn up the carpet and ripped the plaster off the exterior walls. His father, who had bought the house in the 1940s and had since moved to Florida, said he was crazy. Joe Sr. thought adding a dishwasher or replacing the old bathtub would have been a better investment. "But I told him that that wasn't the way to attract high-class tenants," Joe Jr. explained to Nate and Elisa one afternoon, while he repaired some tiles in the bathroom. "I told him the kind of people who pay the big bucks go wild for clawfoot tubs. It's a matter of taste, I told him." Joe Jr. turned to face them, a jar of spackle dangling from his fleshy fingers. "And was I right or was I right?" he asked jovially, a big grin lighting up his face. Nate and Elisa, holding hands, nodded uneasily, unsure of the appropriate response to being so openly—and aptly—characterized as a certain kind of dupe.

Nate had helped Elisa paint the two nonbrick walls a beige that contrasted with the dark brick and the cream-colored rug under her couch. The dining room table they had purchased together at Ikea, but the chairs and a long cabinet by the door had belonged to her grandparents. (Or was it her great-grandparents?) Her bookcases reached nearly to the ceiling.

The apartment's familiarity now felt to him like a reproach.

Elisa had insisted on his presence tonight. "If we really are friends, why can't I have you over for dinner with a few people?" she'd asked. What could he say?

On the couch, Nate's friend Jason, a magazine editor who, to Nate's alternating irritation and amusement, had long wanted to get into Elisa's pants, leaned back regally, cradling the back of his head in his palms. Jason's knees were stretched absurdly far apart, as if he were trying to bore the largest possible impression of himself into Elisa's furniture. Next to Jason sat Aurit, another good friend of Nate's, who had recently returned from a research trip to Europe. Aurit was talking to a girl named Hannah, whom Nate had met before here and there—a thin, pert-breasted writer, pleasant-looking in spite of rather angular features. She was almost universally regarded as nice and smart, or smart and nice. Seated on the loveseat was a woman Elisa knew from college. Nate couldn't remember her name and had met her too many times to ask. He knew she was a lawyer. The weak-chinned suit with his arm draped over her shoulder was, presumably, the banker she was hot to marry.

"We've been wondering when you were going to grace us with your company," Jason said as soon as Nate had both feet in the door.

Nate set his messenger bag on the floor. "I ran into some trouble on the way."

"The G?" Aurit asked sympathetically.

There followed murmurs of agreement that the G, among all the New York subway lines, was especially unreliable.

Nate took the only available seat, next to Elisa's college friend. "It's good to see you," he said, with as much warmth as he could conjure. "It's been a while."

She looked at him levelly. "You and Elisa were still going out."

Nate thought he detected an accusation in her voice—as in "it was before you trampled all over her self-esteem and ruined her happiness."

He forced himself to hold his smile. "In any case, it's been too long."

Nate introduced himself to her banker boyfriend and tried to get the guy talking. If he'd just refer to her by name, Nate would at least be relieved of one anxiety. But the ex-frat boy mostly let her answer for him (equity research, Bank of America, former Merrill Lynch, transition stressful). His preferred means of communication appeared to be nonverbal: a fixed smile and benign, fatherly nods of his head.

Soon—though not necessarily soon enough—Elisa beckoned them to a table crowded with platters and bowls.

"Everything looks delicious," someone said, as they circled the table, smiling beatifically at the spread and at each other. Elisa returned from the other side of the room, carrying a butter dish. Frowning, she scanned the room one last time. A self-satisfied sigh escaped her mouth as she sank gracefully into her seat, the billowy yellow fabric of her skirt fluttering on her descent.

"Go ahead and start," she said, without making any move to start herself. "The chicken will get cold."

While he ate his chicken cacciatore—which, as it happened, was quite good—Nate studied Elisa's heart-shaped face: those big, limpid eyes and dramatic cheekbones, the pretty, bow-shaped lips and profusion of white teeth. Each time Nate saw her, Elisa's beauty struck him anew, as if in the interval the memory of what she actually looked like had been distorted by the tortured emotions she elicited since they'd broken up: in his mind, she took on the dimensions of an abject creature. What a shock when she opened the door, bursting with vibrant, almost aggressive good health. The power of her beauty, Nate had once decided, came from its ability to constantly reconfigure itself. When he thought he'd accounted for it, filed it away as a dead fact—*pretty girl*—she turned her head or bit her lip, and like a children's toy you shake to reset, her prettiness changed shape, its coordinates altered: now it flashed from the elegant contours of her sloping brow and flaring cheekbone, now from her shyly smiling lips. "Elisa the Beautiful," Nate had said without thinking when she hugged him at the door. She'd beamed, breezily overlooking his lateness.

Yet only a short while later, he'd acclimated. Hannah had complimented her apartment. "I hate it," Elisa responded. "It's small, and it's laid out poorly. The fixtures are *incredibly* cheap." Then a quick smile: "Thank you, though."

The familiar hint of whine in Elisa's voice brought back to Nate an equally familiar cocktail of guilt and pity and dread. Also sheer annoyance—that spoiled, ill-tempered quality about her. Her prettiness became an irritant, a Calypso-like lure to entrap him, *again*.

Besides, as he poked at his chicken with his fork, Nate noticed the pores on Elisa's nose and a bit of acne atop her forehead, near her hairline, flaws so minor that it would be ungentlemanly to notice them on most women. But on Elisa, whose prettiness seemed to demand that she be judged on some Olympian scale of perfect beauty, these imperfections seemed, irrationally, like failures of will or judgment on her part.

"What are you working on these days?" she asked him as a bowl of potatoes was passed around for the second time.

Nate dabbed his mouth with a napkin. "Just an essay."

Elisa's round eyes and cocked head implored him to elaborate.

"It's about how one of the privileges of being elite is that we outsource the act of exploitation," he said, glancing at Jason, seated diagonally from him.

The idea for this essay was a bit hazy, and Nate dreaded sounding naive, like the person he'd been in his early twenties, before he'd learned that writing ambitiously, about big or serious subjects, was a privilege magazines granted only to people who'd already made it. But he had recently written a book. He had received a significant advance for it, and even though publication was still many months away, the book had already generated quite a bit of publicity. If he hadn't yet made it, he was getting closer.

"We get other people to do things that we're too morally thin-skinned to do ourselves," Nate said with more conviction. "Conscience is the ultimate luxury."

"You mean that it's almost entirely working-class people who join the army and that sort of thing?" Jason said loudly enough that all other conversation ceased. He reached for a slice of baguette from a butcher block. "Can you pass the butter?" he asked Hannah, before turning back to Nate expectantly.

Jason's curls were tamped down with a glistening ointment. He had the aspect of a diabolical cherub.

"That's not exactly what I had in mind," Nate said. "I mean—"

"I think you're absolutely right, Nate," Aurit broke in, wielding her fork like a pointer. "I think Americans in general are too removed from all the ugliness that goes into safeguarding so-called normal life."

"That's the Israeli perspective, of course—" Jason began.

"That's offensive, Jason," Aurit said. "It's not only reductive but racialist—"

"It *is* offensive," Nate agreed. "But I'm actually not so much interested in security issues as day-to-day life, the ways we protect ourselves from feeling complicit in the economic exploitation that goes on all around us. Take Whole Foods. Half of what you pay for when you shop there is the privilege of feeling ethically pure." He set his wine glass on the table and began gesturing with his arms. "Or consider the Mexican guy the landlord pays to put the trash in front of our buildings twice a week. We wouldn't exploit him ourselves, but on some level we know the guy is an illegal immigrant who doesn't even get minimum wage."

"Joe Jr. does the trash himself," Elisa said. "But he's really cheap."

"Is there a difference between being 'racialist' and 'racist'?" Elisa's college friend asked.

"Same with the guys who deliver our pizza and make our sandwiches," Nate continued. He knew that he was violating an implicit rule of dinner party etiquette. Conversation was supposed to be ornamental, aimed to amuse. One wasn't supposed to be invested in the content of what was said, only the tone. But for the moment he didn't care. "We don't exploit them ourselves," he said. "No, we hire someone, a middleman, usually a small business owner, to do it, so we don't have to feel bad. But we still take advantage of their cheap labor, even as we prattle on about our liberalism—how great the New Deal was, the eight-hour workday, the minimum wage. Our only complaint—in theory—is that it didn't go far enough."

"Excuse me, Nate." Aurit held up an empty wine bottle. "Should we open another?"

"Joe does hire Mexicans to renovate," Elisa said in a tipsily thoughtful voice as she walked to the cabinet by the door. Atop it stood several wine bottles whose necks poked out of colorful plastic bags. They had of course been brought by the other guests. Nate recognized the lime-green packaging of the Tangled Vine, his own neighborhood wine store. This seemed to make his failure worse. He had meant to pick up a bottle on the way over.

Elisa selected a red and returned to her seat. "Can someone open it?" she asked before turning to Nate. "Sorry, Nate. Go on."

Nate had lost the thread of his argument.

Hannah took the bottle from Elisa. "You were saying that we benefit from exploitation but pretend our hands are clean," she said helpfully as Elisa handed her a tarnished copper corkscrew that looked old enough to have accompanied Lewis and Clark on their westward journey. One of Elisa's "heirlooms," no doubt. "I think—" Hannah started to say.

"Right," Nate said. "*Right.*"

His argument came back to him at once. "You know how you read a Dickens novel where these eight-year-old boys work in factories or beg on the streets? And you wonder why didn't anyone give a fuck? Well, we aren't so different. We've just gotten better at hiding it—from ourselves most of all. People back then at least justified their behavior by admitting to their contempt for the poor."

Jason addressed the banker. "If you haven't already noticed, young Nate here suffers from a particularly acute case of liberal guilt."

Jason was currently working on an article about the obesity epidemic, to be called "Don't Let Them Eat Cake."

Before Nate could respond, Hannah turned to him. She was cradling the wine bottle in one arm and gingerly twisting the ludicrous corkscrew with the other. "When people voluntarily pay more to shop at Whole Foods, aren't they, by your logic, trying to be responsible?" she asked. "Aren't they paying more so as *not* to take advantage of cheap labor?"

"Absolutely," Nate said appreciatively. (Someone, it seemed, was actually listening.) "But do those marked-up prices really benefit anyone other than Whole Foods shareholders? All they have to do is put some picture of an earnest lesbian couple on a cereal box and we just assume it comes from some free-love workers' paradise. It's in our self-interest to think so because it allows us to buy good conscience, just like we buy everything else." He paused before concluding. "It's basically a Marxian argument, about the inexorability of exploitation under capitalism."

Aurit frowned. "Who's this essay for, Nate?"

"I don't know yet," Nate said. "I want to write it before I start worrying about whether it will advance my career."

Aurit scrutinized him the way a doctor studies a protuberance he suspects is malignant. "Also, don't people shop at Whole Foods because the food is healthier?"

The wine bottle whooshed as Hannah removed the cork.

"*I* think your idea sounds interesting," Elisa said.

Elisa, Nate thought, was being extremely, even uncharacteristically, nice to him. Maybe they really were, as she had said, turning a corner?

"I think it sounds interesting as well," said the guy half of the couple, whose name, Kevin or Devon, Nate had by now also forgotten but who had, Nate noticed, found his voice as the wine began flowing more freely. "I haven't heard anyone call an idea Marxist and mean it as a good thing in a long time," he said as Elisa "refreshed" his glass. "Not since college."

Nate nudged his own glass into Elisa's line of sight.

While she poured, chair legs scraped the floorboards, ice cubes cracked between molars, and silverware clattered against plates. Nate scanned the books on Elisa's shelf. Her collection was impressive, suggestive of seriousness and good taste. The chick lit and the women's magazines, she kept in the bedroom.

"So, what *is* the difference between racialism and racism?" Kevin/Devon's girlfriend finally asked.

"Racialism," Aurit began enthusiastically, "is not so much dislike or prejudice against a group but the—"

"Hey, guess who I heard got a four-hundred-thousand-dollar book advance?" Jason interrupted. Out of courtesy to Aurit, no one responded.

"—attribution of personal qualities or"—Aurit looked pointedly at Jason—"*beliefs* to a person's membership in—"

"Greer Cohen," Jason finished.

"—a racial group." Aurit's words were orphans. She grimaced when she heard Greer's name. Even Hannah, who had indeed struck Nate this evening as nice as well as smart, raised her eyebrows.

"Good for Greer," Elisa said, like some kind of Stepford hostess whose good manners extend even to those who aren't present.

"Who's Greer Cohen?"

"A writer. Of sorts," Aurit said to Kevin/Devon and his lawyer girlfriend.

Nate's friends then began offering up various, mostly uncharitable assessments of Greer's talent and speculating about whom she'd slept with and whom she'd merely flirted with.

"I do think she's a good writer," Hannah conceded.

"It's not so much her writing I object to," Aurit said. "It's her willingness to trade on her sexuality and call it feminism."

Nate leaned back in his chair and stretched his legs under the table. He felt no inclination to join in. He, too, had recently received a sizable book advance (though nowhere near four hundred thousand dollars). He could afford to be magnanimous.

His glass was empty again. The open wine bottle was on the far side of a vast, primitive-looking wooden salad bowl. He pivoted to reach for it, and as he turned, his torso momentarily blocked out everyone but him and Elisa. She met his eye and gave him one of her sultry looks, tilting her face bashfully downward and smiling a little lopsided smile that was peculiarly suggestive, the shy but flirtatious look a woman might wear when she confessed to some slightly offbeat sexual fantasy.

Nate's body tensed. He became panicky and hyperalert. He felt, he imagined, like a soldier who had been having a rollicking time on guard duty until he heard the crackle of approaching gunfire. Previous reports of improving conditions had proved false. Situation on the front was actually bad, very bad.

The wine made glugging sounds as it hurried out of the bottle and splashed against the fishbowl contours of his glass.

"Careful, buddy," Jason said and laughed. Nate ignored him. He needed fortification for later, when, he was now certain, Elisa would keep him back after the others left, insisting they needed to "talk." Ill-conceived advances would lead to a reprise of old accusations. The night would end as their nights so often had, in tears.

He exhaled loudly. An ex-girlfriend—not Elisa—once told him he was a histrionic breather.

When he looked toward the cabinet near the door to make sure there was another bottle of wine on reserve, he thought he felt something brush his leg, near his kneecap. He made the mistake of turning to investigate.

Elisa coyly withdrew her fingertips.

Nate bolted out of his chair and, as if overcome by a sudden and maniacal desire to study its contents more minutely, made for the bookcase. Borges, Boswell, Bulgakov. He ran a finger along their spines, most marked with yellow "used" stickers from the Brown bookstore.

When he dared to look up, careful to avoid the part of the room containing Elisa, he saw Hannah silhouetted in the kitchen doorway. She was wearing a blue top and narrow skirt. She really did have a nice, slim figure. She was carrying a stack of dishes and had turned partly back to respond to something someone said. She laughed, a real laugh, hearty and open-mouthed.

As it subsided, Hannah's eyes met his. She smiled. It was a friendly smile, a sane smile, perhaps the last he'd see tonight. He wondered if she was dating anyone.

{ 2 }

Nate had not always been the kind of guy women call an asshole. Only recently had he been popular enough to inspire such ill will.

Growing up, he had been considered "nice." He was also a wunderkind of Advanced Placement classes, star debater, and fledgling songwriter whose extracredit homage to Madonna for Math Appreciation Week—"Like a Cosine (Solved for the Very First Time)"—had, unfortunately, been broadcast to the entire upper school. Despite playing on the varsity soccer and baseball teams since tenth grade (granted, his was a Jewish day school), he never quite achieved the reputation of an athlete. He didn't repel girls, exactly. They sought him out for help with bio or calculus, even for advice about their personal problems. They flirted with him when they wanted an ego boost and then they told him about their crushes on Todd or Mike or Scott.

He wasn't much to look at back then. Dark-haired and skinny, he had a pale, sunken chest that he felt made him look cowardly, as if he were perpetually shrinking back. Though he wasn't painfully short, he wasn't tall either. His hands, eyebrows, nose, and Adam's apple appeared to have been intended for a much larger person. This caused him to hold out hope, even as high school progressed, that he might spring up another couple inches, into

the five-foot double digits. In the meantime these attributes didn't
add much to his existing stock of personal charms.

Todd and Mike and Scott were his soccer and baseball teammates. Scott was the most popular guy in their class. He was tall
and broad-shouldered and had that combination of crudeness and
confidence that rendered intelligence not only irrelevant but
slightly ridiculous, a peculiar if not entirely unamusing talent, like
the ability to ride a unicycle. Todd and Mike and Scott were not
exactly Nate's friends—at least not in terms of equality—but they
thought he was funny. They also relied on him for help with
calculus. (Todd and Mike did anyway; Scott never made it past
trigonometry.) Nate went to their parties. Nate got drunk. Jokes
were made about how funny it was that Nate, bard of the math
department, with the 4.0 GPA, was drunk.

Nate pined for girls like Amy Perelman, the stacked blonde
siren of their class, whose bashfully averted eyes and modest smile
were nicely offset by her clingy sweaters and ass-hugging jeans.
Naturally, Amy went out with Scott, although one day she con-
fided to Nate that she was worried about their future: "I mean,
what will become of him? Like, if his dad's stores"—liquidated
designer goods—"don't keep doing well? My dad says that they are,
like, overleveraged. But Scott can barely read—I mean, he can read.
Just not, like, whole books. But I can't see him doing well in college
and getting a regular job. It just wouldn't be him, you know?"

In retrospect, it wasn't surprising that Amy Perelman, who
was not actually stupid but only affected stupidity in her speech
because that was the fashion, eventually ditched Scott and got an
MBA from Wharton. At the time, however, Nate had, somewhat
to his surprise, come to Scott's defense.

"He's a good guy, though. And he really likes you."

Amy looked thoughtful but not quite convinced. "I guess."

In those years, nice-guy Nate, friend to girls in need, devoted
copious intellectual resources to such questions as the verisimili-
tude of various household items to female genitalia. After school,

while his parents were still at work, he roamed the eerily quiet ranch house in search of erotic inspiration, leaving the lights off as darkness began to swirl through its corridors. Slinking like a burglar from room to room, he sized up fleece-lined mittens, condiments, even his mother's pantyhose for possible requisition. One day, in his parents' bedroom, he discovered a surprisingly racy book by a woman named Nancy Friday, and for a time, his equipage also included a "scrunchy" that Amy Perelman had used for her ponytail and which she had left behind in physics lab one day. During lonely afternoons of television and self-ministration, Nate, buoyed by Friday's assurances that women too have dirty thoughts, sniffed the yellow-and-white cloth until the smell of Amy's blonde waves had finally been depleted. Whether he'd literally inhaled it all or whether overexposure had desensitized him, he didn't know. Hoping a hiatus from daily use would restore the hair band to its former glory, he hid it in the back of his bottom desk drawer, behind an old graphing calculator and some tins of colorful, animal-shaped erasers he'd collected in elementary school. Before the experiment could be concluded, he'd forgotten about it— baseball practice had begun, cutting into his autoerotic afternoons. Still, he must have reeked of self-love because around that time Scott branded him "Learned Hand" (a surprising indication that Scott had paid attention in social studies class at least once).

Years later, when Nate and his college girlfriend Kristen had come to Maryland to pack up his old bedroom before his parents sold the house, she'd come across Amy Perelman's scrunchy.

She held it up. "Why do you have this?"

A few blonde hairs, which Nate had once been ever so careful not to displace, still clung to the fabric.

As soon as he realized what it was, Nate snatched the scrunchy from her hand, horrified, afraid that she'd catch something from it, a debilitating skin disease or a whiff of his former self.

"It must be my mom's," he mumbled.

Nate did have one admirer during high school: frizzy-haired

Michelle Goldstein. It wasn't that Michelle wasn't pretty—he'd been interested in girls who looked worse—but there was something painfully self-conscious about her. While it should have been refreshing to see *someone* at their school engrossed in Mary Wollstonecraft's *A Vindication of the Rights of Woman*, Michelle's embrace of culture seemed affected. She had an inexplicable fondness for the phrase *pas de deux*, which Nate had once, frighteningly enough, overheard her use in reference to her "relationship" with him.

Still, at moments, he felt real affection for Michelle. One spring night—it must have been after a school play or concert—they sat together for hours on a bench outside the upper school, gazing down a grassy hill toward the dark expanse of the athletic fields. Michelle spoke, intelligently, touchingly, about the music she liked (moody female singer-songwriters with socially progressive lyrics) and of her intention to live in New York one day, to go often to the Strand—"a huge used bookstore downtown."

Nate wasn't sure if he'd even been to a used bookstore. There weren't any in their suburb, he didn't think.

"You should go to New York sometime," Michelle said.

"I've been. We didn't go anyplace like that."

From his family's weekend in New York, Nate had photos, taken by his dad, of him and his mother huddled together on the Observation Deck of the Empire State Building. They wore newly purchased ponchos and smiled wanly while a cold drizzle fell on their heads.

Michelle smiled sympathetically.

In the light that spilled over from the parking lot, Nate thought Michelle's freckles and straw-colored hair were cute. He nearly reached out across the bench and touched her—her hand or her thigh.

It wasn't even about sex. Nate's life had been somewhat short on friendship, real friendship, distinct from the sort of conditional alliance he had with Scott and company. There had been Howard from summer camp and Jenny, a tomboyish girl on his street who moved to Michigan when he was in sixth grade and from whom Nate had received the occasional letter for several years after, and Ali, also from his neighborhood, who went to public school. He and Nate had drifted apart after junior high. Sitting on the bench with Michelle, Nate felt as if the two of them shared something, some nebulous, slightly melancholic sensitivity that made them different from their classmates.

But at school on Monday, Michelle seemed to have reverted back to her other self.

"I can't believe you got an A on that test," she said after calculus. "What a coup d'état." She gave a little wave as she walked away. "Ciao, chéri."

"Coup," he wanted to shout. "You mean just plain coup."

Yet he and Michelle were constantly lumped together and treated as a couple. Scott repeatedly asked him if her cooter smelled like mothballs because of all the vintage clothes she wore. Michelle's ambiguous social status, neither cool nor uncool, apparently made her his female equivalent. They even went to senior prom together. Nate had been working up the nerve to ask a pretty sophomore, and he felt both resentment and relief when Michelle's asking him foreclosed that possibility. On prom night, he thought Michelle might have been willing to have sex, but he didn't really try, although they made out—more than made out, actually: he had a brief opportunity to assess Scott's hypothesis vis-à-vis the bouquet of her female parts (the word he'd use was *musky*). Nate didn't push because at that particular moment in his life, he didn't want to get entangled with a girl who was slightly repulsive to him. Nor could he imagine sleeping with Michelle and then blowing her off, the way that Todd or Mike might have (although not Scott, who for all his crudity was sensitive and unwavering in his devotion to Amy). There was something that rubbed Nate wrong about Todd and Mike's attitude toward girls— their implicit belief that whatever befell a foolish or unattractive one was her just deserts. Empathy, they reserved for the best-looking girls. (Amy's most minor setbacks, a B-plus or mild cold, elicited coos of grave concern.)

Besides, by prom, Nate had largely begun to pin his erotic hopes on college, where, he imagined, even girls who looked like Amy Perelman would be smart and, more important, *mature*, a word he had lately begun to interpret as "willing to have sex with him." If he were to list the biggest disappointments of his life, freshman year of college would be near the top, right behind the realization, much later, that even something as seemingly sublime as a blow job—his penis in a woman's mouth! *his penis in a woman's mouth!*—could be boring, even slightly unpleasant, under the wrong circumstances or performed inexpertly.

Had he been an urchin rescued from the back alley where he'd foraged for food in dumpsters and solved millennia-old math problems on the inside of torn cereal boxes, he couldn't have been more naive, more uneducated in the social mores of a place like Harvard. And if he'd been a homeless autodidact, he would at least have reaped the social benefit of being exotic. What had seemed normal back home screamed Mall of America, middle management, and mediocrity on a campus where the tone had been set long ago by Puritans with names like Lowell, Dunster, and Cabot. Todd and Mike and Scott, with their gelled hair fanning up from their foreheads and with their polo shirts and BMWs, shrank in size. The kids who seemed to belong at Harvard—the ones who seemed at ease, chatting breezily in the Yard, greeting old friends and throwing their heads back in laughter—drove beat-up Volvos, ordered clothing from catalogs (an activity Nate had previously associated with isolated prairie farms and early Montgomery Ward circulars), and, in a flat English shorn of all regional accent, reeled off the names of places he had never heard of: "Yeah, I've been to Islesboro!" "My uncle has a house there!" "We go to Blue Hill every summer."

Before arriving in Cambridge, Nate had mentally prepared for

Park Avenue, for country clubs, yachts, caviar, for the heedless extravagance of Tom and Daisy Buchanan, but Maine, *Maine* caught him by surprise. Nate was used to summer locales that advertised themselves as such in their names: *Long Beach Island*, *Ocean City*. His new classmates were not playboys or debutantes. They didn't wear blazers; the girls weren't named Muffy or Binky. A fair number had gone to public schools (albeit largely a specific breed of elite public school). They were thin, ponytailed girls who wore no makeup and slouching guys in T-shirts and khaki shorts. They spoke of kayaking and hiking as the ne plus ultra amusements of their young lives. Nate, who had done those things at summer camp, hadn't accorded them any special significance beyond that of the other required activities, such as singing around the campfire and making finger puppets from strips of felt.

When Amy Perelman's family had gone to Vail for spring break, everyone at school knew they stayed at a ski lodge that sounded like some kind of alpine palace staffed by a regiment of liveried bellhops. People at Harvard, on the other hand, referred to their family's "places" in Vermont or New Hampshire as if these were cabins that their parents or grandparents had personally built, log by log, and they seemed almost to compete about whose had the fewest amenities. ("We never have enough hot water because we rely on our own solar generator, totally off the grid.") Amy spoke of the five-star steakhouse her family ate at after a long day on the trails; Harvard people talked of standing out in zero-degree weather waiting for their charcoal grills to heat up, as if their families had never bought into the whole indoor-stove fad. Nate, too, had been skiing. With a group of kids from his synagogue, he spent a weekend on a barren mountain in Pennsylvania that was also home to an abandoned mine. The trip was called a *Shabbaton*. They stayed at a Holiday Inn and ate at the Denny's across the parking lot.

Nate had never thought of himself as disadvantaged. His parents were immigrants, but the kind with good jobs. They worked for defense contractors. He grew up in a detached house with a lawn and a metal swing-set in the back. He attended a private, albeit religious school, where he got an excellent education. His parents had graduate degrees (masters in engineering from Polytechnic University of Bucharest, rather than, say, PhDs in art history from Yale). Growing up, Nate discussed current events at the dinner table; as a family, they watched *60 Minutes* and *Jeopardy!* Apparently, though, some parents read the *New York Review of Books* and drank martinis. In time, Nate would learn to make finer distinctions between the homes of his most sophisticated classmates—the old-school WASPs versus the academic intellectuals (Jew or gentile)—but in the first weeks of college it seemed to him that all of them, from the children of well-known leftist firebrands to the spawn of union-busting industrial titans, spoke the same language. It seemed that way because they did. (Many of them had gone to the same prep schools.) When it came right down to it, these groups were like the Capulets and the Montagues. Whatever their differences, they were both wealthy Veronese families. Nate's family was from Romania.

Before he arrived at Harvard, Nate had read *War and Peace* and *Ulysses* for his own edification, but more important he had shown up without ever having heard of J. Press—so he couldn't mock it. (Eventually, he gleaned that it was a clothing store.) He had only a distant familiarity with the *New Yorker* and no idea how easily an apple could be converted into a device for smoking pot. Nate had been captain of his high school trivia team. He knew many things—for example, the capital of every African country as well as each nation's colonial name, which he could reel off alphabetically—but he did not know the kinds of things that made a person knowing at Harvard in the fall of 1995.

He was, as a result, more than happy to be led about by his suitemate Will McDormand. Will's great-grandfather had been a railroad executive prominent enough to have been personally despised by Eugene Debs. After long days straining to make conversation at orientation activities, Nate gaped at the parade of "dudes" who came to drink with Will. Even chugging cans of Miller Lite and ribbing one another about the pimply girl who had been free with her favors at boarding school, they were clearly the kind of young men who shook hands firmly, made old ladies blush and giggle, and uttered the appropriate condolences at funerals (before escaping to the deserted part of the cemetery to smoke a little weed). They wore expressions of light irony, and their conversation dexterously dodged all serious, intellectual, or sentimental subject matter. When Nate brought up a course he was looking forward to, an embarrassed silence fell over the room.

Nate believed passionately in the equality of man, disdained inherited privilege, and bemoaned on ideological grounds the failures of the French and Russian Revolutions; just the same, during those first few days at Harvard, every time there was a knock at the door, he popped up from the sofa with eager anticipation. He was trying to make out which new arrival was a nephew of a cabinet member and which was a grandson of the Nobel Prize–winning economist, details Will tossed off with a nonchalance that Nate tried to mimic in his replies. (The ransom a kidnapper could have collected if he'd snagged the roomful of guys watching the Red Sox with the sound turned off while the Smashing Pumpkins played on Will's stereo!) Will singled Nate out from their other two suitemates—Sanjay ("Jay") Bannerjee, an affable but slightly stiff kid from Kansas City, who tried and failed to conceal nervousness about the beer drinking, and Justin Castlemeyer, a Young Republican from a small town in North Carolina—both of whom Will treated with a noblesse oblige that, as the semester progressed, grew increasingly smirking. But Will thought Nate was "hysterical." He liked when Nate said "smart things" while pounding shots of vodka, tequila, Jägermeister, peach schnapps, or whatever happened to be on hand. Will particularly liked hearing Nate recite the African countries' colonial names. "You're like a wind-up toy!" he cried. "Again! Again!"

It took Nate a long time to realize that "thank you" was not the only possible response to Will's offer of friendship. For most of his freshman year, he found himself among Will's friends, lusting after surprisingly vacuous girls, who, though they had energy sufficient for sailing expeditions and weekends in the country and though they *got into Harvard*, shrank not only from abstract conversation but from any form of culture unrelated to drinking or the outdoors (including movies with subtitles and anything that fell under the umbrella of "performance"). Every once in a while, in private, to Nate only, one of these tanned, healthy girls made whispery reference to a middlebrow novel that she had once read at her summer house after a wayward guest left it behind. So clearly they *could* read. Nate was aware that there were other kinds of girls on campus, but these girls, the ones Will hung around with, many of them boarding school classmates or daughters of family friends or girls whose families had summered near his for so long that they were "like cousins"—these girls seemed like "the best," the ones who really belonged here.

Other classmates were ruined for Nate after Will made fun of them. Girls who liked theater were "thesbos," activists were "lacktits," and would-be campus journalists were "muffrakers." When Nate spent time with other people, Will seemed threatened. At least that's how pop psychology taught Nate to interpret it. (Years later, Nate would conclude that Will was simply a dick.) "Doing the ugly people thing tonight?" he would ask. "If that's what floats your boat, fine, but if you get tired of limpydick and the barking dogs, come to Molly's suite. We'll be playing quarters— or else tackling the mind-body problem." As if Nate had come to Harvard to play quarters! Yet, inevitably, he'd wind up slinking out of the dorm room where a group would be watching *Mystery Science Theatre 3,000* or a Godard film and head over to Molly's. Where he would play quarters with drunk girls who called him "cute" and asked, in giggly, slurring voices, whether Will was seeing anyone and if he was really as big a player as they'd heard. (Nate couldn't tell if the answer they hoped to hear was yes or no.)

It wasn't until midway through his sophomore year that Nate grew thoroughly tired of Will's world. It was too late. He didn't have much in the way of other friends. He sometimes hung out with his former roommate Jay, but for the most part he'd alienated all the nice, thoughtful people he'd tentatively, kind of, maybe liked freshman year by constantly dropping them for Will. When, through one or another extracurricular activity, he did hang out with other people, other types of people, he couldn't stop thinking in Will's terms. Every time he saw a girl in colored tights, no matter how cute or how into poetry, he thought "thesbo" and heard a howling sound in the background. And the nice kids' outings, to the movies or a lecture on campus and then to a coffeehouse or diner, were depressingly tame, alcohol-free affairs. Many of these fiery debaters and ardent newspaper editors drank a lot of coffee and, in voices that grew squeaky at moments of high tension, discussed the allegorical implications of *Seinfeld*.

It was then that Nate began, really, to read. It seemed to him as if all the reading he had done back in high school had been tainted. Some part of him had been aiming to impress, reaching for a sophistication he had thought would serve him—socially—in college. (Ha.) The spring of his sophomore year, he began to read from feverish loneliness, a loneliness he began to fear would be permanent. After all, if he, if someone like *him*, wasn't happy in college, where and when would he be happy? His disappointment and isolation made him bitter, and he judged the world around him harshly, with the too-broad strokes of a crank. Except for people like Will, who already had enough privilege that they could afford to take it for granted, his classmates were blindly striving to climb up the meritocratic ladder, as if their lives were nothing more than preparation for business or law school—or, if they were "creative," Hollywood writing jobs. Only when Nate read, and occasionally in class discussions or during professors' office hours, did he feel any fluttering of hope. Perhaps his personality wasn't so ill formed if at least he found kinship somewhere, even if it was among the words of men who were long dead. Or in class, which everyone knew was the least important part of college.

In the middle of junior year, he met Kristen. They were in a political science seminar together. From her comments in class, Nate could tell that she was very smart. She was good-looking, too, with the healthy, athletic look common to Will's gal pals. She had the kind of quiet confidence that comes from faith in her own sturdy self-discipline and quick good sense. She and Nate often found themselves on the same side in discussions. Soon they exchanged smiles whenever a particularly fatuous classmate spoke. They began to walk from class together and discovered that their upbringings were similarly modest. New England–bred Kristen seemed intrigued by his immigrant parents. She laughed at his jokes. Still, when he finally mustered the courage to ask her out, Nate fully expected that she'd turn him down—whip out the boyfriend in Hanover or Williamstown or her latent lesbianism or a chastity vow effective until the implementation of universal health care. But . . . Kristen said yes. She'd recently broken up with her boyfriend (Providence).

Kristen was premed, bighearted, the kind of girl who spent winter break doing Habitat for Humanity projects in the Honduran jungle, but she was also hardheaded and acerbic, prone to a withering disdain for foolishness or absurdity that was both winning and slightly intimidating. People instinctively wanted her approval. Between this authoritative air and her sunny good looks, Kristen was, in the world's crude judgment, a catch for Nate, several notches above him in the college social hierarchy. Nate wholeheartedly concurred with the world: he felt himself to be extremely lucky. If Kristen didn't share his love for literature—well, that seemed beside the point, like insisting your girlfriend share your preference for Pepsi over Coke. It wasn't as if she were willing to date only biology majors.

Around the same time that he met Kristen, Nate met Jason, in a literary theory class, and through Jason, he met Peter. In some ways it was sensitive, thoughtful Peter with whom Nate felt a strong connection. But three worked better than two. There was something too breathily eager about two guys drinking whiskey and talking endlessly into the night about books and the corporate-financed rightward shift of the nation and whether it was fair to say that Marxism had been tested or not because Soviet-style communism was such a perversion. Jason as a third leavened the dynamic. His cheerful bluster dispelled Nate's and Peter's bashfulness and gave their outings the social imprimatur of a guys' night out.

Senior year of college, alternating his time between Jason-and-Peter and Kristen, Nate was happy. For many years afterward, he wondered if he was happier then than he'd ever be again. It was so new—the girl and the friends. And he'd waited so long for both. After graduation, he followed Kristen to Philadelphia, where she started med school and he wrote freelance pieces for a left-of-center magazine in D.C. He missed Jason, who worked at a glossy magazine in New York, and Peter, who was getting a PhD in American Studies at Yale. Home by himself—freelancing—Nate felt isolated. Perhaps he expected too much of Kristen. She had a different type of mind, and besides she was busy and tired. Medical school fulfilled her, mentally and socially.

Over time, Nate began to grow frustrated by her lack of literary sensibility, the sheer practicality of her intelligence, as well as a certain rectitude or squareness on her part—in other words, by her essential Kristen-ness, which he had once revered. He visited Jason in New York more and more frequently. He started to notice there were women who dressed differently, who wore neat-looking glasses and sexy high-heeled boots and had cool hair that made Kristen's ponytail seem uninspired. Many of these women seemed to be reading Svevo or Bernhard on the subway. At home, he'd read Kristen bits from Proust, and she'd get this pinched look on her face, as if the sheer extravagance of Proust's prose was morally objectionable, as if there were children in Africa who could

have better used those excess words. Kristen also seemed to disapprove of Nate's homebound lifestyle on a visceral, almost Cal-
vinistic level that she couldn't justify according to any of her core
principles. (In theory she was devoted to the poor and idle.)

But the animosity accumulated so slowly that for a long time
Nate hardly noticed it. He was genuinely shocked when Jason
floated the notion that the relationship might be less than perfectly
happy: "I don't know," he said, "it's just the way you sound when
you talk about her—it's like 'Kristen, sigh, this' 'Kristen, sigh,
that.'" Nate had gotten so angry that it was all he could do not to
walk out of the bar. Never mind that in the past twenty-four hours
he'd silently accused Kristen of being prudish and narrow-minded
a dozen times. Never mind that only seconds before Jason had
spoken, he had been imagining their Goth-looking waitress going
down on him.

That spring, Kristen signed the two of them up to serve as
guides for the blind in a 5K at Fairmount Park. The morning of the
race Nate wanted to stay in bed and read, and then maybe, *maybe*,
have a Bloody Mary or two a little later, as he read some more at a
sports bar with a game on.

"Why does everything always have to be so goddamn wholesome
and sunny and do-gooder-y?" he said.

He wasn't shouting, but he was close.

Kristen was sitting on their desk chair, bent at the waist as she
pulled on her sneakers. She glanced at Nate, not with concern but
with surprise that curdled quickly into annoyance. Then she
returned to the business of her shoes. This angered him even more.

"I'm not fucking Jimmy Stewart," he said, mixing up *Pollyanna*
and *It's a Wonderful Life*.

A spasm of irritation—out-and-out contempt, really—flickered
across Kristen's face.

"If you want to sit around in your underwear all day, go right
ahead," she said. "I'll go get you a beer from the fridge if that's
what you want."

Nate had brought his laptop into bed. Now he closed it and looked at the wall beyond Kristen's head. "That's not what I meant."

Kristen began pulling her hair into a ponytail. "I'm going to go to the race now," she said in the doctor's voice she'd been cultivating: neutral and distancing and only dispassionately empathetic. "I think you should, too, because you said you would, and they're counting on you, but it's your decision."

Of course Nate apologized. Of course he began getting ready. But the truth was he still wished he didn't have to go. He felt he was right somehow, even though he was clearly wrong because he had promised and because it would suck to be blind and he was fortunate to be blessed with the gift of sight.

After that, their squabbles began to feel more like sublimated judgments of the other's entire person. For a while, each fight was followed—on Nate's end, anyway—by a strong internal counter-reaction. He felt uneasy about the precipice to which his resentful thoughts seemed to lead. He wanted to take back, retract, even in his mind, his criticisms of Kristen and restore the mental status quo (Kristen was the greatest, he adored her) that had served him so well, for so long. But as the fights persisted, his subsequent urge to backtrack began to diminish. Meanwhile, Kristen became increasingly interested in spending time with her classmates. Nate found he was relieved to be left to himself. Soon, they acknowledged that they'd "drifted apart."

Their breakup was very amicable—it was as if simply by agreeing to part, their frustrations with each other shrank to manageable dimensions—and although Nate was a little surprised by how quickly afterward she got together with one of her medical school classmates, there was, to this day, nobody he respected more than Kristen in that good, sturdy, upright citizen way.

Nate moved to New York. He had high expectations, both professionally and romantically. The growth spurt he'd longed for had never come to pass, but he had filled out. His proportions had harmonized. He also felt as if he'd been vetted and Kristen's seal of approval would, through some new air of self-confidence, be transmitted to all other pretty girls. After all, when he had still been going out with Kristen and he had, say, exchanged a look with a girl across a subway car, it had felt as if, surely, were it not for the existence of Kristen, he and the attractive stranger would have gotten off the train together and headed to a dive bar for a drink and smart, fizzy conversation. Once single, however, Nate quickly became aware of the vastly complicated chain of events that had to take place before a look translated into a conversation and a phone number, let alone drinks. It turned out that many of these good-looking girls who gleamed so promiscuously on the subway had boyfriends waiting for them aboveground. Or so they claimed.

When he did manage to get a date with a girl he picked up in public, he was usually in for a series of surprises. Yes, those girls with the boxy glasses reading Svevo or Bernhard or, more commonly, Dave Eggers (Nate had to admit that Svevo and Bernhard had always been much rarer sights, even on the F train), were, as a general category, very attractive. And when the sum total of Nate's knowledge of such a woman had been what he gleaned from her clothing, posture, reading material, and facial expression, he had effortlessly filled in the blanks. She would be nonvegan, catless (or at least only one-catted), left-leaning, sane, and critical of the inadequacies of the American educational system without embodying them personally. He had been extremely naive.

It was around this time that he began to understand what was meant by the phrase *low self-esteem*, something he used to think he identified with intuitively. But what he had himself experienced was nothing like the total habituation to being treated badly that he encountered in some of the girls he met his first year in New York. He went out with a girl named Justine, a Pratt student who lived in a tiny studio in Bed-Stuy with a poodle named Pierre and a cat called Debbie Gibson. Several nights after Nate had gently suggested they might not have a future, she called him on his cell.

"I thought maybe you'd want to come over," she said.

It was 2:00 a.m. Nate said he probably shouldn't. "I think— well, I'm not sure I'm over my ex."

Although Kristen had just told him that her new boyfriend was moving into the apartment they had shared, and although he had been, uhm, *surprised* by the dispatch with which this had transpired, what he told Justine was not, strictly speaking, true—he wasn't pining for Kristen. But, it was the best he could come up with on the spot.

Justine started to cry. "I guess Noah was right."

Noah was *her* ex. Apparently, he had told her she needed to get breast implants if any guy was going to want her. Obliged to disprove this prince, Nate said he'd be there in twenty minutes.

The next day he felt ashamed. What did boxy glasses and edgy tattoos matter if you were talking about a girl who suggested, in a heartbreakingly resigned monotone, that he might like to do her with porn on "because that's how Noah liked it"? (Nate wondered how Noah felt about Pierre-the-poodle's wiry-haired silhouette flitting across scenes of spanking and anal penetration as the ill-natured canine chased Debbie Gibson around the room.) Nate felt bad for Justine—because she'd grown up in an infinitely bleaker suburbia than the one he had known; because her mother had repeatedly chosen "the asshole" (her stepfather) over her; because, art school notwithstanding, she grimly expected to be a waitress or secretary all her life ("I don't know the right people"); and because guys like Noah and Nate himself took advantage of her. But pity couldn't be transmuted into romantic feeling, and Nate knew the best thing he could do for Justine was to stop seeing her.

Besides, he had problems of his own. Unhappy with the way one of his articles had been edited, he had—in a moment of pique or high principle, depending on how you looked at it—vowed never again to write for the left-wing magazine that had been his main source of income as well as credibility. This decision had disastrous consequences for his career and his finances.

When he first moved to New York, he'd had some notion that he'd paid his dues during his years in Philly. This turned out to be false, risibly so. Even with Jason's connections at up-market men's magazines, Nate had trouble getting assignments in New York. He took a temp job that became a full-time, indefinitely termed job in the library of a private equity firm, with the intention of writing at night. The job was so demoralizing that he wound up mostly drinking during his off-hours. It was a bad year (closer to two, actually). His industrious parents, who for his sake had emigrated to an unfamiliar land and whose uncreative and not particularly fulfilling labors had funded his lavish education, were, understandably, displeased. They wanted him to get a real job or go to graduate school. Nate was, however, determined to make a living writing.

Looking back, he was proud that he'd "persevered," by which he meant that he hadn't gone to law school. He'd moved to a cheaper apartment, which allowed him to quit the private equity job in favor of shorter bouts of temp work and freelance proof-reading for a law firm. He worked on fiction and pitched articles and book reviews, getting assignments here and there. His critical voice improved. He began to get more assignments. Toward the end of his twenties, it became evident that he'd managed to cobble together an actual career as a freelance writer. The achievement was capped off when a major online magazine offered him a position as its regular book reviewer.

By then, he'd mostly stopped picking up girls at bars (let alone on the subway), having learned that he had a better chance of meeting someone he could have a conversation with if he dated women he met at publishing parties—editorial assistants and assistant editors, publicists, even interns. They weren't all brilliant, but chances were slim that they had an ex-boyfriend named Noah who told them to get breast implants. They'd never met anyone like Noah, not in a romantic context anyway, not at Wesleyan or Oberlin or Barnard. And if they hadn't read Svevo or Bernhard—and let's face it, most hadn't—at least they knew who they were. ("*Zeno's Conscience*, right? Doesn't James Wood, like, love that book?")

Conveniently, such women tended increasingly to like him. The well-groomed, stylishly clad, expensively educated women of publishing found him appealing. The more his byline appeared, the more appealing they found him. It wasn't that they were out-right social climbers so much as they began to see him in a flatter-ing light, the light in which he was beginning to see himself. He was not underemployed and chronically low on cash—he wasn't only those things, anyway. He was also a young, up-and-coming literary intellectual.

Nate felt not only glad but vindicated, as if a long-running argument had finally been settled in his favor. His unpopularity, though persistent, had never seemed quite right. He was not and had never been a nervous, nebbishy sort; his interest in science fiction, never very intense, had peaked at age thirteen. He had always been a rather well-disposed and agreeable sort of person, if he said so himself.

He knew he'd truly arrived when he began dating Elisa the Beautiful. Not long after, he began making rapid progress on the book that had gone on to win him a six-figure advance from a major publishing house, further enhancing both his professional reputation and personal popularity. Water, as they say, eventually finds its level.

{ 3 }

The block of text that appeared on his computer screen was oppressively dense. Nate reached for his coffee mug before he began to read.

The e-mail was from Hannah, from Elisa's dinner party. "I was wondering something," she had written. "The other night you said that the indifference to suffering that was normal in Dickens's times still exists. We've just gotten better at keeping it at a remove. But back then things like child labor were tolerated in a way that they aren't tolerated now. They have, literally, been outlawed. Doesn't that matter?" She continued in this vein for another couple paragraphs before ending on a friendly note: "I had a lot of fun the other night. It was nice talking to you."

Nate's coffee mug contained flat Coke. This was not his top-choice beverage first thing in the morning, but he didn't have the wherewithal to make coffee, in part because he hadn't had the wherewithal to make coffee for so many mornings in a row that he was afraid to face the live cultures colonizing his coffee-maker.

After reading Hannah's e-mail, he set down the mug. Its impact on the desk caused a stack of books to wobble. As he reached out to steady it, the stapler that was perched atop an adjacent stack fell forward, landing on the back of his outstretched hand. He yelped.

Several minutes passed before he clicked back on Hannah's message. He frowned as he reread it. Sober, in the daylight, he felt strangely hesitant to pursue the connection. The reason for this was unclear.

On the other hand, he wasn't awake enough to start writing his commodification-of-conscience essay. And he didn't have anything else in particular to do. When he'd been working on his book, he'd always had something to work on. Even when he wasn't up to writing new material, he could always go back and tweak sentences he'd already written. Now that the book was in the hands of his publisher, he missed that.

He hit REPLY. "Isn't it true, though"—his fingers tap-tap-tapped across his keyboard in a pleasing clatter of productivity—"that we are as acquisitive, if not more, than people were back then? We want comfortable lives, and if we don't have servants, we have laborsaving devices made in China. Only now we want to feel good about it, too. So we make sure the exploitation happens out of sight. China is ideal."

After he pressed SEND, Nate checked for new mail. He was expecting something from Peter, who had recently moved from New Haven to Maine for an academic job. But, no, nothing.

He got up and looked out the window. His street was barren, the trees that lined its sidewalks short and spindly, their leaves sparse even at the height of spring. They had been planted a few years ago as part of an urban revitalization scheme, and they ha about them a sad, failed look, as if no one but civil servants h ever cared for them. Maybe they were also the wrong specie simply poor examples of their type. The wealthy residents of Park Slope, one neighborhood over, would have known bett to let the city plant such gnarled, runtish saplings on their The people of Park Slope probably imported their o verdant, perhaps even fruit-bearing trees.

The smell of bacon wafted through the window. Nate wondered if he'd missed anything the last time he'd scrounged around his cupboards for food.

As he walked to the kitchen, his socks stuck on the hardwood floor. Coffee droplets, dating from the days before he'd sworn off the coffeemaker, had congealed, turning his hallway into a strip of flypaper for dust and balled-up receipts and the tiny paper disks spewed by his hole puncher.

He gazed into his refrigerator, looking for he didn't know what. A ready-made breakfast of eggs Benedict with a strong cup of coffee would have been nice. Alas. Not even a stray carton of rice from his favorite Chinese delivery place, whose motto was *Always YOU Will Find Deliciousness*. He poured the last of the Coke into his mug and threw out the bottle. A rancid odor rose from the trash can. He pressed the lid shut.

From the other room, his computer pinged. Nate hurried back to his desk. "Even so," Hannah had written, "doesn't it matter that forms of exploitation that were openly tolerated in the past have been forced under the table? Doesn't that say something about how our conception of what's acceptable has changed?"

She had a point. Nate leaned back in his chair. It was not a deal-breaking point, but something he'd have to address in his essay. Perhaps as we become more ethically ambitious, we have more incentive to hide our failings from ourselves? He scrawled "Rawls" on a Post-It note and stuck it to the screen of his laptop.

Then he began to consider more closely the personal implications of these e-mails. Why did he feel so wary?

There was Elisa. He didn't think getting mixed up with a good friend of hers would go over well, and Hannah had been at her dinner party. Still, it wasn't clear that they were good friends. He'd ever heard Elisa mention her. And Hannah was older than Elisa, least thirty, closer to his age than Elisa's. And she seemed, just, erent from Elisa, more mature or something. They didn't seem to be bosom buddies.

No, something other than Elisa was holding him back. Nate closed his eyes and pictured Hannah turning around in Elisa's kitchen doorway. She was nice-looking, sort of striking and appealing at certain moments, when her expression was animated, but there was something about the stark line of her eyebrows and the pointiness of her features that wasn't exactly pretty. And while she had a nice body, she was on the tall side and had something of the loose-limbed quality of a comic actor, goofy and self-conscious, good-humored but perhaps also a bit asexual.

If Hannah had been more obviously hot, he was pretty sure that he would have given her more thought before the other night, when she had been the only woman present who was at all a viable candidate for his interest. That had to mean something, although Nate wasn't sure what exactly. When he was younger, he had imagined that as he grew up, he would become progressively less shallow and women's looks wouldn't matter as much. Now that he was, more or less, grown up, he realized it wasn't going to happen. He wasn't even particularly shallow. Many of his friends were far colder and more connoisseur-like in their attitudes toward women's appearances, as if the tenderer feelings that had animated the crushes of their younger years had been spent. What emerged in their place was the cool eye of the seasoned appraiser, who above all knows how to calculate the market rate.

Physical attraction had driven him straight into the beds of Elisa and Juliet. This was not exactly a proof of its wisdom. With Kristen, on the other hand, there had been a brief window, before they'd spoken, when he thought she was a bit plain, slightly rabbity and prudish-looking. Later, when Kristen was achingly beautiful to him, his harsh initial assessment became hard for him to believe.

The problem, he realized, wasn't Hannah's looks.

Nate wandered back to the window, pulling up blinds all the way and squinting at the milky white sky. The problem was that he was not particularly interested in the kind of relationship he'd had with Kristen.

He thought of Juliet, the look on her face the other day right before she turned away from him. Then, later, Elisa. *Jesus.* When the others had left, she'd tried to kiss him. "I don't think it's a good idea, for either of us," he'd said, disentangling himself. She was upset, whether embarrassed or angry, he didn't know. He was both. He couldn't believe she was going to put them through this *again.* While she cried and dredged up old grievances Nate thought had been put to rest, he downed the rest of the wine and then started in on a bottle of vodka he'd bought her ages ago and found still lying on its side in the back of her freezer. An hour later, she was still going. He was by then so angry he was tempted to fuck her—just to shut her up. But he didn't. He had done his share to create this situation, and he knew it. After a while, they both calmed down, and he coaxed her into her bed. "Just so you know, it wasn't about sex," she said from under the covers. He was leaning on her bedroom door, about to slip out. "I just wanted to be held," she said. "I wanted, for a little while, not to feel alone. You know?" "I know," he said. As he picked up his messenger bag and closed the door to her apartment, he too wanted to cry.

Contrary to what these women seemed to think, he was not indifferent to their unhappiness. And yet he seemed, in spite of himself, to provoke it.

When he was twenty-five, everywhere he turned he saw a woman who already had, or else didn't want, a boyfriend. Some were taking breaks from men to give women or celibacy a try. Others were busy applying to grad school, or planning yearlong trips to Indian ashrams, or touring the country with their all-girl rock bands. The ones who had boyfriends were careless about the relationships and seemed to cheat frequently (which occasionally worked in his favor). But in his thirties everything was different. The world seemed populated, to an alarming degree, by women whose careers, whether soaring or sputtering along, no longer preoccupied them. No matter what they claimed, they seemed, in practice, to care about little except relationships.

The sun had come out from behind the clouds. A bead of sweat rolled down Nate's neck and was absorbed into the limp fabric of his undershirt. As he pulled off the T-shirt and tossed it to the ground, it occurred to him that maybe Hannah just wanted to be friends. Maybe he was being presumptuous?

He returned to his computer and tapped on the spacebar. When the screen came to life, he skimmed Hannah's e-mails again. Dickens this, child labor that. Even if she weren't offering outright to suck his cock, she was, in a sense, doing just that. It was in her careful, deliberate friendliness even as she disagreed, in the sheer length of her initial note. These e-mails were invitations for him to ask her out. If he went along, sooner or later his dick would wind up in her mouth.

To Nate's surprise, the thought of Hannah going down on him caused a slight flutter in his crotch. Interesting. Wearing only gray boxer briefs, he swiveled his chair away from his desk so he could stretch his legs and contemplate a blow job from her—for research purposes, to ascertain his level of interest.

He was distracted by an ominous crack in his wall, inching downward from the molding above his bed. Arrow-shaped, it seemed to point accusingly at the squalor below. Parts of his black futon mattress were exposed because the ugly black-and-white sheets, purchased at one of those "department stores" that sell irregular goods in not-quite-gentrified urban neighborhoods, were too small for the mattress and nightly slipped from its corners, tangling themselves like nooses around his ankles. His green comforter spilled over onto the floor, a corner dangling into an abandoned mug.

Because his apartment had no living room, his bedroom was his main living space. Someone had once told him that not having a couch was an effective way to get girls into bed, though that presumed bringing a girl here wouldn't immediately repel her. At the moment, his apartment was like an ungroomed human body, with fetid odors seeping out from dark crevices and unruly patches of overgrowth sprouting up here and there. Nate wasn't big on cleaning or on having someone else in to do it. It wasn't even that he didn't want to shell out the sixty or seventy dollars every couple months. It tormented his conscience to see a stooped Hispanic lady scrubbing his toilet; he held out until the level of filth was unbearable. When finally she came, Consuela or Imelda or Pilar looked at him with big frightened eyes, as if a person who lived this way was most probably dangerous. He didn't blame her. Casting about in his own detritus, Nate often felt ashamed. When there was an unexpected knock at his door, he felt as panicky as if he had to hurriedly pull up his pants, untie the pantyhose from around his neck, and hide the inflatable woman doll in his closet.

After a moment, Nate gave up on his "investigation." He climbed back into bed—to gather strength.

Jason would say to fuck Hannah if he wanted. But Jason—with his finger, Nate made a circle the size of a dinner plate in the air above his pillow—wasn't the right person to consult about this sort of thing. Although he was technically good-looking (and three—three and a half—inches taller than Nate), Jason lacked the good-with-women gene, the thing that Nate had come to realize he had, even back in the days when they mainly wanted to be his friend. For all his gonzo talk, Jason was prissy, almost squeamish when it came to physical contact. He would break off making out with a girl to tell her she should use higher-powered lip balm. "What?" he'd say, genuinely baffled, if you called him on this kind of thing. The belief that he was entitled to only what was most desirable was so deeply ingrained that Jason not only felt disgust at women's minor flaws but took for granted that his disgust was reasonable. "How could I make out with a girl whose lips were like sandpaper?" he would ask. Okay, Jason, fine. Alienate every single fucking woman who gives you half a chance. Go home by yourself and watch porn. *Again.*

Yet Jason gave Nate advice: "Stop overthinking, dude. You're acting like a girl." Nate hated, really hated, being told he thought too much. Jason wasn't the only one who said it: hippie-dippie types who romanticize the natural and the "intuitive" also prefer feeling to thought. But not thinking was a way of giving oneself license to be a dick. If Nate consulted only his "feelings," he'd fuck Hannah without regard for anything else.

Nate sniffed the air several times rapidly. Something was rank. It wasn't the apartment. It was his sweat, musty and animal. He leaped out of bed. For a while now, his stomach had been hissing and yowling like a pair of mating cats. He'd need to go get something to eat soon. Showering was a good idea, forward-thinking.

Afterward, he stood in front of his bathroom sink with a towel wrapped around his waist. In the steamy mirror, his body appeared to be in a state of panic. His nipples were pink Os that the wiry hairs on his chest, pointing every which way, appeared to be riotously fleeing. He had developed a small paunch that protruded sullenly above the white towel. His eyebrows, thick and bushy like the hair on his head, were in need of a trim. Elisa had introduced him to the concept of eyebrow grooming, just as she'd introduced him to many other aesthetic innovations, such as socks that didn't climb halfway up his calves. "Like tomatoes on a vine," she'd said, frowning at the ring where his socks ended and his leg hair came bounding out, wild with gesticulative fervor.

In the mirror, Nate tightened his jaw and pressed his lips together. The expression was suggestive of a cable news pundit taking a moment to consider his response to a thorny question: When will Al Qaeda strike next? Does Iran have sufficient quantities of plutonium for a nuclear weapon? Although Nate had never ceased to consider his nose problematic (bulbous and peasantlike, like that of the dissipated monk in a farce), his literary agent, a brash, jolly doyenne of the industry, had told him he had a telegenic face: intelligent without being priggish, attractive but not, she told him cheerfully, so attractive as to undercut his credibility. This last point Nate heard with slightly less good humor than she had delivered it with.

While getting dressed, he glanced at his laptop. He still hadn't decided how to respond to Hannah. As he pulled on a pair of brown socks, he noticed that one had a dime-sized hole near the seam. He rotated the fabric so the hole wouldn't catch his toe as he walked. Then it occurred to him: he was a man with a book deal. Recently, on the strength of that book deal, he'd even hired an accountant, a singular development in the life of a person who had for years come close to qualifying for the earned income tax credit. Other people, people like Jason and Peter, took for granted a much more exalted sense of what they deserved. Jason prized his well-being too highly to consign his foot to a hole-ridden sock. And Peter, struggling academic though he was, probably wore hand-sewn silk socks he special ordered from an aged Italian sock maker. Weren't Nate's feet entitled to the same consideration? Nate cast off the brown socks. He found another pair in his drawer.

Before leaving, he checked his e-mail one more time. Just mass mailings from various news outlets. Annoyed, he hid the mail program. In its place appeared the last Web site he had visited. A naked woman stood with her breasts pressed against a brick wall, her ass jutting out behind her as she tottered on tiptoes.

It had been a long time—nearly two months—since he'd slept with anyone. At a party the weekend before, he probably could have slept with, or at least fooled around with, a young editorial assistant, yet he'd decided at the last minute to cut out of there, to go home, by himself. Recently he had been undone by the mere dread of tears, female tears, theoretical future female tears that might never even come to pass. (Not every woman he hooked up with liked him!) In the midst of hooking up, all he needed was a moment's fleeting sobriety for his mind to conjure up the fraught, awkward scene that might ensue after one night or two or three, when he tried to skip out of her apartment without committing himself to seeing her again, not meeting her eyes because he knew she knew what he was doing. And then the call a few days later, when, in a studiously cheerful voice, willing herself to be optimistic, she'd casually suggest that they make plans to do something. Holding the phone next to his ear, Nate would feel not only bad but culpable. Had he led her on, acted just a tad more interested than he was out of some perverse combination of tact and strategy and unwillingness, for both their sakes, to ruin the moment? Once this happened—once his mind stepped out of the drunken, groping present to contemplate this bathetic, déjà vu–inducing future— the whole thing might just become . . . undoable. *Unbelievable.* This was Nate, whose unflagging hard-ons had formerly caused him to worry that he was a latent sex addict, liable to wind up arrested for masturbating in a Florida porn theater. But, instead of setting his mind at ease, his new sexual temperance filled him with another kind of anxiety. It made him feel like a wuss.

Fuck it, he thought as he grabbed his wallet and keys off the dresser. Maybe he should go ahead and fuck Hannah, as well as every other willing girl from Red Hook to Williamsburg. Maybe he'd start at the coffee shop, with Beth, the cute girl who worked behind the counter.

{ 4 }

The light was dim and reddish at the bar Hannah chose on Myrtle (once known as Murder) Avenue. The music, an early 1990s alternative album distantly familiar to Nate, wasn't too loud. A large exposed pipe ran along the ceiling. Tables were topped with old-fashioned desk lamps, an upscale touch in a place that was on the whole studiously dingy, a dark, heavily curtained wannabe dive. As Jason said, you can tell a real dive by its bathrooms. If they don't reek, it's no dive, no matter how much graffiti is on the walls.

Hannah arrived a few minutes after eight, apologizing for being late. "I have no excuse," she said as she slid onto the bar stool. "I live just down the street."

Nate caught a whiff of coconut shampoo.

While Hannah deliberated between a Chianti and a Malbec, with her head tilted away from his and her lips slightly puckered, Nate noticed that she looked a lot like a girl he knew in high school. Emily Kovans had been in the tenth grade when he was a senior. He could still picture Emily sitting outside on the strip of grass between the upper school building and the cafeteria. Her long, dirty blonde hair, shiny like Hannah's, but lighter and less auburn, had a bit of string braided into it, and she wore bunches of silver bracelets and rings with colorful stones. Her sandals sat beside her; her small feet poked out from under a long, flowery skirt. Nate hadn't generally been drawn to hippie chicks, but for months he nursed a tender longing for little Emily Kovans. Even the memory filled him with a strange, airy feeling.

Hannah murmured thanks as the bartender set down her glass. Nate asked her about the neighborhood.

"I love it," she said. "Of course, the last time my parents visited they saw a drug deal go down in front of my building." She smiled as she combed a hand through a smooth curtain of hair. "They're not so keen on it."

Nate continued to study her face for hints of Emily. The resemblance came and went, depending on the angle. After a moment, Hannah's smile began to falter. Nate realized it was his turn to say something.

"Mine dislike all of Brooklyn," he said.

Hannah cocked her head. "How come?"

With his thumb and forefinger, Nate rotated his glass on the bar. "Even the son of my mother's chiropractor lives in Manhattan," he said. He lifted his gaze to meet Hannah's. "And he, as my mother likes to point out, didn't go to Harvard."

Hannah tittered. "Nice."

"They get that I moved here when I was broke," Nate continued. "They can't figure out why I stay. I told them I like it. That all my friends live here. I told them that the whole publishing industry lives in Brooklyn."

Hannah was still smiling. "And?"

"And I fell into a trap. My dad says, 'See? It's just like I always told you—no one makes money writing. Except for Stephen King. And as far as I know he doesn't live in Brooklyn.'"

With a jaunty little toss of her chin, Hannah flipped the hair off her face.

Nate was back in high school. History class, Mrs. Davidoff's gravelly voice describing FDR's battles with the judiciary (Scott, covering his mouth with his hands and forming the words *Learned*

Hand every time she mentioned the courts) as Nate gazed out the window at Emily.

He couldn't remember when he'd last thought of Emily Kovans. In this dark bar, where the smell of cigarettes wafted from people's clothes and a pink neon martini glass glowed sullenly on the wall, he remembered not only Emily but what the world had felt like to him then. He could see what he hadn't seen at the time: how much his thrilling and uniquely angst-free crush had been bound up with youth, with the particular headiness of a Harvard-bound senior in the months of April and May—college and adulthood glimmering before him like rewards for good behavior. (How naively he had believed what his teachers and school counselors told him about the joys of college.) He didn't know then that the ability to feel the kind of sincere and unqualified longing he felt for Emily would pass from him, fall away like outgrown skin. His current self was considerably more louche—buffeted by short-lived, largely prurient desires, whose gratification he no longer believed would make him happy, at least not for long.

"I used to love this song."

Hannah's voice brought him back to the present. Nate listened. *Those sheets are dirty and so are you,* a vocalist intoned to cheerful, California-surfer pop accompaniment. It was from a different album than the one that had been playing before. He didn't recognize it.

"I listened to it all the time when I was in high school," Hannah said. "Freshman year of college, too."

She told him that she'd grown up in Ohio and had gone to a big public school, the kind where cheerleading was taken seriously.

She took a sip of wine. "You can imagine why punk seemed really cool."

"Ohio, huh?"

"Yup."

She ran a finger along the seam of a cocktail napkin she'd folded into a triangle. "Most of my friends from home are still in Cleveland. Maybe Chicago, if they were ambitious."

She said she'd gone to Barnard on a whim and wound up staying in the city for journalism school. "Nobody I know from home writes or does anything close," she said. "They have regular jobs, at banks and insurance companies. Things like that."

She rested her chin on her palm. A thin silver bracelet slid down her arm and disappeared into the sleeve of her sweater. "What about you?" she asked. "Did you feel remote from this world before you got here? Or is your family . . . ?"

Nate knew what she meant. "Did I tell you what my dad thinks of writing as a profession?"

Hannah had a warm, throaty laugh.

Nate was charmed by something he couldn't quite identify, a tone perhaps, a sort of pervading archness. Now that he was alone with her, he found Hannah to be a little different than he'd expected. He'd formed an impression of her as the kind of cheerful, competent person one likes to have on hand at dinner parties or on camping trips, but she struck him as more interesting than that.

"I definitely didn't grow up in a fancy intellectual environment," he told her. "But I was determined not to stay in Baltimore. I interned in D.C. one year, and I met kids whose parents were politicians and *Washington Post* columnists. I knew I wanted that, what their parents had. I felt like if they had it, there was no reason I couldn't."

Hannah leaned in, poised to be amused. "What was it you wanted exactly?"

Nate caught a glimpse of cleavage beneath the neckline of her loose-fitting V-neck T-shirt.

He toyed with a whiskey-coated ice cube inside his mouth, pressing it against his cheek. He didn't have a game plan for the evening. He hadn't even made a conscious decision to ask her out. The day after he'd gotten her e-mail, he'd simply been restless. In the same spirit that he flipped through stacks of takeout menus, he scrolled through the names on his phone, reaching the end—Eugene Wu—without seeing one that appealed to him. Everyone's shtick felt tired, overly familiar. Hannah offered, if nothing else, novelty. He wrote back to her suggesting they continue the conversation in person.

"What did I want?" he repeated. "You really want to know?"

"I really want to know."

He toyed with a whiskey-coated ice cube inside his mouth, pressing it against his cheek. He recalled old daydreams: a generically handsome, professorial man with a strong jaw sitting in a wood-paneled office, a line of students waiting out front and a beautiful wife on the phone. Sometimes, the office wasn't wood-paneled but chrome and glass, with a secretary who patched his calls through and a wall of windows opening onto the skyscrapers of New York. There was also a little hut in Africa where he'd dispense antibiotics and teach the villagers to love Shakespeare.

"On the one hand, to do something interesting," he said. "And on the other, to be admired for it."

Nate remembered something else: the belief that success was something that just happened to you, that you just did your thing, and if you were deserving, it was bestowed by the same invisible hand that ensured that the deli would have milk to drink and sandwiches to buy. Wouldn't that be nice? Nate sometimes envied people less clear-sighted, people so seduced by success itself that their enthusiasm for successful people was wholly genuine. Nate knew perfectly well when he was currying favor—or trying to—and he was more than capable of feeling dirty about it.

"I used to think—" he started to say. But he didn't know how to finish. He began fiddling with one of the buttons on his shirt. "It's more complicated than I thought, the whole thing—ambition and writing," he said finally. "More sordid."

Hannah laughed. "Sold your soul lately?"

"Only in bits and pieces."

"Lucky you," she said. "I've tried. No takers."

Like him, Hannah was a freelance writer, but Nate was pretty sure she wasn't as far along yet. He remembered that she was trying to get a book contract. "They'll come," he assured her.

When Hannah got up to use the bathroom, she walked with her shoulders hunched and her head tilted slightly down, as if she were accustomed to rooms designed for shorter people. She was wearing a cardigan sweater over her T-shirt and jeans tucked into boots, a style that had reminded Nate of Wonder Woman when girls started adopting it en masse a year or two earlier. Her outfit seemed almost deliberately unsexy. But she had what seemed like a nervous habit of pulling the two sides of her sweater more tightly closed, which had the effect of making her (not insubstantial) breasts more prominent. As she walked away, the long sweater prevented him from getting a fresh read on her ass.

"Want another?"

Nate swiveled his head. The bartender, a young woman, was staring at the place where Nate's face would have been if he hadn't been watching Hannah walk away. She wasn't so much pretty as stylish, with a slightly beakish nose and pouty lips. Her dark hair was separated into two long ponytails that hung on either side of her face.

"Yeah, thanks," he said. He nodded at Hannah's empty glass. "And another Chianti for her."

"She was drinking Malbec."

"Malbec then."

She leaned over the bar to scoop up Hannah's crumpled cocktail napkin. *Her* cleavage was frank and undisguised. The top few buttons of her plaid shirt were undone, and even though she had on a tank top underneath, it too was low cut.

She glided off to the other end of the bar. While he and Hannah had been talking, more people had filtered in; the room swam with their long, swaying shadows. A disco ball cast roving splotches of red and blue on the walls of the long, narrow space.

When Hannah returned, she glanced at her wine glass. "Thanks. Next round is on me."

Jason had a theory that girls who offer to pay on dates suffer from low self-esteem. They don't feel they deserve to be paid for; it's a sign there's something wrong with the girl. Nate wasn't sure he agreed. Sometimes, it was just nice, only fair—especially if you weren't Jason, who had never been short on cash because he was, Nate was sure, on the receiving end of significant income supplements from his parents or grandparents. Not that he and Jason discussed such things openly. No one in their circle did.

Jason would never go out with Hannah anyway. He was only interested in women who were very conventionally attractive, a preference he had once defended on the grounds of social justice: "If smart people only mated with smart people, class structures would ossify. There'd be a permanent underclass of stupid people. But when smart men mate with beautiful women, smart or not, you undermine that kind of rigid caste system. Dumb rich kids do everyone a favor by eroding any justification for birth-based privilege." Jason was a jackass. Still, the thought of his friend's appraisal—Jason would probably call Hannah a seven ("coworker material")—bothered Nate. He didn't like the idea of dating girls Jason wouldn't. That seemed wrong, since Nate was clearly the better person—more successful as well as more deserving.

This was not a helpful line of thinking. "What's your book proposal about?" he asked Hannah.

"What? Oh . . . *that*." She began to adjust the folds of her cardigan. "Class and college in America," she said finally. "It's kind of a history and analysis of a national obsession. The Ivy League as our own version of aristocracy." She nodded at him. "Nice shirt, by the way."

Nate looked down. He'd unbuttoned the top buttons of his Oxford. Underneath, he was wearing an old T-shirt. Just visible were the crimson-colored letters *A-R-V*. He laughed.

Fuck Jason. Nate was having a good time.

"When does your proposal go out?" he asked.

Hannah touched a hand to one of her earrings, a silver dangling thing. "I'm not finished yet," she said. "It's taking longer than I hoped."

Nate nodded. "It's a lot of work. You want to make it as strong as possible."

A moment later, he made a throwaway comment about how it's sad that so few people read these days. "It's hard not to feel irrelevant in a world where a book that does really well sells maybe a hundred thousand copies. Even the lamest television show about time travel or killer pets would be canceled instantly if it did that badly."

"Oh, I don't know," Hannah said, turning to face him on the bar stool. "I think it's vanity to want it both ways. You know, to want to write books because that's your thing but also to want to be treated like a rock star."

She held her wine glass rather elegantly if precariously by its stem, at nearly chin level. There was about her manner now a certain devil-may-care majesty not quite of a piece with her earlier timidity.

"Are you really so indifferent to the fate of books?" Nate asked. "You said the other night you love Nabokov. Wouldn't it be a bad thing if people stopped reading *Lolita*?"

"I think people who are likely to appreciate *Lolita* will read *Lolita*," she said, her expression challenging—flirtatious. "I don't care about the rest. I mean, I don't care what they do for fun."

It flashed through Nate's mind that Hannah's position wasn't very feminine. She sounded more like an aesthete than an educator, and women, in his experience, tended by disposition to be educators. He felt intuitively that she was paraphrasing someone else (a professor? Nabokov's *Lectures on Literature*?) and that the someone was a man.

"You're saying most people are philistines and no amount of education or cultural outreach will change that?" he asked.

She raised an eyebrow. "Not exactly. I mean, who even says 'philistine' anymore?"

"You know what I mean."

"I don't think they are worse people because they don't like novels, if that's what you mean."

"You don't?"

"They could be, I don't know, scientific geniuses or Christians who devote their lives to charity. I don't see why being a person who reads novels makes me or anyone else superior."

"Do you really mean that? Or are you just paying lip service to the idea because it's politically correct?"

Hannah laughed and her cardigan fell open, revealing the contours of her breasts through her T-shirt.

"I mostly mean it," she said. "I try to mean it."

Nate realized he was having a conversation with Hannah—that is, he wasn't going through the motions of having a conversation with her while privately articulating her tics and mental limitations. When it came to dating, his intelligence often seemed like an awkward appendage that failed for the most part to provide him with whatever precisely was wanted—dry, cynical humor; gallantry; an appreciation for certain trendy novelists—but nonetheless made a nuisance of itself by reminding him when he was bored. He wasn't bored now.

"Is it snobbery to think that *Lolita* is better than a television show about pets?" he persisted.

"It's snobbery to think you're a better person than someone else just because they don't happen to get off on the world's most elegant account of child molestation."

Her eyes flashed in the light cast by the disco ball.

Nate suggested they order another round.

As the bartender brought their drinks, he remembered something. "I didn't know you and Elisa were friends," he said.

Hannah looked at the black Formica bar. With her fingertips, she pushed her wine glass along its surface, guiding the glass like a hockey puck on ice.

"We're not really," she said. "To be honest, I was surprised when she invited me to her dinner party." She looked up. "Pleasantly surprised, I should say."

This made perfect sense. Elisa wasn't great at maintaining friendships with women. She often pursued new female friends eagerly, but from year to year there was high turnover. Nate didn't think it a coincidence that half the guests at her dinner party had been his friends rather than her own.

"What about you?" Hannah asked. "You and Elisa . . . ?"

"We used to date," Nate said quickly.

Hannah nodded. Nate nodded back. He suspected that Hannah already knew about him and Elisa. For a moment, they continued to nod at each other.

"It's great you're still friends," she said.

She suggested they go outside for a cigarette. Nate was glad for the chance to stand up.

It had been a chilly June; the outside air was cool. He and Hannah stood with their backs to the bar. Across the street, in a brightly lit new bodega, a table was piled high with pineapples and bananas. Its back wall was lined with stacks of Nature's Harvest toilet paper wrapped in bucolic green cellophane. Next to the bodega stood a shabby, glass-fronted insurance office.

Hannah sifted through her purse and passed Nate a pack of cigarettes. He held the yellow box at a distance from his body, like a teetotaler forced to handle a martini glass.

"I didn't know you smoked," he said.

She continued to dig through her bag. "Only when I'm drinking," she said. Her voice had become a bit singsong. She'd kept up with him drink for drink. That had surprised him.

The traffic light turned green. Two yellow cabs with their empty lights on shot past, hightailing it back to Manhattan. Hannah retrieved a plastic lighter. Nate watched as she put a cigarette in her mouth, cupping it with one hand and lighting it with the other. When she inhaled, her mouth formed a small O. Her eyelids drooped languidly. Pleasure seemed to ripple through her.

"You're like a junkie."

Without meeting his eye, she gave him the finger. The gesture surprised Nate into laughter.

"I just get so sick of the antismoking thing," she said. "It's so totalitarian."

Before he knew what he was doing, Nate leaned in and kissed her. He descended upon her so swiftly that she made some sort of girlish, giggling noise of surprise-cum-accommodation before she began kissing him back. He felt the cigarette fall to the ground.

Her mouth tasted mildly of ashtray. It didn't bother him. He liked that she found the antismoking thing "totalitarian."

He began walking her backward until her upper back touched the brick front of an adjacent building. He leaned into her, one hand on the wall above her head for support, as his other moved down to the curve of her hip. Then, abruptly, he felt a tightening in his chest, as his body reacted to a thought before it had fully formed in his mind. Without at all wanting to, he had begun to wonder whether this was a good idea, if the spontaneous affection he felt for Hannah weren't a signal that this was the last thing he ought to be doing.

No. The hand on the wall balled into a fist, scratching against the brick; the other found its way to where the small of Hannah's back dimpled and flared into her ass, which was indeed nice, *very nice.* Through his shirt, he felt her hand climbing up his back. He told himself to shut the fuck up and enjoy the moment.

Nate held his coffeepot up to the light. Its bottom half was a mash-up of pale brown stains with dark outlines, a fossil record of every pot of coffee he'd made since the last time he cleaned the thing. He began scrubbing the inside with a warm sponge.

After a little while, his thoughts turned to Hannah. He'd had fun with her the other night. That wasn't so unusual. He generally liked first dates. What was unusual was the impression of her he had taken away, one of both reasonableness and intellectual depth. Although it wasn't something he'd admit aloud, he often thought women were either deep or reasonable, but rarely both. Aurit, for example, was deep but not reasonable. Kristen was reasonable but not deep.

Sometimes he wondered whether he was a bit misogynistic. Over the years, various women had complained that almost all the writers he admired were not only dead and white but male. Although this was pointed out to him with prosecutorial glee, Nate didn't think it meant all that much. Women had faced systemic barriers to education and opportunity for most of history. They hadn't written as much.

What he didn't say—why aid the prosecution's case?—was that the kind of writing he preferred seemed inherently masculine.

The writers who impressed him most weren't animated by a sense of personal grievance. (They were unlikely to, say, write poems called "Mommy.") Of course that wasn't an accurate characterization of all, or most, writing by women. Still, the fact was that when he read something he admired, something written today—fiction, nonfiction, didn't matter—there was about an 80 percent chance that a guy wrote it.

He thought women were every bit as intelligent as men, every bit as capable of figuring out how long it would take for train A to crash into train B if the two were moving toward each other at an average speed of C. They were as capable of rational thought; they just didn't appear to be as interested in it. They were happy to apply rational argument to defend what they already believed but unlikely to be swayed by it, not if it conflicted with inclination or, worse, intuition, not if it undercut a cherished opinion or nettled their self-esteem. So many times, when Nate had been arguing with a woman, a point was reached when it became clear that no argument would alter her thinking. Her position was one she "felt" to be true; it was, as a result, impermeable.

Even self-consciously intellectual women seemed to be primarily interested in advocacy, using intellect to serve a cause like feminism or the environment or the welfare of children, or in the interpretation of their own experience. Take Aurit. She was one of the smartest women—people—Nate knew. She was clear-sighted and original, and not, like a certain type of woman, intellectually timorous; she was comfortable challenging conventional wisdom. But her subjects—Zionism, Judaism, patriarchy—stemmed from her life. When she tried to do more abstract writing, the result was comparatively thin. She wasn't interested in international relations or Middle Eastern politics; she was interested in growing up in a crazy, conflicted Israeli family that functioned like a two-headed monster, liberal socialism and primitive tribalism everywhere bumping up against each other. In other words, she was interested in being Aurit. And that was fine. But it was a difference.

Of course, if you pointed this out to Aurit, she'd be furious. And for Aurit, the fact that something made her feel bad was reason enough to reject it. She didn't even like it when Nate mentioned things outside her ken. If he got to talking about philosophers she hadn't read—which is to say, most of them—her face would grow taut, tight-lipped, with a pulsing around the temples, as if Nate, in talking about Nietzsche, were in actuality whipping out his cock and beating her with it. Even Jason—and Aurit was surely a better person than *Jason*—was far more fair, intellectually.

And that was Aurit, who was brilliant. If Nate was honest, he also thought that women as a general category seemed less capable of (or interested in) the disinterested aesthetic appraisal of literature or art: they were more likely to base judgments on a thing's message, whether or not it was one they approved of, whether it was something that "needed saying."

By now, the coffeepot was reasonably transparent.

Nate set it aside and inspected the coffeemaker itself, examining the caked-up grounds that clung to it. When he turned the lightweight plastic apparatus upside down, compartments came flapping open, swinging wildly on plastic hinges. The machine began to slide from his hands. Crouching quickly, he caught it, hugging it against his stomach. He set it in the sink and began jabbing at it with the limp sponge.

When he finished, he left the coffeemaker to dry on the counter next to the carafe. As he walked to his bedroom, he took off his damp T-shirt. The air in the bedroom was thick with a restless gloom as wan late afternoon sunlight mostly failed to pierce a thick blanket of clouds. A light layer of condensation dotted the windowpane and gave the room a sealed, hermetic feel.

He felt a wave of affection for his little garret. Its particular brand of squalor appealed to him on a basic level. Real squalor was not this but the barren utilitarianism of his parents' suburban condo, where various unseen appliances hummed monotonously like hospital monitors. Or it was the plasticky faux-elegance of

the ranch house they'd lived in when he was growing up, an immigrant's version of the American home, culled from TV shows of a
generation earlier, with artificial flowers and a living room that was
rarely used. Even the tasteful, high-end prewar co-ops that some of
his friends had purchased in recent years, with their baby gates and
wine refrigerators (wine refrigerators!), were to Nate more squalid
than his little apartment, which was, in contrast, the home of a
person who lived for things other than the sort of domestic and
domesticating coziness that almost everybody seemed to go in for.

He'd done some cleaning. That helped. Nate's day-to-day life
was characterized by bursts of productivity punctuated by downward slides into lethargy, loneliness, filth, and gloom. His bad
moods had a self-perpetuating quality. He hadn't a job or consistent routine to stop the slough, and his general recourse—drink—
tended to be helpful only in the short-term. Still, Nate had never
really been incapacitated by his moods, not for more than a day or
two, and ever since his book had sold, his low bouts had been both
less frequent and less severe. If his relative success hadn't exactly
made him happy, it had, on average, made him less unhappy.
Today the approach of a deadline had spurred him out of inac-
tivity. He had a book review to write, and write fast. In preparation, he'd launched into hyperproductive mode. In the past several
hours, he had gone for a run (five miles in forty-one minutes and
thirty-eight seconds), mailed an overdue RSVP card to a friend's
wedding, dropped off his laundry, and ventured to the grocery
store, where he'd bought beer, milk, three Celeste Pizzas for One
(on special), and an ample supply of Total Raisin Bran and Lucky
Charms (his breakfast of choice was a bowl of Raisin Bran followed by a "dessert" of Lucky Charms).

Feeling entitled to a moment of repose, Nate pulled his bedroom window open and leaned outside, breathing in mouthfuls of
moist air. His apartment's two windows—one in the bedroom and
one in the kitchen—were the only features that a yuppie might
covet. South-facing, they let in lots of sunlight, and from the sixth

floor, the view was decent—if you looked above the roofs of the neighboring buildings and into the skyline rather than at the street below. But his block was more dear to him for its ugliness. Its proximity to fashion—appealing bars and restaurants, coffee shops, his friends—was convenient, but its unfashionableness was what he loved. At the corner, a tire repair shop's yellow awning read, "Open 7 a.m. to - -" On Sunday mornings, the storefront church across the street drew a crowd of black women whose calf-length skirts clung to their legs in the breeze.

Such vestiges of the neighborhood that this had once been were especially touching now. In his own building, people who had lived for many years in dark, mildewy apartments with cracked linoleum tiles watched from their doorways as surrounding units were gutted, then redone with gleaming new windows, hardwood floors, and stainless steel appliances—and a different type of tenant, the kind who paid several times the unrenovated rent. Nate had moved in a few years before the current wave of ubergentrification; that his own apartment had hardly been improved was a source of pride.

Still, like the newer arrivals, he only superficially lived among the poor. They walked the same streets and rode the same subways (the buses, however, were largely ceded to the underclass), but the two groups might have existed on different layers of the earth's atmosphere that only from a distance appear to be on the same plane. A store called National Wines & Liquors, Inc., where both liquor and cashier were enclosed behind bulletproof glass, was not actually a competitor to the much newer Tangled Vine, which specialized in organic and local wines and exhibited the work of area artists at its Thursday-evening tastings. Even at the bodegas, where all paths in fact converged, the different strata of residents rarely handled the same merchandise. Nate reached for the *New York Times* (which they had only begun to stock relatively recently—when he first moved to the neighborhood, he had to walk to Park Slope to get it), while the cabbies and construction workers grabbed the *Post*. He bought six-packs of beer to take home rather than single-serving forty-ounce cans. Only the cash that passed back and forth across the counter touched all hands.

From the street, Nate heard the guttural throb of an unmuffled engine, followed by the screech of brakes. Nate could hear shouting but not the words as a pair of young women crossed the street in front of a stopped car.

He thought again of Hannah. After they'd kissed the other night, they'd gone back inside the bar and finished their drinks. He walked her home, and they made out a little more in front of her building. Even in retrospect, he found her—her easy willingness to contradict him, her unfeminine but not at all unflattering outfit—strongly sexy.

But he should cool it. He had a bad habit of initially zeroing in on one or two things he liked about every new girl he found himself interested in, as if to justify his attraction. This one (Emily Chiu) was not just beautiful in a petite and delicate way he found particularly compelling, but he and she had also had, on first meeting, an intense and bonding conversation about being children of immigrants. That one (Emily Berg) was funny. A third was dazzlingly impressive in a certain sane and competent and businesslike way. (Yes, early on, he'd thought maybe he would fall for Juliet.) But early impressions were unreliable. Juliet, for example. She prided herself on being a person who had the courage to speak her mind, who called things as she saw them, but after a few dates, Nate had felt *aggressive* was perhaps a more fitting description. She was a repository of truths both obvious and rude: a friend should go on a diet, a struggling coworker should accept his limitations and stop trying to be "some hotshot reporter he's not cut out to be." She rarely asked Nate questions about himself except to wonder if he'd been to such-and-such restaurant and to marvel when the answer was no. They couldn't seem to hit on many topics of mutual interest; Nate spent much of their time together affecting interest in subjects that held only moderate appeal for him: personnel issues at the *Wall Street Journal*, the vast number of business reporters who lacked a solid understanding of business, the relative merits of whole grains versus refined ones. Also, the high percentage of New York men who were, according to Juliet, intimidated by successful women.

There was nothing *wrong* with Juliet—Nate had no doubt that many other men found her desirable—but it had been obvious that he and she weren't right for each other. Still, when he realized that he had been mistaken in his initial impression—of Juliet or of any of the women he dated—he invariably felt like a jerk for having seemed, initially, more enthusiastic than he would turn out to be.

Of course, these women ought to have listened when he told them he wasn't looking for anything serious. But on a certain level, it didn't really matter if it was stupid of them. Ethical people don't take advantage of other people's weakness; that's like being a slumlord or a price gouger. And treading on weakness is exactly what dating felt like, with so many of these women—with their wide-open hopefulness, their hunger for connection and blithe assumption that men wanted it just as badly.

Based on what? On whom?

The outside air began to chill his bare chest. Nate edged back inside, ready now to begin. The book he was reviewing was written by a left-leaning Israeli novelist. In the past few weeks, he had read all of the author's earlier works and other related books but not, until today, the book he was actually reviewing. He quickly grew absorbed in the text, rarely looking up as the sun sank behind a jagged gray horizon of six- and seven-story buildings. He was already growing disenchanted with the text—it was rife with sentimentality, its politics were pat and self-congratulatory—when he realized he was squinting to read in near darkness; he switched on his desk lamp. He finished the book around midnight and began making notes. Several hours later, he turned out the lamp to take a short nap. He was back at his desk, bent over his laptop, when the first hint of salmony orange began tingeing the darkness outside. He walked to the window. Even the storefront church looked austere and dignified in the dawn mist. *The city doth now, like a garment, wear / the beauty of the morning, silent, bare* . . . He vowed to pay attention to the sunrise more often, when he hadn't been up all night. Which is what he always said when he'd been up all night.

By midmorning, the sun was brilliant, hard and glinting. What clouds remained were reduced to stringy tendrils kicked around by the breeze. Nate shut his blinds to block out the glare. By then, he was laying out the heart of his argument. While he shared the author's outrage at certain developments in contemporary Israel, there is, he wrote, an inevitability about the country's rightward shift. When a nation claiming allegiance to liberal-democratic principles is founded on explicitly nationalistic grounds, the contradiction is bound to come back to haunt it, even if nationalism is dressed up as Zionism. Because Israel was from its birth riddled with evasion—like the United States, in terms of slavery—there isn't firm ground on which to argue with the growing number of Israelis, particularly Orthodox Jews and Russian immigrants, who dismiss liberal principle as mere weakness. Eventually, a true reckoning, not a mere hand-wringing, will be necessary. (Aurit, Nate realized, was going to hate the piece.)

Every once in a while, as he considered a phrase or conceived a counterargument, he stood up to pace, clasping his hands together behind his head as he roamed his apartment's small perimeter. In the late afternoon, he opened his blinds and looked outside. Cloud shadows passed so quickly over the tops of buildings that he had the sensation of being himself in motion.

It was early evening when he sent off the completed review. He felt like he'd emerged from some dark, intimate chamber. He showered and then left a trail of wet footprints as he walked back to the bedroom with his towel around his waist, his cheeks tender and pink from the razor. He resisted the urge to e-mail his editor with a few minor corrections that had come to him as he shaved.

Instead, he picked up three cereal bowls, two mugs, an empty can of Bud Light, an orange ceramic plate full of pizza crusts, and several greasy paper towels. It didn't seem like much detritus for twenty-four hours of pretty much straight work.

Sitting at a nearby sports bar an hour or so later—his hunger sated, and his interest in the Yankees game on the flat-screen TV waning as their lead over the Orioles grew larger—he felt a yearning to see Hannah. He wanted to talk to her about his review, which he was largely happy with. He'd made a glancing reference to Nabokov that he thought she would appreciate.

He toyed with the idea of calling her to see if she wanted to join him. But that was ridiculous. He was practically falling asleep on the bar stool and felt drunk after a single beer. There was also the fact that he was wary of starting something.

He left a few dollars under his glass and nodded good-bye to the bartender, a gruff, muscular guy about Nate's age. As he emerged onto the street, a deliveryman on a bicycle whizzed by, causing him to step back. It occurred to him how ridiculous he was being, how *neurotic*. He was making way too big a deal out of this. He made up his mind to call her the next day.

The restaurant they met at was one of those bistro-style places, with red leather banquettes and a black-and-white tile floor, a decor inspired by *Casablanca* and French colonialism. When Nate arrived, Hannah was leaning on the bar with a drink in her hand. A ray of sunlight from the window cut a stripe on her slender back and then, as she turned to face him, across her chest and shoulders.

She was dressed in a fitted blouse and a narrow skirt that wasn't exactly a miniskirt but didn't quite reach her knees. She looked nice. "You look nice," he said.

"Thanks."

Nate tugged at his T-shirt, only to notice that his gut jutted out a bit in the front. He sucked it in and saw that his jeans, fashionable ones that Elisa had picked out for him, sagged from too much time between washings. His pockets, full with wallet and cell phone and keys, bulged unattractively.

"Expecting rain?" Hannah asked.

She nodded at the umbrella he was carrying and tilted her head toward the window. Bright blue sky was visible above the rooftops.

"Maybe I got bad information," he said.

He told her he'd been given the umbrella that afternoon by the girl who worked at his regular coffee shop. Someone had left it weeks before.

"Can't beat free, right?" he said. Then he squinted at the umbrella. It was oversized, with a purple-and-white canopy. "Well, it is maybe a little conspicuous."

When Hannah smiled, the Emily Kovans resemblance struck him again.

"I hope I'm not turning into my dad," he said after they'd been seated at a table in the back of the restaurant. "He likes to brag about how he never has to buy dishtowels or washcloths because he just takes the ones they give you to use at the gym."

Hannah asked what his parents were like—"when they aren't stealing household items, I mean."

Nate immediately wanted to take back what he'd said. He didn't like the derision that habitually crept into his voice when he talked about his parents, as it had the last time he'd seen Hannah, when he'd mocked their attitude about Brooklyn. Seeking to entertain, he too often found himself making fun of their middle-class immigrant ways: their un-PC remarks about minorities, their defensive, almost childlike assertions of superiority over Americans and the American culture that they so often misread, their too-naked concern with money and frequent suspicion that people intended to take advantage of them. All of those stories were true, but when Nate trotted them out something didn't translate. He felt more empathy for his parents than his tone implied, and he suspected that what he was really trying to say was "I'm different— I'm of Harvard, of New York, not of these rubes." This had been especially bad with Elisa. Perhaps he never forgave her for the remorseless quality of her laughter when he'd told her about how, long ago, they had oohed and aahed at the furniture in the window of a rent-to-own store. They had said the cream-and-gold lacquered coffee table and the bed with the swan-shaped head-board reminded them of Versailles.

"They're not so bad," he said to Hannah as a waiter dropped down menus. "They're nice people."

She was more forthcoming. Both her parents had grown up on the west side of Cleveland ("the wrong side"). Her father was the brainy son of an autoworker who'd wooed and won a popular girl, Hannah's mother, when they were students at Kent State. "She literally was homecoming queen," Hannah said. Her father was a corporate lawyer. She had two older sisters, both well-adjusted and successful, "more midwestern" than she was. They were married; one lived in Chicago and the other in Cleveland. East side.

When they finished their cocktails, Nate ordered a bottle of wine.

"What a proper meal this is turning into," Hannah said. "Very WASPy."

She told him that she'd visited a friend's Cape Cod beach house a couple weekends before. She described the house's wine cellar and the bedroom she'd stayed in, which opened to a screened-in porch that led to the beach. She said she couldn't quite believe she was there. Nate remarked that the rich enjoy being hospitable to smart, artsy types. They need an audience of people discerning enough to truly appreciate all they have. It helps them to enjoy it more. Hannah suggested that he was being overcynical. Her friend's family had money. Why should that make her hospitality more suspect than other people's? Nate said that he didn't mean to insult her friend. He was talking on a macro level.

"Oh, a *macro* level," Hannah said. "I see then."

Nate was immediately embarrassed. Why had he used that word? He had a bad habit of getting carried away, unwittingly revealing his pedantic precision, the academic cast of his mind. In writing, he could cover this up with deceptively casual language, a hard-won conversational tone that often eluded him—in conversation. In contrast, Hannah had about her, in spite of her slight shyness, an air of cool; it was in her amused, ironic, slouching posture, her default arch tone, even in the careless way she held her drink.

"I mean—" he began.

"I know what you mean," she said. "I just think any overarching theory based on a misconception, or an exaggeration, is bound to be off."

She smiled innocently.

Nate laughed. Why did women say men were threatened by women who challenged them?

The waiter poured the last of the wine into their glasses. When they left the restaurant, the buildings and sidewalks were slick and shiny. Nate wiped a large drop of water from his forehead. Hannah looked indignantly skyward.

Nate waved the umbrella victoriously. "I knew it!"

Hannah rolled her eyes, with the sort of mock exasperation women like to affect when they're flirting. As she got under the umbrella with him, her hip brushed his. She was so close Nate could almost feel her hair on his face.

"Let's go to your place," he said.

Hannah's expression became searching. She pushed her hair back behind her ear and pulled back from him as much as she could while remaining under the umbrella. She seemed to be considering the question very seriously. Nate was tempted to touch her, but something, perhaps the fact that she was busy "considering," held him back, as if to do so would constitute an illegitimate interference, like jury tampering.

"I want to see your book collection," he said instead.

"Gag me."

"I'm taking that as a yes."

The cab he hailed seemed to move like a bumper car on the shimmering street, spewing water as it slid to a halt about twenty feet in front of them. They ran toward it, laughing drunkenly as they scrambled into the backseat. The small, balding driver grumbled when they told him they were going to Brooklyn and, muttering into his cell phone in a South Asian language, banged a fist against his doily-covered steering wheel. This also struck them as extremely funny.

Crossing the bridge, Nate turned to take in the Manhattan skyline behind them. The chains of white lights lining the cables of the other East River bridges were like dangling necklaces beneath the brightly lit towers, a fireworks display frozen at its most expansive moment. The view, familiar and yet still—always— thrilling, in combination with the plastic smell of the taxi, made him feel almost giddy. He had sort of a Pavlovian reaction to cabs. He rarely took them except on his way to bed with a new girl.

Hannah's apartment was right off Myrtle, on the second floor of a walk-up building. Nate waited near the door as she circled the living room, switching on a succession of small lamps. The space lit up only gradually, as she got to the third or fourth one. Its wood floors were scuffed, but the walls were a very clean, stark white with original moldings at the top and very few pictures on them. One wall was lined with bookshelves. On the other side, a half-wall separated the kitchen from the living area. The room seemed unusually spacious for New York, in part because it had relatively little furniture. There was, Nate noticed, no couch. No television, either.

Hannah gestured for Nate to sit near the window where two mismatched upholstered chairs sat on either side of a small, triangular table. On the windowsill sat an ashtray.

A breeze blew through the window screen. The air, heavy with moisture, smelled clean and fresh. Hannah put some music on a record player, a stoned-sounding guy on a guitar, his voice ethereal and sad.

"I thought you were into punk," Nate called as Hannah walked toward the kitchen.

"What?"

She turned around. "Oh, right . . . the Descendents. Different epoch."

Epoch. Nate liked that. The music wasn't bad, either, though it reminded him of Starbucks.

The breeze rustled up the air again. Nate leaned back in his chair, experiencing the pleasant sensation of being outside time and normal life. It was officially the first day of summer, and for a change his mood was in sync with the calendar. He felt free and heady, the way he had when he was young, when summer was a long possibility, a state of mind, not a period when work was slow because editors were on vacation.

Hannah moved around the apartment with dizzy cheer, pivoting shakily on the balls of her feet every time she changed direction. On her tiptoes, she retrieved a bottle of bourbon and two thin, blue-rimmed glasses from a kitchen cabinet. She placed the glasses on the little table next to Nate and began to pour the bourbon, holding the bottle high above, like a bartender, the long, amber stream glimmering in the lamplight. As she moved from one to the other, she spilled a little so that a dotted trail of liquid linked their drinks.

Nate picked up the one closer to him. "Cheers."

He noticed some blue-and-white china crockery on Hannah's countertop. "That reminds me of stuff my mother brought with her from Romania," he said. Though he'd brushed her off when she asked, he'd wanted to tell Hannah about his family ever since she told him about hers. She wasn't at all like Elisa.

He told her about the redbrick ranch house they'd lived in

when he was growing up. After school, Nate and his mother would sit at the table, a Formica thing, in their sunny 1960s kitchen and drink tea—this was before his mother worked full-time. He remembered stirring in sugar cubes from a porcelain bowl with delicate fluting around the rim and gold-plating inside. Because the little bowl was one of the few things she'd been able to take with her when she and his father emigrated, it was regarded in their household as a treasure of inestimable value. In retrospect, he told Hannah, it was striking how his mother conveyed something aristocratic about her life in Romania, something very Old World and romantic, in spite of the poverty, the anti-Semitism, the dreariness. "She still has some of that European snobbery," he said. Over tea, she had told him that children there don't read "this, this"—and she'd scrunched up her nose—"*Encyclopedia Brown*." She gave Nate a copy of *Twenty-Thousand Leagues Under the Sea*. It was also over tea that she first spoke to him about the novels she loved. She'd tossed her long, honey-colored hair over her shoulders as she explained how Anna Karenina simply couldn't take it anymore. Mr. Karenin was a good man, but his kind of goodness—and Nate could remember the way his mother grasped his arm with a bony hand as she said this—his kind of goodness could be stultifying. The rim of her teacup had been stained with red lipstick.

"I guess she didn't have many friends back then," Nate said quickly, feeling suddenly that he'd said too much. "She and my dad are really different."

Hannah nodded.

Nate was relieved that she didn't question him about his parents' marriage, and what, as an adult, he had come to think of as his mother's somewhat self-serving interpretation of it.

He got up to peruse her bookshelves. "You've got a lot of Greene."

She had mostly old paperback editions, their titles printed in modish 1960s fonts above Graham Greene's name.

"I did grow up Catholic," she said.

She had padded to his side, bringing with her the sweet scent of bourbon. Nate turned and kissed her.

A moment later, she pulled away. She looked at the ground. Lamplight glinted on her long eyelashes, giving her face a languorous, abandoned aspect. The next words out of her mouth spoiled the effect. She told him that he was welcome to stay over if he wanted, but she'd rather not . . . well, you know. She bit her lip. "I probably should have told you before you came over."

Nate stepped back as if he'd been reproached. He wished she wouldn't look so nervous. He wasn't some brute who was going to fly into a rage because she wouldn't fuck him. He looked toward the kitchen.

"That's fine," he said. "Whatever makes you comfortable."

"It's just . . ." Hannah's eyes shot from the ground to his face. "Just that we don't know each other that well. That's the main thing."

Nate began to crack the knuckles of his right hand with his left one. He'd live without sex, but he really didn't want to get drawn into a long and uncomfortable conversation about it.

"Hannah," he said. "I get it. It's not a problem. Really."

He must have sounded impatient because she seemed to bristle. She flashed a quick smile. "Great," she said.

Nate put his hands in his pockets. He began looking at the bookshelf again.

"Just tell me one thing," he said after a moment. "Does this have to do with your being Catholic?"

For an instant, Hannah looked taken aback. Then she raised an eyebrow. "No. It has to do with your being Jewish."

Nate laughed, a real and hearty laugh. When he stopped, the awkwardness he'd felt the minute before was gone. Hannah, too, seemed to have gotten past her irritation. She leaned against the bookshelf, looking amused. Nate touched her cheek.

"If it really is all right, I'd like to stay."

She nodded. "It's all right."

{ 6 }

Nate and Aurit had a go-to restaurant. Located halfway between their apartments, the place was moderate enough in price to suit him but not so devoid of culinary pretension as to be unacceptable to her. It was also, somewhat mysteriously, as far as Nate was concerned, hip. Certain medieval touches—dark walls, tall wooden benches, torchlike lighting from iron ceiling fixtures—had a themey-ness that could easily have gone the other way.

Nate arrived first and was seated at a table near the kitchen.

Aurit showed up ten minutes later. She scanned the room. "I don't know why you'd want to sit here when there are booths free," she said.

Nate glanced at the time on his phone.

After they changed tables, Aurit began telling him about a party she'd gone to the weekend before. "I overheard these two ugly, completely lame guys talking, at full volume, about which woman there they most wanted to go home with. I wanted to be like, 'Do you not understand that people can hear you? Do you imagine that you are speaking in some exotic tongue?'" She shook her head. "Did I mention they were ugly?" Another night, she'd had dinner with a friend, who "is otherwise nice but has this habit that drives me up the wall. You remark on anything, and she starts *explaining* it to you, as if you

are totally clueless. You say, 'So many people are moving to the
South Slope these days,' and she says, 'Well, it's more affordable
than other neighborhoods,' and you're like, 'Thanks, and by the
way, I'm not an *idiot*.'" Nate laughed. "It's actually amazingly annoying," Aurit continued. "But it's also kind of tragic. She must alienate
people all the time without having any idea why."

Their waitress had white-blonde hair with dark roots and elab-
orately tattooed forearms. After she took their orders, Aurit asked
Nate what had been going on with him. He told her about his
book review, leaving out aspects that he thought she'd find objectionable.

"Hmm . . . uh huh, uh huh . . . That's interesting."

She seemed far more interested when he mentioned that he'd
gone out with Hannah again. She leaned in. "Do tell."

Nate described their date, surprising himself by how effusive
he sounded. Aside from that one tense moment, it had been a really
nice night.

"That was, when, Wednesday? Thursday?" Aurit asked. "What
about since?"

She was buttering a slice of bread. When Nate didn't immediately answer, she put the bread down. "Nate. Have you not called
her?"

Sometimes Aurit reminded him of the Lorax, the glowering
little Dr. Seuss character who climbs out of tree stumps to hector
the greedy capitalist. Like the rook in chess, she was short and big
on top, with large maternal breasts and broad shoulders that were
like the top of a triangle, tapering to petite hips that she liked to
show off in close-fitting jeans. She had dark skin and attractive,
small, almost gaunt features. Her black hair was short, but it had a
baffling quality of not seeming short, or at least not striking Nate
as androgynous the way short hair sometimes did. It had lots of
wispy layers so that there was always plenty of it around her face,
longish pieces that fell almost to her chin and were always tum-
bling forward and being pushed back behind her pixieish ears.

Aurit had long ago explained to Nate that the two of them had never gotten romantically involved because when they started spending time together, he was going out with Elisa. By the time he and Elisa broke up, it was too late: he and Aurit were already in the "friend zone." For a long time Nate had believed this because Aurit said it so authoritatively and it sounded plausible and he was in the habit of thinking that Aurit had more insight than he did into such things. Until it occurred to him that he'd never been attracted to her. He had been perfectly capable of finding women other than Elisa attractive. She just wasn't one of them. This realization had scared him a little. He'd nearly been convinced of a false account of his own feelings merely because Aurit was so emphatic. He was also relieved. Aurit had a way about her. If she had wanted him for her boyfriend, there was a good chance that, attraction or not, he would at this very moment be carrying her shopping bags.

The waitress arrived with Nate's burger. She brought Aurit a large plate of shootlike leaves and then retreated quickly, as if to forestall any additional requests.

"What is that?" Nate asked Aurit.

"You haven't answered my question," she said. "How many days has it been?"

Nate leaned forward for a better look. "Is it arugula? Bamboo shoots?"

"Four? Five?"

"Clovers of some sort? Do you get anything else with it?"

"Do you get off on making her wait? I'd just like to know what men are thinking when they pull this sort of thing."

"Are you on some kind of extreme diet? Should I be worried?"

Aurit was too proud of her slim figure to let that go. "It's a *pizza*."

"Maybe where you come from, they call that pizza. Here in the United States, we call it a grassy knoll."

"For your information, it's a prosciutto and arugula pizza." Aurit used her fork to rake off a section of shrubbery. Nate saw that underneath there did appear to be a fairly standard pizza

with cheese and prosciutto. She set down her fork, and the arugula layer fell back in place.

"So . . . *Hannah?*"

Nate began pouring ketchup on his burger. "Why are you bent
on giving me the third degree? I only went out with her twice. I
haven't even slept with her."

In Hannah's bed that night—*four* nights ago, as a matter of
fact—they had alternately talked and engaged in what felt like a
prolonged and fairly innocent bout of adolescent groping. It had
been pretty nice, though. Perhaps he was getting old, but there had
been surprising consolation in the knowledge that he was not going
to wake up with the chalky feeling of embarrassment that often
followed drunken hookups. In the morning, he'd hung around for a
while. He walked home along a street he particularly liked, with
mansions set back from the sidewalk. Built by nineteenth-
century industrialists, the mansions had degenerated, in the mid-
twentieth century, into single-room-occupancy boardinghouses.
Recently, the neighborhood had turned again, the SROs converted
to upscale apartment buildings. On that summer morning, the
shady street was lush and fragrant. Nate had felt unusually cheerful
as he made his way home.

"So, what?" Aurit said. "It doesn't matter? You can just do
whatever you want because you didn't slip your thing in?"

For god's sake.

Nate put the bun on his burger, picked it up with both hands,
and took a bite. He winced as some ketchup squirted out from
under the bun and onto his hand. He could feel Aurit's eyes on
him. She had a very particular way of staring. She was still except
for a slight widening of her pupils, which managed to suggest that
her mind was hard at work, trying to accommodate some new and
terribly damning truth she'd just discovered. Nate looked intently
at the bun of his burger, imagining he was on a gently rocking sail-
boat. The only thing on the boat with him was a big, juicy cheeseburger. The idyll was short-lived.

"It's just great, Nate," Aurit said. "While writing the book review of the year and whatever the hell else you've been doing, you happen to go out with a girl a couple times, spend the night with her—who cares if you actually slept together?—but for you, it's out of sight, out of mind. As soon as she's not in the room, you're back in Nateland. What about her?"

Nate wished he'd called Jason instead. You could eat a fucking cheeseburger with Jason.

He eyed the opposite wall, where some kind of menacing lancelike weapon was on display.

"I think it would be a little strange if Hannah were all that invested after two dates," he said finally. He felt that responding at all was giving in to Aurit, but he didn't see an alternative that wouldn't set her off even more. "I don't think you're giving her much credit."

"Two dates that you said yourself went really well," Aurit said. "So she's thinking about you and wondering if maybe she imagined it, maybe she was crazy for thinking you guys had a lot of fun, because otherwise why haven't you called?"

"Maybe she's thinking I haven't called because I've been busy. Which happens to be true. Or maybe she hasn't thought anything because *she's* busy. She's a smart girl and has stuff going on. I really don't think you're being fair to her, turning her into this sad creature who is sitting around waiting for my call. Maybe she doesn't even like me much." Nate arranged his features into a smile he hoped was charming. "Shocking as it may seem, not every woman finds me irresistible."

Aurit plucked a single sprig of arugula from her pizza. "No offense, Nate, but you sound really defensive."

He dropped his burger to his plate.

Aurit began making dainty little strokes with her fork, clearing away tufts of salad greens from the surface of her pizza. She cut a tiny triangular bite. She was about to put it in her mouth when she spoke instead.

"The thing is, Hannah seems cool, like someone you might actually like." Aurit spoke in a deliberately soothing tone, wagging the fork with the pizza across the air above her plate. "You usually pick the wrong women. You see someone pretty, and you come up with a reason to find her interesting. Then, when it doesn't work, you act like the problem is 'women' or 'relationships,' instead of the women you choose . . . Like that ditzy Emily, who might as well have been sixteen years old."

"Which Em—?" Nate started to ask. But she obviously meant Emily Berg. He closed his eyes for a moment. "I really don't want to talk about this," he said when he opened them. "Can we please drop it?"

He knew that Aurit would interpret his reaction as "defensive." He was not defensive. He was frustrated by her (unjust) dig at Emily and her facile analysis of his personal life—delivered, naturally, with unwavering certainty of tone.

"Fine," Aurit said.

"Thank you."

Nate took a bite of his burger.

"It's just that I don't understand," Aurit said. "It seems to me that when you do meet someone suitable and you have a nice time with her, you should tread carefully, take it seriously . . ."

Nate felt like he was the subject of a highly sophisticated type of torture in which the torturer listens to your objections, even seems sympathetic, and then continues to administer electric shocks.

Aurit had once espoused a system of categorizing people that he found useful. She said some people were horizontally oriented, while others were vertical. Horizontally oriented people were concerned exclusively with what others think, with fitting in or impressing their peers. Vertically oriented people were obsessed only with some higher "truth," which they believed in wholeheartedly and wanted to trumpet no matter who was interested. People who are horizontally oriented are phonies and sycophants, while those who are entirely vertically oriented lack all social skill—they're the ones on the street shouting about the apocalypse. Normal people are in the middle, but veer one way or the other. Nate was tempted to tell Aurit that she had been sliding into tone-deaf vertical territory.

"Can we please talk about something other than dating?" he said instead. "I mean, there is a lot more in the world than who wants to date whom and 'Oh my god, have you called her yet?' We might as well be on fucking *Sex and the City*."

Aurit raised her eyebrows and tossed her head back, chin up in the air, so that, diminutive as she was, she seemed to be looking down at him from some kind of perch. "Oh, I'm sorry, Nate. I forgot how deep you are. Silly me, I can't believe I bored you with my girlish prattle. Maybe we should talk about nuclear disarmament."

How did he come to be in the wrong? Nate didn't know what happened, but now there was no help for it.

"I'm sorry," he said. "I'm just tired."

"Whatever." Aurit shrugged. "It's fine. I just hate the way so many men treat 'dating' as if it's a frivolous subject. It's boneheaded." She smiled frostily and tilted her head in his direction, lest there be any uncertainty about who exactly she was calling boneheaded. "Dating is probably the most fraught human interaction there is. You're sizing people up to see if they're worth your time and attention, and they're doing the same to you. It's meritocracy applied to personal life, but there's no accountability. We submit ourselves to these intimate inspections and simultaneously inflict them on others and try to keep our psyches intact—to keep from becoming cold and callous—and we hope that at the end of it we wind up happier than our grandparents, who didn't spend this vast period of their lives, these prime years, so thoroughly alone, coldly and explicitly anatomized again and again. But who cares, right? It's just girl stuff."

Classic Aurit. Take whatever she was personally interested in and apply all her ingenuity to turning it into Something Important. It never occurred to her that there was anything more worth caring about or thinking about than upper-middle-class women's

search for happiness, in the cozily coupled, fatally bourgeois sense
of the word. She thought if she could just convey *how much this
meant* to women—articulate it once and for all—the world would
come around. Never did she realize how limited her perspective
was, how insensible she was to all that fell outside the sphere of
her own preoccupations.

"I don't know," Nate said in a tone intended to be placating even
though he was about to disagree. "It's easy to overstate the importance of whatever you're personally affected by. It's like mothers
whose kids don't test well think standardized tests are the worst
thing in the world. I just don't think dating is quite the scourge of
modern life you're making it out to be. I don't think it's that big of
a deal. It's just one aspect of life and certainly not the most important one."

"No, you wouldn't think it was that big a deal, would you?"
Aurit mused. Her voice was no longer pissy but thoughtful, as if
she were a naturalist classifying a homely new species. "Next time
you feel lonely, my guess is that you'll think it's a pretty big deal.
But as long as you're feeling calm and collected and you're able to
focus on your book and your highly intellectual, oh-so-important
book reviews and whatever else, I can see why it reinforces your
sense of self to act as if you're too deep to care much."

Nate was amused. "I'm boneheaded is what you're saying."

Before Aurit could respond, the waitress approached. "You
done?"

"Uh, *no*," said Aurit, who was poised to bite into a forkful of
pizza.

The waitress scowled and walked away. Aurit's nostrils flared.
Bad service was a source of great frustration for her, an irritant
that might at any moment set her off, like science was for the
medieval church.

"When she comes back, I'm going to tell her there was too
much arugula on my pizza."

"Hi guys."

Both Nate and Aurit looked up. Standing beside their booth was Greer Cohen—Greer Cohen whose book advance had aroused such animosity at Elisa's dinner party. Greer was smiling gaily, as if running into them was the best thing that had happened to her in weeks.

Seeing Greer wasn't such a surprise, really. In Brooklyn, everyone turned up everywhere. Though the parts of Brooklyn congenial to people in their demographic had expanded dramatically in a widening web of faux-dives and mysteriously hip restaurants, to Nate the place seemed never to have been smaller, so dense was it with people he knew.

"I thought it was you guys," Greer said, in her girlish, vowel-elongating lilt.

Greer's manner of speaking was not merely flirty but flirty like a teenage girl with bubblegum in her mouth and a tennis skirt and tanned thighs.

"We heard about your book," Aurit said. "Congratulations. That's a great opportunity."

Greer smiled and shrugged a little bit, as if to say "Who me?" As though the book deal had simply fallen into her path, and she'd barely taken the time to notice it. Now, *Greer* was a horizontally oriented person. Even her sexiness had something artificial in it. Some people reeked of sex; Greer, in spite of a tomboyish style of dress, reeked of a manufactured sexiness more tartish than slutty, like a pinup girl from the 1940s.

The last time Nate had seen her, at a party, they had gotten into a long and tiresome argument. Nate had said that in a certain sense, and only in a certain sense, it's harder for men to say no to sex than it is for women. When a woman says no, nobody's feelings are hurt. Men expect to be shot down. But when a man says no, the woman feels as if he's just said she's fat and undesirable. That makes him feel like a jerk. Greer thought he was being a sexist asshole who didn't think women should hit on men and refused to grasp the seriousness of sexual harassment and rape. Nate thought she was

strident and unsubtle, either deliberately misunderstanding him for
effect or simply unable to grasp the distinction he was making.

Now, however, as Greer described her book to Aurit ("it's partly
a memoir about my teenaged misadventures but also sort of an art
book with photos and drawings and song lyrics"), he was entranced
by her cleavage. She began nodding vigorously at something Aurit
said. Greer's breasts, snug in an olive-green tank top, were his favorite size, just big enough to fill a wine glass (a red one). When he
tried to meet her eye, they were squarely in his line of vision.

"It was good to see you guys," she said finally. "I'll see you later."

Nate watched Greer's heart-shaped ass bounce in tandem with
her jaunty little stride as she turned the corner into the bar area.

"Did I tell you Hans is coming to town in a couple weeks?"
Aurit asked.

Aurit's boyfriend Hans was an affable German journalist who
wore circle-rim glasses and sometimes struck Nate as more of a
prop of Aurit's than a figure in his own right. His existence in her
life, however semimaterial given the long-distance nature of their
relationship, gave her authority to lecture others about their
romantic lives.

Nate was still contemplating Greer's ass. "That's nice."

Sunlight sloped through the windows of "Recess, open 7 a.m. to 9
p.m." (no ungrammatical dashes there), and collected in glittering
eddies of dust underneath chairs and behind display counters
laden with coffee beans.

Whatever his feelings about gentrification, Nate appreciated the
abundance of coffee shops that had lately appeared in his neighborhood. It was hard to believe that, once upon a time, the pale,
bleary-eyed freelancers and grad students who gathered daily at
places like Recess would have typed away all by themselves, grimly
holed up in rooms of their own. "Sometimes you just want to see
another human being, you know?" Nate had tried to explain to his

dad, who clucked about the waste of money and extolled the virtues of the home espresso machine. Nate didn't tell his father that working at Recess prevented him from looking at porn, easily boosting his productivity enough to earn back what he spent on coffee.

Nate had chosen Recess on the dual bases of proximity (a block and a half from his apartment) and Beth, who worked behind the counter. He met Beth's eye now. She smiled and looked questioningly at his computer. He shrugged and made a face, as if he were trying to work without success. In fact, he'd been scanning an e-mail from a national office supply retailer. It seemed there had never been a better time to buy a home copy machine.

In truth, he was having a hard time focusing. His mind kept drifting. Personal stuff. Hannah.

He had not called her the day after his dinner with Aurit. He had waited until the day after. The extra day was sort of a fuck you to Aurit. She had been a real pain in the ass that night. But . . . calling Hannah seemed like a good idea. It was the right thing. He had spent the night with her. She'd made him breakfast. On the phone, Hannah's voice, contra Aurit's dire prognostications, had not been full of tearful reproach, even though he had taken—gasp—six days to get in touch with her. She sounded a bit sleepy at first, her consonants not quite distinct. After a pause just long enough to alarm him, she said, "Sure, let's do something."

Since then, Nate had been busy making revisions to his review of the Israel book and filling out a long, detailed questionnaire from his publisher's marketing department. The fact that in February his book was going to be in stores across America was beginning to feel more real. When he thought about seeing Hannah, he felt a mild sense of anticipation. Not only did he like her, but they'd be on good behavior with each other, not touchy and peevish the way he and Aurit had been the other night, but the new-person versions of themselves: attentive, polite, and good-humored. This iteration felt to Nate like not just his better self but his real self, except that, like a skittish housecat, this magnanimous and engaged person materialized only occasionally, under very particular circumstances. New people brought him out. So did the receipt of good news. Nate had never been more tolerant of other people than in the weeks following the sale of his book.

But he and Hannah were soon going to move past new-person territory. That whole bit about not wanting to sleep with him, about not knowing him well enough, made clear that she wasn't looking for something casual. He had tacitly agreed to her terms when he asked her out again. (This was the real reason he'd hesitated about calling her, which he would have told Aurit if she hadn't immediately begun haranguing him.) After the other night, it would be harder, more awkward, for him to tell Hannah he wasn't looking for anything serious. Also something had stopped him from delivering such a line either time they'd gone out. He had sensed it would be, for Hannah, a deal breaker—that she wouldn't bat her eyelashes and say, "I'm not looking for anything serious either" the way a lot of girls did, as if this were part of the challenge of dating. Each time he'd been out with Hannah, he had found himself reluctant to say anything that would throw water on their fun, flirty dynamic. No doubt he'd feel the same hesitation tonight.

Outside, the brakes of a bus squealed. Nate set his elbows on the table and rubbed his temples with the heels of his palms. Aurit wouldn't have been any help anyway. She didn't understand (she willfully refused to understand) that in the little mental space where she stored fond images of cuddling, Nate saw himself struggling to read in bed while some alien presence breathed moistly at his side and asked if he would be ready to turn off the light soon. He imagined gazing in farewell at his apartment as he closed the door and left for some girlfriend's place "because it *is* more comfortable, isn't it?" He saw touchy-feely sex and dutifully concealed porn and movie nights—well-reviewed indie comedies on Netflix, or maybe, if they were feeling especially ambitious, a documentary.

Nate was devoted to humanity in the abstract—to human rights, equal opportunity, the eradication of poverty. He was, in theory, sympathetic to the limitations of others: you had to take into account root causes, the punishing handicaps posed by stupidity, an infantilizing consumer culture, et cetera. But when he trained the microscope more closely, human beings took on, in his view, an increasingly unattractive cast. They appeared greedy, grubby, hypocritical, self-deceiving. Sex, the sexual impulse, was a lure—an illusion engineered by an animal organism that sought only to perpetuate itself. The makeup, the hairstyling, the waxed limbs and gym-toned musculature, the urbane posturing and protective veneers of youth and achievement and even kindliness— weren't they all merely cover for the pathetic, grasping "I" underneath? It wasn't misogyny. Men laid similarly bare, stripped of pretensions, would be equally unappealing. But Nate wasn't both attracted to and repelled by men. Men didn't force him into contact with their least attractive aspects. The cesspools of need, the pockets of self-pity, the most vain and ugly of the thoughts that roiled Nate's male friends as they lay awake in the middle of the night remained largely hidden from him, like foul odors sucked into the exhaust fans of modern bathrooms.

But maybe he was kidding himself. Certainly abstract ideas hadn't prevented him from enjoying many other things he found philosophically objectionable, such as consumer goods from China, jet travel, Tori Amos. If he wanted to be in a relationship, no argument would change his mind. Perhaps the salient issue was not *why* but simply *that* he didn't want to be in a relationship. His work fulfilled him, and his friends provided all the conversation and companionship he needed.

Was this so wrong? Why do women get away with pathologizing men for not wanting girlfriends? There are entire Web sites written by supposedly smart, "independent" women who make no bones about calling such men immature at best, assholes at worst. Nate wanted to argue, if only he had someone to argue with, that women want to be in relationships because on a gut level they don't like being alone. They aren't noble, high-minded individuals, concerned about the well-being of the nation or the continuity of the species. They simply swoon at images of cooking dinner together, of some loving boyfriend playfully swatting their ass with a dishtowel while the two of them chop vegetables and sip wine and listen to NPR (preferably in a jointly owned prewar apartment with an updated kitchen). And that's their prerogative. But what right do they have to demonize a counterpreference? If Nate's idea of a nice dinner involved hunching over his kitchen table with a Celeste Pizza for One and a copy of Lermontov's *A Hero of Our Time*, who is to say that his ideal is worse?

Nate knew what the response would be: maturity, it's what adults do, et cetera, et cetera. But the same women who are so quick to call men immature when they don't order their lives around snug domestic relationships would never call a woman immature because she doesn't want to pop out babies. They resent the hell out of anyone who implies there's anything wrong with *her* choice. No, women only pull out that talk about mature adulthood when it's convenient, when they want grounds to resent some poor guy who doesn't want what they want. It isn't merely inconsistent: it suggests an unwillingness to take seriously other people's preferences. As such, it's a tyrannical impulse. And somebody really needs to say so.

Out the window, sunlight reflected off the windshields of parked cars. Nate finished the last of his coffee and set his mug down.

The problem was that no matter how unfair they are, no matter how insanely bent on domestication, Nate was unable to entirely discount the claims of women—those he slept with or might sleep with. If only, like those cock-swinging writers of the last century—Mailer, Roth, et al.—he could see the satisfaction of his sexual desire as a triumph of spirit, the vital and needful assertion of a giant, powerful virility whose essence was intellectual as well as erotic. Either Nate was less poetic, unable to rise to such dazzling heights of imaginative fancy, altogether more pedestrian and earthbound—and no doubt he was—or he was less self-dramatizing. He didn't, couldn't, adorn his basic desire to get off, *to squirt his stuff*, with such baroque justification; so it was harder to see why his desire ought to trump everything else, trump women's post-coital unhappiness. The dreary voice of Kant, insisting on impartiality, and the egalitarianism of the age—every person equal as a claimant to empathy—were, for him, lodged too deep.

"You okay, Nate?"

Nate turned to look at Beth's broad, friendly face, the kind of face that retained a whiff of the well-loved girl who hung pictures of horses on her bedroom wall. "You've got this big scowl going on," she said.

"Just focusing, I guess. How're you?"

She waved the rag she was holding. "Oh, you know, another day in paradise."

On his table, Nate's cell phone began to vibrate, flailing like an overturned cockroach struggling to right itself. When he reached for it, Elisa's face stared back at him. In the screen shot, her pouting lips were painted a deep red, and her blonde hair was messily pulled back from her face, with just a few stray clusters falling forward. The flash had flushed her skin, and the angle was askew because she had taken the picture herself with an outstretched arm. She still looked beautiful. But if she had been trying to endear herself to him by setting this picture to appear when she called, she'd miscalculated. The implicitly accusing expression on her face always filled him with dread. He hit DECLINE.

Then he opened a new message window on his computer. "I'm sorry," he wrote to Hannah. "I got swamped with edits on the Israel book review. I'm not going to be able to get together tonight."

He added a few pleasantries, signed his name, deleted his name, replaced it with the letter *N*, deleted the letter *N*, and finally settled on the lowercase *np* as signifying just the right amount of intimacy.

As soon as he pressed SEND, relief washed over him.

7

The next night an acquaintance of Nate's was reading from his new book at a bookstore in Lower Manhattan. Nate arrived early, in part because his friend Mark had called and asked Nate to hold a seat for him.

Jason showed up soon after and took one of the seats next to Nate's. "Hey, man, you're coming out after, right?" Jason's voice dropped to a stage whisper. "I've got gossip. I can't tell you here."

Nate had once suggested to Jason that there was something prurient in the intensity of his interest in other people's lives. In response, Jason had paraphrased Bellow paraphrasing Allan Bloom: "When I do it, it's not gossip. It's social history."

Nate's friend Eugene Wu arrived and started to sit on Nate's other side. Nate was about to tell Eugene that the seat was saved for Mark. He stopped himself. Eugene was a suspicious, bilious sort of person. He was apt to take even this as a personal affront. There was something fey about seat saving anyway.

Mark walked in just as the author was being introduced. Nate waved his arms and made a sad clown face, trying to suggest that he had done his best. The author began to read. Nate tried to focus, but Mark distracted him. Forced to stand beside a rack of foreign periodicals, he visibly shifted his weight from one leg to the other while glowering in Nate's direction. Nate tried to avoid looking at that part of the room.

Afterward, a large group walked to a nearby bar. On the way, Nate wove in and out of various conversations. The thrashing of car horns and the whoosh of traffic lent a pleasant urban ambience as the group ambled along Houston Street in the humid dusk. Nate felt a wave of contentment. Sometimes he remembered how lonely he had been in high school and the early part of college, even in his early years in New York, after he and Kristen had broken up. Surrounded by friends and reasonably established, he felt lucky. He knew he'd been lucky.

The inside of the bar was scarcely populated, with only a few diehards watching baseball on a flat-screen TV and another group gathered around a pool table. But its large, gravelly backyard was packed. Standing under a scraggly tree, Nate got into a conversation about payday loans with a girl named Jean. She was writing an article about urban poverty.

"I had to take out a couple over the years," Nate told her.

"Really?" she said. "You're not exactly the target demographic."

Jean wore cute faux-librarian glasses and had a cheerful abundance of curly hair that bounced energetically when she nodded, which she did frequently, as if to offer encouragement to the person she was speaking with.

"I had some bad years," Nate said. "I couldn't always afford to wait two months for some magazine to get around to cutting me a check."

As Jean groaned in sympathy, Nate started to roll up his sleeves. He wished he'd worn a T-shirt. The warm air was thick, a physical presence.

"Can I ask why you didn't just get a cash advance on your credit card?" Jean asked.

"I forgot my PIN," Nate said.

Beyond Jean's shoulder, he noticed a very cute brunette. She was talking to a girl he knew slightly, and she seemed to be looking in his direction. The gravel beneath Nate's feet crunched as he shifted position to get a better view.

"Seriously?" Jean asked.

Nate turned back to her. "I figured if it was one I knew by heart, it would be too tempting," he said. "I made up a random one, wrote it down, and lost the paper."

Jean pushed her glasses up on her nose. "Did you think about retrieving it from the credit card company?"

"I kept answering the security questions wrong."

"You're kidding," Jean said.

"My mother's Romanian. Her maiden name has a lot of vowels. I may also have been drunk. They didn't ask so many questions at the payday loan place."

Jean had a guffawing laugh, which, while not particularly feminine, seemed uninhibited and heartfelt at least.

She was someone Nate liked, someone he was always happy to see at a party. Yet he inevitably ran out of things to talk about with her. She knew a lot about obscure bands and indie actors, but she almost never spoke personally or volunteered an opinion not in accord with right principles and liberal piety. After a while, this unwavering good nature left Nate tongue-tied.

The brunette went inside the bar.

Nate patted Jean on the shoulder. "I'll be just a minute."

The girl—and she was indeed young enough that Nate didn't think calling her a girl was politically incorrect—was leaning over the bar, the soles of her feet rising out of her ballet slippers as she stood on her tiptoes.

Nate took the place next to her. "I think we're with the same group. You were at the reading, right?"

She sank back into her shoes. She came up to, maybe, his chin. "Yeah," she said warily.

"So you'll help?"

"With what?"

Nate pointed with his thumb at the bartender. "You stand a better chance of getting his attention than I do."

Her name, Nate soon learned, was Cara. She had graduated from Stanford a couple of years before. She had since gotten a master's degree in writing from Johns Hopkins. She was interning at an august literary magazine and looking for a full-time job. She was open to something in publishing or magazines, but it was hard, in spite of her degrees.

"It's really awful that there aren't more full-time jobs for people in our field," she said. "I'd even take an assistant-level job."

To Nate, this sounded more than a little entitled. But she was young, and it was no easy task—getting started professionally— and she seemed sweet. It helped also that she was model pretty.

They returned to the backyard with their drinks. It had grown appreciably darker. One by one, windows in the surrounding tenements switched from black to yellow as inside lights were turned on.

Nate and Cara leaned against a brick wall. She let on that she knew who he was, that someone had pointed him out to her and she'd read something of his, or at least heard it spoken of. Naturally Nate was flattered. She told him she lived in the South Slope with roommates. She liked it. She had never felt like a true Californian. And Baltimore? No, she couldn't say she much liked it, even if it was Nate's hometown.

After a couple of minutes, Nate found himself eyeing Jason and Eugene, who were huddled together on the other side of the patio. He still hadn't heard Jason's gossip. He was growing a little bored, but he wasn't ready to extricate himself. Cara was petite. Her dark hair fell in long, loose waves around her face, which was delicate and appealing, with well-shaped lips and thick but shapely eyebrows. Olive-skinned, almost Persian-looking, she wasn't just good-looking; she appeared intelligent, soulful. And clearly she was smart. She would have to be. It was impossible—*wasn't it?*—that she could actually be as boring as she seemed.

What began, after a few more minutes, to irritate him was that she didn't even attempt to be engaging—made no effort toward wit or color in her replies. Only an attractive young woman would take for granted a stranger's interest in the minutiae of her life.

Perhaps she was shy.

He asked how she liked the internship. Her answer was not unintelligent, yet it struck Nate as academic and passionless. At another point in his life, he would have felt a challenge in her stiffness—that air of complacent acquiescence rather than enthusiasm. He would have tried to get her to say something inflected with feeling, if only gossip or a complaint about her coworkers. He would have done so in part because he wouldn't have wanted her to come away thinking *he* was boring. But he didn't feel motivated to make that kind of effort. He thought of Hannah and felt a pang—of something, he didn't know what. He didn't choose to examine it.

He was getting ready to slip away when he found himself telling Cara that he pretty much had no choice but to live in New York because he was a terrible driver. "I couldn't live in a place where you need a car to get around."

"Did I hear you mention driving, Nate?"

Mark approached, holding out his hand to Cara. "Hi, I'm Mark," he said, his tone self-effacing, as though he doubted whether someone of Cara's importance would want to meet him. That was part of his shtick.

"Did Nate tell you his theory about driving?" Mark asked.

He sounded bored, lugubriously so, as if he'd told this story a hundred times and was sure she wouldn't be much interested.

Cara shook her head no.

"Well, let me tell you. He's a *terrible* driver."

She smiled. "So he said."

She already looked more animated than she had when Nate had been alone with her.

A magazine editor, Mark was thin, slight, with tidily cut dark hair; he was always neatly dressed in business casual. He looked at first to be almost trifling, but he had cultivated a dry, everyman persona that he played to great advantage.

"He says—" Mark began, his voice thick with disapproval. He broke off, as if overcome, and started again. "He told me and our friend Jason a couple years ago, when we were on a road trip, that his brain is like a Mack Truck."

Cara's smile was now a little confused. Nate was shaking his head, but he began to laugh, partly in embarrassment, partly in amusement. He'd nearly forgotten this story. He had to give Mark credit as far as Cara went. Mark was bringing far more panache to the job than he himself had.

"Nate says that good drivers are people who can put their brains on cruise control. Their brains are like small Japanese cars. He, on the other hand—well, his brain is this huge roaring engine that needs to be constantly monitored. It's too powerful to be put on a default setting where it can seamlessly change gears or pick up on a stoplight ahead."

Mark shook his head reproachfully. Cara, hands on her hips, pivoted toward Nate, for some sort of defense.

Nate tried to look endearing. "What he's not telling you is that those two—he and Jason—were on my case all weekend about my driving. I had to say something."

Mark frowned at Nate before turning back to Cara. "Personally, I thought it was extremely elitist. I was very offended."

"Also," Cara said with sudden energy. "I think trucks *do* have cruise control. I mean, airplanes do, right? Autopilot? Why not trucks?"

"Smart!" Mark turned to him. "What do you have to say to *that*, Nate?"

Nate held his hands up. "Whether they do or not, I concede. It was a stupid theory."

He had finally started having fun.

When Cara left to use the bathroom, Mark turned to him. His face was submerged in shadows cast by the tabletop umbrellas. "I think she kind of dug me, but if you're—I mean, you got there first."

"Go for it," Nate said. He meant it. He still felt a little bad about the seat-saving incident. That wasn't the main thing, though. "We didn't have much to say to each other."

Even in the semidarkness, Nate could see that Mark looked surprised. "I'd do her no matter what she has to say."

"Best of luck."

Nate went inside for another drink. While he waited at the bar, shrill peals of laughter rang through the beery air. Nate felt sticky, also rather glum. It was hard to say why. The night simply seemed empty, almost pointless.

When the bartender handed him his drink, he finished it too quickly. It was his third or fourth, and consumed so fast, it was enough to nudge him from buzzed to drunk. He ordered another immediately.

He awoke the next morning to embarrassing recollections— going up to Jean and putting his arm around her, for one. "So, what is your deal?" he'd asked. "Who are you, really?" She'd laughed, but he had felt her edging back from him. He wasn't, he had realized even through the haze of his drunkenness, coming off as bold and daring, only buffoonish. And sweaty. He also had a distinct memory of passing Cara on his way out. There was something pitying in the way she looked at him.

After four Advils, a large iced coffee, and the passage of several hours, he felt significantly better. In the early afternoon, he called Hannah.

"Well . . . ," she said slowly, when he asked her to reschedule the date he'd canceled. "It's not really a great week for me." Nate played dumb, cheerily suggesting the following week. Hannah said she was busy then too. But there was a slight laugh in her voice that gave him confidence. "What about coffee at ten a.m. on Tuesday?" he asked. "You can't be booked for ten a.m. on a Tuesday, can you? It's not like you have a job or anything—by which I mean no offense. I don't have one either."

She conceded that she might have a free evening that she'd forgotten about.

When he arrived in midtown, at Bryant Park, Hannah was already sitting with a book at a small green café table, lightly thumbing the edge of the page as she read. Her hair, lighter than usual in the sunlight, fell forward, on either side of her face. She glanced up from her book as he approached. When she stood up, the spindly metal chair she had been sitting on rocked on the cobblestones.

"Hi."

Nate felt uncharacteristically nervous as they smiled at each other.

"I brought you something," he said, reaching into his back pocket. He pushed a copy of Graham Greene's *Travels with My Aunt* across the table. "I noticed you didn't have it," he said, looking not at Hannah but at the book.

"Oh! That was nice of you. Thank you."

The concert they had come to hear wouldn't begin for another few minutes, but the park was full of activity. Across the wide swath of grass was the carousel, and to their left, in an old-timey booth, a "sandwich artisan." A few kids, maybe six or seven years old, were playing on the grass nearby. "Look!" cried a little Asian girl in pigtails and a white dress. She was speaking to two blond boys, twins. The little girl leaped from a chair, her skirt billowing up from her split legs. The boys didn't even pretend to care. They ran off, and she followed, pigtails flying behind her. "Wait!"

Back in the 1980s, the sociologist William Whyte said that you couldn't have found a more villainous-looking crew of dope dealers than the ones who hung out at this park if you hired them. Nate told Hannah that, and she laughed.

"Did you write something about him?" she asked. "I seem to remember reading something. It was . . . good."

Nate was pleased she'd read it. The piece was one he liked, about the materialism of the age.

The musicians began to play. Hannah turned to face them. She had suggested the free evening concert. "They're going to play some late Beethoven quartets that are really wonderful," she'd said. Nate was less keen on these kinds of performances. He thought there was something grating about upper-middle-class New Yorkers' love of high culture in city parks. It was so full of self-congratulation, as if a few lousy performances made up for systemic economic inequality. "Uh huh," Hannah had said. "You know you sound like one of those, uhm, *philistines* who doesn't see the use in art, right?" That had shut him up.

Now, Nate began to wonder what Hannah had really thought of his essay. There had been something coy, something withholding, in the way she'd said it was good.

The music stopped. Nate nearly started clapping before he realized it was only the end of the movement. Hannah whispered that the next one would be slower. Nate nodded meaningfully. When the musicians resumed playing, he closed his eyes to filter out distractions. Hannah had told him that these quartets were bridges between the classical and romantic periods. That was interesting. But the crisscross slats of the metal chair were gnawing the flesh on the back of his legs. It seemed as if the chair had been designed back in the 1980s to keep the dope dealers from getting too comfortable.

He was contemplating some of the wording his editor had suggested for his book's catalog copy when people abruptly started clapping. As soon as he realized, he began banging his hands together with great zeal.

He failed to convince. "I take it you aren't a classical music lover?" Hannah asked.

Nate let his hands drop. "I took piano lessons as a kid. I guess they didn't take."

When they left the park, he and Hannah were swept into a mass of people exiting an office tower. All around them briefcases bumped against thighs; cell phones clicked shut. They passed a subway entrance, and the crowd began to thin. They walked west, toward the setting sun.

Hannah told him that she played the cello through college. She asked what kind of music he liked.

"Honestly, I'm kind of an idiot about music," Nate said. "I usually wind up liking what people tell me is good." He glanced at her, a little shyly. "I liked the music you played at your apartment the last time."

Shielding her eyes from the sun with her hand, Hannah turned to him. "Elliott Smith? I wouldn't have guessed."

"What can I say, I like sad music."

She tossed her hair over her shoulder. In the sharp light, it glinted red-gold. "Interesting."

It was one of those cheerful dusks. Puddles that pedestrians would have had to make long arcs around the day before had dried up and disappeared. Convivial laughter rose from sidewalk cafés and echoed through the streets, which, in the fading heat, seemed to unfurl at the edges and relax into evening. People moved jauntily as if choreographed. As he and Hannah stepped from the sidewalk into a street, Nate touched a hand to her lower back. He felt glad to be exactly where he was.

8

The following week he brought Hannah to his apartment. The bulbs were out on his stairwell's third and fourth floors; he and Hannah climbed in near darkness. His door, when he pushed it open, emitted a piteous, multisyllabic whine.

"I hope you're not expecting much."

Hannah peered into the kitchen. Then she walked down the narrow hallway toward his bedroom. Nate trailed behind her. He had tidied in preparation for her visit, but his apartment cleaned up was unconvincing, like a career hoodlum dolled up for court by his lawyer. The rag he had used to wipe his desk and dresser sat in a heap on the windowsill. One of his dresser drawers, too crammed to shut all the way, had fallen wide open. He had hastily made the bed, but a triangle of garish black-and-white sheet poked out from beneath the comforter.

"It's nice," Hannah said slowly. She pointed to the wall above his desk. "I like that picture."

Nate had found the print, El Greco's *View of Toledo*, on the street. The angry blue sky and hilly green cityscape had appealed to him. He'd fixed the frame with duct tape.

"Thanks."

He came up behind her and placed his hands on her jeaned

hips. Leaning his head against hers, he closed his eyes and breathed in the scent of her hair.

After the concert the Friday before, they had gotten dinner and gone back to her place. Nate had stayed the rest of the weekend. On Saturday, they went out for breakfast and then walked around her neighborhood. They drank Bloody Marys at a well-air-conditioned Moroccan restaurant that was nearly empty between the brunch and dinner shifts. Afterward, he tagged along on her evening plans with a couple of her girlfriends from journalism school, skipping a party that he didn't much want to go to anyway (half the people who would be there he'd seen at the reading the week before). Sunday afternoon, Hannah practically pushed him out of her apartment. "I totally intended to work on my book proposal this weekend: If I don't get on it, I'm going to be writing health news my whole life." She had a regular freelance gig writing a weekly roundup of health news for the *Times*'s Web site.

Now, she relaxed against him, her hips pressing into his. Nate began to get hard. In the course of the weekend he'd spent at her apartment, she had rescinded the ban on sex.

He hadn't exactly changed his mind about wanting to be in a relationship. But now that he'd met Hannah, now that he found that he liked her, he couldn't see any other way to be. It was with the pleasure of cynicism defied that he had come to believe that she was in fact different from other women he'd recently dated. Though she came from the same sort of upper-middle-class background as most people he encountered socially, she seemed to him to be sort of savvy, not as blinkered as many of the women he knew—there was nothing precious or sheltered-seeming about her. Smart rather than "smart," she was neither timid nor humorless in her thinking. She didn't venture opinions with a question mark at the end. He'd looked up her work online and was surprised he hadn't noticed her stuff more before. Her reviews and essays were lucid, well-informed, and often wonderfully acerbic. She had a voice of her own, an energetic moral outrage tempered by irony and warm, self-aware humor. And she was nearly as well read as Jason and Peter and even Nate himself. (To be honest, that had surprised him.) She was fun, too—quick to smile and to laugh.

She also had a way of insinuating that she hadn't entirely made up her mind about him that he enjoyed. He felt as if she was taking his measure, according to some exacting standard of her own devising. He respected her for it. He felt instinctively that her standard was a good one, that she was, in some essential way, *good*. Not just in the sense of being kind to orphans and kittens, nor in the do-gooder sense in which Kristen had been good, but good in some other way. Honest, fair-minded, unsnobbish.

A gunshotlike crackle cut through the room. Fireworks, no doubt left over from the Fourth of July holiday several days before. The rumbling soon gave way to the shriek of car alarms and shouts from the street below.

"Sorry about that," Nate said, letting go of Hannah and pushing the window partly shut. "My neighbors take America's independence very seriously."

Hannah walked to the milk crate next to his bed and began examining the books stacked on it.

"Do you want some wine?" Nate asked.

"Sure."

As he walked to the kitchen, Nate yawned. It was late. They'd already been out to dinner.

The wine he'd purchased earlier from the Tangled Vine was in a plastic bag on the table. He uncorked the bottle and retrieved a pair of wine glasses, holding them in one hand with the stems crisscrossed.

Hannah was standing expectantly, even docilely, in the middle of the bedroom. Nate set the wine and the glasses on the crate before he went to her.

The first time they'd slept together, as well as the second, the following morning, had been urgent, feverish, as if there had been a tremendous amount of buildup, rather than just a few weeks' worth. He wanted to take it slower this time.

He kissed her. She was nearly his height. He barely had to bend down. He slid his hands around her waist and beneath her shirt. Her back was taut and sinewy. He found the clasp of her bra: he felt her hands on his back, gently kneading the flesh under the elastic of his boxer briefs and moving along his belt line. The area was tender, and he enjoyed her touch, but he grew conscious of being a little thicker there than he would like, a little paunchier on the sides and in front, and he tried to pull in his abdominal muscles.

He nudged her toward the bed. His desk lamp lent the room an institutional cast, so he switched it off. He began unbuttoning his shirt. His eyes adjusted to the dark, and he saw Hannah watching him from the bed. Holding his gaze, she slipped her shirt over her head.

Nate poured wine into one of the glasses and handed it to her. While she sipped it, he sat down beside her and touched her breasts. She gave the glass back to him, and as he drank, she began to unfasten his jeans. He set the glass down. Then he took hold of her, pushing her onto her back and tugging at her jeans as he pressed himself against her.

As he had been the previous times, he was quickly swept up in a current of feeling, the intensity of which surprised him. His most recent encounters before Hannah—months ago now, and with women he'd scarcely known and had had little desire to see again—had been strangely tensionless, almost masturbatory.

He and Hannah had plain missionary-style sex, no theatrics, and it was—for him—really good. He thought it was for her, too. Her body seemed keenly responsive to his touch. That was part of what made it so good for him—that, and its lack of artificiality: he wasn't conscious of playing a part, conforming to expectation. The intensity, mysterious as it was, and the temporary forgetting of self, was real. After he came, he buried his face in her neck as waves of tenderness, embarrassingly strong, washed over him.

For a few minutes, they remained quietly curled in each other's arms. Then Nate began to recover himself. Quotidian thoughts pressed upon him. He became aware of feeling clammy and got up to throw out the condom.

Returning to the bed, he took in the sight of her, sprawled out before him. "You have such a nice body," he said. "People must tell you that all the time."

He could see the taut muscles of her stomach tense up as she laughed.

"I'm, like, totally tired of hearing about it," she said. She turned on her side. "If there's one thing women get sick of, it's being complimented. We're just so secure about our bodies."

Nate poured more wine. They began to talk, for some reason, about her ex-boyfriend Steve, whom she'd been with for four years. Nate pressed her for details. She had an intelligent, novelistic way of describing people that he enjoyed. "He had this culturally conservative streak," she said. "He read a lot. He was a lawyer, but he read philosophy, fiction—even poetry. I respected that, but after a while the gentleman-scholar thing got on my nerves. It seemed like he was trying to recreate something, like he had a little too much nostalgia for the past, for aristocracy and class privilege, really."

She said Steve was practical and organized and critical of her for being too careless, making her out to be some kind of hapless wild-child. Over time, their relationship devolved into a series of proxy battles. "In the last year we were together, I could feel him constantly inspecting me from top to bottom. A missing button or tiny stain was an *aha* moment in which my fundamental failure as a person was exposed." She began toying with a lock of her hair. "But I'm not being fair. The truth is I was doing the same to him at the end—building a case as to how rigid and unsubtle and bullying he was. He was always accusing me of rolling my eyes or smirking at him. I guess I was."

An hour had gone by. They had lost interest in the wine. Nate brought glasses of water from the kitchen.

He found himself telling her about Kelly Krebs, the girl he'd lost his virginity to between freshman and sophomore years of college.

"We met at the beach. Ocean City. She was a type I'd never really known before—middle-class, all-American, gentile. Not all that smart and not at all concerned about it. She thought it was weird I went to Harvard. I think she was embarrassed for me."

Because of her ski-slope nose and because she attended a second-tier state college, his friends from high school called Kelly a *grit*, which he explained to Hannah was a Baltimore term for a hick. ("They called her that to her face?" Hannah asked, aghast. "No, no," he assured her. "Of course not. Just to me.") He told her that it said more about his friends' provincial, suburban Jewishness—to say nothing of their dickishness—than it did about Kelly. They lumped all gentiles together (except for the very rich ones, from whose ranks senators and presidents were culled). Kelly was no hick. Her dad was an accountant. Her mom worked part-time in a boutique. To Nate, who had none, she had what seemed a superabundance of siblings. Their house in Towson, a suburb adjacent to Nate's, was a crowded jumble of sports equipment—hockey sticks tilting out of umbrella stands, kneepads abandoned on the coffee tables—and unmissable signs of female habitation. Jars of nail polish were left open, their contents spilling onto the pages of fashion magazines. There always seemed to be a hair dryer on upstairs. His own house seemed funereal in comparison. The Krebses were warm; as a family, they seemed happy. Nate liked them. He was especially taken with Mr. Krebs, a plump bearded man with a booming voice who coached Little League and soccer and was constantly shepherding one or another Krebs child to a sporting event or to the mall. Nate had rarely encountered a father as cheerful as he was.

Nate could see that as a family the Krebses were proud of their salt-of-the-earth-ness, their friendly, unpretentious American-ness. Nice as they were, they exuded their own brand of self-satisfaction. He compared them to his own parents, with their pride in their bookish intelligence, their sobriety and self-restraint. He had wondered if everybody took the quality they had and treated it as the most important thing—used it as a basis for feeling superior to others.

Nate had been on his back, looking at the ceiling. He turned to Hannah. "The answer, I decided, was yes."

She was leaning on her elbow, with her chin in her palm. "It sounds like the germ of relativism."

He began fondling her breasts. While he'd been talking about the Krebs family, Hannah had reached for her shirt. He'd swatted her hand away. "Please don't," he'd said. "I can't tell you how happy it makes me to look at your breasts."

She asked what happened with Kelly.

"She broke up with me for a guy from her college. I was a little relieved, to tell you the truth."

It must have been close to three o'clock by then. At some point, Hannah went off on a writer she thought was overrated. He happened to be the son of a very prominent journalist.

"Couldn't it possibly be," Nate said, "that you just don't like his stuff as much as some people do? Or is every article you dislike proof of an industry-wide conspiracy—a plot on behalf of nepotistic overlords to keep down good, hardworking, talented writers, such as, ahem, Hannah Leary?"

She laughed. It pleased him that her laughter was not a prelude to hurt feelings or sulkiness.

"Maybe you have a point," Hannah said. "Maybe it's a defense mechanism on my part."

Nate reached for a clump of her hair and gently pulled her close to him. They started to fool around again.

Nate wanted to freeze and preserve an image of her, from afterward. She was standing naked at his window with her back to him. Her hair fell in clumps against her flushed skin as the orange tip of a cigarette glowed pensively in the dark.

It was after four when they finally fell asleep. Nate's nose was buried in her hair, an arm draped over her side. His hand rested on her breast, and her ass brushed against his now limp dick.

The weeks that followed ran together in what seemed like a near-continuous stream of conversation and sex, punctuated by bouts of sleep and work. Nate was productive, workwise, perhaps even more productive than usual (he finished the commodification-of-conscience essay). But the hours at his computer, the occasional evening he spent by himself, resting with a pizza and a book, even his weekly soccer games at the park, felt almost like extensions of sleep. The time he spent with Hannah—narrating his life, listening to her do the same, exchanging opinions, fucking—seemed like the real awake time.

He told her about his book, the way it had evolved in the years he'd spent working on it. He'd first intended to write a scathing critique of the suburbs, featuring an immigrant family with one child. A son. This son was intended to be the book's central character, from whose lips precocious wit and wisdom would flow and whose struggles—girls and popularity—would arouse readers' sympathy. He told her how the novel had started to come together only when this "insufferable" character had been shunted to the sidelines, in favor of the parents, with their quietly troubled marriage and off-kilter but also in certain ways sharp-sighted responses to American life. Hannah told him that growing up she'd felt underestimated. "People expect girls from good middle-class families to be smart—but what they mean by smart for a girl is to have nice handwriting and a neat locker and to do her homework on time. They don't expect ideas or much in the way of real thought." She said, for her, writing had been a way to be heard.

One night they went to a party hosted by a girl Nate was friendly with and Hannah knew slightly.

When they arrived at Francesca's apartment on the Lower East

Side, Francesca ran up to Nate and hugged him. "I want to introduce you to my friend Nicholas," she told him. He reminded her of Hannah's name. "Hannah, that's right. It's *so* nice to see you," she said. She turned back to Nate. "Nicholas is a huge fan of yours. He's looking forward to your book."

Francesca pulled him to the other side of the room. He lost sight of Hannah.

"Nicholas is very big in Canada," Francesca whispered.

Nicholas was a burly, mustachioed guy with an unlit cigarette hanging out of his mouth. After he and Nate exchanged a few words, Francesca laid a hand on Nate's arm. "What would you like to drink?"

Something in her smile made Nate suspect she wasn't personally pouring out gin and tonics for all her guests.

Several years older than Nate, Francesca was a prettyish, stylish writer who'd been extremely successful with her first book at a young age. After that, she'd been less successful, but she was well known. And she made a point of knowing everyone. It was only recently that "everyone" had come to include Nate. When he'd been a struggling freelance writer who did some legal proofreading on the side, she'd been merely polite.

In those years, Nate had often been dismayed not by Francesca in particular but by the vast number of women whose legs, like the doors to an exclusive club, parted only at the proof of a man's success. Now that he was—barely—on the other side of it, the tendency depressed him for other reasons. There was something in the almost wolfish way that Francesca was looking at him that nullified whatever attractiveness was there.

"Don't worry about it," he told her. "I know where the kitchen is. Nice to meet you, Nicholas."

He didn't find Hannah in the kitchen, but Francesca's apartment had a back window that opened to a fire escape and a flight of stairs.

The roof was strung with white Christmas lights that ran from an extension cord inside the apartment. Francesca's building was flanked on one side by a tall fortresslike structure with few windows. On the other sides, jagged rows of shorter buildings spread out around them.

Nate saw Hannah standing near the edge of the roof. She was talking to Eugene Wu. Nate walked up to them and looped his arm around her waist. "Hey," he said. Hannah flushed slightly and pulled back. Nate realized that this was probably the first public gesture of couplehood he'd made. They'd largely spent time together one-on-one. Amused by her reticence, he kissed her temple lightly.

Hannah ignored this. "Eugene was just telling me that yoga is the new Orientalism," she said. "It's a good thing I do Pilates."

Nate had to strain to hear her over the roar of an air-conditioning unit atop one of the neighboring buildings. "Same difference, isn't it?" he said loudly.

"Pilates was invented by an American," Eugene said. "In the 1920s."

Nate gaped at him. "How do you know that?"

Eugene held out one of his arms for their perusal. "How do you think I stay so lean?"

When Hannah broke away to talk to a friend she hadn't seen in a while, Eugene turned to Nate with his arms crossed in front of his chest. "I didn't know you were dating her."

From his tone Nate suspected that Eugene had asked Hannah out before and had been shot down. Eugene had long been eager to date a bookish girl, a member of the literary set; for him, Hannah, pretty (if not a knockout by Jason's standard), pleasant, and smart, would have been a natural object of desire.

"It's recent," Nate said.

"Hmm . . . ," Eugene said. "Well, she has a nice rack."

Nate didn't know if Eugene was trying to indicate that he wasn't envious or if he was simply pissing on Nate's fire hydrant. Eugene existed in a state of permanent aggrievedness. He felt it his duty to nip at the happiness of those more fortunate. He resented that Nate had gone to Harvard and had a book deal; he acted as if money and girls and writing gigs had been handed to Nate with his diploma. In fact, their professional lives had been similarly scrappy until several years ago when Nate got the regular reviewing gig and then sold his book. Still, Eugene was smart—and more serious, less exclusively careerist than many people he knew.

"What about you, Eugene?" he asked. "You dating anyone?"

"I'm thinking about going online," Eugene admitted.

Surprised, Nate tried to remove from his expression anything that Eugene, in his prickliness, might perceive as mocking. "Go for it," he said. "Can't hurt, right?"

Soon after Hannah returned. Then Nate saw Jason's large silhouette emerge from the fire escape stairs. Jason looked around for a moment before he came lumbering toward the corner they'd staked out.

When he had told Jason he was dating Hannah, Jason's response—"she seems like a nice girl"—had been so bland that Nate had silently seethed, hating himself because the number seven flitted across his mind. He hated himself even more as he heard himself extol Hannah's virtues: *she's really cool! fun! smart!* An undertone of desperation had found its way into his voice. Jason had nodded, doing nothing that Nate could call him out on, and yet something in his smile had reminded Nate of a WASPy hostess "overlooking" a breach of etiquette.

"Hannah," Jason said as he approached. With mock formality, he held out a hand for her to shake.

Hannah scrunched her eyebrows quizzically, but she smiled and matched his tone. "Jason," she said, giving him her hand. "It's nice to see you."

"You look lovely. As always."

"Thank you."

Nate began rubbing the stubble on his chin. There wasn't anything he could do. Either Jason would be a dick—he'd call it "shaking things up"—or he wouldn't. As a distraction, Nate let himself get drawn into a hair-splitting and incredibly geekish argument with Eugene about libertarianism. After a few minutes, he turned to Jason.

"Can I use your phone to look up something?"

"Dude," Jason said. "Get your own. You're like the last person in New York to not have a smartphone."

"Jesus."

Hannah reached into her purse. "You can use mine."

Nate took the phone from her and turned to Jason. "Do you see how it's possible to do someone a favor without commentary?"

Jason smiled exultantly. "Commentary is what I do," he said. "I'm a *social commentator*, remember?"

Jason had recently been interviewed on CNN about his essay on obesity.

Hannah let out a short, skeptical laugh. "Harassing Nate about his cell phone is social commentary how?"

Nate looked at her in surprise. The awkwardness he'd been dreading had materialized—from an unexpected corner. His "girl-friend" was stepping in to defend him. He wished she wouldn't.

"Hannah, Hannah, Hannah," Jason said. He was leaning on the roof's railing with his arms extended on either side of his body and his ankles daintily crossed. When he smiled, his wide jawline formed a gratuitously large canvas for his fleshy lips. In his head's narrower, more delicately constructed upper half, his eyelashes fluttered in a show of affability as disingenuous as the upturn of his mouth.

"There comes a point"—Jason unclasped his hands from the metal rail and lurched toward them like a cuckoo emerging from inside its clock—"when a technology becomes such a part of the mainstream that it is no longer, strictly speaking, optional. This is a social phenomenon; diagnosing it is like diagnosing narcissism in the 1970s. The moment of smartphone saturation, or you might say, of *cultural transubstantiation*, occurred at or around August of 2008, at least for people in our demographic—"

"That's ridi—" Nate tried to cut in.

"*After that,*" Jason said, "not to have one is a statement. Especially when, like our friend Nate here"—Jason gestured grandly in Nate's direction—"you aren't exactly poverty-stricken. At least not anymore." He flashed Nate a quick, malicious grin before turning back to the others. "For Nate, today, not to have a smartphone is a high-pitched scream that he is a square peg who refuses to be wedged into a round hole. And that," Jason said, looking directly at Hannah, "is an invitation to the rest of the clan to shame him. That's how the social order is maintained."

"So in giving Nate a hard time, what you're really doing is embodying a repressive social order?" Hannah's eyebrows were raised and her voice was mocking, but her expression was amused, even a bit flirtatious. "You're like the guy who sewed the *A* onto Hester Prynne's dress?" She turned to Nate and Eugene. "And that's his defense?" she concluded with a shake of her head.

Nate felt his body relax. She'd been perfect.

Jason shrugged in defeat. "No one likes the enforcer," he said. "I guess that's just the way it is."

Nate pulled Hannah closer to him, feeling pleased both with her and in some more obscure way with himself.

"Incidentally, Hester sewed on the *A* herself," Eugene said.

"Thank you, Brainy Smurf," Nate said. He turned to Hannah. "Jason's very big on social order these days," he said, resting his hand on the place on her hip where her jeans ended and feeling really turned on. "He thinks it's gotten a bad rap—"

"—because of, you know," Eugene cut in, "Hitler. Mussolini."

"Social order, huh?" Hannah said to Jason.

Hannah's back was lightly touching Nate's shoulder. Her body language, tilting away from the group, suggested she was ready to shrink away from the spotlight, glad for its attention to refocus on Jason, who sighed loudly, though in fact he enjoyed nothing so much as pontificating, even if he had to play the buffoon to do it.

"As Aristotle said, man is a political animal—"

"I'm going to get a drink," Eugene said.

"Man alone is worthless," Jason continued. "Hairless, shivering, and physically puny, he's no match for animals or the elements. Only through our collective intelligence, through *society*, has man risen. The mistake people make is to consider human evolution from the perspective of the individual. The happiness of individuals is, evolutionarily speaking, irrelevant; what matters is the health of society."

Nate circled Hannah's waist with his arm and cocked his head so that his forehead was touching hers. Her hip grazed his upper thigh, and her hair brushed against his chin and neck. He wanted to get even closer, but as it was, he was already a bit too turned on. He took a few deep breaths.

Above, the strings of white Christmas lights cut diagonal stripes across the darkening sky; several stories below, city traffic streamed around them. Jason droned on.

When they returned to Hannah's apartment, Nate apologized for Jason. "He doesn't mean any harm. He's just kind of a blowhard. Some people have golf, some have girlfriends, Jason has his mouth."

"I like him, actually," Hannah said. "He's . . . *ebullient*."

"Ebullient?" Nate smiled. "I'll tell him you said so. He'll like it."

They were lying on top of Hannah's bed, staring up at her ceiling as if at the stars. Nate told her that in college he thought he had less in common with Jason than with his friend Peter, but that over the years, the balance had shifted.

"Jason's weird, especially about women, but he's not a bad guy," Nate said. "He's more, I don't know how to put it exactly—substantial, maybe?—than a lot of people. He doesn't look over his shoulder to see what other people think, the way someone like Mark does." Hannah knew Mark; he had edited her writing at the online magazine where he used to work. "Mark's great, of course," Nate continued. "Good at what he does and really funny—but his first allegiance will always be to his reputation."

Hannah asked what Peter was like.

"Smart. Lonely. He really wants a girlfriend. He lives in Watertown, Maine—he got a job teaching up there. There aren't very many single women in Watertown. And, well, he's kind of awkward with women."

Nate realized that in the past couple weeks he and Hannah had talked about many aspects of their lives, but they hadn't spent much time on their friends. "What about you?" he asked. "What are your friends like?"

Hannah told him that her close friends dated back to journalism school and her days as a newspaper reporter. They were reporters who covered politics and business. Although she and Nate had a number of common friends and acquaintances, she felt her foothold in Nate's literary circle was tenuous. For the past few years, since she and Steve had broken up, she had felt a little bit lonely, intellectually. Her choice to try and write a book while taking miscellaneous freelance gigs was mysterious to many of her journalist friends in a way that it wasn't, couldn't possibly be, to Nate.

Nate stroked her cheek with his thumb. "I find that strangely touching," he said. "I mean, it makes me glad that I can do that for you. Understand that part of you. I promise you're doing the right thing. Your book will be terrific."

She kissed his chin. "Thank you. That's really nice."

The desire Nate had been holding back since the party started to well up again, and he began to touch her breasts through her tank top. But he could tell she was distracted.

"What are you thinking about?"

She turned on her side, so they faced each other. She didn't answer right away.

"Nothing really," she said finally. "Just that you've been kind of great. I mean, it's been really great, these past few weeks." She touched his chest lightly through his T-shirt. "I've been really . . . happy."

He curled a finger into her hair. "Me too," he said. "Me too."

9

Like Freud, Aurit had a coherent theory of the universe. From a single foundational myth, she had derived a large and growing labyrinth of substories, all internally logical and surprisingly convincing, as long as you accepted her initial premises. The most important of these was the belief that being part of a couple was *the* primary marker of psychological health. On such a basis, she came up with far-reaching analyses of everyone she encountered. This one, she would announce, was sexually dysfunctional due to a painful formative relationship. That one was stunted by a series of early professional successes that kept him committed to the same immature belief structure he'd possessed during his period of peak glory. (Single men were deemed particularly lacking in emotional well-being.) Aurit took her analyses very seriously, often liking, disliking, or feeling sorry for people based almost entirely on the narratives she constructed. In particular, the men who'd hurt her most had become objects of such a virulent strain of pity that one might suspect her motives for dating them had been philanthropic.

Nate was reminded of this the following Saturday afternoon. He and Aurit were walking to Prospect Park, where some friends were hosting a picnic to celebrate their recent City Hall marriage. Aurit wanted to hear all about Hannah.

"It's been, what? A month? A little longer?"

"Something like that." It had been six weeks since he and Hannah first went out, about four since they'd begun to see each other in earnest.

"I'm really glad for you, Nate."

Aurit was nodding and smiling at him like he'd made it through naptime without wetting his pants.

Suddenly, it was essential to Nate that he complicate Aurit's narrow viewpoint. "It's not *that* big a deal. Who knows what will happen?"

Aurit had just purchased an iced coffee. Through the plastic lid, she had been stabbing at the caramel-colored liquid with her straw.

"Oh?" She looked up at him. "Is something wrong?"

"No. I just don't want to blow it out of proportion, that's all."

Aurit frowned. "Uh huh."

What he wanted to get across was a general demurral from Aurit's romantic monomania. He didn't see his getting together with Hannah as quite the epic, life-defining event that Aurit's relationships were for her. His new relationship, though consuming when he was with Hannah, wasn't the only thing on his mind, especially as time wore on and he became more acclimated to her presence in his life. Particularly in the past few days he'd had new preoccupations. He had gotten a journalism assignment that he was pleased about, a big and well-paid piece for a glossy magazine. Jason had recommended him for it. He had also had the germ of an idea for another book. And it wasn't only writing. The relationship, nice as it was, shared space in his mind with other things— with his interest in thinking abstractly, about things other than his personal life, for one, even with his interest in sports. But he couldn't think of a way to explain this to Aurit that wouldn't seem to her to imply discontent with Hannah.

They walked in silence. The plastic bag with the bottle of wine Nate bought for the picnic bumped rhythmically against his knee and shin.

"Is she coming today?" Aurit asked finally.

"No. She wanted to do some work. She's working on a book proposal."

Aurit nodded. Then she took a big sip of her drink and glared into the plastic cup.

"Ugh. An iced mocha shouldn't taste like chocolate milk."

Nate had nothing to say to that.

For the last day of July, the afternoon was lovely—not too humid, the sky a non-washed-out shade of blue—and the scene, as they entered the park, was idyllic, almost too idyllic. Technically, Prospect Park's natural amenities (wooded hills, rolling meadows, crescent-shaped pond with requisite ducks and swans) probably didn't outshine those of other parks in other cities. But unlike the parks Nate had known growing up in the suburbs, frequented almost exclusively by delinquent teens, gay cruisers, and sundry procurers of crack, this one didn't feel rickety and abandoned. ("When people have their own backyards, they grill alone," Jason had said once.)

Prospect Park teemed with cheerful people doing cheerful things: walking, running, biking, playing Little League, watching Little League, eating drippy ice cream cones while watching Little League. Groups of young professionals toting canvas bags from local bookstores staked out places on the grass next to Caribbean families with plastic coolers full of elaborate foods that somehow all smelled of plantains. The park was a liberal integrationist's wet dream: multiracial, multiethnic, multiclass.

When he and Aurit arrived at the picnic, a rapid-fire exchange of effusions ensued. "Congrats!" "It's official!" "Thanks for coming!" "Have something to eat!"

On an adjacent picnic blanket, Jason was holding court. "I'm sorry to have to tell you, but no amount of quality day care or liberal education is going to produce a nation of self-critical adherents to the Golden Rule," he was saying. He was speaking to two bemused-looking women and paused only long enough to nod at Nate and Aurit. "It's just not in everybody's DNA. Virtue is its own reward for some—but not for everyone. And that's a good thing. There are a lot of things that moralists are incapable of doing."

"Like what, building pyramids?" Aurit muttered. "It's amazing what you can do if you're willing to use slave labor."

"Exactly!" Jason said. "Pyramids, the settling of the New World, industrialization. Think of the brutality!" He beamed. "Moral people wouldn't have pulled off any of it. And then where would we be? Not sitting here in lovely Prospect Park with our cushy jobs and preening social consciences."

The women he was talking to—or at—exchanged a glance. "What about the victims of these immoral people?" asked one, a friendly-looking redhead.

"Of course, there's a social tax we pay for having psychopaths running around," Jason conceded. "But society needs the cunning to make things happen, just like it needs the conscientious to enforce the rules, to keep the thing from turning into a game theorist's nightmare. Just like it needs *artists*"—he spoke the word with mocking emphasis—"by which I include writers, musicians, and the like, to attract would-be loners to the communal campfire and fold them into the clan."

"That's a moving theory," the redhead said.

The argument petered out. The redhead, whom Nate sat down next to, told him she was a grad student in art history. Before she went back to school she had been an editor at his publishing house. She and Nate began running through various common acquaintances.

Jason turned to him. "Where's *Hannah*?"

Nate's jaw tightened. He knew Jason thought he had the temperament of a sad, whipped schmuck, a conviction that certain women might have found hard to credit but was nonetheless unshakable as far as Jason went. (Jason had, in the past, attributed this to Nate's "squirrelly, smarmy" need for everyone to like him.)

"We're not attached at the hip," Nate said.

He turned back to the redhead. After a few minutes, their conversation began to run dry. He wished there were a way to politely exit, but she was so smiley and friendly that Nate didn't want to hurt her feelings. Finally, she nodded at the red wine he was drinking. "I think I'm going to look for some white," she said.

"Of course!" Nate said.

He remembered something he wanted to ask Mark. He flicked Jason's upper arm. "Is Mark coming today, do you know?"

Jason shook his head. "Dunno . . . I haven't seen him for a while. You know he started dating someone, right? The hot little ticket from that reading? Carrie? Cara?" He whistled. "*Cute girl.* Hey, wait. Didn't you talk to her first?"

"Maybe," Nate said, tugging a blade of grass from the ground. "Yeah. I guess I did."

"And you didn't . . . ? Oh, that's right." Jason smirked. "*Hannah.*"

Before Nate could respond, a woman he had dated briefly years ago came up and said hello. She was now married with a small child, which she had brought along with her. When they dated, Nate had thought that she was a little too maternal for his taste. The well-being she projected now, as she held up the little blond thing for him to admire, seemed to confirm his intuition. When she put the child down, it lurched toward a squirrel. Laughing, she tottered off after it. "Good to see you!" she called behind her.

Nate accepted some carrots and hummus from a plate being passed around.

"Did I tell you Maggie started dating someone?" Jason asked.

Maggie was a girl Jason worked with. He had made out with her once the year before and talked about it frequently.

"The guy sounds like a real douche," Jason continued. "Some kind of freelance Web site designer or something that basically anyone could do in their spare time."

The sun had emerged from behind a cloud. Nate lifted a hand to shield his eyes. "Not that you care, right?"

"I care about Maggie a lot," Jason said, swatting one hand against his arm. "*Fucking mosquito.* Maggie's happiness is extremely important to me."

"Right . . ."

Nate's cell phone rang from inside his jeans pocket.

"The girlfriend?" Jason asked as Nate fished for the phone.

Nate hit the DECLINE button to make Hannah's name disappear from the screen. "You know, Jase," he said. "I was trying to remember. When actually was the last time you got laid? Who was president? Did you have dial-up or broadband?"

Jason stared at him for a moment. Then he smiled broadly. His distended lips reminded Nate of the bellies of starving children. "I can't help it if I have high standards," he said.

The group was called to attention to toast the couple.

Afterward, Jason turned to him. "I get the feeling you think I don't like your new girlfriend."

"I didn't—" Instinctively, Nate started to deny that he'd given the subject any thought whatsoever, but Jason continued over him.

"That's not true. I might have thought she was a little mousy at first, but I was wrong. I think she's a cool girl."

Nate was surprised to hear this—also surprised, and a little embarrassed, by just how glad he was to hear it. He nodded with studied casualness. "She is cool."

"I was surprised, at first, only because I didn't think she was your type."

This was clearly a provocation. Nate knew he should ignore it. "What do you mean, not my type?" he asked.

"You know . . ." Jason said. "You usually go for—I don't know how to put this—sort of girly, high-maintenance women. You know, like Elisa."

"That's ridic—!" On the other side of the picnic blanket, Aurit, in conversation with someone Nate didn't know, glanced up at him. Nate lowered his voice. "—ulous. Don't you think I liked Elisa in spite of her being, as you put it—so generously, I might add—'girly and high-maintenance,' and not because of it?"

"Well, I'm sure you think so—"

"There were a lot of reasons I liked her. Not one of them had to do with her being high-maintenance. That did have something to do with why I broke up with her."

"Calm down," Jason said. "All I'm saying is that we're hard-wired to respond to certain things—I know I am—and not all of them are what I'd call good."

"Kristen wasn't girly or high-maintenance."

"No, she wasn't," Jason agreed. "Anyway, it doesn't matter. If you're happy, that's great. As I said, I think Hannah's a cool girl." Without giving Nate a chance to respond, Jason turned away. "Hey, Aurit, can you pass some of those vegetables?"

"Speaking of Elisa," Jason said a moment later, "what'd she say when you told her you were doing her friend?"

Nate started to react to that last bit but checked himself. "I haven't told her yet," he said. "I'm going to."

Jason was nibbling on a broccoli floret with a delicacy that was almost effete, especially in contrast with the leer that took shape on his lips. "Tell her if she needs a shoulder to cry on, she can call me," he said. "I've always got time for her tight little ass and big blue eyes."

"For fuck's sake."

Nate did meet up with Elisa several days later. He'd been putting it off, and indeed he should have done it sooner. She had already heard about Hannah from someone. To Nate's surprise, she was mad not at him but at Hannah.

"I thought she was my friend," Elisa said.

"She feels bad," Nate said. "She really likes you. She assumed it was cool since you and I are friends."

"I'm sure she feels *awful.* A person who dates her friend's ex, who she met at her friend's own house—at her friend's *dinner party* . . . I'm sure she feels terrible."

Nate studied the grain of the wood on the bar. They were at a steak place, in midtown, near Elisa's office. He was beginning to wonder whether this get-together was a good idea. Making such a big to-do about him and Hannah seemed to confer undue legitimacy to Elisa's anger.

Elisa was aggressively stirring her martini. "What a bitch."

"That's not fa—"

But as Elisa turned her eyes from the smoky mirror behind the bar to meet his, Nate let the words trail off. Sometimes, it hit him all over again, the rawness of Elisa's unhappiness. For all her beauty, she looked—around her eyes—haggard, stricken.

"I'm sorry, E," he said softly. "I really am. I didn't think you guys were close. I didn't mean to hurt you."

Elisa's lower lip protruded sulkily. She didn't so much shrug as raise a thin shoulder, causing her collarbone to jut out above the wide neckline of her blouse. Apart from her eyes, she looked as pretty and fashionable as ever, with her blonde hair swept up in a loose bun. She was wearing a long, loose white shirt and tight-fitting black pants.

"You'll meet someone," Nate said.

Elisa looked at him, her perfect features perfectly still. As one beat passed and then another, her expression seemed to deepen until her face projected a profound weariness.

"Maybe," she said finally.

Nate braced himself for her to start in on familiar accusations. He had poisoned her future relationships. She could no longer trust that a guy who claimed to love her wouldn't change his mind at any moment. He had made her feel that she wasn't smart enough or good enough. How was she supposed to recover from that?

But she must have sensed that for now she already had Nate's sympathy. There was nothing to gain by taking that tack.

"By the way," she said. "I'm sorry about last time. My dinner party, I mean. And afterward. I had too much to drink. I shouldn't have put you in that position. It's just . . . I don't know, things have kind of sucked lately. I've been feeling really down."

Nate shifted his weight on the well-padded bar stool. In his chest, various emotions—guilt and pity and simple sadness—swelled miserably. He almost preferred when she berated him.

"Don't worry about it," he said. "I'm sorry you haven't been happy."

Elisa shrugged again as she scrutinized one of her hands and began repositioning a ring that had slid off-center.

Nate sought something diverting to say. "What's the boss up to these days?"

Elisa very subtly shook her head as if in wry amusement, as if she knew he was changing the subject because he was a coward, but was by now resigned to his immaturity. With touching pliancy, she launched into an anecdote.

Elisa worked for a Very Important Magazine. Nate, as she well knew, liked hearing about the goings-on there. She told him about a well-known writer who'd pissed off her boss, the editor in chief, by withdrawing a piece rather than submitting to his editorial suggestions. The writer had then published the piece in a competing publication, incorporating many of those suggestions.

"He's never writing for us again," she said.

"No, I would think not."

Elisa looked deliberately at him. "What about you? It's only about, what, six months until your book comes out? You must"—her eyes twitched—"you must be really excited."

Nate stared at the row of single-malt scotches lined up on the shelf behind the bar. He had written much of his book while he had been with Elisa. In a way, she had been essential to his writing it. Although she had sometimes complained about the time he took away from her to work on it, she had always believed in the book and in his ability to pull it off. During periods when the writing wasn't going well, when he had seriously doubted it ever would, her faith had mattered a lot, had maybe been crucial. Then, before the book was finished and sold, he'd broken up with her.

"I try not to obsess about it," he said.

Elisa pushed her empty glass to the back of the bar. It was immediately whisked away by a bow-tied attendant. Nate began to call him back to ask for the check.

"Why are you in such a hurry?" Elisa asked.

Something familiar snapped back into place as her resigned tone gave way to one of complaint.

Nate held up his hands. "I'm not."

"Is *Hannah* expecting you?"

"No! I just—oh, never mind. Let's get another."

"Not if you don't want to."

"I want to!" he insisted. "I do."

It was after ten when he walked Elisa to her subway station. As she disappeared down the steps, Nate felt the kind of relief that has a physical component, like the release after a long run. On his way to his own subway station, several blocks west, he sent Hannah a text. *Is it weird that I miss you?* They'd seen each other only that morning.

Her reply came a moment later. *Yes, it's weird.* Seconds after, another arrived: *(but I kinda, sorta miss you too).*

After the evening with Elisa, Nate wanted nothing so much as to rebuild his mood in a different key. The light, easy banter he and Hannah tended toward—the implicit reassurance of her presence that he wasn't a heartless ingrate—was particularly appealing.

Before he got on the train, he wrote back. *I can be there in 45.*

10

That night, Hannah asked what the deal was with him and Elisa. They were sitting in the chairs by her window. Nate paused before answering.

He had met Elisa three years ago at a publishing party. She had arrived with the editor in chief of the Very Important Magazine. Nate asked his friend Andrew about her. Andrew said she was the editor in chief's new assistant.

When her boss left, Elisa remained. Nate downed two or three thimble-sized glasses of wine. She was standing next to the food table, in front of a small mountain of fruit.

"Hi, I'm Nate."

She popped a red grape into her mouth. "Elisa," she said, almost drowsily.

For the next few minutes, she answered his questions, but she seemed slightly put out by the obligation he had imposed on her. Eventually, she asked what he did.

He said he was the book critic for an online magazine. She asked which one. He told her.

She eyed him. Nate tugged at the collar of his blue Oxford shirt. He noticed that one of his shoes was not merely untied but radically untied, as if he had only just now wrested his foot from a steel trap. Its gaping, brown tongue hung crookedly, crisscrossed with faint indentations where the laces should have been. He stepped on that foot with the other, swaying slightly, like a top-heavy kebab.

She told him that she'd recently finished a master's degree in comp lit from the Sorbonne. Before that she'd been at Brown. This was her first job in publishing. She wanted to write. She'd love to get coffee with Nate sometime. *She would?* Yeah, she'd love to talk about publishing.

Coffee turned into dinner and, a few days later, a sunset run over the Brooklyn Bridge and then a party at a Harvard friend/ hedge fund guy's Upper West Side triplex and a Saturday night at the Brooklyn Museum. Nate was terrifically impressed by her. She dropped casual references to the work of aging intellectuals who contributed to the *New York Review of Books*. The polysyllabic names of avant-garde eastern European filmmakers rolled effort-lessly from her tongue. Her father was a well-known professor whose books Nate knew by reputation. By that point in his life, Nate had dated any number of editorial types. Elisa seemed dif-ferent, unusually serious and well informed, especially for some-one so young. And so attractive.

Even Nate, who had had to be told by Jason not to wear pants with pleats, could tell somehow that among all the well-dressed young women of Brooklyn, Elisa looked especially nice. She knew where to buy anything, which stores were not so much expensive as tasteful, and also what was okay to buy at Target (from what Nate gleaned, things that started with the letter *T*: Tupperware, tights, toothpaste). In theory, Nate disdained "bourgeois status signifiers," but in practice he took pride in Elisa's whiff of smart chic. She radiated the effortless worldly ease of the popular girl. She was clearly first-rate, top-shelf, the publishing world equiva-lent of Amy Perelman in high school and Will McDormand's best-looking gal pals at Harvard: she was the thing that was clearly, indisputably desirable.

Her demeanor was smooth and preoccupied, even slightly sullen, and she spoke at times with an unnerving, almost anhedonic lack of affect. She often seemed bored. This edge of perpetual dissatisfaction made it all the more thrilling for Nate when he cajoled her into laughter and good humor: to impress her, one felt—he felt—was really something.

Back then he didn't have a book deal. His book-reviewing gig ensured a regular paycheck, but to call it modest, relative to the cost of living in New York, was an overstatement bordering on a lie. To get by, he needed to hustle for all the additional assignments he could get, both proofreading and writing. He worked alone, in his dirty apartment. Some days, he didn't bother to shower. He blew his nose with toilet paper. Cheap toilet paper. (Once when he was visiting from New Haven, Nate's college friend Peter had surreptitiously nabbed a few squares from the roll and folded them into the breast pocket of his shirt. He waited until their friends were assembled at a bar to pass them around. "Just feel it. Can you believe that *this*—the world's most diaphanous sandpaper—is what our Nate uses to wipe his ass? Talk about self-loathing.")

Nate had no health insurance, hadn't had it for years. After a while, he'd come to take for granted that he was the kind of scruffy, marginal person whose well-being was not deemed important by society. Elisa's well-being, on the other hand, was incontrovertibly important—to her, to her parents, to the magazine that lavished her with extensive dental, optical, and mental-health benefits. The universe itself seemed bent on accommodating her, with free drinks from bartenders, gentle treatment from otherwise gruff cab drivers, and kindly offers of advice from avuncular grandees of magazine publishing who never returned Nate's e-mails.

Nate was usually still sleeping each day when Elisa, lovely and carefully groomed, sailed past the guards in the lobby of that midtown Manhattan skyscraper, zoomed up to the zillionth floor in the express elevator, and took her seat at a desk with her nameplate above it. There, she answered phones, calmly assuring nervous writers that her boss would get back to them. She escorted various Important People into the big corner office. She sat in on certain editorial meetings and even, when asked, offered ideas about the magazine's content. For the most part, though, her work was administrative. It was, nonetheless, the start of a career. She was taking great care not to become someone fringy like Nate, at home in his underwear, sweating up his sheets, pondering such questions as whether he should take the earned income tax credit if he qualified, or if that would be wrong, since it was clearly intended for real poor people, not Harvard grads who eschewed regular jobs to pursue their idiosyncratic intellectual ambitions.

When he met up with Elisa at the end of a workday, he felt like he'd clawed his way out of a Morlockean underworld. With her, he was treated differently at restaurants. Other men sized him up with their eyes. Waiters and maître d's were more deferential. Even among his circle of friends and acquaintances, his stock rose subtly.

So it hardly seemed to matter that she was not a particularly nice girlfriend. Unless they coincided with hers, Elisa treated his desires as perverse whims, wholly negligible. An expensive restaurant she liked was a healthy indulgence; his craving for barbecue was "disgusting." A somewhat down-market local barbecue chain he especially liked? "Out of the question." After social engagements, she enjoyed regaling him with a list of criticisms of his behavior. She seemed to think that everything he did was first and foremost a reflection on her. When, at a dinner party, he made a bad joke, Elisa was mad at him for embarrassing her. "What made you think that would have been funny?" she demanded as soon as they'd rounded the corner from the Park Slope brownstone where they'd spent the evening. Nate was forced to admit he had absolutely no idea why he had thought that responding to someone's comment that we are living in an age of anxiety by saying that he thought it was the Age of Aquarius would be funny. As soon as the words had escaped from his mouth, he was humiliated by their lameness. This provoked no sympathy from Elisa. She thought he owed it to her to be someone she could respect. That meant not making bad jokes. It also meant being affectionate but not too affectionate, complimentary but not too complimentary, smart but not pedantically so, and a host of other things.

When Elisa felt that someone had wronged her, she was outraged. Apparently, she was the only person in all of New York with any manners; everyone else behaved like an animal, especially to her, which was very hard for her to understand because—and this was news to Nate—she "bore no ill will toward anyone." She was furious if Nate didn't wholeheartedly support her in her indignation toward such-and-such coworker, who had made a comment at lunch, which, though it seemed fairly innocuous when she repeated it to Nate, struck Elisa as unforgivably barbed. To suggest even the possibility of a misunderstanding, let alone an overreaction, was, as far as Elisa was concerned, to undermine her.

She seemed to have no internal sense of justice. When Nate got annoyed because she was late to meet him or because she seemed to him to be acting bored as he told her something he felt was important, he instinctively evaluated his irritation, tried to assess whether it was reasonable or fair, under the circumstances. (Perhaps she hadn't realized that what he was saying was important to him? Perhaps he hadn't been clear?) She, on the other hand, treated her emotional responses as infallible. His self-criticism, she seemed to perceive merely as a weakness to be exploited. "No," she'd say. "You really weren't clear."

Nate's only other serious girlfriend had been Kristen, who was, whatever else you might say about her, an extremely fair-minded person. Elisa was a bit baffling to him. But for a long time, none of her limitations mattered. Nate had grown up on the Old Testament. He didn't expect his god to be reasonable or merciful. He may have privately grumbled about her demands, he may have tried to reason with her or cajole her, but Elisa's presence in his life, in his bed, her beauty (sometimes when he was with her he was simply overcome with the desire to touch her silky blonde hair or perfect doll face), the particular pains and pleasures of being with her: these had become, for him, existentially necessary.

Although Elisa was intelligent—and fluent in the things sophisticated people were supposed to be fluent in—Nate had realized fairly early on that her writing was often stilted and awkward. Her ideas tended toward strained attempts at a sort of academic profundity. There was also something brittle about her love of intellect and intellectualism and, more important, *intellectuals*, like Nate. This passion of hers had impressed him at first. But it was, he learned over time, a form of success mongering, a specialized form, but success mongering all the same. Long before he was ready to call it quits with her—long before even a seed of the thought had entered his mind—he began to assemble a picture of her much less flattering than his initial impression. Her taste, for example, was great—inasmuch as it was received, inasmuch as she absorbed what was fashionably highbrow. She really liked, say, Svevo—was able to see myriad virtues in Svevo—once she was primed to like Svevo, once she knew that Svevo was someone she was supposed to like. Once her father, the professor, or her boss, the Very Important Editor, had sung the praises of Svevo. But other times, railing against the "male literary establishment," she'd assert (to Nate, never to her coworkers) the value of some schmaltzy if well-meaning piece of middlebrow fiction about a girl and her mother, or a girl and her best friend, or a girl and the black woman who helped to raise her, who together combated predatory males and social injustice and ultimately learned the redemptive power of love. Those were the books she really liked, Nate realized after a while. The Svevo, the aging intellectuals of the *New York Review of Books*—all that, it turned out, was for show, even if she was putting on the show for herself as much as for anyone else.

Nate wished, for her sake, that she'd relax about it, realize it was okay not to be some kind of highbrow intellectual. She'd surely be happier at a different type of magazine, a less stuffy one, perhaps one of those Web sites for smart, independent women, where she wouldn't have to disguise her tastes and where, freed from the need to posture, her verbal cleverness, her knack for snappy aperçus, would come into play. (She was always criticizing him in the most *clever* and *imaginative* terms.) But, no, the high opinion of people like her father and her boss meant too much to her. She had to do something they valued, not something that she valued. Nate felt tenderness toward her when he saw her situation in those terms. Elisa was a beautiful, intelligent woman trying desperately to make herself into a slightly different kind of intelligent woman.

Incidentally, this was also the answer to the question that had so perplexed him initially: the matter of why she was with him. At that moment in her life, Elisa was, he realized, almost pathologically attracted not to status or money or good looks but to literary and intellectual potential. Nate possessed many of the same mental qualities as her father and her boss. And he had to admit that, no matter how much Elisa criticized his dress, manners, personality, and habits, her faith in his mind had been strong and constant.

She was a good influence on him in certain ways, compelling him to go to plays and concerts and gallery openings and well-reviewed restaurants in obscure corners of the city. His default had always been the neighborhood bar. In retrospect, though, Nate supposed that even when they'd been at their best, even as she'd clung to his arm sweetly when they walked from the subway to the pizza parlor in a once-Italian neighborhood in deep Brooklyn, even when they'd sat together drinking hot cocoa on a stone bench outside the Cloisters, staring across the Hudson at the red-brown New Jersey Palisades, even at those moments he had been on some level cataloging her inadequacies for future reference. By the time they'd been going out for seven or eight months, she'd become an increasingly frequent topic of conversation between

Nate and his friends. "Is it normal for your girlfriend to have what's basically a temper tantrum if you make plans for a Friday night without consulting her?" he would ask. "What does it mean that when she pronounces judgment on someone, my first instinct is to assume the opposite is true?"

After he and Elisa had been together for about a year, his dissatisfaction overwhelmed whatever it was—love? need? infatuation?—that had attached him to her. "When a friendship ceases to grow, it immediately begins to decline," said the amoral Madame Merle, and so it seemed to Nate. One day he found that Elisa's hold over him had loosened. He could contemplate her being mad at him without the thought triggering successive jolts of anxiety that inexorably, almost against his will, directed his energies toward effecting reconciliation.

Initially he treaded lightly—said no to more of her proposed outings, stayed at his place when he felt like it, made plans to go away with Jason and Mark one weekend without checking with her first. He brushed off her annoyance and waited to see if the old anxiety would reassert itself. It didn't. Elisa quickly sensed the change, with, it seemed, the same gut-level instinct that some animals sense an approaching storm. She became nicer, more accommodating. She suggested a barbecue restaurant, albeit a trendy one reviewed in the *Times*. She stifled her irritation when Nate told her he wouldn't spend a week at her parents' summerhouse because he wanted to work on his book. She slept with him more often and even bought lacy lingerie and garter belts and teddies with furry pom-poms over the breasts, and the sight of her thin, too-thin, body in these costumes touched him as much as it turned him on. "For me you did this?" he marveled, as she approached him in a red-and-black-striped corset that called to mind the costume of one of Zola's prostitutes. He had always enjoyed sex with Elisa. From the beginning, her aloofness, that bored, preoccupied quality she had, combined with the intensity of his attraction, had imbued it with a sense of quest, of contest; his satisfaction on those occasions when he'd succeeded, and she'd squealed beneath him, had been almost unparalleled in his erotic life. These occurrences became more frequent.

But except for sex, Nate's ardor did not appear to be coming back. The things that had bothered him most about Elisa—her selfishness, her criticism, her demands—were disappearing one by one, and still he felt no slackening in the pace with which indifference, even distaste, was overwhelming everything else he felt for her.

Then he ruptured his Achilles tendon and was on crutches. He stayed with her for a couple weeks because there were fewer stairs to climb to reach her apartment. She behaved beautifully, picking things up from his place, cooking for him, anticipating almost all of his needs. Nate returned to his apartment as soon as he possibly could. Being at Elisa's he had felt like a criminal harbored by the person he has wronged. He had by then almost entirely ceased to feel romantic interest. In its stead: a dispassionate appraisal of her merits and demerits that wasn't entirely to her credit. Even the sex, that blissful second honeymoon, had sputtered out. Increasingly conscious of his changed feelings, Nate couldn't escape the sense that he was taking advantage of her, taking something on false pretenses. He began to shrink from sleeping with her.

When finally he broke up with her, she was more upset than he'd expected. Although he pretended at sympathy, he felt it in only the shallowest sense: he saw her cry and in the moment felt bad. On another level, her tears gratified him: *So now you think I'm such hot shit? What about six months ago when you gave me crap the whole weekend we spent at my parents' house because they were too "shrill," and gave you a headache, and you had too little to talk about with them?* But he didn't say anything. He knew that if she said she was sorry, if she promised to change even more than she had already, it wouldn't matter.

She called him the next day, sounding alarmingly distressed. He agreed to meet her for coffee a few days later; this prospect calmed her down. Over coffee, he told her again that he was sorry but it was just too late, no, he didn't know why, it was nothing she did, he simply needed to focus on finishing his book and probably he wasn't fit to be in any relationship, maybe there was something wrong with him—anything to avoid the truth: that over time he had come to see her as overprivileged and underinteresting.

"It's just—" Elisa set her coffee cup in her saucer and looked at him with watery eyes. "I never really felt loved before. I thought this was it."

Something tugged at him. Back when he had been enamored with her, and incredulous that she had chosen him, hadn't he done a thousand little things to make her feel as fully, as wholly loved as possible? He had thought it would give him more of a hold on her.

But, then, he told himself, wasn't that just what happens in a relationship? It wasn't as if he had intentionally misled her.

They agreed, that day, to remain friends. But Nate soon found himself growing frustrated. Nearly every time they got together she brought up their failed relationship, insisting she just wanted to clear up a few things. When the conversation didn't go the way she wanted—and what she wanted sometimes seemed to be no less than for him to declare that he'd made a mistake in breaking up with her—she'd get upset. With tears came mawkishness and recrimination, unanswerable questions intended, it seemed to him, only to make him feel guilty. "You don't think I'm smart enough, do you?" "How am I ever supposed to trust anyone after I let myself trust you, after you *made* me trust you?" Meanwhile, he remembered with perfect clarity how little sympathy she'd had for him when she had been the one with more power.

Over time, though, another current of feeling began to build within him. No matter how much he told himself that he had done nothing wrong with regard to her, not according to the standards that he and everyone he knew lived by (if anything *she* was in the wrong in her clinginess and undignified hysteria), on some intuitive level, Nate began to feel culpable. A stentorian, Faulkner-like voice within him insisted on seeing the relationship in stark moralistic terms. He'd been drawn—this voice intoned—to Elisa because of her beauty, because she seemed first-rate, because of her well-known father and shining pedigree, and he, nerd, loser that he'd long been, had always suspected that people like her, people like Amy Perelman, with their good looks and popularity, had something he didn't, something impenetrable by intelligence alone, a sort of magic and grace, a wordless wisdom about how to live, and a corresponding access to unknown pleasures. Unlike with Kristen, to whom he'd felt a real kinship, Nate had glommed onto Elisa from reptilian ambition. And then, like a dog that sniffs at a foreign object before deciding it doesn't interest him, he trotted off, on to other attractions. Except his experiment hadn't been so painless for Elisa. Perhaps the strength of her attachment wasn't even as strange as it had once seemed to him. Before him, Elisa had dated a string of guys she seemed to have chosen on the basis of their good looks and propensity to treat her badly. Although he was less good-looking, Nate had apparently hit some sort of sweet spot, being both a nicer boyfriend *and* more desirable in terms of professional prospects than the parade of broad-shouldered sociopaths who'd preceded him. And as Elisa, not without basis, rated her claims to worldly admiration higher than she rated Nate's, it was easy to understand why she had felt secure in his affection.

If she was now sort of pathetic—shameless in her lack of pride and in her unreasonable anger—wasn't all that of a piece with everything he had long known of her? She had been spoiled by her good looks and good fortune; she lacked inner resources; she was petulant and childish when things didn't go her way. He had known all that since practically the first time they'd gone out. If he had wanted her when he knew she was immature, could he really use that as a reason to throw her over now, just because he no longer wanted what else she had on offer? Well, yes, he could, the answer was obviously yes—but still it made him feel bad.

Most of the time, Nate quieted the fundamentalist preacher's voice in his head. It was not to be trusted—it was simplistic, it was self-aggrandizing, according him a godlike power over others; it assumed, problematically, that he was smarter and stronger than Elisa and thus solely responsible for everything that happened between them. Yet his attitude did become more sympathetic toward her. He could always, in an effort to justify himself, list the ways in which she was lacking as a person (she was shallow and her concerns, even her disappointments, were narrow; her ill-concealed pride in her upper-class family was itself vulgar; she was acquisitive, not so much for money as for status and a "suitable"— i.e., alpha male—partner, et cetera), but what, really, did it signify? She may not be a particularly admirable or noble-minded person, but she was indisputably a person. She bled if you pricked her. Although he didn't buy Elisa's most histrionic claims as to the irreparable damage he had supposedly done her—all told they had only been together for a year and a half, they hadn't even lived together—Nate did come to acknowledge that he had hurt her badly. He promised to try, to really try, to be kinder to her, to help her if he could. Even though from his perspective the best possible thing would be to just drop out of each other's lives, he promised her he wouldn't "abandon" her.

But he messed up. He not infrequently found her maddening, particularly when she started in on her favorite/his least favorite topic of conversation: their relationship and all psychic wounds appertaining to it. He took too long to return her calls. The worst of it, though, was that he slept with her far too many times after they broke up, convincing himself that it was okay, that she "understood" the situation. Drunk, lonely, horny, feeling for her a tepid nostalgic affection, he'd contrive for a moment not to see what was obvious: that, apparently, he was willing to fuck with her head, to lead her on a little, because he wanted not just sex but to revel for a short while in the balm of her continued, perhaps even increased, affection. (She seemed to forget that for much of the time they'd actually been together, she'd found him lacking.) And for all he knew, she did understand the situation perfectly, better than he did. Maybe she had never for a single minute thought that this backsliding would amount to more than sex. Still, if she wasn't yet entirely over him, Nate knew he hadn't exactly helped. At least, he had stopped—that is, they had stopped sleeping together. They had agreed not to do it anymore.

This hadn't, of course, prevented her from coming on to him the night of her dinner party. But as she said, she'd been unhappy. A lot of that had nothing to do with him. Life had changed for Elisa since he and she had first met. Three and a half years was too long to be an assistant, even to the editor in chief of a Very Important Magazine. But her forays into writing for the magazine had been painful. Her pieces had been received by editors somewhat poorly and had been so extensively rewritten that she'd been stung. Nate tried to convince her that this was not unusual. Most people her age don't start off writing for magazines of this caliber. They work up to it over time. That was what he had done in his twenties. But Elisa had always been successful at whatever she'd undertaken; she wasn't emotionally prepared for failure of any sort. Without much in the way of humor or humility to put it in perspective, the crash of her expectations was crippling. She clung all the more tenaciously to her job: although she found it at times demeaning, she relied utterly on the prestige of the magazine, and of her boss, to feel important—that is, safe.

While she was still beautiful, she'd lost some of the freshness that she'd had when he first met her, when she was brand-new to the city and adult life and the literary scene, when she'd first entered their social universe as an unknown and nubile young commodity, whose good looks ensured a warm and enthusiastic welcome. Over time, the very quality that he had been drawn to, that indisputable first-rate-ness, had begun to diminish. She had become another attractive, unhappy single woman who could be seen at certain types of parties, complaining about her job and the men she'd been with. She was also known as his ex, which, accurate as it was, was not quite fair. He wasn't classified in the same condescending way as her ex.

Nate rubbed the back of his head.

What was the deal with him and Elisa? Hannah had asked. Sitting in the chair across from him, she smiled encouragingly as she waited for his answer.

She had told him about her ex. But his relationship with Elisa would be difficult to explain. There were things he wasn't proud of. Also, Hannah knew Elisa. He'd feel unchivalrous divulging certain unflattering facts about her to the woman he was currently sleeping with. Besides, he was suddenly very tired.

"We went out for a while," he said, standing up to signal he was ready to move to the bedroom. "It didn't work out. Now we're friends. I guess that's about it."

11

What had begun as an unusually cool summer by August turned into a very hazy, sticky one. Nate retrieved his clunky old air conditioner and installed it in his bedroom window as he began to work seriously on the magazine assignment that Jason had helped him get. Most days, he went for a run in the park, usually before eight, and then worked straight into the evening, rarely allowing even himself the pleasant distraction of Recess. Often he'd meet up with Hannah for a late dinner. Sometimes he felt he didn't have time for that, and she'd come over around eleven to spend the night. Though he occasionally regretted not having time to see his friends, he was happy during those weeks. He always felt most alive, most himself when he was immersed in a project.

When he turned in the piece at the end of the month, Hannah said she wanted to cook him a real dinner. "To celebrate the article," she said. Nate said that sounded nice.

In the meantime, he started in on a list of chores he'd put off while he was working on the piece: Buy birthday present for his mother. Renew driver's license. Switch banks to avoid punishing new fees recently imposed by current bank. Bills. Haircut. Laundry. Tedious stuff.

Perhaps that was why he wasn't in the greatest mood when he arrived at Hannah's for dinner. He couldn't think of any other reason.

She was stirring herbs into a pot of pasta.

He peered in. "Wow. Real clams. In their shells and everything."

She looked amused. "That's how they come. In shells."

Nate followed her to the table. She was wearing a dress he didn't remember having seen before, clingy and black.

As they began to eat, he complimented the pasta. She started talking about cooking and the "psychodrama of taste." Her mother and one of her sisters constantly got into these ridiculously heated squabbles about whose favorite cookbook was better or whether organic really was healthier. What was actually at stake, Hannah said, was the question of which of the two was more tasteful, classier—the mother with her white tablecloths and coq au vin or the sister with her butcher's block and Alice Waters–inspired recipes.

"Your sister wins," Nate said. "Definitely."

"You're not a neutral judge—you're her generation, more or less. And you've never tasted my mother's coq au vin."

Nate smiled, but it was a little forced. He didn't know if it was his imagination or if there was, tonight, some change in their dynamic, a diminution of the lively, crackling energy that usually infused their talk. Maybe he just didn't feel like talking. He turned back to the pasta. Not all the clams had opened. It was good, though. So was the salad she'd made to go with it.

When they finished eating, Nate began clearing dishes. As he returned from the kitchen, Hannah stood up to refill her wine glass. Then she reached over the table to refill his.

"That's okay."

She looked up, her mouth a surprised O.

"I don't really feel like it," he said, a note of apology finding its way into his voice as it occurred to him that she'd cooked him a nice meal and put on a dress. This, this dinner was a *thing*. In not drinking—in not getting into the spirit—he was failing to do his part.

Hannah clasped the wine bottle with both hands. A small crease appeared between her eyebrows. For an instant, Nate saw her in an unfamiliar light—vulnerable, needy. His guilt flickered into annoyance. Why a thing? Says who? Why should he be made to feel bad just because he wasn't in the mood to make a romantic fuss about a Tuesday night? He felt like reading. Or fooling around online. So what?

But just as quickly as it had appeared, the furrow in Hannah's brow disappeared.

"Okay," she said.

She shot him a quick smile as she pushed the cork back in the bottle. Nate, rocking on his heels, his thumbs hooked into the belt loops of his jeans, smiled back.

She turned and walked to the kitchen. Nate watched as she stood on her tiptoes and reached up to set the bottle on top of the refrigerator. Her black dress rode up her thighs. Her ass, in the clingy fabric, looked good.

A part of him wanted to feel it against his body, to get up behind her and whisper his thanks for the meal. But he was afraid that if he did, he'd raise expectations that, at the moment, he wasn't up to following through on.

"Do you mind if I check my e-mail?" he asked.

"Go ahead," Hannah said, walking back to the table. "I'll just hang out here." She lifted her glass. "With my wine."

The next morning, Nate put on running clothes and jogged toward the park. He was conscious of trying to evade, literally to outrun, a feeling of restlessness.

The night before had been sort of a drag. He'd sat by himself at Hannah's desk for a while, fiddling on her laptop, but he'd been uncomfortably conscious of her movements in the living room. He'd been glad when after about half an hour she came into the

bedroom and asked if he wanted to watch a movie. He did. The film, an indie comedy that they watched in bed, on the laptop, cheered him. Temporarily. He'd woken up to the same feeling of dullness.

Yet everything was going well. Strong blurbs were coming in for his book. On the phone a few days before, his father had made an uncharacteristically approving remark about Nate's career choices. (His years of underpaid freelance work, previously seen as "bumming around," had been recast as evidence of "entrepreneurial spirit.") And he was getting laid.

When he went too long without sex, he invariably felt depressed. The pent-up sexual energy seemed to corrode his self-esteem. One-night stands mostly failed to satisfy. (Since the main criterion one selected for was willingness, perhaps this wasn't surprising.) Casual dating, he had learned, didn't work all that well either. Too many hurt feelings. What he had with Hannah—sex with a woman he liked—was better, clearly, than any of the other options.

Of course, it was a lot more than sex, what he had with Hannah.

The air, as he entered the park, was thick with humidity. When he stepped onto the running path, he glanced at his phone to check the time, then sped up.

Free-floating ennui wasn't something Nate experienced much until the past year. Before he'd sold his book, his adult life had been so circumscribed financially and so uncertain professionally—yet so charged with the beating pulse of his ambition—that he hadn't hungered for drama. Through no choice of his own, bohemianism, in the sense of not always knowing how he'd pay the rent, had been thrust upon him. The fear of failure had been real and constant. He supposed some part of him missed it, missed the urgency.

The running path, a utility road, really, curved through a wooded area. The foliage crowded out all signs of urban life. For a moment, Nate just listened to the sound of his footfalls on the asphalt.

A few days ago, he'd received a solicitation from the nonprofit that maintains the park. He'd felt a pang of guilt when he tossed the letter in the trash, but he had a tall stack of solicitations from various do-gooder outfits.

Once he would have thrown them all out unopened. It had seemed obvious they were intended for someone else. Someone more like the rest of his Harvard classmates. Someone who wasn't broke. But though he was far from free of financial worry, Nate knew he no longer had quite the same excuse of poverty as he used to have. Yet he felt depressed whenever he thought about writing out a check to any of these worthy organizations, of then making a note of it for his accountant to get the tax deduction. He would have denied it, even to himself—deemed it a laughable affectation—but it seemed to him now that he had always secretly believed that in the way he lived (he refused to say his "life-style"), in his freelance, un-health-insured, sparsely thinged life, he was in a small way registering a rejection—of conformity, of middle-class convention, of not just acquisitiveness but enslave-ment to the idol of "security." Nevertheless, he'd wound up in the same place as everyone else. Was this—latte liberalism—his ines-capable fate? Surely it was. It was sheer vanity to pretend other-wise. What'd he think he was going to do, foment revolution with his precious essay about the commodification of conscience? Still, no matter how worthwhile the cause, no matter how many dissi-dents were spared torture or children saved from preventable disease, he never could send in his hundred dollars without feel-ing like he'd crossed over and that something had been lost along the way.

Nate realized he'd slowed down. About a hundred feet in front of him, a blonde woman with a long ponytail was moving at a good clip. She had shapely legs and a long narrow waist. She reminded him a little of Kristen. He began using her as a pacesetter.

It was useless to lament what he'd lost—if he'd lost anything, if it weren't pure self-indulgence to think this way. He'd been extremely lucky. Sure, writing his book hadn't been entirely easy. To finish it, he'd eventually quit his biweekly book-reviewing gig, which had been the only claim to status he'd had in the eyes of the world. Even Elisa, who'd believed in the book, had wondered if giving it up was a mistake. "You never know what'll happen," she pointed out. But the reviews hadn't paid enough to justify the time and energy they required. He'd gone back to temping, which paid more, per hour, and required less mentally. He had proofread. He had done what he had to—for the sake of something that existed only as a Microsoft Word document, a sprawling tale of a young immigrant family grappling with life in the American suburbs in the 1970s and 1980s, a work he'd been revising and rewriting since he was in his midtwenties without ever having earned a penny from it. But writing his book—at least after a certain point, years in, when, by shifting its focus from the son to the parents, he'd finally seemed to find the thing's pulse and the novel began to take shape almost of its own accord—had also been the greatest pleasure of his life. That a publisher was then willing to pay him for it, pay him generously, was nothing to complain about. He'd do it again for free, in a minute. Many of those late nights, when he'd paced his apartment, his mind roaming the world he'd painstakingly created and could finally inhabit—moving within it from character to character, feverishly distilling into words thoughts not his own but theirs—had been ecstasies of absorption and self-forgetfulness.

Of course, life couldn't always be lived at that pitch. Day-to-day life was bound, sometimes, to be mundane, full of workaday tasks and minor decisions. *Amnesty International or Doctors Without Borders? Dinner in or dinner out?* Some nights were bound to contain little more than a movie on Netflix.

As he emerged from the wooded part of the park, the heat began to wear on him. He started counting out his breaths.

The gap between him and the Kristen-like runner narrowed. He sped up even more, fighting his body's yearning toward comfort. As the path wound around the pond, the tall yellow grasses that lined its shore waved slightly in spite of the air's stillness. Nate overtook the blonde.

When he began to climb the last and longest hill of the running loop, thought was edged out by the need to focus on his breathing. All he could do was register in short, sensory bursts of intake the scene around him: leafy trees on his right, meadow on his left, an Asian chick in a Duke T-shirt running in the opposite direction, a swarm of passing bicyclists.

At the top of the hill, he was breathing hard. He forced himself to run faster. The last eighth of a mile, slightly downhill, was more tunnel-like, lined with trees on both sides. Each time his foot hit the pavement, he silently repeated the word *will*, as in *I will*, as in *willpower*, as in the thing that had made him get off his ass and write, night after night, when he'd been in his twenties, working those interminable temp jobs, long before writing the book had been fun, when all he'd wanted to do was get wasted, or at the very least do something passive, like read.

He reached the end of the loop and almost collapsed at the waist. Panting, he stumbled past a gaggle of Orthodox Jewish girls in long sleeves and long skirts. After a moment his breath became more regular. He checked his time on his phone. Twenty-seven minutes, twenty-two seconds. Not his best for 3.42 miles. The humidity had gotten to him.

Although he had come up with an idea for another book, by early September he hadn't made any headway on it. He decided he needed more time to hash out the idea before he'd be ready to start writing. In the meantime, he yearned for something else to do. Because his review of the Israel book a couple months before had gone over well, he wrote to his editor at that publication and asked to review an upcoming novel by a prominent young British author. He was a little surprised not to get a response right away.

It came several days later. It wasn't the one he was looking for. Eugene Wu had been given the assignment. Nate couldn't believe it. He had done such a good job with the Israel book. (He thought he had anyway.) He had pretty much assumed this one was his for the asking. He couldn't believe he'd been turned down in favor of *Eugene*.

He and Hannah were having dinner with Aurit that night. On their way to the restaurant, Nate told Hannah about Eugene getting the assignment, but he downplayed his disappointment. He didn't want her pity. And it was embarrassing. He hated that being passed over in favor of Eugene bothered him as much as it did. It suggested a pettiness and an insecurity that he associated with mediocrity. It was not exactly the light in which he wanted Hannah, who was nobody's fool, to see him. Besides, between the two of them, he had always played the role of the more successful writer. He had been the one to champion *her* work, to build *her* up. For their roles to be reversed, even temporarily, would only add to his sense of indignity.

The restaurant they were meeting Aurit at had opened only recently. Aurit had chosen it. But the dinner had been his idea. He wanted Hannah and Aurit get to know each other better. Although Aurit got on his nerves in a thousand different ways, he had never ceased to consider her one of the most intelligent and interesting women he'd ever met. Over the years, he had compared various women he'd dated to her, in terms of conversation. Until Hannah, the comparison had not tended to flatter the woman he was sleeping with.

While he and Hannah waited for Aurit to arrive, Nate scanned the menu and saw that the place was more expensive than he would have liked. He felt a twinge of irritation.

He had lately started to worry that he was spending too much, little by little letting his standard of living edge upward, as if his book advance money could never be depleted. As he'd just been reminded, freelance journalism assignments were unpredictable. And no matter how much he sometimes romanticized the past, he really didn't want to ever have to temp again.

"Hello! Sorry!" Aurit trilled a few minutes later as she sent semi-ironic air kisses at them.

A large leather purse and a pair of sunglasses and a set of headphones were peeled away and placed in a pile on the table. Once unencumbered, Aurit collapsed into the chair next to Nate's. "I've been on the phone with my mother," she said breathlessly. "Here's the thing about my mother . . ."

The story that followed dated back to childhood. Aurit's mother, in this telling, had long nursed an idea of herself as very sensible and self-sacrificing and unfrivolous. She propped up her self-image by constantly invoking a comparison between herself and these other women, "who've never had a job, who never, *ever* cook—they hire caterers whenever more than two people come over—who shop all the time, who resent their daughters' youth, who never read. As a kid, I bought the whole thing. It's only over time that I started to wonder where all these vapid, lazy, superficial women are. I've never encountered anyone quite so bad, let alone an army of such women, except maybe on *Dallas*. Then I realized the only place they exist is in her head, where they play a very important role. She can justify almost anything she does because she truly, deep-down believes she's more than entitled to have her 'modest' wishes granted, given the extreme and almost unparalleled excellence of her character, relative to other women."

Both Nate and Hannah were laughing.

Aurit shook her head. "It's like someone who surrounds himself with people who are less intelligent than he is so he can feel smart. Only she does it in her head. *So* fucked up."

"I know just what you mean," Hannah said.

It soon became evident to Nate that Hannah and Aurit liked each other. This had not been a given, particularly not on Aurit's end. Aurit was very picky and frequently evinced what seemed, to him, to be an arbitrary dislike for people he liked, especially women. But Aurit's approval didn't make him as happy as he'd hoped. Throughout the meal, he experienced a disorienting and rather emasculating feeling of being subsumed by a klatch of gabbing women. Aurit's and Hannah's combined selves created a stronger pull than either woman on her own. Instead of settling halfway between Nate's sensibility and Hannah's or Aurit's, the conversation was weighted toward the feminine. There was a giddily confidential, almost salacious quality to it. Moreover, Aurit and Hannah seemed to have decided beforehand to express only unequivocal agreement with whatever the other said. (When Hannah said she bought only cruelty-free chickens, did Aurit have to nod and coo quite so agreeably?—when, as Nate well knew, Aurit felt nothing but scorn for "Americans' childish sentimentality about animals.") Their enthusiastic supportiveness created a close, cloying atmosphere that made Nate clamor to get out.

"Did you have an okay time?" Hannah asked when the two of them were walking back to her place. "You seemed kind of quiet."

"It was fine."

He glanced through the open doorway of a restaurant kitchen. A white-smocked Hispanic man was stirring a steaming pot. "I just think Aurit sometimes dominates the conversation," he said. "Not to mention the way she pronounces judgment on everyone but herself. Does she really think she's above reproach?"

Hannah laughed. "She's, uhm, *your* friend."

"Yeah."

He and Hannah didn't speak much as they walked along quiet streets of brownstones. Nate knew there was a slight edge to his silence. His conscience told him he should say something to set Hannah's mind at ease—say he was tired or something. He didn't. Although his irritation was directed primarily at Aurit, it was sprawling enough to take in Hannah at the edges. There had been, in her effort to be agreeable, something slightly insipid, a sort of relaxation of her usual quick, decisive judgment. She had gone along with Aurit, matching Aurit's girly, gossipy tone. She wasn't usually like that. But this criticism was so ungenerous that it made him feel guilty. Hannah had, after all, been gamely trying to get on with his friend while he had mostly been sullen and not much help.

As Hannah unlocked her door, it occurred to him that they had been spending a lot of nights at her place. He'd prefer if they alternated between his and hers. Tonight, her place made sense, because of the location of the restaurant, but still . . . he wasn't thrilled. Inside, he checked the status of the package he'd sent his mother for her birthday. (It was, as it had been several hours earlier, in transit.) Then he checked the results of a baseball game and scanned the lead stories in the *Times*. When he finally got into bed, he and Hannah began fooling around. He wasn't really in the mood, but he went along from tact or inertia.

Soon Hannah was going down on him. It wasn't working. He started thinking about Eugene and the review. Then he thought about how he hadn't heard back from the editor he'd written to about his commodification-of-conscience essay. He remembered the day he'd gotten Hannah's first e-mail, when she'd quibbled with him about the idea. He'd thought to himself that sooner or later his dick was going to wind up in her mouth. Well, here it was.

He shut his eyes, trying to squeeze out all this unpleasant consciousness. He craved blankness, an absence of everything except for the sensation of Hannah's mouth on his cock. After a moment, he gave up. He guided Hannah away from him, pulling her face to his so he could kiss her.

Not long after, she drew back, tucking herself in like the letter *S*. "I . . . uhm . . ."

"Hmm?" he said.

"I was wondering . . . Is there maybe something you want me to do differently when I, you know, do that? I just wondered . . ."

She bit her lower lip.

"Oh!" Nate said.

As it happened, he had, more than once, felt slightly dissatisfied on this very score. It hadn't reached the level of "problem," but he had been fleetingly conscious of a small frustration. Strategically timed grunts and moans and gentle manual guidance he'd offered (by way of his hand on her head), intended to point the way toward some minor recalibration, had not been effective. But the complaint had always evaporated in the course of things, when they moved from one act to another. There is, after all, more than one way to skin a cat. Still.

"Uhm . . . ," he began.

He had always had a hard time talking about sex. That is, he had no problem discussing sex in general terms or sex as an intellectual or psychological or historical concept. When he was younger, he had enjoyed discussing various real or ideal women's bodies with his friends. But the other kind of sex talk, about what felt good and what didn't—this thing of *giving instructions*, saying, "touch me this way," "please do this, not that," even "faster" or "harder"—he found, had always found, excruciating. The prospect made him feel lecherous and animalistic and most of all unsexy, as if whatever modicum of sexiness he possessed was derived from careful, curatorial self-presentation.

Typically, the only way he could do it, state aloud what he wanted, was to go all out, sort of become a different person—the kind who could tell, not ask, a woman to take him all the way in her mouth or to suck his balls or to get on her back and spread her legs. His voice, when he said these things, sounded different, hard and flat, stripped of its usual amiability. To get to this state, he had to drum up a certain amount of contempt for the woman (because he didn't speak to any human being this way, in any other context). He'd feel himself slip out of a more civilized, woman-respecting mind-set, as if this way of being weren't really of him but merely an acquired habit, like separating out bottles and cans for recycling.

It wasn't really a place he liked to go. It didn't matter that many women claimed to like being treated that way, to get off on it. In fact, that depressed him. After he came, he inevitably felt a bit disgusted, with himself and the situation, by which he meant, in large part, the woman he was with.

There had to be another way.

Hannah was sitting upright, naked, her eyes cast downward and her hair falling forward on her face.

Nate pulled the bedsheet up around his waist, covering himself. "I, uh . . ."

Their eyes met. Hannah's expression was meek and almost beatific in a kind of nervous desire to please.

Nate saw that it was hopeless. It had been a long day. He was tired. He didn't, just then, have it in him to look into those big, kind, cruelty-free-chicken-buying eyes and tell her he'd like her to suck his balls first and to please apply gentler but more consistent pressure with her mouth and to go deeper and, simultaneously, to flatten her tongue so it sort of cradled the seam as she moved up and down his shaft, and, finally, that it would also be great if she could caress the skin between his scrotum and his anus with her fingers.

"What you do is great," he said.

"Because you could tell me if . . ."

"There's nothing to tell."

From somewhere outside Hannah's apartment, a boom box whose insistent bass Nate had barely been conscious of was abruptly switched off.

He rolled onto his back and stared at the ceiling. He wanted to be outside, in the fresh air. He liked Hannah's apartment, but he'd never particularly liked her bedroom. She had one of those big, freestanding wooden mirrors, draped with scarves and belts and other feminine things, from which wafted all sorts of artificial floral vapors. The sight of it had always depressed him, recalling to him the fusty home of his childhood piano teacher, a Quakerly widow with a long gray braid down her back. Then there was Hannah's closet. Teeming with hanging clothes and stacks of blue jeans and sweaters crammed into every available space, with a brigade of boots and pumps and sneakers in clear plastic pouches bounding downward from racks attached to the doors, the closet haunted him even unseen. It almost too neatly embodied so much that was unattractive about women: mustiness, materialism, clutter.

He also realized that he disliked the corduroy throw pillows on her bed, one of which was currently wedged under his shoulder.

He wanted to get up, to walk through the cool night to his apartment, to get in his own bed, by himself, with a book, porn on his computer if he wanted it. *Why did she have to be so unsexy about it—so like a wounded dog? How the hell was that supposed to have made him feel?* But he knew if he tried to leave, he'd just implicate himself. The only guaranteed way to avoid a scene— "what's wrong? why are you upset?"—was to stay put, act normal. Cuddle. What did it matter anyway? Soon he'd be asleep, and then it would be morning.

He tossed the throw pillow from the bed and pulled Hannah close to him. "You smell good," he said. He wasn't sure who fell asleep first, which probably meant he did.

12

Ooh, kale," Cara said. "I never could find kale in Baltimore."

Nate and Hannah and Mark smiled in sympathy. They were seated in the backyard of a new and trendy farm-to-table-type restaurant. The night had been billed as a "double date."

It was a pleasant September evening. The restaurant's yard was lit up by hanging lanterns and furnished with splintery-looking wooden tables and benches. A waiter arrived and began expiating upon a variety of specials featuring early autumn vegetables. The young man's checkered shirt and high-waisted pants reminded Nate less of a farmer than a scarecrow.

When the waiter left, Nate tore off a piece of hard-crusted bread. "How's the job search?" he asked Cara.

She set down her menu. "Terrible. That's to be expected, I guess. Everyone I know who is my age is vastly overqualified for the jobs that are out there. I mean, answering phones?" She shook her head. "It's a real problem."

Nate murmered something that passed for assent.

"Cara's honors thesis on Baudrillard won the top prize in the comp lit department at Stanford," Mark said brightly.

"Is that right?"

When Nate met Hannah's eye, he was relieved to see from her expression that she found Cara as grating as he did. Under the table, he took Hannah's hand, pressing his fingers into her palm and running his thumb along her knuckles.

After their (non)conversation about blowjobs the week before, he had avoided her for several days, claiming to be busy or tired. He knew his annoyance wasn't fair, but he had wanted the awkward recollection, and the unfamiliar feeling of her apartment as stifling, to fade from his mind. It had—basically. Maybe they'd begun to see each other a little less than they once had, but surely that was to be expected as time wore on.

The waiter brought their drinks. Cara said something about video games. Their popularity portended badly for American society. She mentioned Europe and sighed in a way that suggested young men never played video games there.

"I don't know," Hannah said. "The people I know who play a lot of video games could be up to a lot worse. You know, doing actual harm to others. At least this keeps them occupied." She shrugged. "Maybe I just know some fucked-up people."

Nate chortled.

Cara was less amused. Her face was slow to change expression, like an old clock face behind which heavy wheels had to turn. It took a moment for the set of her eyebrows and lips to register perplexity.

"That's one way of looking at it, I guess," she said.

Mark jumped in to say that Hannah was onto something with the "distraction from worse" argument. "There's a lot of evidence to suggest that people are less violent than they used to be."

As soon as he realized that he'd basically taken up the opposing side, Mark looked nervously at Cara. Nate recognized the anxious solicitude of a guy who gets laid only when certain conditions are met. Poor Mark, Nate thought.

"I'm not saying that video games make people violent," Cara said a little pettishly.

Suddenly, Nate felt a bit sorry for *her*. She was pretty, self-possessed, and intelligent enough, but she was fresh out of school and repeating opinions that were no doubt fashionable there. In time, she would catch the tone of New York. Her schoolmarmishness was provincial. Here it was all about the counterintuitive. She'd learn. Besides, being pretty, self-possessed, and intelligent enough would go a long way, and if she wasn't well connected before she started dating Mark, she would be now.

Their waiter walked briskly past, foodless. Nate squelched a yawn. Time seemed to be moving very slowly. Even Mark was different in Cara's company. His sense of humor seemed blunted, as if he couldn't simultaneously exercise it and ensure Cara's minute-to-minute happiness.

Nate felt a stirring of appreciation for Hannah. He knew that if he had been single, had been eating dinner alone with Mark and Mark's new girlfriend, he would have gotten a little depressed. Cara would have seemed, however solipsistically, a stand-in for women in general—his future, more or less. He was glad to have met someone so . . . reasonable, so *not ridiculous*, someone he liked as much as he desired.

When, finally, they were dividing up the check, Nate happened to catch a sidelong glance at Cara. He was momentarily struck by just how good-looking she was. But then Mark had always been a very shallow guy, in terms of women. Then, it occurred to Nate that Mark could very well feel sorry for *him*, just because technically Cara was better-looking than Hannah (although Hannah was, as far as he was concerned, far more appealing). Still, it was a weird thought, and he pushed it aside. Sometimes he wished he could turn his brain off.

Back at his apartment, Hannah told him that her friend Susan was coming to town from Chicago that weekend.

She was sitting Indian-style on his bed, with a weeks-old issue of the *New Yorker* in her lap. "Do you want to have brunch with us on Sunday?" she asked.

Nate was standing in the doorway. He combed a hand through his hair.

This invitation didn't do much for him. Hannah had described Susan as one of those people who sees her life as a long series of injustices perpetrated against her by various assholes. If you take issue with her account, you're one of the assholes. A real charmer, she sounded like.

Besides, he wasn't big on brunch as a social to-do. This one was easy to imagine: 11:00, wait in line with all the other yuppies at hip new restaurant, make tired conversation about whatever Susan does for a living and how New York compares to Chicago; 11:30, order a Bloody Mary, still standing outside, still waiting to be seated; 12:00, at the table, order inadvisable second Bloody Mary in attempt to stave off creeping boredom/existential despair; 12:30, split the check and silently regret blowing thirty dollars (the extra ten for the second Bloody Mary) when he would have been happier with the six-dollar Sunday Special (two eggs, bacon, home fries, and toast) at the nongentrified diner on his street.

Hannah had already taken out her contacts. She peered at him from above the rims of her glasses. Her hair was in a ponytail. Nate's glance flitted to the milk crate beside his bed. On it sat a stack of upcoming books that he wanted to go through with an eye to pitching reviews or essays. Reading in a leisurely, exploratory sort of way was just the kind of thing he enjoyed doing on a Saturday or Sunday, perhaps at home, perhaps at a sports bar with a game on in the background. He'd intended to spend last weekend this way, but it had gotten away from him. He wasn't entirely happy about that. When you're single, your weekend days are wide-open vistas that extend in every direction; in a relationship, they're like the sky over Manhattan: punctured, hemmed in, compressed.

Nate scratched the back of his head. "I don't know," he said. "I'm not sure what I'm doing."

He smiled nervously.

"Okay," Hannah said.

Nate couldn't read her expression, but instantly he felt apprehensive. Hannah turned back to the magazine. Almost unconsciously he remained where he was.

After a moment, Hannah looked up. *"What?"*

He stepped back. "Nothing!"

"God! I can't stand this!"

"Can't stand *what*?"

"You! Standing there, waiting for me to get mad at you because you don't want to get brunch." She made a face at him. "I don't care. I don't care if you come or not."

"Okay . . . ," Nate said slowly. "But you asked me if I wanted to come, so I just naturally assumed that you cared, at least a little bit?"

Hannah took off her glasses and held them in her hand. "It's like you want to make me out to be some kind of demanding, hysterical girlfriend," she said. "That's not who I am."

Nate was momentarily confused. He certainly hadn't expected her to be *this* angry. Then it sunk in what she was accusing him of. He heard his voice rise as he spoke. "Can you maybe tell me how exactly I made you out to be 'demanding and hysterical'? Was it something I said? Because I don't remember saying a damned thing."

"It's like . . . you just . . . ugh!"

Hannah stood up, and the magazine slid from her lap, landing in a heap on the floor. "It's just this vibe."

"A *vibe*?" Nate repeated, the word inflected with weeks of unspoken tension.

Hannah flushed.

Her discomposure had the effect of making Nate feel more composed.

"As far as I recall," he said coolly, "you asked me a question and I answered, and now you are mad at me for assuming, like a complete asshole, that you cared about my answer."

Hannah closed her eyes and inhaled through her nose. "What I mean is that it's not some test. I care like I care if we get Thai food or sushi whether you come or not."

"Great. Brunch. Not a test. Noted."

"Will you quit it with the sarcasm? *I get it.* It's not about brunch. It's how you've been acting. I feel you putting me into this box. I am not that person, and I resent you for making me out to be that person."

They were now standing head to head, with only about a foot of space between them. Nate felt energized—wholly awake.

"You realize I have no clue what you are talking about," he said. "What person am I making you out to be?"

She didn't blink. "The person forcing you to give up your freedom."

"Wait, am I the one in the box? Who's in the box? You or me?"

Nate felt himself shifting his weight from one leg to the other the way he did when he played football.

"Fuck you, Nate," Hannah said. "Just fuck you. You know what I mean. Or you would if you were being honest."

He threw up his hands in a pantomime of disbelief. "Excuse me for listening and trying to understand what you're saying."

"Fine." She shook her head. "Have it your way. I'm just being ridiculous."

Nate didn't contradict her. They stared at each other. "I'm going to brush my teeth," he said finally.

"Great."

The bathroom's fluorescent light was oppressively bright. A few of Hannah's long hairs were stuck to the grimy white porcelain of his sink. Nate felt a little shaky as he lingered over his teeth. He'd been mean, he knew he'd been mean, but she'd started it. There was no denying that. *Making her out to be demanding and hysterical?* He hadn't done *anything.*

He decided to floss. It occurred to him that maybe she'd have gotten up and gotten dressed. Maybe she'd pack up her things and leave. He approached the bedroom warily. Hannah was on the bed.

"I'm sorry," she said. Her voice was contrite but not otherwise emotional. "I'm sorry I blew up like that."

Nate was surprised to find himself disappointed. Not that she hadn't left—he hadn't really expected her to—but that she seemed normal again. When she'd been acting crazy, he'd had license to give vent to that pent-up tension, and yet to be also beautifully, effortlessly *right*. Something he'd learned with Elisa: it was not always unpleasant to deal with a hysterical woman. One feels so thoroughly righteous in comparison. Now he felt as if he were deflating. Although he hadn't been conscious of being turned on before—he'd been fairly disgusted by Hannah's hair in the sink—he felt his cock slackening, as if without his noticing it, he had been a bit hard.

"It's no big deal," he said. "Don't worry about it."

"I think we should talk about it."

"Everyone needs to blow off steam sometimes."

"I mean, the reason why."

Of course she did.

Nate sank into his desk chair, feeling dispirited, vanquished. He crossed his legs and then immediately uncrossed them.

"I'm sure it seemed to come out of nowhere to you," Hannah said in a fair and reasonable tone of voice, an aggravatingly fair and reasonable tone of voice. A voice that compelled him to be fair and reasonable too. "I think I reacted the way I did because I felt like you were waiting for me to burst into tears about brunch with Susan. It just seemed narcissistic or something. I don't know, it just pissed me off."

In spite of himself, Nate smiled.

She went on. "It's just that lately I've had this sense that something is different. With you, or with us, and I keep waiting for you to say something . . . I don't want to be the kind of girlfriend who analyzes every little thing or makes us talk things to death—I really don't—but if something is up, I wish you'd just tell me. I don't expect things to be exactly like they were when we first started dating. But don't *oblige* me, like you're the put-upon boyfriend." Hannah sat up very straight; her tone became more insistent, almost defiant. "If you don't want this, fine. I'm not some girl who is dying to be in a relationship."

Nate leaned back in his desk chair so its two front wheels were raised off the ground. Pretty much every relationship conversation he had ever been party to included more or less the same caveats. Apparently, no woman in the early twenty-first century is the kind of woman who (a) wants a boyfriend or (b) wants to talk about her relationship, no matter how much she (a) wants a boyfriend and (b) wants to talk about her relationship.

As he rocked the chair back to face her, Nate cleared this unnice thought from his mind.

"Hannah," he said gently, "I'm not 'obliging' you. I don't know what gave you that idea."

She tugged at her ponytail. "It's just—well, I hope you know that I don't think we have to spend every second together. I don't *want* to. But if you make excuses not to see me, as if you think I'm going to get mad at you, or if you skulk around and act guilty because you don't want to have brunch with my friend, it makes me feel like it's a bigger deal, like there's something else you're trying to tell me."

With his foot, Nate traced a circle on the floor. He said, "I thought you might be disappointed, that's all. I didn't mean anything by it."

Hannah nodded. "That's fair," she said. "I overreacted. I'm sorry."

She looked the way she sounded—sincere. An uncomfortable feeling had come over Nate. Now that he'd been accorded the full power to forgive, he didn't feel sure he deserved it. Even when they'd been fighting, he'd had some inkling of the box she'd been referring to. He might have feigned a bit more ignorance than he could honestly claim. But then the whole thing had happened so fast—he had just been defending himself.

"Don't worry about it," he said, feeling that the least he could do was be gracious. "I'm just glad you're not mad. And I'm sorry I was mean before. I guess I felt attacked."

"I can understand that," Hannah said. "And I'll drop this, I promise, but just to be clear . . . I don't care about Sunday. Susan isn't a close friend. But"—she paused and looked at him intently, her hazel eyes round and luminous in the light from his lamp—"if you *are* on some level unhappy, it would be better to say so now, before—"

"Hannah."

Nate rested a hand on each of her knees. Whatever mild dissatisfaction he had felt recently had been displaced by the fight, by Hannah's feistiness, by the moment's intensity.

"I like you. I want to be with you. The only thing I'm trying to tell you is that I don't want to have brunch with your friend Susan on Sunday. I hate to say it, but you didn't really make her sound all that appealing." He cocked his head. "You might want to work on your sales pitch next time."

"It's just that lately you sometimes seem a little—"

"I've been a little stressed," he cut in. "I thought by now I'd be well into another book, but I'm not. All I've got is an idea, and even that's vague. I feel as if I ought to be working night and day until I figure that out. I don't have a regular gig the way you do with the health news."

Hannah hugged her knees to her chest. "You want to do the health news?" she said. "Be my guest."

Nate sat down beside her on the bed. When she stretched, he could make out her nipples through the thin fabric of her T-shirt. "You know what I mean," he said.

The issue seemed, to him, to have been resolved, but they continued to talk for a while longer. This didn't really surprise him. In his experience, women, once they got started, exhibited a rather insatiable desire to confess, elaborate, iron out, reveal, and so on and so forth. Nate exerted himself to be patient. Hannah was generally an extremely easygoing girlfriend, more easygoing than anyone he'd dated since Kristen. He didn't begrudge her a little girlishness. They went to bed on good terms.

But she brought it up again the next time he saw her. They were on the subway, coming back from Manhattan.

"I feel kind of ridiculous about the other night," she said. "Getting so mad and then making us talk and talk. I hope you don't think I'm really . . . I don't know . . ."

The words trailed off, and she smiled helplessly as she waited for him to rescue her from her own sentence.

Nate's thoughts had been far removed from relationship issues, and he didn't feel like getting drawn into another of those conversations. He also didn't like being pressured to provide reassurances on demand, being made to perform his affection at someone else's bidding, like a trained seal. Besides, it seemed that in soliciting assurance—after everything that had been said the other night— Hannah was allowing herself to give in to a neurotic compulsion. That wasn't something he wanted to reward.

"It's *fine*," he said in the kind of cold, flat voice that only someone with serious Asperger's would take at face value.

Hannah's expression indicated to Nate that she did not suffer from Asperger's syndrome.

Nate looked away, a little repelled by the near panic he'd seen on her face. He was also afraid that if he looked at her, he'd feel bad and apologize, and he didn't want to feel bad or apologize. He didn't want to feel like the big bad wolf just because he wouldn't play this particular feminine parlor game.

He stared across the aisle at a little boy who slept with his head on his mother's shoulder. The boy's small calves were visible between the bottom of his pants and his socks.

After a minute, Nate's irritation faded, dissolving almost as quickly as it had come on. She'd been a little insecure; it wasn't the worst thing.

"Sorry," he said, turning to her. "I didn't mean to snap at you."

The panic had been wiped clean from her face. Her expression was blank, hard. As she considered his apology, she seemed to relax.

"Don't worry about it," she said. "It's not a big deal."

Nothing more was said, and for the rest of the evening, they were resolutely light and cheerful.

{ 13 }

Nate held his cordless phone to his ear with one hand as he half-heartedly sponged his kitchen counter with the other. He found his parents easier to talk to if he engaged simultaneously in other tasks.

He spoke first to his father, who was not actually that hard to deal with. All Nate had to do was be polite and impersonally pleasant, the way he would if he were talking to a well-meaning but nosy stranger, someone he met, say, in the line at the Department of Motor Vehicles.

"Did you get the next payment from your publisher yet?" his father asked. "You know that every day they hold on to that money, it's accruing interest that is rightfully yours."

"They made the payment, right on schedule," Nate assured him. "My agent has the money. She'll write me a check."

"Minus fifteen percent," his father said in a tone that suggested that this was a "Gotcha!" moment.

"Yes, dad. Minus fifteen percent."

"You know, Nathaniel . . . ," his father began. No argument could convince him that, as an aeronautical engineer, he might not have sufficient knowledge of the publishing industry to determine that the services of a literary agent were unnecessary.

Nate switched the phone from one ear to the other and rested it between his shoulder and his ear so both his hands were free. He began lifting up the grills of his stove and scrubbing the surfaces underneath with a Brillo pad.

"Have you given any thought to self-publishing the next one?" his father asked. "I've read that a number of established authors are starting to do that. Once they have a following, they don't need the publisher's name. This way, all the profits come to you. Eh?"

"I'll look into it."

Nate walked to the window and pulled up the blinds. Sunlight streamed into the kitchen.

His mother got on the line. She began telling him a story about the people at her work, how they were all moony about some television series "on HBO or Showtime or some such nonsense."

From a hundred and eighty miles away, Nate could feel her gathering energy, the satisfying torrent of contempt she was whipping herself into.

"They say that it's as good as a nineteenth-century novel," she said, her speech growing more rapid. "And these are supposed to be the 'smart' young people. They went to Georgetown and Columbia—practically Ivy League schools."

Through the window, the leaves on the trees' topmost branches were already beginning to fall off.

"Like Tolstoy!"

"That's nuts . . . ," Nate agreed.

But his tone was too mild. He felt rather than heard his mother's silence.

Unlike his father, his mother required that she and Nate be in vociferous accord. In colorful, overheated language, she framed life as a drama between "we" and the rest of the world, otherwise known as "those idiots." As a child, Nate had loved being on her side. Not only was she beautiful, with her long, honey-colored hair and tightly belted dresses, not only did her exotic French and Russian novels and aristocratic unhappiness appeal to his imagination, but her side was also so clearly the right one. It was the side of sensible governance: potholes filled in, corruption punished, Democrats elected, Israeli passenger planes and cruise ships not hijacked (the last position reiterated often after sixty-eight-year-old, wheelchair-bound Leon Klinghoffer was pushed overboard from the *Achille Lauro* when Nate was in the fourth grade). Hers was also the side of intelligence. (She had a moral disdain for stupidity and instinctively regarded Nate's classmates in the slow reading group with suspicion, as children of dubious character.) She stood for the appreciation of culture, especially literature, theater, and museums. When Nate got older, it was her smugness that bothered him. He was put off by the invocation of this all-thwarting "they," and the certain knowledge that all problems would be summarily solved if only "we" weren't obstructed at every turn. But if he questioned this presumption, his mother took it as an attack or clucked that he was too young and naive to understand. Their adult relationship was built on his willingness to humor her. Unless he was able to summon the energy and patience to appear to join her in this cloistered, airless "we," he—the son for whose sake she had left her home to start over in a new country—was rejecting her. With his dad, all he had to do was not argue.

Blinking into the sun as he gazed out the window, Nate knew he had failed. She'd sensed condescension in his tepid agreement. *He went to Harvard, and now he thinks he's too good for me.* She sucked in her breath sharply, as if it were her very soul she'd offered up to him and which she was now withdrawing. As clearly as if she were standing before him, he could see her nostrils flare once or twice.

It was too much, he knew—what his mother wanted of him. It wasn't fair or reasonable, his friends would tell him. But neither had her life been fair or reasonable. In Romania, she'd been denied all sorts of academic honors because she was Jewish. She wasn't even permitted to major in literature, as the humanities were

THE LOVE AFFAIRS OF NATHANIEL P.

almost entirely closed to Jews. She'd slept on a couch in the living room of her parents' one-bedroom apartment in a concrete tenement until the day she married Nate's father, whose family was a little better off. Then she'd come here and worked as a computer programmer—so that Nate could attend private school, so that he could go to a good college.

Nate leaned his forehead against the glass windowpane. "How have you been, Mom?"

"Fine." Her voice was tight and small.

He closed the blinds and shuffled back to the sink, sliding a little on the linoleum in his socks and tightening his grip on the phone. They were the reason he had this stupid cordless phone. His parents had insisted on a landline—"in case of an emergency." The only people who used it were the two of them and the telemarketers.

"You think I'm old-fashioned," his mother said after a moment. "Narrow-minded."

The sigh that punctuated this remark was a finely honed symphony of self-pity.

"*Mom*," Nate said. "I don't even *have* a TV. Of course I don't think you're narrow-minded."

She let out a small chuckle. "I guess we're both a little bit backward."

"I guess so."

There was another, less fraught silence.

"How's Hannah?" she asked finally. *Henna* was how it sounded from her lips.

Nate squeezed the water from his sponge.

"She's okay."

Several evenings later, he was sitting in Hannah's living room, reading Eugene's review of the British novelist's new book.

"Nate?"

The review was good—very good, Nate had to admit. Eugene was good.

"Nate?" Hannah said again.

Reluctantly, Nate laid the article down. Hannah was standing with her hands in her back pockets. "Yes?"

"What do you feel like doing tonight?"

Nate closed his eyes. What did he and Hannah usually do together? For a moment, he couldn't remember. Then he thought of the long nights of animated conversation they used to have, over the summer—nights when they'd never needed to "do" anything. He wasn't in the mood for that sort of . . . *communion* of togetherness. Certainly not.

He thought maybe he felt like watching baseball. The playoffs were approaching, and there was a game he was mildly interested in for its potential negative impact on the Yankees.

Hannah said sure, they could go to a sports bar.

They went to a place called Outpost, an unfortunate name, in Nate's opinion, for a newish establishment that appeared to be patronized almost exclusively by the white people who'd begun to move into the historically black neighborhood in which it was located.

The game hadn't started yet. When they sat down, Hannah told him she'd decided to take on some copyediting work for extra money. She started describing the exacting requirements of the publisher she was doing the work for.

Was this his life now? Nate wondered as she spoke. Sitting across from Hannah at various tables, in various restaurants and bars? Ad infinitum. Was this what he'd committed himself to the night they'd had that fight about brunch and he'd reassured her, told her that it was safe—that he was into this?

He tore off the slip of paper that kept his napkin rolled up and began toying with his knife and fork.

He tried to focus on what Hannah was saying—still about the copyediting job—but he found himself wondering how much she needed the money. At the rate she was going, she'd never finish her book proposal. Besides, her father was a corporate lawyer. He didn't doubt she could get money from him if she needed it. A nice luxury if you had it.

Though it was the last day of September, the evening was warm. Hannah had taken off her jacket. Underneath she was wearing a strappy tank top. It became her. She had nice shoulders. But when she moved her arms in emphasis of some point, Nate noticed that the skin underneath jiggled a little bit, like a much older woman's. It was odd because she was quite fit. He felt bad for noticing and worse for being a little repelled. And yet he was transfixed. The distaste he felt, in its crystalline purity, was perversely pleasurable. He kept waiting for her to wave her arms again.

When she finished her story, he just nodded.

He was hungry. Where was their food? he wanted to know. "Why do you think it's taking so long?" he said.

Hannah looked a little surprised by his vehemence. She raised her hands, her palms facing up. "No idea."

She asked him a few questions about what he'd been up to. His answers were short. He couldn't rouse himself to match her mood of cheerful pleasantry. If she were a stranger—a mere friend or acquaintance—it would be nothing, nothing at all, to fall into the rhythms of polite if banal conversation. But it was different with Hannah. Being with her had rarely entailed that kind of obligatory social performance; to start treating it that way now seemed like a defeat. Or a capitulation.

Hannah tried to fill the vacuum. As she flitted from topic to topic, Nate began to feel as if he were watching her from a remove, evaluating her. Even though she spoke with a fair amount of wit— she was telling a story about a friend's "almost aggressive tactfulness; she doesn't wait until you finish talking to start agreeing with you and supporting you"—something in her tone, an eagerness to please, a quality that was almost pleading, grated on him.

"Nate?" she asked finally.

"Yeah?"

"Is everything okay? You seem kind of . . . I don't know . . . *distracted*?"

"I'm fine," he said. He flashed a quick smile to compensate for what was unconvincing in his voice.

A moment later, Hannah got up to use the ladies' room. As he watched her walk away, he noticed that the jeans she was wearing made her bottom half look bigger than her top half, her hips and ass strangely wide and flat. He wondered why none of her girl-friends had told her this, about the jeans. Why hadn't she herself noticed? After all, a huge, full-length mirror took up a quarter of her bedroom.

When she returned, she asked if he was mad at her.

As if she had done anything that would have entitled him to be mad at her. Why the fuck did women, no matter how smart, how *independent*, inevitably revert to this state of willed imbecil-ity? It wasn't as if he had the emotional register of a binary sys-tem, as if his only states of being were "happy" and "mad at her."

"No," he said. "I'm not *mad* at you."

She drew back.

Before anything more was said, the waiter brought their burgers. *Finally*. The game began. As he ate, Nate turned his attention to the television screen above the bar. He began to feel better.

"That really hit the spot," he said of his burger.

Hannah was doing something on her phone and didn't look up.

Nate pretended not to notice. "How's yours?"

She raised her gaze slowly and blinked several times, as if trying to determine by this means if he could really be such a moron. "You're asking me how my burger is?"

"*I'm sorry*," he said. "Sometimes I get grouchy when I'm hungry. It's no excuse, but I am sorry."

"Whatever."

"I should probably start carrying nuts in my pockets."

He saw the barest hint of a smile. She immediately suppressed it. But it was a start.

In the process of wheedling Hannah back into good humor, Nate, too, was revived. Having a project—getting back into Hannah's good graces—dispelled boredom and silenced that critical voice. He told her (because women love talking about personal life) about Aurit, who was flipping out because Hans was still balking about moving to New York.

"She treats his concern for his career like it's a transparent excuse. I've got to get her to quit that before she really pisses him off."

By the time their plates were cleared, all traces of Nate's former mood were gone. He appreciated that Hannah had gone along with his desire to watch baseball. He had a good time.

On the walk home, Hannah turned to him. "Nate?"

"Yeah?"

"What was the deal before?"

He tensed. He'd already said he was sorry. And what had he done, really? Spoken sharply to her? In fact, all he'd actually said was "I'm not mad at you." It could hardly be deemed a vicious comment. Maybe he'd been a *little* curt before. But. Come. On.

"I don't want to be overly dramatic," she said. "But . . . I don't want to be treated that way. If you're unhappy about something—"

"I'm not."

What was he supposed to say? That maybe she should do some tricep curls so her upper arms didn't jiggle? Buy some jeans that had been vetted from all angles? He sounded, even to himself, like some sick fetishist of female emaciation. He sounded like a real bastard.

He took her hand. "I don't know what came over me. I'm sorry."

"You know, Jason," Aurit said. "There's a certain type of man who likes to be with women he feels intellectually superior to."

"Who says models can't be smart?" Jason shot back, glancing at Nate for support.

The three of them were standing by an open window at their friend Andrew's new apartment. Andrew and his boyfriend were throwing a housewarming party. Jason was telling them about the Lithuanian model that the art director of his magazine had promised to set him up with.

"For your information," Jason said, "Brigita studied electrical engineering in Vilnius."

"It's like Lydgate in *Middlemarch*," said Aurit, apparently unimpressed by electrical engineering. "'That distinction of mind which belonged to his intellectual ardor did not penetrate his feelings and judgment about furniture, or women.'" Aurit smiled sweetly at Jason. "Lydgate ends up with the dumb blonde, by the way. She ruins his life. His career, too."

Jason wrapped one of his long arms around Aurit's shoulders. "Aurit, darling, you're so cute when you get riled up. Like Mighty Mouse. But I've got to tell you, Lydgate's the best character in that book. Also"—he paused to take a sip of his beer—"*of course* George Eliot would think the way you do. She's not exactly unbiased. Smart women have a personal stake in vilifying men who fail to appreciate smart women. Trust me, men can do great things no matter who they marry."

"Jesus, Jase," Nate said.

"Think about it," Jason said. "If so-called companionate partnership between two intellectual peers were the measure of a man's worth, there'd be maybe two first-rate men in all of history— Eliot's own pseudo-husband and John fucking Adams."

Aurit had slipped out of Jason's grasp. She eyed Jason coolly. "Does the fact that you have no soul ever worry you, Jason?"

Nate snorted.

Their group broke up. Nate migrated from the window. The living room was packed. In the scrum of bodies, Nate spotted Greer Cohen, looking rather fetching in tight jeans. Before he could wave hello, he felt a tap on his shoulder. It was Josh, a guy he played soccer with. Josh worked at a publishing house, and he congratulated Nate; he said he'd heard good things about his book, sensed growing excitement.

"Thanks, man," Nate said.

"It comes out in February, right?" Josh asked.

Nate nodded. Then he saw Eugene Wu. He told Eugene that he liked his review of the British author. Though he tried to conceal it, Eugene seemed pleased. After a bit, he and Nate got into a protracted argument about the relative proportion of women with breast implants in New York versus in red states. Nate realized he was having a good time. It occurred to him that he had more fun at parties when he had a girlfriend than when he didn't. Being in a relationship spared him from having to hit on girls, from getting into long, boring or boring-ish conversations with girls he barely liked in the hopes of getting laid. He was free to talk to the people he actually wanted to talk to.

As he left the party, he called Hannah. "Hey," he said into his cell phone when she picked up. She sounded as if she might have been sleeping. "What are you up to?"

Although they hadn't had concrete plans to see each other, he had told her earlier in the day that he "might" call. He had contemplated asking if she wanted to join him at the party, but he hadn't. He didn't really know why. He just hadn't felt like it. Besides, she'd been the one who said, when they'd fought over brunch, that they didn't have to spend every minute together.

He paused in front of a subway entrance and asked her if she wanted him to come over. She hesitated. "I'll probably be in bed," she said. "But you're welcome to come. If you want."

The night air smelled pleasantly of burned leaves. It was starting to feel like fall. Nate decided to walk to Hannah's instead of taking the train. On his way, he stopped at a deli and bought her a Hershey bar because he knew she liked them, preferred them to fancier chocolates.

"I'm sorry I didn't call earlier," he said when he arrived. "I just got caught up in things."

She was wearing an oversized Kent State T-shirt, and her hair was loose, a little messy. "It's no big deal," she said. "I had a chance to do some reading."

Nate sniffed. He could tell she'd smoked a cigarette recently.

They sat on the chairs by her window and caught up a bit. He hadn't seen her for several days. She told him she'd been feeling a little down lately. She ran her fingers through her hair. She said she thought she needed to get back into her book proposal, something that she could really throw herself into. She hadn't been writing enough lately. Maybe it would cheer her. Nate felt a flicker of guilt. He suspected that he, that things between the two of them, might also have a role in her mood. He knew he'd been a little distant. But he agreed with her plan. "Work is always a big help for me," he said. "In terms of mood. That and sports, doing something physical."

She raised her eyebrows. "Do you know how many Pilates classes I do?"

Her tone was challenging. It reminded him of how she'd been on their early dates. Lately she'd been . . . more tentative, almost nervous.

He ran his eyes down her scantily clad body. "I know you look hot," he said. "C'mon." He took her hand, pulling her toward the bedroom.

In bed, he peeled off her T-shirt and underwear. The taste of cigarette in her mouth as they kissed wasn't ideal—over time her smoking had begun to bother him more—but it wasn't a big deal. He fondled her a little. Soon he was on top of her, sliding into her easily. At first, he felt great. But he was drunk and a little desensitized. He needed more. He began riffling through various mental images. He saw Hannah lying naked on his bed, one of the first times they'd slept together: an abandoned look on her face that he'd never forgotten, the way she'd arched her back as he approached, pushing up her breasts. This held his attention for a moment. Then he became conscious of a clock ticking and the whine of a bus outside. He turned his mind to Internet porn, a petite brunette who looked a little like Greer Cohen in a hiked-up businesswoman's suit getting it from behind on a big wooden desk.

Beneath him, Hannah's eyelids were crinkled shut. Then her eyes opened. For an instant, she and Nate looked directly at each other. She froze, as if she'd been caught. What he saw, before she masked it, was total vacancy, absence, as if she were a log floating down a river, as if she were scarcely conscious that he was fucking her.

Nate, leaning his weight on his elbows, looked away from her face, craning his neck and staring angrily at the wall behind her. If she wasn't having the best sex of her life, he couldn't help but feel it wasn't all his fault. She was too . . . merely acquiescent. Her bedroom persona was meek, pliable. Even her body, her pale flesh, had a soft, quivering quality—melting, enveloping, but lacking something . . . some plasticity, some pushback.

After a moment, he turned her over on her hands and knees. He felt a pang as he positioned her this way. It was one thing to do it doggie style when the sex was energetic and smutty, when it was in keeping with the joint mood. This wasn't that. This might as well be masturbation. It had nothing to do with her.

As her glowing white ass lurched back and forth, the loose flesh of her thighs flapping from his momentum, he couldn't help but think that there was something humiliating—to women— about doing it this way. But for him it was better, in terms of sensation. Besides, she was probably relieved that she didn't have to look at him. The expression on her face now was probably worse than absent. It was, no doubt, resigned.

He pounded harder. Hannah's hair, moist with sweat, parted in clumps on either side of her neck. Finally, he felt an orgasm build, and he reached underneath her to cup her breasts, thrusting a few last times as the waves of his climax coursed through him.

Afterward, he curled up against her. His orgasm had swept his irritation away. He felt a little bad for the way he'd pawed at her. He hadn't really done much to get her into it. *Next time* . . . He wrapped his arm around her in atonement, nuzzling his chin into the crook of her shoulder as he lay behind her. He felt spent and peaceful as he began to drift into sleep.

He only half woke up when he felt her wriggle from his embrace and slip out of bed. He heard the bedroom door close and opened one eye in time to see a yellow stripe appear underneath as she turned on the living room light. He fell back asleep. He woke up again when Hannah got back into bed. It seemed to him like a long time had passed.

"Is everything okay?" he asked.

"It's fine," she said. "Go back to sleep."

But there was something aggrieved in her voice, an unstated recrimination that, even in his half-asleep state, awakened a sense of dread. Tomorrow, he decided as he began to fade back into sleep, he'd call Jason or Eugene, see what they were up to. He was in a guy mood.

{ 14 }

One night, Hannah told him she had slept around in high school. This was news to him. They were on their way back from a movie, and he'd made a comment about women in slutty Halloween get-ups. It was getting to be that time of year.

Hannah said that when she was a sophomore, she slept with a senior, a football player she felt sorry for because, though sweet, "he was so very stupid."

"I thought these probably *were* the best years of his life," she said. After that, various of his teammates wanted to go out with her. She went out with them, each of them, in turn. She shrugged as she told him this. "It seemed sexist and old-fashioned to act as if chastity really was a virtue like the born-agains thought."

She was a little tipsy—they both were—and her manner was flirtatious, but also defiant, as if she were daring him to be so prudish as to chastise or pity her. As if. Nate was titillated by this story, more turned on, in fact, than he'd been in a while.

When he'd been with Elisa, he had learned that contempt is very compatible with lust. Anger, even actual dislike and flashes of hatred, seemed to be a close enough approximation to sexual passion that the result was virtually the same. Guilt, on the other hand, is a very unsexy emotion. But now . . . It wasn't just that he found Hannah's blasé attitude toward her virginity sexy, the way atheism and Marxism and other antiestablishment, intellectual isms are sexy in an attractive woman. It was something far more corrupt. The image of those empty-headed, teenage douche bags fucking Hannah, passing her around from one to the next, of her *obliging* them because she was *nice*, turned him on like porn turned him on. Her dumb naïveté, that bovine, Marilyn Monroe–like credulity, transformed her from the Hannah he knew to a girl who allowed herself to be used and shared, a stupid chick who ought to be fucked. And that night Nate fucked her, fucked that other Hannah.

It was the hottest sex they'd had in a long time. From a certain perspective (say, a pornographer's), it may have been the hottest sex they'd ever had.

The next morning, Hannah woke up bright and cheerful. She suggested making eggs. Nate had to admit there was nothing obviously offensive in that. But as she sat there, with the sheet around her chest, her head cocked as she waited for his yea or nea, she struck him as cloying, overweening, as if there was nothing in the world she wanted to do more than make him goddamned breakfast. What she really wanted, he felt, was to have a cozy morning in—to bathe in post-coital togetherness.

"I *don't want eggs*," he said.

The happy expression—also much of the color—fled from Hannah's face.

"Okay . . . ," she said. "Well, I'm hungry. You want me to go and get bagels?"

"It's your house. You can do what you want."

She made a face and then shook her head quickly, so her hair fanned out. "Okay. *I'm* hungry. *I'm* going to get a bagel."

With her back to him, she began pulling jeans on.

"A whole-wheat everything with cream cheese and tomato . . ."

She turned around. She looked as if she might give him the finger. Nate smiled hopefully.

"Please, please? Take money from my wallet. Sorry to be testy. I didn't sleep well." He picked up one of the corduroy pillows on her bed and threw it across the room. "That thing was eating my face all night."

Hannah stared at him for a moment. "Fine."

When she was gone, Nate fell back into bed and gazed at the ceiling.

At moments Hannah seemed to trigger something sadistic in him. He could swear he didn't want to hurt her, but sometimes, when she looked at him in a certain way, or that eager note crept into her voice, a perverse obstinacy rose within him; to go along, to do what she wanted, felt treacly—intolerable.

The sheer white curtains on her window twisted in the cool October breeze. Nate stood up and looked outside. He felt ungainly, comically masculine, as the gauzy curtain grazed his bare chest.

He noticed the stack of books on Hannah's bedside table. *The Letters of Abelard and Heloise, A Sentimental Education, The Kreutzer Sonata*. Was he imagining it, or was there a theme? Books about lovelorn women, men whose feelings were shorter-lived. Maybe he was being paranoid. Maybe his girlfriend just had impressive taste in literature.

Nate heard the key turning in the lock, then Hannah's footsteps, quick and determined, as she moved through the apartment. He waited for her to come to the bedroom, intending to make up for his churlishness earlier.

After a minute, she pushed open the bedroom door. "Your bagel is on the table."

Before Nate could respond, she threw a clump of bills and coins at him. Then she turned around and slammed the door behind her.

As he collected his change from her sheets, Nate wondered if Hannah had intentionally echoed a john throwing money at a prostitute. He hoped so. It would reflect a certain malicious imagination that he couldn't help but admire, aesthetically.

He pulled on his undershirt and stepped tentatively out of the bedroom. On the table, he saw a white paper bag, bearing the words *La Bagel-Telle*. Hannah was nowhere in sight; after a moment, he heard the shower running in the bathroom. He sat down to eat his bagel. The irony was he really would have preferred eggs.

Elisa wanted his advice about an upcoming job interview, for a position at a weekly newsmagazine. When they met up, Nate wondered if excitement about the job was the whole difference. Because something was different.

"You seem good," he said. "Happy."

"Thanks."

Her face was tilted over her wine glass, and she looked up at him from the top of her eyes. Nate remembered her looking at him in just that way when she went down on him. He felt a fluttering belowdecks and automatically shifted in his seat.

As soon as he realized this, he blinked and rubbed his forehead. It had been a long time since he had reacted this way to Elisa.

She set her wine glass down and cocked her head. "How's Hannah?"

Nate shrugged as he took a sip of his whiskey. "Fine." He paused, sucking on an ice cube. "Actually, things haven't been so great with us lately."

"I'm sorry," Elisa said. But the crooked way she smiled suggested that this was just what she had hoped to hear. "Poor Hannah."

In spite of the bad character on display, Nate felt unusually fond of Elisa right then, protective and affectionate, feelings born of long familiarity. He leaned his elbow on the bar and smiled at her, resignedly as if to say, "What can you do?" Meanwhile, in the virtual reality chamber of his mind, he began to replay various scenes of fucking her. He had a large cache of raw material from which to draw.

They hung out for quite a while, until nearly midnight—bent over the bar, laughing a lot, gossiping about Elisa's coworkers and other mutual acquaintances, pulling apart not just their writing but their disordered personal lives, irritating habits, and personal unattractiveness. Nate allowed himself to slip out from Hannah's influence, the moral quality that would have made him ashamed to be this catty, this cruel in her presence. Her fairness, her lack of pettiness were things he liked about Hannah generally—he certainly respected her more than he respected Elisa—but the fun he was having felt deserved in light of the strain he'd been under in his relationship.

When he and Elisa said goodnight at the subway entrance, Nate felt a touch of wistfulness. He gave her a quick peck on the cheek.

"Good luck with the interview, E," he said. "You deserve it."

The following day he met up with Hannah.

"Did you have fun last night?" she asked as they walked to a bar. "You were with Elisa, right?"

She didn't sound jealous. Nate instinctively attributed that to savvy, not to an absence of jealousy. Immediately, he felt defensive—also a little annoyed to be put on the defensive when, thoughts aside, he had done nothing wrong.

"Yeah," he said, daring her with his tone to complain. "I did."

"Good," she said, just as coldly.

They were on their way to meet some of her friends from journalism school. At the bar, Nate's mood improved. Hannah's friends were by and large down-to-earth, hard-drinking reporters who spent a lot of time at City Hall or on the police beat or hanging out with Wall Street types. He soon lost sight of Hannah, but it was okay—they were a fun crowd. After a while, though, he got what Hannah had meant, back when they'd first started dating, when she'd said that she had felt a little bit isolated intellectually. He could see that there were aspects of her personality that she wouldn't be able to express with these friends. The thought made him feel tender toward her.

He spotted her talking to two women by a Ms. Pac-Man machine. He made his way to her and placed his hand on her hip. "Hi."

"Hey."

Her tone was clipped, almost hostile. After a moment, he realized she was drunk.

She started getting aggressive with him, treating his light remarks as criticisms and responding disproportionately, hitting him "playfully" but actually using a bit too much force. When she said she was going to get a drink, he suggested that maybe she didn't need another.

"Who are you to tell me what to do?"

He shrugged, and she went to the bar.

At his apartment later, she became downright belligerent, muttering hostile, not-quite-coherent reflections on him almost under her breath, as if to herself as much as to him. Her tone was false, full of a surly and world-weary and utterly put-on cynicism, a strange, unnatural bravado.

"You know that Irina and Jay and Melissa are *nice people*," she said. She spoke as if these were fighting words. Which, he supposed, they were. "That's what actually matters," she continued. "You know that the other stuff is all vanity, right? Writing, I mean."

She made a sarcastic comment about Nate's "artfully crafted sentences," which, she said, mimicked true feeling without knowing what it was. He imitated the stylistic devices of writers he admired without realizing that for those writers these weren't mere devices but means of expressing something true.

It was brutal stuff. Nate didn't take offense. She was obviously lashing out at him for the way things were between them. All he felt was mild disgust at her lack of control. Mostly he just wanted to go to sleep.

As they were getting into bed, she told him that he was treated like a big shot because he was a guy and had the arrogant sense of entitlement to ask for and expect to get everything he wanted, to think no honor too big for him. The funny thing was that Nate thought there was a great deal of truth in this. But he thought *she* could stand to ask for more. His main criticism of her, in terms of writing, was that too often she wasn't ambitious enough. She should treat each piece as if it mattered, instead of laughing off flaws proactively, defensively, citing a "rushed job" or an "editor who'd mess it up anyway," or referring to the insignificance of the publication ("How many people even read such-and-such magazine anymore?"). On top of it, she didn't seem to be writing much at all lately, aside from the routine stuff she did for money. In spite of what she'd said the night she told him she'd been feeling down, she didn't seem to be making progress on her book proposal. Still, he unreservedly thought she was extremely talented. She deserved more recognition than she'd gotten. It wasn't fair. He told her so now. Then he leaned over to turn out the light.

"That's nice of you to say," she said as the room went dark. "Every time I want to paint you as a total jerk, you go and say something nice. That's what kills me."

On the ceiling, dark shadows were indistinguishable from dust. Nate wondered for a moment if he should break up with her. But he liked her. And he didn't want to hurt her.

He turned onto his side. He was too tired to think about this right now. He'd think about it when his head was clear. Tomorrow. Later.

In early November, Peter came to town from Maine. Nate was sure Peter would like Hannah and looked forward to introducing them.

With women he didn't know well, Peter affected an exaggerated courtliness that some found off-putting and pretentious ("toolish," Aurit once said bluntly). But, over a dinner that also included Jason, Peter won Hannah over when he remarked that Flaubert had been responsible for untold numbers of men getting laid. "When Leon overcame Emma's last qualm with the remark that 'all the women in Paris do it,' he nailed it. Forget love, forget morality. Appeal to vanity . . ." Hannah laughed, delighted by this observation. That, in turn, delighted Peter.

At some point, they got to talking about the name Lindsay and how none of them had known any girls named Lindsay at Harvard or Yale, but apparently, according to one of Peter's academic friends, NYU was teeming with Lindsays, and could names possibly reflect such minute social distinctions? Nate glanced at Hannah, but she didn't appear to be outraged by their snobbery. She looked amused. When she spoke, there was just enough irony in her tone to chasten them but not so much as to seem humorless.

They ordered a couple bottles of wine and several rounds of cocktails. By midnight, Hannah was starting to get a little sloppy. Eager to let a good thing be, Nate corralled her into a cab. He was feeling happy and affectionate. As the taxi careened down Ninth Avenue, he leaned close to her and touched one of her eyebrows with his thumb. "You're so much fun," he said.

When they got back to her place, she disappeared into the bathroom. Nate got into bed. Several minutes later, she returned, wearing a tank top and high-cut underwear.

Then Nate looked at her face and saw that she'd been crying. She had tried to cover it up. No, that wasn't quite right. She looked as if she'd made a halfhearted attempt to cover it up but what she really wanted was for him to know that she was upset and ask what was wrong.

Although tears, even off-screen tears, were a new development, this didn't really surprise him—or rather his surprise was limited to the comparatively minor question of "why now?" when they'd had a really good night, when they might very well continue to have a really good night. As she searched for something in one of her over-stuffed drawers, her eyeliner smeared and her lips pursed, Nate felt not pity but exasperation. *You're hurting your own cause,* he wanted to shout to the crying, not-crying Hannah. *Can't you fucking see that?*

But her droopy vulnerability gave her the moral high ground. "Are you okay?" he asked.

"I'm fine."

"Why don't you come to bed?"

He spoke in the patient, patronizing tone of a person accustomed to dealing with the mentally feeble.

She swallowed and looked down, blinking as if in pain or embarrassment. Then—something happened. An idea or a mood seemed to take hold of her. Her face brightened, and her demeanor became less glum, more definite—animated.

"Come on," she said, her eyes glittering. "Let's go in the other room and have a drink."

Her voice had an inexplicable, almost lunatic pull. As he followed her into the living room Nate's irritation gave way to curiosity to see what would happen next.

Without turning on the light, she went and got the bourbon from on top of the refrigerator and then the two blue-rimmed glasses. Nate sat down by the window. The only sound in the apartment was the refrigerator's hum. Hannah returned from the kitchen and sat in the other upholstered chair, tucking her naked legs underneath her. She poured out the bourbon and handed him a glass.

He wasn't really in the mood to drink, hadn't been since the moment at the restaurant with Jason and Peter when he realized he needed to keep an eye on her drinking.

Hannah downed nearly half of hers in one gulp. She shuddered.

"It's so fucked up," she said. The words were clear and lucid, but her voice had a bitter, reckless quality. "I see it, but I can't do anything about it."

"See what, Hannah?"

She looked at the window. Their reflections in the glass were faded and translucent, crisscrossed by the slabs of brick on the apartment building across the street. She turned to face him, the liquid in her glass a luminous amber.

"I don't even smoke around you anymore. How great is that?"

"Do you want a cigarette? If you want one, go ahead and have one."

"Shut up! You're so patronizing. That's what I thought when I first met you. I thought you were so smarmy and self-satisfied and not that interes—I remember thinking, *How many times is he going to mention fucking Harvard?*" She laughed. "I never thought I'd—" She shook her head. "Oh, never mind."

Her voice had become singsong, as if she were speaking to a slightly daft elderly person.

When she spoke again, the pleasant quality was gone. "What was that tonight?" She fixed her eyes on him. "You were *so* affectionate."

Nate's grip on his glass tightened. Whatever was coming, he didn't want.

"Why?" Hannah continued. "Because your friend Peter liked me."

The pulsing of the blood in his temples felt like an aggressively ticking alarm clock.

"No offense," Hannah said. "But it kind of made me sick. I mean, what kind of person are you that your friends' opinions are so fucking important?"

"You're drunk, Hannah."

"And who am I that I go along with it? Perform for your friends so you'll . . ." She shivered as the words trailed off. "I'm ashamed of myself, too, just so you know."

Nate looked out the window, at the yellow crescent of light cast by a streetlamp.

"The thing is, the last guy I dated"—Hannah began to speak earnestly, as if they were in the middle of hashing out something important together—"he was a writer. You probably know him—not Steve—this was just someone I went out with a few times. But, see, he had a trust fund and a great apartment, and one day we were there, and he had these Hispanic guys doing some work on his roof deck, and I asked him if he ever felt weird, you know, because he sat around all day and half-worked on his writing while these guys were right outside his sliding glass door, in the heat and everything. And he said, 'Yeah, all the time,' but, like, because that's what he was supposed to say. Because then he went on and said that writing poetry was hard work, just like being a day laborer is hard work, and the guys on the roof wouldn't want to trade with him, any more than he'd want to trade with them. And that was it, that was how he talked himself out of feeling uncomfortable about all his advantages. So callow, you know?" She looked at Nate intently. "You're not like that. No, you're sort of decen—"

"That might have just been something he said in the moment, not the sum total of his life's thought on inequality," Nate suggested.

"Maybe," Hannah said. "He was kind of a callow guy, though."

Nate smiled. He knew who the guy was. And he was an asshole. A tall, good-looking asshole.

Hannah squinted at her empty glass and then reached for the bottle of bourbon. Nate nearly told her to cool it but at the last moment stopped himself. Did he want to be that guy? They weren't in the restaurant, in public, anymore. Why the hell shouldn't she drink? Why shouldn't he?

He swallowed the contents of his glass. "Pour me some, too, if you don't mind."

Hannah brightened. "Sure!"

"Can I ask you something?" she said after she set the bottle down.

"Sure."

"What happened?"

Then, as if she knew that Nate would be tempted to feign ignorance, she added. "With us, I mean."

Nate supposed he'd known all along—when he'd agreed to accompany her to the living room—that this was where things were going. This was what they'd come out here for. Yet he still felt an impulse to pretend he didn't know what she was talking about—to deflect or postpone this conversation.

"I don't understand," she said. "Did I *do* something?"

When Nate spoke, his voice came out raspy, more pained than he expected. "I don't think—no."

He wished he could blame it on her—assign a cause. But he knew it was him. Whatever had happened, it was him.

"No, you didn't do anything," he repeated.

He looked at her. She was pale. The expression on her face so precisely mirrored how he felt, the sense of helplessness that had come over him. Almost without being aware, he got up and walked to her chair, perching on its arm. His irritation had faded. He felt protective and tender toward her. He was glad. It made him feel human and humane.

She scooted over, and he slid down beside her on the seat of the chair.

"I think, maybe, I'm just not very good at relationships," he said.

"Maybe we should just admit it's not working," she said. "I mean, right? A month ago if someone told me what things would be like between us, I would have said, no, I'd never stand for that. But I keep negotiating down what I think is okay. I like you—my problem is that I do like you. There's something about you . . ." She stopped and then sat up straighter. She started again in a new, more decisive tone. "But this thing, this thing that we've become, is sapping something from me."

Nate turned to her bookshelf. He began trying to make out individual titles in the dark.

"You can't be happy either," Hannah said.

No. As he tore his eyes from the books to meet hers, he was, as a matter of fact, nearly overwhelmed by sadness. It gusted over him. He felt almost unbearably lonely. He wondered whether he was flawed on some deep level, whether—in spite of all the friends who seemed to think he was a good guy (and he *was* a pretty good friend), in spite of being a fairly decent son—there was something terribly wrong with him. Did romance reveal some truth, a fundamental lack, a coldness, that made him shrink back at just the moment when reciprocity was called for?

He shuddered. As he drew in his breath, he took in the scent of Hannah's hair. It smelled of coconut—of what he now knew to

be the cheap drugstore coconut shampoo she kept in her bathroom, the kind of shampoo that would make Aurit or Elisa curl
their lips in disdain.

He remembered how much fun he'd had with her in the beginning, their early dates, how she'd made him laugh, how she'd surprised him by being so . . . *interesting.* He thought of how she'd
been tonight, at the restaurant with Jason and Peter. (And it wasn't
because Peter liked her. It was because she had been herself, the
person he had fallen for.) Even the callow bit. He knew what she
meant. And that was the thing, actually. He usually knew what
she meant. And he felt that she usually knew what he meant. From
the beginning, he had felt at home with her.

He leaned his forehead against hers. "I'm sorry about how
things have been. But let's keep trying, okay? I can do better."

She stared into the dark, empty air of her apartment.

He traced her bottom lip with his thumb. "I like you a lot," he
said. "You know that, right?"

In fact, he felt right then that he loved her. *Of course* he loved
her. Had he merely been punishing her for some unknown crime?
For being nice to him?

She didn't respond right away, just continued to stare off. "I
need to feel like you're trying, too," she said finally. "I need to feel
like I'm not in this alone, the only one who cares about what's going
on here."

He held her chin with his thumb and looked into her eyes.
"You're not," he said. "You're not the only one."

He felt her relax. "Okay," she said, nodding. "Okay."

He pulled her to him. Her chest trembled as she released her
breath. He held her tighter. He felt close to her, perhaps closer to
her than he'd ever felt, as if they'd been through something together,
seen each other not just at their best but in some real capacity, and
they were still here. She—she hadn't given up on him. He buried his
face in her hair, mumbling something about love.

15

Nate was at the counter, asking Stuart—Beth wasn't working today—for a refill when Recess's glass door swung open. In walked Greer Cohen, an autumn breeze swirling around her. As the door clicked shut, the rustle in the air subsided. Greer remained at the center of a small whir of activity. A sweater and various bags, one containing a rolled-up yoga mat, swung from her shoulders. Wild locks of wavy hair spilled out from a loose bun.

"Nate!"

Her smile expressed such pleasure that Nate couldn't help but feel touched. "Greer," he said. "What brings you here?"

"Yoga. Down the street."

Stuart was waiting behind the cash register for his money. Other patrons were looking up from behind their laptops. Greer's fluttering energy and lilting, girlish voice ruffled the still air of the coffee shop.

Nate slid a bill to Stuart and then put a hand on Greer's upper arm to guide her out of Recess's central corridor. When he felt her small arm through her sweater, a tremor passed through him. Until that moment, he hadn't consciously noted that Greer had become a recurring figure in his fantasy life, a sort of marquee name among the myriad other pretty girls who wafted in and out of various scenarios.

As she allowed herself to be led backward, Greer smiled up at him with what felt—absurdly—like complicity.

Nate asked about her book. They began talking about the day-to-day process of writing at such length.

"So much staring at the screen," Greer said. "I'd shoot myself if it weren't for yoga."

The girlishness of Greer's smile did not at all offset its suggestiveness.

"I feel you," Nate said.

Over time, he had revised his opinion of Greer upward. She was warm, friendly. You had to give her that. And her book deal was not nothing. It took no small degree of skill, in terms of basic writing ability and self-presentation, to manage that. Such savvy wasn't the same thing as real talent, but it was something. About her writing itself he had nothing to say. It wasn't his kind of thing.

They continued to chat for a few minutes. "You're dating Hannah Leary, right?" she asked at one point.

Nate shifted his eyes. "Yeah."

Greer's smile merely altered around the edges, becoming more conspiratorial.

"We should get a drink sometime," she said as she was getting ready to go. "Talk about book writing."

There was a new flurry of activity as a business card was produced from one of her bags. Greer grabbed a Magic Marker from the bulletin board and began scrawling on the back of the card.

She handed it to Nate. On the front, it said "AMD Global Brand Management." "Ian Zellman, Senior Strategist" was printed below. Nate looked at Greer questioningly.

She shrugged. "Just some guy."

Nate turned the card over. Greer hadn't written her name, just the ten digits of her cell phone number. He put the card in his pocket, not without a feeling of satisfaction at having triumphed over Senior Strategist Ian Zellman.

When Greer was gone, Nate was left in a pleasant state of bewilderment. He didn't know why Greer was so flirtatious with him. Perhaps she was attracted to his supposed intellectual cachet? Greer had sold her book for more money than he'd sold his, and would probably sell more copies, but as a memoirist of adolescent promiscuity, she lacked a certain . . . respectability.

He went back to work on the review he was writing. He forgot about Greer until later that night.

He was out with Jason, who was talking about Maggie from work. Maggie was thinking about moving in with "that douche," the Web site designer.

Nate slipped his hand in his pocket. He found the card with Greer's number on it. He ran his fingers along its edges.

He had cheated before. On Kristen. They were living in Philadelphia at the time, but he had been in New York for the weekend. He'd gone to a party at an apartment in what had at the time seemed to be deep Brooklyn but was actually very close to where he now lived. The only person he knew was the guy he came with, who by midnight was nowhere to be seen. Jason, at whose place he was crashing, was supposed to show up at some point, but until then what was Nate supposed to do but talk to girls? Why would a guy want to talk to him? He flirted in the habitual, desultory manner of someone who expects it to come to nothing. He was on a beer run with a girl he'd been chatting with when she turned and fell into him, pushing him into the limestone wall of an apartment building. Nate felt, as he halfheartedly kissed her back, only a startled impulse not to hurt the girl's feelings, in part because she wasn't even that pretty. He broke away quickly. But back at the party, he found himself acutely aware of the girl, attuned to every instance when his arm or thigh brushed against her. When she went to speak to someone on the other side of the room, he followed her not just with his eyes but with some animal instinct. It was as if, in order to crowd out all thoughts of Kristen, he had to blow up his desire into something outsized, over-the-top, something that simply didn't allow for reflection. In fact, the girl was merely a cute-ish, chipmunk-cheeked, slightly neurotic, casually but not convincingly slutty aspiring film . . . whatever it was people who want to work in film aspire to be. All the same, Nate was pretty much in a blinding fury of desire when they took a cab back to the apartment she shared in Alphabet City. Not-Kristen had her tongue in his mouth, Not-Kristen was unfastening a cheap red bra that clasped in the front, Not-Kristen had a bumpy constellation of moles around her collarbones and a loosy-goosy tummy—all of it only contributed to her intoxicating unfamiliarity. At some point, when she had him in her mouth, she created so much suction that the phrase *menacing vise grip* had come to mind. Nate had had to gird himself to bear it manfully. When they fucked, her multisyllabic mewing sounds were stagy, meretricious, as perfectly timed to his thrusts as if they were playing Marco Polo. And yet it was thrilling.

The thrill was harder to fathom the following day. On the bus back to Philly, Nate stared out the tinted window at the traffic on the Garden State Parkway. The sky was dull and gray, his face in the glass wan and abject. Whatever frustration he'd felt in his relationship had vanished. His life with Kristen seemed full of fresh air and intelligence and promise. Her austere beauty, the crispness of it, seemed to mark her as one of the elect. Why had he done this thing that could fuck it all up?

The bus lurched. The smell of other people's fast food made him feel sick.

When Kristen pulled up to the bus station, Nate began furiously adjusting the straps of his backpack. Although he told white lies with the same facility as anyone who is generally successful and liked, he had never been a skilled liar when any sort of personal gain was at stake. He'd speak the words as if they were in scare quotes, as if to distance himself from whatever he said.

He reminded himself, as he tossed his bag into the backseat, that he didn't really have to lie. He had only to omit certain pieces of information. In the car, he passed into a state of becalmed terror. In bed later, Kristen apologized for being tired—thankfully. Sex would have been one more, exhausting semi-lie, but he would have felt too guilty to say no if she had initiated.

A few days later, when they were driving out to a suburban shopping center, Kristen turned to him. "You stayed with Jason over the weekend, right?"

The back of Nate's neck grew rigid. "Yeah."

Kristen's brow was furrowed. Beads of sweat formed under Nate's T-shirt as he waited. And waited.

"That's what I thought," Kristen said, after she made her left onto Delaware Avenue. The clicking of the turn signal ceased. "But I thought you might have stayed at Will McDormand's. I'd love to know what Will's apartment is like. Probably he has, like, a fireplace and an Andrew Wyeth painting in his living room and a mirror on the ceiling of his bedroom."

Nate snorted. "That sounds right."

But his heart was still thumping.

The worst part, though, *wasn't* that it was hard. The worst part was that it wasn't hard enough. Nate felt guilty, yes, but the knowledge that what Kristen didn't know wouldn't hurt her made this easier to bear than even a much more minor offense, such as snapping at her when she interrupted his reading to ask some unimportant question, like whether they should go to Ikea that weekend or if he'd call the phone company about the erroneous bill they'd received. In those instances, the hurt was immediate and palpable and instantly made Nate feel bad. But after this far more serious infraction, Nate experienced much less internal fire-and-brimstone than he expected. He saw that cheating could easily become if not routine, then at least more doable. In spite of the self-loathing, in spite of what was a little bit disgusting about the girl, and what he imagined would be a little bit disgusting about most girls one was likely to cheat with, the fun of it, the variety of it, was enticing: to have what he had with Kristen *and*, every once in a while, a little bit of that—that crossing into the unknown and unfamiliar. Possibilities occurred to him. He thought of a Goth-looking waitress at a nearby bar who he'd long suspected was flirting with him.

What stopped him was the realization that it was a bad road to go down. It wasn't only that he'd grow comfortable lying. He would also have to justify his behavior to himself: caricature Kristen in his mind, exaggerate her limitations and "prudishness," repeat pop-psych mantras about the uncontainable nature of male sexuality, as certain middle-aged men did, men who tended to strike Nate as not only sleazy but pathetic and distinctly unattractive. He could see, too, that it would destroy the best thing he had with Kristen. While she might not be hurt by what she didn't know, the need to hide key facets of his private life would mean he'd have to be on guard, think before he spoke, lest he contradict himself or reveal something unwittingly. Besides, it was 1999, and the specter of Clinton loomed large: the accomplished statesman turned into a joke because he couldn't keep it in his pants. Nate had made a conscious decision not to do it again, not to cheat.

He put Greer's card back into his pocket and turned to Jason. "Why don't you just tell Maggie how you feel about her?"

Jason looked surprised. "Don't you know?"

Nate realized he didn't, not exactly. He'd chalked it up to Jason's general weirdness about women.

"Spell it out for me."

Jason's Adam's apple quavered as he took a long sip of beer. He set the glass down on the table and leaned forward. "It's Saturday morning," he began, sweeping his arm in front of him with oratorical flourish. "I open my eyes and push off a floral comforter. Sunlight is pouring through a window, reflecting off a gigantic Ansel Adams photograph hanging on the wall. Where am I? I wonder. Oh!"—he cupped his ear—"what's that I hear? A scampering little footstep? It's Maggie! She comes skipping into her bedroom, cute as a button, in her Sewanee T-shirt and flannel pajama bottoms, full of little teeny bumpy nubbins. In her hands, she's holding a plate full of fresh-baked banana muffins, and she smiles up at me"—Jason paused to flutter his eyelashes, which he did with unexpected skill—"her little-biddy button nose is sweetly pink-tipped, and her smile is so sweet, it breaks your heart. And you know what happens? My cock shrivels up so small, it's like a tiny, little pink shrimp, like a fucking toddler penis. All I want is to get the hell out of there as fast as I can, get the fuck to some dank club full of models and do some coke. And I hardly even like coke."

"How do you know, Jase? Seriously. How do you know you wouldn't be happy?"

Jason traced the rim of his glass with his finger before looking up at Nate. "Well, Miss Lonelyhearts, even if there's only an eighty percent chance that's what would happen, I couldn't do it. Maggie's a really good person. And it may be hard for you to believe— you think you're the only one women fall for, you vain fuck—but she really likes me."

Nate started to respond—to defend himself—but then shut his mouth. Jason's sensitive side, on the rare occasions when it emerged, seemed infinitely fragile, like glass so fine that even discordant notes of speech could cause it to shatter.

"No," Jason said, his voice returning to a more familiar register. "What I need is a model with a really good personality. Too bad Brigita turned out to be such a dud."

Nate grunted sympathetically. They turned back to the chips and guac they were sharing.

After a while, Jason asked how things were going with Hannah.

Nate glanced at the flapping chef's door between the bar and the kitchen. "Fine. Good."

Since the night he and Hannah had stayed up drinking bourbon, things had been better. She was resolutely unmopey. She called him less, would sometimes fail to return his calls until he became increasingly eager to see her. He had taken her out for her birthday, bought her a scarf that Aurit helped him choose. Things were fine. And yet he sometimes felt her eyes on him, watching too closely, trying to read his mood, clearly worried that he was growing bored or distant. When he was especially affectionate, he picked up on an anxious, guarded happiness that she tried but failed to conceal, as if he were a drug addict or a gambler and she the long-suffering wife who detected signs of reformation. This seemed humiliating, for both of them.

Nate suppressed a sigh as he stood up. "I'm going to the bar," he said. "You want another?"

"Yeah."

"What I wonder is whether fashion really has gotten more ironic," Hannah said over brunch a few days later. "I mean, the nerd glasses and mom jeans and the eighties-inspired clothes."

Nate nodded absently.

"Or does it just start to seem ironic as you get older, because you've seen all the trends come and go, and you can no longer take them seriously? You've watched the waistlines of jeans move up, up, up and then down, down, down and now up again. And the glasses! They got smaller and smaller until it seemed like you needed glasses just to see your glasses, and then, boom, one day they are all of a sudden big and owlish again? But maybe to twenty-year-olds, who haven't become jaded by this cycle, those big glasses just look cool? Not ironic, but just nice, the way people our age genuinely thought tapered jeans looked nice in the nineties?"

While Hannah was talking, an attractive woman had entered the restaurant. She had a long mane of light-brown hair, thick but smooth and shiny, the kind of hair that awakens a primitive appreciation for good health and breeding. Her face was nice, too. The hair's-breadth difference between the exact set of her features and classic beauty (her nose was a little wide, her chin too prominent) didn't make her any less attractive. She was wearing a blazer that gave her a cute, grad-student sort of look but was cinched at the waist and short enough so that her legs looked extremely long. When she passed their table, Nate saw that her jeans clung tenaciously to her ass, which appeared to have benefited from years of horseback riding and lacrosse.

He turned back to Hannah. She was staring at him with her mouth open.

Nate looked away, taking refuge in his coffee mug, where oily droplets clung to the surface like small, prismatic reflecting pools. He'd looked at another woman. Big fucking deal. He didn't have the energy right then to deal with this unbearable, this *boring* tension between the two of them.

He started talking about the cover of his book, about how he wanted a few minor changes made, to rearrange the order of some of the blurbs and make the font color of the jacket copy more vivid against the book's background.

Now Hannah seemed to be nodding absently, playing with a glass saltshaker, rolling it between her thumb and fingers. This struck Nate as rude. She was, supposedly, his *girlfriend*, and this— his book—was only the biggest thing in his life. It wasn't as if he were talking about fashion.

The waitress appeared. "French toast over here, and eggs Benedict for you. How are we doing otherwise? Do we need more coffee?" She nodded her head as she spoke as if to guide them to the correct answer. Then she picked up the little white jug of cream from their table, tilting it toward her so she could peer inside. "I'll get some more. Ketchup for your potatoes? You got it. Be right back!"

Nate resumed his narration about the book jacket. He was glad he'd rejected the first design. He had felt bad doing it—he didn't

want to be troublesome—but he felt it looked old and stodgy.
Oscar, the designer, had done a brilliant job in the end. The new
cover conveyed seriousness but also freshness, hipness.

Nate was in the middle of making this last point when Hannah
cut him off. "I can't do this, Nate."

"Do what?"

"Sit here and be your cheering section. I'm not in the mood to
ooh and ah about your *big* book and all your little successes."

"That's a nice thing to say," Nate said. (In fact, he felt relieved
that she'd given him an opening to vent his irritation.) "That's a
really kind, considerate thing for your girlfriend to tell you as you
try to discuss something that's just slightly important to you. Do
you want to talk about fashion again? Would that be more interesting to you?"

Hannah swallowed and closed her eyes. When she opened
them, they trained in on his with angry precision. "Why don't
we talk about the woman you were checking out? She *was* very
pretty."

"For Christ's—"

"Don't bother," Hannah said. "I know how this plays out.
You're going to tell me—or better yet, not tell me, just *imply*—
that I am being irrational, that I am neurotic and jealous and
impossible. After all, don't all liberated people in the twenty-first
century know that it's no big deal for men to check out women?
It's just biology. Only some impossible, ridiculous woman would
mind."

Nate glared at the table.

Hannah kept talking. "But we both know you weren't just
checking her out. You were being incredibly, *spitefully* obvious
about it. You were broadcasting your contempt for me, or your
boredom, or whatever. Don't worry, I got the message."

From other tables, laughter, strands of animated conversation
curled through the air. Nate felt sweaty, conspicuous, as if Hannah

were making a scene, even though she wasn't speaking loudly. There was an intensity that marked out their conversation from the others. *Which of these pairs of diners enjoying high-end hipster comfort food doesn't fit in?*

"So now I'm stuck," Hannah was saying. "If I complain, I look ridiculous, but if I ignore it, am I really then supposed to sit here and act like I'm all gooey-eyed and happy for you because you are just so successful and your book is so exciting? That kind of makes me feel ridiculous, too. Either way, I'm screwed."

"Jesus! I—I—can we please just eat our food?"

"I have an idea," Hannah said. "I can play the game you're playing. See that guy over there?" She gestured toward a man in a leather jacket sipping coffee on a stool at the bar. "Isn't he good-looking? He's so *tall*. I think I'm going to chat him up."

Nate met her eye. "Go right ahead."

Hannah winced and then shook her head. They eyed each other for a long, languorous moment, reveling in the cool pleasure of open hostility. Then Hannah leaned her face down into her hands, covering her eyes with the tips of her long, tapered, cellist fingers. Her hair fell forward on her cheeks. When she looked up, Nate sensed her anger was spent. This frightened him.

"Never mind," she said. "I can't do this. I don't want to."

With his fork, Nate moved some egg around his plate.

"I've tried playing that game," Hannah continued. "Pretending I don't care. And you know what? It worked. You always responded to it."

Nate willed himself not to move a muscle in his face, not to let on that he had a pretty good idea as to what she was talking about. To admit it seemed intolerably humiliating, a too-open acknowledgment of the dinky little rinse-and-repeat melodrama their relationship had devolved into.

"But I don't want to do it anymore," she said. "You'll always win this game because I'm only playing at it, and you—well, you . . ." She dropped her knife and fork, which apparently she'd been holding for quite some time like some kind of ritualistic accoutrements. They clattered as they landed on her plate. "Well, I don't know what you're doing."

Her eyes shone.

Nate realized, with some surprise, that he'd never actually seen Hannah cry, not in all these months. The closest had been the time when he could tell she'd been crying.

"And by the way," she said, no longer on the verge of tears but with feeling. "I think it's stupid. The whole thing is stupid. It doesn't reflect well on you."

Nate had lost the will to fight. "No, certainly not," he said quietly. "Listen, why don't we get out of here?"

A few minutes later, they set out for the park in the center of Hannah's neighborhood. Without touching each other as they walked down the street—their hands were buried deep in the pockets of their jackets—they spoke pleasantly, about topics of no consequence.

Hannah nodded toward a kitchen store on the other side of the street. "That's new."

"It's convenient," Nate said. "Next time you need a frying pan or something."

He looked away when they passed the bar they had gone to on their first date.

The park felt barren, the grass a dull green and the trees skeletal, their leaves long since shed. He and Hannah walked to a bench on the crest of a hill. For a while, they were silent.

"I guess we both know this isn't working," Hannah said finally.

Her hands were still in her pockets, but her arms were extended on her lap, so her jacket was pulled forward and made a sort of tent in front of her. Nate nodded slowly, careful not to show too much eager assent.

"I don't know why," she said. "I've tried and tried to figure it out, but after a while, I guess the only thing we can say for sure is that it isn't working."

Her voice was even, unemotional, but her eyes, when she turned to face him, were so imploring that Nate had to look away. He felt sure that she wanted him to contradict her, as he had that night in her apartment. But he couldn't do it again. The intensity of feeling he'd experienced that night hadn't lasted. The facts had become too obvious. Relationships shouldn't be this hard. *Nobody* thought so. He'd have to be crazy. And the simple fact was he no longer wanted this.

Greer popped into his mind: the way she'd smiled at him at Recess, the way he'd *felt* when she smiled at him. That had to mean something—that real, spontaneous longing. The card with her number on it was sitting on his dresser. "Global brand management?" Hannah had remarked dryly, when she'd noticed it there, amid the bitten-up pens and the torn-off dry-cleaning tags. "Thinking about a career change?"

The thought of Greer made him feel guilty. Why should it, though? It wasn't as if he'd called her. Yet it did. As much as he was beginning to feel relieved—and indeed he felt an easing of a deep, almost muscular tension that he hadn't even known was there—he simultaneously began to feel, as if in exact counterreaction, both sad and ashamed.

"I'm sorry," he said. He made out a faint and fleeting bit of condensation in his breath.

"I guess I haven't been exactly perfect either," Hannah said. She took her hands out of her pockets and hugged her body with her arms. "I'm not mad at you. I've been mad at you, but I don't think I am anymore. I don't see the point."

Nate shifted his position on the bench, feeling uncomfortably as if she did have reason to be mad at him, though he couldn't say what it was precisely. He knew he'd hurt her, yet he felt bound by twenty-first-century chivalry to pretend he didn't know it, lest he seem presumptuous or arrogant.

"You know I think you're great," he said.

She merely raised her eyebrows. He felt the triteness of his words.

"The thing that bothers me," she said after a moment, "is that in the beginning, *my god*, you couldn't have been more into it. But since then . . ." She turned to face him. "*Why?* Why did you start this if you didn't care enough to try and make it work?"

Nate tried not to sigh. *Start this?* Obviously, they'd both had a hand in starting it.

"I did try."

"*Really?* Did you ever spend three seconds thinking about what the problem was and whether there was anything you could do to make it better? It was like you had nothing at stake, like you were a passive bystander."

Nate wished he didn't have to have to listen to this. He felt he'd heard it, or some variant of it, a billion times.

"And you always had your book," Hannah continued. "Whatever happened between us was not going to affect you much one way or the other because the most important thing for you is that your book is coming out. It's hard to compete."

"Are you saying that's a bad thing? Caring about my book?"

"I—no! Of course not. There was a power imbalance, that's all I meant. It wasn't fun being on the wrong side of that."

Nate wondered if it would be patronizing to suggest that she might be better off if she cared about her book more. It could be difficult to stay motivated sometimes—he knew that—especially when you were unhappy. But he also knew that you had to push through. He had. He had written his book even on days when it was the last thing he felt like doing.

He decided it would be better not to say this.

He stared through the bald trees to the stalls of the farmer's market that assembled at the park each week. On this gray day, it looked like the threadbare marketplace of some bleak eastern European village. He could smell the diesel from the row of idling trucks that transported produce and workers from upstate. It reminded him of dreary Sunday afternoons as a child, driving back with his parents from visits to his cousins in New Jersey or to the houses of his parents' Romanian friends in the D.C. suburbs, of looking out the car window at drab, shabby landscapes and being crushed by a sadness caused at once by everything and nothing—a general sense of life as a bleak, lonely, rather hopeless affair.

He thought of his immediate future, of being single. He remembered the night he and Mark had hit on Cara, the feeling of dullness that had come over him when he had contemplated his single life, the incessant, relentless flirting, its underside of loneliness and cynicism.

"Sometimes I think I've lost something," he said to Hannah. "Some capacity to be with another person, something I used to have." He laughed mirthlessly. "I feel pretty fucked, to tell the truth."

Hannah looked incredulous. "I don't know what to say to that. What am I supposed to say?"

Nate was stung by her tone. "Never mind," he said. "I'm feeling sorry for myself. It's stupid."

Hannah shut her eyes. When she opened them, she spoke slowly. "I feel like you want to think what you're feeling is really deep, like some seriously profound existential shit. But to me, it looks like the most tired, the most average thing in the world, the guy who is all interested in a woman until the very moment when it dawns on him that he has her. Wanting only what you can't have. The affliction of shallow morons everywhere."

"Jesus! If you're going to—"

"I'm sorry," Hannah said. "I'm being harsh, but give me a break. If what you say is true, if you just have some 'problem,' it kind of sucks for me, too. I can't sit here and try to make you feel better. It's like the robber asking his victim to sympathize with his uncontrollable compulsion to rob people." She squinted up into the pale sky. "Give me a few years, until you're on your deathbed or something."

Nate made a chortling sound. So did Hannah. Their eyes met. Her smile was strangely companionable, as if they were old war buddies.

He knew with near-perfect certainty that there would come a time when he would be feeling down and lonely and crave more than anything Hannah's company, her warmth, her intelligence, her humor, her ability to understand him. On that night, as he returned home to his empty apartment, he'd regret this day. But he also knew that on all the other nights—the, say, forty-nine out of fifty nights when he wasn't unhappy in that particular way— he'd be glad to be free of this, of the heavy, unfun yoke of it. This thought made him feel bad all over again.

"I'm sure a lot of it *is* my fault," he said. He smiled ruefully. "And by a lot, I mean all."

"Ah, the self-deprecating dude routine," Hannah said. "'What a lovable fuck-up I am.' The annoying thing is that it makes you look good, but it doesn't get *me* anything."

The return of bitterness in her voice took Nate by surprise. Each time he thought they'd moved beyond reproaches, she turned angry again. He foresaw a potentially endless loop. He was also getting hungry—he hadn't eaten much at breakfast—and it was growing chillier outside.

"I guess we should get going," he said.

Hannah turned her face away from his. A wall of straight red-dish brown hair moved up and down as she nodded slowly. "Yeah."

He pretended not to notice as she wiped her cheek with the back of her hand. The truth was he felt a flash of resentment. It seemed manipulative.

16

Nate had a long and intimate relationship with guilt.

He felt guilty when he passed by the neighborhood homeless guy, a bespectacled, middle-aged man with a salt-and-pepper Afro whose lilting refrain—"Can you spare a dollar, bro?"—echoed as you walked away, like an effect on a dance remix. He felt guilty when, in a Manhattan office building, he saw an elderly janitor stooped over a mop, joints creaking, jowls hanging over his collar. He felt guilty when a blank-faced Hispanic or Asian man refilled his water glass at a restaurant. He thought of ten- and twelve-hour shifts, of returning to squalid apartments shared with a dozen others. He felt guilty on the subway, when, as the train moved deeper into Brooklyn, more and more white people got off. Eventually almost everyone who remained was black—and tired. Overworked, underpaid. He felt guilty when circumstances forced him to get up early on a frigid winter morning, and, hurrying along wind-swept streets, he saw Southeast Asian vendors blowing on their hands as they set up their coffee carts. What had he done to deserve his easier—his easy—fate?

His intelligence was just something he'd been born with. Luck of the draw, like being beautiful. It was a rationalization to say that he'd worked hard. It was like being given a fine knife and taking the trouble to polish and sharpen it: it's great that you make the effort, but someone had to give you the knife. And it wasn't just intelligence. Nate felt guilty when he thought about his grandparents and great-grandparents in eastern Europe—shtetls and pogroms and worse.

In such a context, the small-scale romantic disappointments of privileged single women in New York City did not even remotely make the cut. Yet the day after he and Hannah broke up, Nate was riled by a strong sense of guilt.

At the park, he'd been so—well, he hadn't been able to see beyond a great cloud of irritation, which had seemed not only to justify his actual behavior but much worse behavior as well. He'd felt that he behaved remarkably well, that, in an effort to extricate himself from such a subtle and uncomfortable snare, he could have been much meaner. There had been times with Hannah, in the past month or two, when he had found himself feeling so harassed that it had seemed an act of heroism that he hadn't told her exactly what he was thinking in the bluntest possible terms. And yesterday, at brunch and after, he'd been at moments so aggravated that his endurance of the whole breakup scene had seemed, on the whole, a display of magnanimity. He hadn't said "enough" and taken off, as many guys would have. Many guys would have told her she needed to chill out—implied she was obsessive, fucked-up.

Yet, now, as he wandered around his apartment, shuffling listlessly from room to room, Nate didn't feel so hot. He felt guilty about various things. Checking out that woman at the restaurant, for one. For the way he'd been in general.

He was also baffled. So many times, as their relationship had begun to deteriorate, he had gone from being irritated by Hannah to feeling remorse once his irritation passed. He'd always thought that in the aftermath, when he felt bad, he was clearheaded, seeing the situation for what it was. Only now it seemed to him that he'd been in some kind of fugue state the whole time, going back and forth from one mood to the other, without ever stopping to consider what was driving the insane back-and-forth. Instead, he'd just avoided her for stretches.

At the park, he had thought Hannah was unreasonable when she accused him of not trying, but now he wondered if he had, at some point, stacked the deck against her—decided he didn't want her and then set things up so she'd justify his slackening interest. Because he knew—of course he knew, he wasn't stupid—that his behavior had contributed to, if not entirely caused, her insecurity. And of course her insecurity (*Are you mad at me? Can I please, please make you breakfast?*) just made her more annoying. But it had felt as if he couldn't help the way he behaved. When he had behaved badly—snapped at her, checked out that woman, whatever—he had been acting from some overpowering compulsion. And yet he had once liked her quite a bit.

He stopped pacing and stood by the window, blinking at the paper-white sky. The truth was he hadn't stopped liking her. Even now. That was what had been, what continued to be, so confusing.

The stentorian voice inside his head told him he'd been a jerk. He'd known his behavior had confused her. He'd watched her diminish, grow nervous and sad, become in certain ways someone he didn't recognize. Whenever he'd felt bad about it, he told himself that he wasn't forcing her to stay with him. She could break up with him any time she wanted.

But now he thought of something Aurit had said—written, actually, in a truly excellent piece of expository writing. She'd described her parents' fucked-up dynamic, how her father's response to any criticism was "if you don't like it, leave." Aurit argued that for the person with more power in a relationship to refuse to take seriously the unhappiness of the other, simply because nothing is forcing them to, is the ultimate dick move: "It's like if the United States in the 1950s said, 'Sorry, black people in the South, but if you don't like the way you're being treated, you can go back to Africa.'"

On the other hand, Hannah *wasn't* a disenfranchised minority,

Nate thought, leaving the window and padding from the bedroom to the kitchen. Why should he have had more power? He didn't ask for it. When he remembered that, he began to resent her, for her meek willingness to put up with his bad behavior. For her willingness to be his victim. Sure, she'd snapped back, gotten pissy, but these had been empty little torrents, the indignant flailing of a small animal caught in a trap. By and large, she'd put herself at his disposal, made it easy for him to hurt her. And now he had to be his own judge and jury. But he had his own feelings to worry about. It wasn't fair to make him responsible for both of them.

That made him feel a bit better, for a little while. Then it occurred to him that she'd put up with him because he had wanted her to. Until he didn't. He had always stopped being a dick to her as soon as he sensed he'd crossed the line and she might actually walk away. She'd allowed him to torment her in this way because *she liked him*. Maybe she even loved him.

The thought made him wince.

Because, come on, was he ever going to find someone with no annoying tics or physical imperfections? What real criticism did he have of her? That she sometimes drank too much? So did he. That she seemed not serious enough about her writing? The truth was that before their downward-spiraling relationship seemed to consume her, she had struck him as quite serious. That she was sometimes insecure? *All* women were sometimes insecure. The ones who claimed they weren't were craziest of all.

He pictured Hannah, at Francesca Whatshername's rooftop party. He remembered how she'd held her own against Jason. He remembered how, well, just how *happy* he'd been that night.

He decided to call Kristen. If a person as upstanding as Kristen, a person who also happened to be a very strong and intelligent woman—*a pediatric oncologist*—a woman who had lived with him on intimate terms for more than three years, thought highly of him, he couldn't be quite so awful a person as he felt like now.

Kristen picked up on the second ring. Her voice was warm and rich—and deeply familiar, still. It moved him even after all this time. "Nate!" she said. "It's nice to hear from you."

One of her dogs barked in the background. "Corky—our newest," she told him. "He's only a year—German shepherd mix. A real handful."

Kristen lived in Boulder with her husband, an MD/PhD who did something very laudable and impressive, Nate forgot exactly what, at the medical school. (Ran some kind of innovative and also highly compassionate clinic?)

Kristen said she and David were fine. Great, in fact. The new house was also great, although they'd barely unpacked. "No time."

But she found time to rescue and care for three dogs?

"I guess," she admitted.

"And run?"

"I did the Denver marathon in September," she said, a little sheepishly.

Nate laughed fondly. "You don't change, Kris."

He heard David calling her name. "Just a sec," she said to Nate. Away from the mouthpiece, she began talking to David, her voice garbled and indistinct. While he waited, Nate pictured dinner at Kristen and David's: candles on the table, the dogs sprawled on plaid cushions, boxes piled up on the hardwood floors.

"Tell me how you are," she said when she got back on the line.

Nate stood by the window, drawing circles in the condensation. Outside, twilight was descending on the angular, postindustrial Brooklyn landscape—a choppy sea of billboards and cranes and squat, gray tenements.

"I've been better."

He told Kristen he'd broken up with yet another nice girl. "Really nice. Nicer than most actually."

But it just stopped working. He had felt—it was hard to explain. Things had gotten "heavy." He'd been conscious of not living up to some expectation. Not being into it enough, into her enough, he supposed. He'd felt, after a while, as if he were constantly letting her down, as if she were always mad at him. It was no fun. By the end, the relationship had been suffocating. That had to mean something, right?

"Nate!" Kristen said. "Of course it means something. Suffocating is not good."

"Right!"

"I'm sure there was a reason you didn't want to move forward with this, uhm, Hannah, even if it's not clear to you now what it was."

Something in Kristen's pinched tone—he could picture her nose slightly wrinkled—told Nate that she assumed Hannah was, well, sort of awful in some way that would be obvious to anyone but him.

But what if—and he couldn't say this, not to *Kristen*—there was nothing wrong with Hannah? What if the problem was just that she didn't do it for him anymore, at least not enough? Perhaps the reason his relationship with Hannah had dragged on as long as it had, so much longer than his other recent attachments, was that usually his attraction waned in tandem with his interest in the girl herself. Women usually began to grate on him at around the same time he found himself losing interest in sleeping with them. This confluence had filled him with a pleasing sense of his own lack of shallowness. The problem with Hannah, he now felt, was that the drop-off in his attraction, in his excitement about her, had not corresponded to his feelings about her as a person. It had showed him up, to himself.

To Kristen, he just said, "What if the reason I felt so conflicted is because I'm, I don't know, just messed up somehow?"

"You're not messed up, Nate."

Right. Nate had forgotten that in Kristen's world, being messed up meant you were a six-year-old kid with a tumor the size of a grapefruit. And when he realized this, he once again (this always happened at some point when he spoke to Kristen) couldn't get past the knowledge that to her, his problems were that of a decadent New Yorker who whiles away his time on self-indulgent personal drama. He felt he could hear the way Kristen would summarize this conversation to David when they sat down for their candle-lit dinner. Good old Nate, single New York guy, can't seem to settle down. Smart, right? David might ask. Yes. But very, well, you know, neurotic, self-involved. Nate would be cast as an amusing counter-point to their virtuous, community-oriented lifestyle, his problems, his unhappiness, reaffirming the rightness of their way of life.

This was not helpful. Nate turned so he was leaning with his back against the window.

"I also feel kind of guilty," he said, the glass cool through his T-shirt. "I couldn't make up my mind." He thought of the night he and Hannah stayed up drinking bourbon at her apartment. "Or rather I kept changing my mind. I think I was kind of a jerk."

"Isn't that what dating is?" Kristen asked. "Trying to make up your mind?"

"I guess."

"Nate," Kristen said emphatically. "You dated her for, what, four months? Five? You get a pass for being unsure about the per-son for the first few months. Be more careful next time. But give yourself a break. It's not as if you led her on for years and now she's too old to have children."

"Yeah."

Kristen, Nate realized, didn't have much sympathy for the romantic travails of women. Although she was good, so very good, the sphere of her sympathy was a bit circumscribed. She had always lacked a certain kind of imagination. She was so sensible and self-disciplined; the only indulgence she allowed herself was contempt for those who didn't manage their lives as competently—or as shrewdly—as she managed hers. (He thought of her string of boy-friends, each lined up almost before the old one was cut loose, a trend that continued right up to David.)

Having to her satisfaction dispatched with the subject of Hannah, Kristen began describing Corky's latest shenanigans, which involved a garden hose and a neighbor's gargoyle. (A *gar-goyle*? Where the hell did they live, anyway?) As he half-listened,

Nate supposed he, too, was not sympathetic to Hannah's plight in theory. It was just that, theory aside, he actually *felt* bad.

After they got off the phone, Nate continued to wander through the gloom of his darkening apartment, choosing not to turn on the overhead lights, as if to keep his external reality in tune with his internal one. He remembered the first night Hannah had come here. They'd stayed up late, talking. They'd fucked. More than once. The second time, it must have been three or four in the morning, and they'd been talking for hours. He'd started kissing her, and then he was on top of her. He couldn't believe he initiated sex. He was exhausted. His cock had spoken against the judgment of his brain, which was afraid that he wouldn't be able to do it or that it would feel like work. But it didn't. It was good—really good, actually.

In the kitchen, he opened his refrigerator, then stared into it, listening to its hiss.

On one of the metal racks, there was a bunch of limp celery Hannah had bought for him. She thought he might like it as a snack with peanut—no, almond—butter. She didn't realize that when he was hungry he didn't have the patience even to clean and cut celery. But he liked the almond butter. It *was* better than peanut butter. He shut the refrigerator door.

It wasn't all guilt, what he was feeling.

"I always thought she was . . . well, kind of . . ."

Nate leaned in. "Yeah?"

"Well . . ."

"What?"

"Weird."

"*Weird?*"

Jason's forehead was scrunched up in thought. When, finally, he spoke, his voice had a strained quality, as if he were trying to distill very complicated, highly abstract ideas into mere words.

"Don't get me wrong. I like Hannah. But I just didn't see you with her. You guys seemed on edge together. Like, her voice would get sort of squeaky when she was talking to you. Sometimes, she seemed nervous around you. I don't know. It just struck me as weird. I didn't see you two being happy together. You didn't really *seem* happy."

Nate and Jason were sitting in a windowed alcove at a bar near Jason's apartment.

"But maybe it's me?" Nate said.

"What do you mean?"

"Maybe it's my fault I wasn't happy. Maybe I—I don't know—stopped trying."

Jason sat back in his chair and rubbed the side of his head, rumpling a section of his hair so it stood up like bristling fur. "Say you did 'stop trying,'" he said. "It was probably *because* you weren't happy. Right? It's not as if you're a masochist." He kneaded his hands together. "Trust me, you're not a masochist. You're pretty good at looking out for your interests."

Nate began picking at some masking tape that had been applied to the armrest of his chair. He listened to the pelt of rain on the windowpane. He felt defensive on Hannah's behalf, as if Jason were letting her down. (*Weird?* Nate had thought Jason liked her—genuinely liked her.) He remembered how Jason had said long ago that he didn't think Hannah was his type. What was it Jason had said? That he tended to like girls who were "girly and high-maintenance." The recollection sparked a sour suspicion that Jason was pleased to have his prediction bear out.

Nate would have preferred to talk to Aurit, but she was in Germany. After getting off the phone with Kristen, he'd also considered calling Peter in Maine, but there seemed to be something kind of girly about calling everyone he knew to discuss his breakup. Also, he would have had a hard time talking to Peter about this. Peter, in the arid expanse of his own romantic life, came at these things with different assumptions. Peter took for granted that if a woman was cool and attractive and liked you, you'd want to be in a relationship with her. So had he, once.

What Nate wanted now was to change the subject. Which was easy enough. Soon Jason was outlining his next essay. A hit piece—on meritocracy.

Nate pressed his palms against the tabletop. "You aren't arguing that the problem is that we don't really have one—but that meritocracy itself is bad?"

Jason nodded enthusiastically. "Fairness in a meritocracy is just homage to exceptional talent. For the unexceptional—by definition, the bulk of people—meritocracy is a crueler system than what it replaced—"

"Than slavery? Feudalism?"

"For every Jude the Obscure," Jason continued over him, "prevented by a hereditary class system from going to Oxford, there are a thousand other stonemasons who lack Jude's intelligence. Meritocracy is great for guys like Jude, who had talent. For the others, it's bad news."

"Wait," Nate said. "How are the other masons injured if Jude gets to go to Oxford? Is this like how straight marriage is injured by allowing gay marriage? Because I don't get that either."

"They're exposed as lacking. Duh." Jason shook his head. "If everyone remains in the station he's born to, there's no shame in it, but if it's in one's power to rise, the failure to do so becomes a personal failure."

"Oh, I see," Nate said, relaxing into the pleasant contours of impersonal argument. "It's better for everyone, but especially for the poor themselves, to know and accept their places. I think I've heard this argument before. From all sort of apologists for aristocracy. Queen Victoria, maybe?"

Jason exhaled loudly. "The difference—and this should be obvious—between me and some clenched-ass Tory is that the Tory denies Jude's existence, refusing to believe that there is any outsize talent in the 'lower orders.' Or, if he acknowledges it, is hostile toward that talent. See upper-class anti-Semitism."

"Still," Nate said. "You'd keep Jude down—to prevent other

blue-collar workers from feeling bad about themselves. Maybe you should spare the people your lack of hostility."

Jason shrugged good-naturedly. "We all have our own way of showing love."

Nate got the next round. This bar had the distinction of being patronized in about equal numbers by both black and white residents of Jason's neighborhood. Jason came here often, something Nate had been reminded of earlier in the evening when he witnessed the bartender greet him. For a moment, Nate had seen Jason as the bartender must have—as a good-looking, well-dressed, gregarious guy, a well-liked regular.

Nate walked back to their chairs slowly, carefully holding their two full beers.

After a while, the conversation came back around to relationships.

"As a rule, men want a reason to end a relationship, while women want a reason to keep it going," Jason declared, waving his glass. "That's why, after the fact, men look to all the things that were wrong with the relationship, to confirm the rightness of ending it. Women, on the other hand, go back and search for what might have been different, what might have made it work."

Foam was dripping down the side of Jason's glass. Nate felt a wave of affection for his friend, who without making reference to it was staying out too late, drinking too much, on a work night because Nate needed the company.

"Men and women on relationships are like men and women on orgasms, except in reverse," Jason continued boisterously. "Women crave relationships the way men crave orgasm. Their whole being bends to its imperative. Men, in contrast, want relationships the way women want orgasm: sometimes, under the right circumstances."

By the time they left the bar, Nate was in a much better mood.

Walking home in the rain, he thought of what Jason said and remembered a disagreement he and Aurit once had. She was railing about a guy who had broken up with her. She felt he was mistaken about what he wanted. She said that men and women both need relationships just as badly; men just don't know it. They misattribute their unhappiness to other causes, which is frustrating for women, who watch men make choices that harm both of them. Nate had argued that the word *need* loses its meaning if you define it that way. If you think you don't want to be in a relationship, and find happiness in other things like friends or work, how can anyone claim that you're suffering from a deep-seated longing to be in a relationship?

Nate had arrived at his building. He climbed up the stairs and unlocked his door, fumbling a little with the keys. When the door opened, he felt a wave of fondness for his humble apartment and for the simple pleasure of being in it, alone.

No, he certainly didn't *need* to be in a relationship.

The next morning he woke up fairly early, paid his electric, cell phone, and Internet bills, and bought his bus ticket to Baltimore for the Christmas holidays. Then he had coffee with the editor of a literary journal who was eager to publish his commodification-of-conscience piece. On the way home, he stopped at the grocery store. When he returned to his apartment, his fingers were red from the twisted straps of the various plastic bags he was carrying (he always forgot to bring a canvas bag—partly on purpose, because it was a little wussy). The day was clear, and his apartment was bathed in a flattering golden light. The shrill voices that had assailed him yesterday had mostly packed up and gone home.

On his computer, he found an e-mail from Aurit, from Hamburg. He'd written to her the day before. "I'm in a hurry," she wrote, "but wanted to say that I'm really sorry to hear about you & H. Maybe sorrier than you. I wish we'd talked beforehand. I feel as if you might not have spent enough time thinking about what might have caused the 'bad dynamic' you described. Is it worth thinking about? Or is it too late? Either way, I hope you don't mind if I write to her. I feel bad for her. Talk soon, A."

Sorrier than you? What the hell was that supposed to mean? Goddamn Aurit. He deleted the message, lest it disturb his rapidly improving spirits.

He picked up Ian Zellman's card from where it was lodged in his sheets. The night before, after he got home from the bar, he'd drunkenly taken it off the dresser and carried it to bed with him, contemplating calling Greer right then and luckily not actually doing it. Now he sat on his bed with his phone in his hand. Rays of sunlight cut stripes through the bedroom air. Greer picked up on the second ring. Her phone voice was girlish and cute, yet somehow sultry, too. Her laughter thrilled him. As they spoke, his chin was pressed bashfully against his shoulder; he ran his hand through his hair and smiled broadly.

A couple days later, in Manhattan for a meeting with his book editor, Nate ran into Amy Perelman, from his high school. He hadn't seen her for five or six years, since soon after she got her MBA. Now she worked for an investment bank. She told Nate she was in M&A, which seemed "really unsexy a few years ago when everybody was making big money in derivatives and other things that no one understood," but in retrospect she was glad not to have "gotten into that whole game." She shook her head sadly as she told him that bonuses were still down. It took Nate a moment to realize that she wasn't speaking ironically, pretending to be a tone-deaf investment banker.

She said she was engaged. The simpering way she held her hand so he could see her ring struck Nate as uncouth, sort of provincial. He was not in the habit of being offended by flirting, but he couldn't help but feel that there was something aggressively condescending about the way Amy halfheartedly flirted with him. She behaved not as if she were attracted to him but as if she were still the most popular girl at school and he the adoring acolyte, as if with her every small smile she were throwing pennies that he'd scramble to pick up off the ground. Besides, while she was still technically quite pretty, she really didn't do that much for him anymore. With her too-heavy makeup and the artificial tint of her blonde hair, she looked older than many of the artier, noncorporate women Nate knew in Brooklyn who were the same age.

It didn't help that she failed to pick up on his relative success in life. When he'd seen Amy last, he was a struggling freelance writer who lived in a tiny garret in Brooklyn. "Not much has changed," he told her now, although, he added quietly, he did have a book coming out shortly. She responded as if she didn't really get it, a bland "That's great." Maybe she thought he was self-publishing or something? So he maneuvered to mention that he'd written something for a particularly prestigious magazine. "That's cool," she said, but he could tell it didn't mean much to her. Nate knew she didn't intend to be disparaging. (She did say that she'd "heard Brooklyn had gotten really nice.") The things that made him feel successful in his own circle simply had little resonance outside that circle. It bothered him that Amy's inability to see him the way he wanted her to—as a success, as her equal—got to him. Why should it matter?

Nate marveled at this encounter most of the way home. He never thought there would come a day when Amy Perelman, whose yellow-and-white scrunchy might very well still be sitting in a box in his parents' condo, would be so unattractive to him. What made it even more striking was that not long ago, he'd happened to run into another girl from his high school. He was at a reading near Columbia when he saw Michelle Goldstein, the frizzy-haired, theater-loving girl he'd rolled his eyes at back then, Michelle Goldstein, of *pas de deux* and *coup d'état*.

At his apartment, as he flipped through his mail, he laughed. Not at Michelle's expense, but at the general idiocy and affectation of youth. Because Michelle, all these years later, had been really *nice*. She was a labor lawyer. She seemed very earnest and left-wing, like an old-school Upper West Sider. Which is where she lived, with her husband and son. The husband, she told him, was an actor. ("Not quite aspiring—he's very talented and does a lot of really wonderful off- and off-off-Broadway work—but let's just say, we don't need a full-time nanny. Which is good, because we can't afford one.") They lived in an old rent-stabilized place on 104th and Riverside that her husband had been in for years, previously with roommates. She complained about how "rich" the neighborhood had gotten. Michelle's hair, casually pulled back, was still a little bit frizzy, and her jeans were kind of mommish, but she was appealing, far more appealing than Amy Perelman.

Nate was still thinking about this when he walked to his computer and scanned his in-box. There was a message from Hannah. Without pausing to think about what it might contain, he clicked on it. A new window appeared. He sat down.

Dear Nate,

At the park the other day, I told you I wasn't mad. I don't think I was lying. I think I was numb.

Later I got mad. The first thing that pissed me off was the way, when I said this isn't working, you *nodded*. What the fuck? What did it mean to you a few weeks ago when I told you that the only way I wanted to stay with you is if you promised you were in this too? I for one meant that I didn't want to be in a relationship with someone who was going to fucking nod when I proposed breaking up with him. (I also get angry when I think of that night at my apartment. Why did you persuade me to stay with you if you didn't really want it? Were you playing some kind of game?)

So, yeah, I've been angry. At you—but also at myself. Because I never thought I'd let myself be treated this way. I know I deserve a lot better and frankly I've gotten a lot better from other guys.

I didn't expect to feel this way about you. Before we got together, I'd heard things about the way you treat women. And at first, I thought you were really full of yourself. I thought you took for granted that I was dying to go out with you because you think you're such hot shit. I hated that.

I bring this up because later, when things started to suck, I kept thinking about that time, before I'd fallen for you too hard to get out so easily. It was as if I hoped the fact that I hadn't put myself totally in your power from day one might somehow protect me from getting hurt later. It didn't, obviously. Eventually I let go. I trusted you. The way I feel right now, I wish I hadn't.

I don't mean to be melodramatic. I know that relationships often don't work out. But I remember how things were, not that long ago. They were pretty great. At least, I thought so. I felt like there was something real between us—like I really knew you and got you. Is that really stupid of me? I can't help wondering, did I do something wrong? Was I too difficult? Not difficult enough? Should I have called you out on it as soon as I felt like you were, I don't know . . . *changing*— instead of taking you at your word when you said everything was fine? I can't stop wondering, and yet I know it's messed up that I'm thinking this way, as if it were my job to make it work, as if I was supposed to figure out what you wanted and adjust accordingly.

The only thing I know is that when I tried to talk about what was going on with us, it felt like you always wanted to shoot it down. I began to get nervous about irritating you—I felt you pulling away and I didn't want to alienate you even more, so I didn't push us to talk more. In retrospect I regret that. It was obvious something was wrong for a while. Looking back, it seems stupid that most of the time we just ignored the elephant in the room.

I wonder—had we talked, really talked, would things have been better? Sometimes I think of things that are so obvious to me, and I hate that they aren't, or weren't, obvious to you. Such as, why do you think it was that we had a good time when we hung out with Jason and Peter? It was because they were nice to me—they acted like they actually wanted to hear what I had to say, which you barely did at that point. (Thank you for that, by the way—for the way you've treated me lately.)

But then I think of how sad you looked at the park when you said that you worry you no longer have the ability to be in a relationship. And it makes me wonder if you are as upset and confused about this as I am. If so, maybe we should talk now, try and figure what

happened. Maybe it's not too late to deal with this honestly and
openly.

Part of me thinks I shouldn't send this, that I've already been
burned enough. But I'd rather not become that scared of being
honest.

H

There were a number of things Nate felt like doing when he
finished reading this e-mail. One was slamming the metallic top
of his computer shut and throwing the thing against the wall.
Another was running hard for about ten miles, uphill. A third was
reading some very bracing, very austere, very *masculine* philoso-
pher. Say Schopenhauer. One thing it decidedly did *not* make him
want to do was get back together with Hannah.

Nate hadn't been attentive to every sentence; he wasn't able to
be. Reading the e-mail was so unpleasant that he found himself
skimming. He felt as if doing so were a courtesy to her, as if he had
caught her in an embarrassing posture and were politely averting
his eyes. (The part where she mentioned other guys? He shuddered for her—it sounded so . . . *desperate*.) But he'd read enough,
more than enough. He got it. The letter—its conclusion, the thing
about "talking more," "dealing with this honestly and openly"—
struck him as willfully deceived. Anyone could see that they'd
given their relationship any number of chances and that their conversation at the park had been decisive. The e-mail was confused,
disordered, veering back and forth between anger and a wild,
almost desperate compulsion to pull the arm of the slot machine
yet again and hope for a different outcome, based on what? Because
he'd said he worried he might be incapable of being in a relationship? When he told her that, he'd been speaking truthfully, but,
come on, it was a fear that seized him every once in a while and
then passed almost entirely from his mind. It wasn't worrying him

at all right now. And it certainly didn't make him want to keep at a relationship that was so clearly dead.

Besides, the e-mail was a visceral reminder, as if he needed one, of the reasons he didn't want to be with her. Hannah's letter brought back all the feelings of guilt and dread and discomfort he'd come to associate with her.

But the letter conferred an obligation. She was clearly upset. He owed it to her to do something. In the next several days, Nate debated writing back, but he saw almost immediately there was no way he could produce an e-mail of equal length, and a few lines of text from him, with her message hanging below, in its grand textual abundance, would look so paltry, so meager, an insulting little pellet atop her voluminousness. It wasn't only that he didn't have the patience to write at anywhere close to equal length. The truth—and this scared him a little—was that he didn't know what he would say. There was a certain moral vanity in her implicit assumption that everyone could sit down and whip out something like her letter, as if everyone's feelings were so known and upstanding. He couldn't have produced such a letter no matter how hard he tried. Even after all the hours he'd spent pacing his apartment the other day, he didn't really know what he thought or felt, and what he did know was confused and, frankly, somewhat upsetting. What he had learned, in the subsequent few days, was that his unhappiness was eminently containable, if managed correctly. That meant not dwelling. It meant moving forward.

Since writing was out, Nate figured he should call her. On a number of occasions, he was about to do it. But he kept putting it off. He couldn't decide if they should have it out on the phone or if he should propose coffee. Probably the latter, but then a part of him wondered if maybe that wasn't a good idea. Coffee would run longer than a phone call. She'd want him to say a lot of things he didn't much want to say. Not just for his own sake. He didn't want to be forced to say things that would hurt her feelings. The only really honest thing that he had any desire to tell her was, he suspected, the last thing she wanted to hear. He wanted to say that he was sorry for not having broken up with her sooner, for not having seen sooner that it wasn't working and wasn't going to work. He shouldn't have nodded at the park. She was right about that. He shouldn't have been with her at all at that point. In retrospect, he felt he'd had a failure of nerve that night at her apartment; they should have broken up then. But he didn't think she'd appreciate hearing this. And other than that, he didn't know what he'd say. Besides, the endless stream of postbreakup conversations he'd had with Elisa was an object lesson in the way these things could backfire. He didn't want to get into another drawn-out and in the end unhealthy dialogue. And Hannah wasn't Elisa. She was more mature, one expected more of her.

Maybe a phone conversation, short and sweet, was better?

Each time he made up his mind to do one or the other, phone call or coffee date, he couldn't quite bring himself to pull the trigger, and he told himself he'd decide for sure later; he'd do it—one or the other—later.

A week after Hannah sent the e-mail, he came strolling back from Greer's on a lovely, sunny Friday morning. He was in a good mood—it had been a good night, a very good night. He saw another e-mail from Hannah. He knew immediately he'd fucked up. He should have done *something*. The subject line was blank. Nate clicked on the message.

> God, I can't believe I am such a moron. I can't believe I wrote you that e-mail in some moment of god knows what. I just wanted to say I take it back. You're a bigger asshole than I ever imagined. I can't believe you couldn't even be bothered to respond. Anyway, there's just one other thing I wanted to tell you. You're really bad in bed.

{ 17 }

So you're dating Greer now?"

Nate and Aurit were walking along Fifth Avenue in Park Slope, their scarves flapping in the wind as they squinted against the midday sun. Aurit had just gotten back from her trip, a week in Israel and two in Germany.

It wasn't just disapproval Nate picked up in her voice. He knew she'd disapprove of Greer. She thought Greer was shallow and twitty. So had he, before. What bothered him more was something withering in the way she pronounced the word *you*, as in "so *you*'re dating Greer now."

"Greer's really smart," he said as they approached thier destination. He regretted the words as soon as they were out of his mouth.

"I don't doubt it," Aurit said. She pulled open the restaurant's glass door. "I mean, she's been so successful in her career. Remind me, how much did she get for her sex book?"

Then they were enveloped in the restaurant's warm air, rife with the scent of maple syrup. A hostess with an Australian accent directed them through a narrow aisle to a table in the back. By the time they sat down, that particular strand of conversation was lost. After Aurit's long trip, there was much to be discussed. Hans was finally going to move to New York.

"That's fantastic," Nate said.

Aurit told him how this had come to pass, the conversations she and Hans had had, the plans they'd made.

Later, she asked if he'd spoken to Hannah.

"You haven't talked to her?" Nate asked.

"I asked you first."

Nate poured sugar into his coffee. "Don't be like that."

"Fine," Aurit said. "She and I have e-mailed. Briefly. She didn't say much."

"Well . . . ," Nate said. "I think she may be a bit nuts."

The table wobbled when Aurit set her mug down. "Don't go there, Nate. It's ugly. Especially because *she* was so classy about it. She didn't say anything bad about you." She looked at him pointedly, jutting her chin out. "What happened?"

"She basically told me I'm the biggest jerk who ever lived." Nate ran a hand through his hair. He tried for a casual "What can you do?" smile. In fact, the way things with Hannah had so quickly devolved made him intensely uncomfortable.

Aurit cocked her head. "What'd you do, Nate?"

"Nothing."

"Don't be an unreliable narrator. What'd you do to piss her off?"

"Literally, I did nothing. That was the problem."

"Uh huh . . ."

"I didn't respond to an e-mail she wrote."

"Did you apologize?"

"You didn't see the e-mail she wrote me in response to my nonresponse. I think we've gone past the point of apologies."

Aurit shook her head. "Nice."

Nate considered making a joke about how lying in wait for him on the streets of New York was an army of hostile women, with Juliet at its head. Even Elisa, who pretended to be his friend, was half in the enemy camp. Now Hannah, too, had joined its ranks. Meanwhile, on the other side, there was still only one Nate. He didn't make the joke, though. He did not in fact feel jokey about

it. He felt bad. When he thought about it. He tried not to think
about it.

"In her e-mail, Hannah tried to be low-key," Aurit said. "But I
got the feeling she was pretty upset. Honestly, I'm surprised you're
so cavalier about it." She studied Nate with curiosity. "You guys
were together for, what, five, almost six, months?"

"Five," Nate mumbled.

"And you seemed to really like her. Like, a lot."

Nate looked at the place on the table where his plate had been.
"It probably won't last long with Greer," he said suddenly, surprising himself. "It's probably just a short-term thing."

He and Greer had slept together on their first date. Because Greer
had been extremely flirtatious the whole night, this hadn't surprised Nate. What had surprised him was that she burst into tears
immediately after. He'd felt confused and concerned and also,
strangely, fascinated—by her mutability, the way she moved seamlessly and unselfconsciously from a sort of tarty affect to that of a
naïf. It had been like watching a reptile shed its skin; it held him
transfixed. The night had an otherworldly quality, veering back
and forth from one mood to another. When Nate left in the
morning, he felt as if he'd lived through a whole lifetime.

When he came to pick her up for their third date—Greer
inspired in him old-fashioned gestures of chivalry, which was odd
because in another sense he felt as if he were coming almost entirely
because he wanted to sleep with her again—he found her not yet
dressed to go out. Her hair was askew. She'd been crying again. The
combined force of a comment from her editor, an incident on the
bus in which an overweight woman had accused Greer of shoving
her, and a conversation with her sister had "annihilated" her.

For an instant, Nate was uncomfortably reminded of Elisa—
that never-ending river of tears. He felt an impulse to flee. He
didn't flee. He didn't even really want to. His most vivid impression

of that night was from much later, well after Greer had been consoled: the glint of her belly-button ring in the moonlit bedroom as her body rose and fell on top of his.

The fling stretched into a longer and longer fling.

Nate had been wrong about the nature of Greer's interest in him. She hadn't been drawn to his "intellectual cachet." She had, she told him, felt some kind of powerful, "almost kinetic," physical attraction to him. Nate, unaccustomed to seeing himself as an object of erotic fascination, was incredibly turned on by this. He was also inclined to believe her. A memoirist, Greer was a skilled narrator of her own emotions. And what she said dovetailed so neatly with what he'd felt, the attraction to her he'd nursed for quite a while, before they got together.

Long ago, he had placed Greer into the category of people who had gleaned amazingly little actual knowledge in four years at Sarah Lawrence or Vassar or Gallatin or whichever fancy progressive school they'd attended, where that much-heralded goal of modern pedagogy, to teach students "how to think," was considered better achieved without the interference of actual facts. Her ignorance of things that had happened—certain illustrious sackings, schisms, famines, et cetera—was almost touching. She was equally unfamiliar with many books and ideas widely deemed to be of world-historical import. But Greer had ideas of her own, all sorts of them. They just weren't rooted in any context beyond that of pop culture and a certain strand of women's literature. She had also perfected an imperturbable irreverence, an earnest and sincere belief in her superiority over stuffed shirts. Like Nate. Greer was no phony. Unlike Elisa, she didn't pretend. Greer stared you in the face and said, "Really? You're asking if I've read *War and Peace*? Do you really not know the answer?"

As he had told Aurit, Greer was smart. Like a finely honed sports car, her mind wasn't weighted down with unnecessary encumbrances, but she was naturally gifted in the dialectical mode of argument, quick to point out the holes in your logic and to come back with counterarguments. When dialectic failed her, she had at her disposal another powerful tool: tears. This rhetorical device she considered perfectly legitimate: tears fell under the rubric of sincerity.

If Greer wasn't rigorous or self-critical, she was impassioned and empathetic, with great reservoirs of feeling about the issues she cared about. Her personality, like her writing, was lilting and engaging. And what Nate had once taken to be a certain artificiality on her part, he came to see as theatricality, which was different and was part of what made being with her so vivid. He soon found himself charmed by her quirky interests—her unpredictable enthusiasms for, say, piñatas this week, or tiny little postcards that fit only one sentence the next. He noticed, too, how other people responded to her. She had a way about her—a charisma, a storytelling verve, an effortless cool in dress that was as fashionable as Elisa's chic but far less fussy, an instinctive social ease that she used benevolently, lavishing attention upon the shyest and most awkward members of a group. One night she played the guitar for him. Her hair was in a messy ponytail; a thin strap of her tank top had fallen on her upper arm. She was, as she sang a Liz Phair song—her voice small, unschooled, but achingly pretty—about the sexiest, most touching thing he'd ever seen. Sweet and tough and sad and hot all at once.

Not only was she unimpressed by it, Greer was inclined to think Nate's "intellectual whatever" was kind of a bore, a sort of masturbatory exercise that she tolerated with pretty much the same condescension that he tolerated what he was apt to describe, in his mind, as the "puerile, self-indulgent navel-gazing" that characterized her work. Every once in a while these attitudes toward each other's writing slipped out in stray remarks, usually during fights, which they began to have nearly as soon as they grew more serious.

Although she prided herself on being honest, Greer wasn't always, strictly speaking, truthful. She didn't invent wholesale so

much as scramble and rearrange to suit her current purpose, facts
reconfiguring themselves like marbles in a tipped bowl. She was
hardly aware she was doing it. In the moment, she believed what
she was saying wholeheartedly. For her, that was enough. She also
slid easily into manipulation when backed into a corner. She felt
no qualms about that either. So it was that a minor argument
about his being late or failing to do some small thing she thought
he ought to—say, pick up his cell phone when she called—would
escalate. She'd make all sorts of outlandish claims; he'd become
so enraged at her "dishonesty" or "manipulation" or simply her
"triviality," that he felt entirely justified dispensing with tact. All
sorts of pent-up criticisms came pouring out, many of which had
nothing to do with the ostensible subject of the fight. Once he
uttered aloud the phrase *puerile, self-indulgent navel-gazing*. It bothered her more than the words *stupid* and *cunt*, both of which had
also found their way out of his mouth. (For Nate, those moments
had been, frankly, thrilling, the words accompanied by a frisson of
illicit pleasure. It was liberating, the idea that you could talk to a
woman this way and nothing worse would happen than that she'd
yell back that you were a "fucking piece of shit asshole.")

Somewhat to his surprise he and Greer came out of these fights
scarred but also purged. In between exaggerating her flaws, accusing her of a much greater degree of dishonesty et al. than she was
in fact guilty of, things slipped out. He told her, for example, that
it was the most annoying thing in the fucking world when she
asked, *in that voice,* "Are you mad at me?" In turn, Greer told him
about fifty other, much worse things that he did. Apparently, he
was a real asshole. He had innumerable ways of belittling her and
women in general. He bullied her when they argued, which is
why she sometimes started to cry. She was not, she explained,
trying to evade the issue. She was merely frustrated, and if her
tears made him stop bullying, made him *stop and listen to himself,*
so much the better. It wasn't so much that she convinced him—

Greer's feminism often struck him as conveniently self-justifying and inconsistently applied (that is, reliably applied in instances where it bolstered her position and otherwise ignored)—but the fear of setting her off did exert a strong pull on him to modify his behavior. Invariably, their fights ended, for Nate, in relief at realizing that Greer was not in fact nearly as unscrupulous or unintelligent as in anger he had painted her. Also, predictably enough, hot sex. Not even make-up sex so much as making up by way of sex. A moment would come when Nate would simply realize the absurdity of what they were fighting about; his anger would just *turn*. By that point, Greer—perhaps because she too was tired of fighting, or perhaps because she was turned on by how hot he had become for her—could usually be brought around pretty quickly.

Greer was needy—that is, she needed an audience—but it was not always clear to Nate why she needed him in particular. Sometimes, he'd glance at her, see anew how sexy, how charming she was. Anxiety would creep over him. Wouldn't she rather be with a guy who was better looking and more fun, someone less ponderous and academic? After a couple months, he asked her, why him? Yes, he remembered what she'd said about attraction, but why— why was she attracted to *him* instead of someone else? She picked up one of his hands in hers and ran a finger along his palm and up and down his fingers. She told him that his helplessness and incompetence in maneuvering objects in the physical world were endearing. "Sometimes, I look at your big, clumsy hands—these fingers . . ." She smiled and kissed the tip of his index finger. "Your hands remind me of bear paws . . . I watch you chop vegetables or button your shirt, and, I don't know, I'm just filled with affection." What she said was sweet, but Nate was still partly unsatisfied. It felt exogenous to him, to the real him.

But he knew what she meant about being touched by vulnerability. Greer's littleness appealed to him. He enjoyed beyond reason being able to encircle her so thoroughly in his arms. He felt protective, especially in her darker moods, when she cried after sex or was rendered helpless by some minor setback. In these moments, the world ceased to be filled with innocent amusements (teeny tiny postcards! piñatas!) and became a sinister X-rated carnival of rapacious, leering men vying constantly to fuck her: "It makes me sick!" And they'd sit on the floor, her knees pulled into her chest, as Nate held her, stroking her small, hunched-over back with his big hands.

In February, his book was published. Although Nate had privately nursed fantasies of being single when this happened, it turned out to be better to have a girlfriend for that. At the parties on his (brief) book tour, he tried to remember the names of people he hadn't seen for years or had just met a few minutes before. He felt inadequate when he couldn't or when he wasn't enthusiastic enough in his chatter. The whole process was exhausting and unnerving—he often felt embarrassed or ridiculous—and he was glad to have someone to call afterward, or better yet to curl up with at the hotel with a movie on. He felt closer to Greer, even grateful to her, after being together through this.

A certain twee quality to her mental landscape, a histrionic, self-dramatizing tendency that occasionally grated, the goddamned manipulative tears—all these bothered him at times. But Greer was nice, sweet-natured, especially when all was going well, when she felt liked, not just by Nate but in general. She was as sensitive as an exotic plant transported from its natural ecosystem, but when she got what she needed, she was radiant. Day-to-day, they were happy. Nate was rarely bored. With Greer, there was always some distraction, a crisis or a fight or some fantastic scheme of hers. Such as wanting him to watch her fuck a woman.

What Greer lacked in strict rectitude, she made up for in more feminine virtues, such as warmth and compassion. Like Hannah,

she was lively and fun to be around. Unlike Elisa, she was willing
to do things he enjoyed. She also had a strong caring impulse. She
liked to cook for him and to generally see to it that he was well
taken care of. Initially, he found this surprising in a girl who was
so wild in bed (though the whole sex-between-Greer-and-another-
woman didn't happen, and as time wore on, and their dynamic
changed, it grew increasingly unlikely ever to happen).

Greer had met his parents briefly at his book party, but in the
spring he took her to Maryland to spend time with them. He was
struck by how much nicer to them she was than Elisa had been.
They didn't, on the whole, like her, he could tell. Or, rather, his
father liked her okay, and his mother, who was critical of all the
women he dated, hardly bothered to conceal, underneath an impe-
riously cordial bearing, a sniffy personal distaste. Nate, full of
tenderness and gratitude for how hard Greer tried, attempted to
paper over his mother's coolness.

Although that kernel of uncertainty kept him keenly awake to
his feeling for her—he couldn't help fearing that Greer's inexplicable attachment to him would turn off as suddenly and as mysteriously as it had turned on—he was also, over time, afflicted from
the other end, by her jealousy. Whether he liked it or not, this was
a fact of life, part and parcel of being with Greer. The fear of a jealous fit imposed limitations on not only his behavior but his conversation. Nate toned down his praise of other women, even of
their writing. Aurit became a sore subject. ("I've never been
attracted to her!" Nate insisted. But Greer, he finally realized, was
astute enough to know that. She was jealous not of Aurit's sexual
appeal but of the respect he had for her, grudging and qualified
though it seemed to him. "You treat whatever Aurit says as if it
has special weight because she said it," Greer said once. "If I say
the same thing as she did, you act like her agreeing with me gives
what I said legitimacy.")

Greer was always on the lookout for ways she was being belit-
tled or denied her due. Never would Nate have checked out

another woman when he was sitting across from her. He didn't
know if she'd wave her steak knife in the vicinity of his heart or
start crying, but it didn't matter because it never happened.

They celebrated their six-month anniversary. "I guess you
don't have a problem with relationships after all," Aurit remarked
one day, on one of the ever-rarer occasions that she and Nate got
together, just the two of them. "I guess you just hadn't met the
right person."

Although Aurit had mostly come around on Greer—had come
to respect her feminism and emotional insight, even if the two of
them hadn't really hit it off as friends—something in her tone
irritated Nate. "Maybe it was just the right time," he said, largely
to contradict her.

Aurit narrowed her eyes. "Do you know that you often subtly
undermine Greer when she's not around?"

"Well, I can't very well do it when she is around, now can I?"

Aurit didn't look especially amused.

"Relax, I was kidding," he said. "I just think timing has something to do with it. Don't you?"

"I wouldn't know," Aurit said. "For women, it's almost always
the right time." She spoke rather edgily. Hans was just then considering going back to Germany because he still hadn't found a
job in New York. "The thing that I think sucks," she added after a
moment, "is that whenever you—men, I mean—decide that it
is the right time, there's always someone available for you to take
up with."

"I don't think that's true," Nate said. "What about Peter? Or
Eugene?"

"Eugene has a toxic chip on his shoulder. And Peter lives in
Buttfuck, Maine."

Despite what he'd said to Aurit, Nate did feel that he'd simply found the right person. After the first few months—which,
between the sex, her moods, and their fights, had been for him a
dizzying adventure—he and Greer began to fight less. Over time,

ground was ceded, claims granted. Now he always took Greer's calls when he was out. He was supportive in certain required ways. (He had learned, for example, that it was *not* ridiculous for her to want him to come over in the middle of the night because a friend of a friend had been mugged the evening before and she felt scared.) If sometimes he felt frustrated by her demands, he felt something else, too: his very exasperation contained the suprisingly pleasant reassurance that he was reasonable, far more reasonable than she was. Besides, he had come to accept that he was happier, more productive, less distracted by loneliness and horniness with a girlfriend than without. If that meant he had to make certain compromises for the sake of the relationship, so be it.

There were times when he was embarrassed by Greer, when he cringed a little inside. She could be too much—too cutesy and childish, too likely to proudly proclaim a poorly thought-out and poorly informed opinion, too self-enamored to see that she sometimes betrayed a glib superficiality that at its worst bordered on vulgarity. But these were just isolated moments, flashes of feeling that passed quickly. And who was he to judge? He—bookish, moody, work-focused as he was—certainly wasn't perfect. Perhaps what disturbed him more was an occasional feeling of loneliness. Sometimes Greer, in perfect innocence, would say something that devastated him, a remark that in its substance or even in its mere elisions expressed volumes of casual, reflexive indifference to, even derision toward, many of the things he cared about most. Certain aspects of who he was were simply incomprehensible to her. It was all just "intellectual whatever." For Greer, writing was a way of monetizing her charisma. It allowed her to spend her time thinking about what she most liked thinking about: herself, her feelings. It was impossible for him to explain to her what it was for him, what certain books, and a certain type of thinking, were to him. He didn't really try. It'd probably come out sounding wrong anyway—hollow. Pretentious.

Such talk wasn't really what their relationship was about anyway. Their conversations were flirty and cheering, a change of pace, especially after a day of work. With her, Nate went into Greer mode, which was lighter, more indulgent, sillier than his normal way of being. This granted him a certain amount of privacy. He retained a separate self, distinct from his Greer self, which was untouched, free, no matter how obliged his physical person was to, say, come to Greer's aid when she got scared. And the truth was, even then, when he trekked out to her apartment in the middle of the night, he was almost always glad to see her. Even after the passage of so much time, the particular way that Greer was pretty called out to him deeply. There was about her, in her smile, her sweet little laugh, her light, birdlike touch, her very littleness, something that didn't just turn him on but made him positively feel—well, something he'd never felt before.

One day Greer asked if he'd broken up with Hannah for her. Nate made the mistake of saying not really. "It was on its last legs anyway."

"So am I, like, your rebound thing?" she snapped. "I know you think she's *so* smart."

"Greer! I was never even serious about Hannah. You and I have already been going out for longer than she and I went out for."

Nate learned a few days later that Hannah had sold her book proposal. Greer had probably heard that, too; it was probably what set her off. Privately, Nate was glad for Hannah. He had a fondness for her that was not really changed by the way things had broken down at the end. He thought of her sometimes, thought of things he'd like to tell her, observations she'd appreciate, and felt a pang of disappointment when he realized that was impossible. Sometimes he thought of the good times they'd had together, but more often, those memories were drowned out by the recollection of his unhappiness toward the end.

He felt guilty when he thought of various women in his past (although he was pleased, and somewhat egotistically relieved, to hear, from both Jason and Aurit, that Juliet's wedding announcement was in the *Times* one Sunday). When he thought of Hannah, he felt something else as well. He and Hannah had related on levels that he and Greer didn't. This was not, for Nate, a comfortable thought. His relationship with Hannah had shown him things about himself that he wasn't entirely proud of, about what he really valued in a woman and what he claimed to value but in fact could live without.

When he and Greer had been together for a little over a year, they decided to move in together. It seemed to make sense. Things were going well with them. His lease was up. Even he had to admit his apartment left something to be desired. Greer's wasn't great, either.

In the midst of packing, he took a break to go to Cara's birthday party. Over time, Cara had grown on him some. She was a nice person. Nate had even, at Mark's request, helped her get a job, putting in a good word for her with a magazine editor who needed an assistant. The important thing was that she and Mark were happy (although, out of her hearing, Mark did spend an awful lot of time riffing about how "women" lack humor).

Before the party, Nate was to have dinner with Jason and Aurit and Hans, who had decided to stick it out in New York after all, and Peter, who was in town, and Peter's new girlfriend. He'd actually met someone up in Maine. She was nice, Peter's new girlfriend, an archivist in Portland. Cute, too, if a little out of place in New York, in her ponytail and fleece jacket.

Greer had texted him earlier in the day to say she wouldn't be joining them. Nate felt a little guilty that he was relieved. When Greer hung out with his friends, she invariably wound up feeling bad. She thought they didn't think she was smart enough for them, or for him. There was no way for Nate to explain that that wasn't it. It was a matter of conversational style. Greer liked to charm and entertain with her Greerness, to regale the group with tales of her latest quirky hobby or comic misadventure—her half-ironic interest in astrology and consequent visit to a psychic, her run-in with a neighbor who complained about the garlic smell emanating from her apartment when she cooked. Maybe a pet theory about reality television or 1990s teen movies. The kind of impersonal argument, aggressive back-and-forth, and different brand of humor that he and Jason and Aurit and Peter engaged in made Greer feel left out, even rebuffed. But contrary to what Greer thought, his friends liked her fine. They were happy to pay tribute to her charm for five minutes in the beginning of the evening and at interstices throughout, between conversations, but the bulk of the time, they simply wanted to talk normally—that is, in the way that was normal for them. There was no way for Nate to explain this to Greer without hurting her feelings.

Over dinner, Jason told him that Elisa had been promoted at the newsmagazine where she now worked.

At Greer's request, Nate had ceased to be in touch with Elisa. This turned out to be for the best. Elisa derived satisfaction from the fact that Greer found her so threatening that she forbade Nate from seeing or speaking to her. From Jason, Nate learned that Elisa remarked on this whenever the opportunity arose. Nate didn't doubt that the triumph of that was more than adequate compensation for giving up what even Elisa must have known was a pretty dysfunctional friendship. (Besides, she had been a lot happier since taking the new job; she'd started dating a reporter there.) Nate, for his part, was mostly relieved to be free of the burden of Elisa, without having had to make the decision to drop her himself. And Greer, naturally, enjoyed this proof of her power to effect speedy sacrifice.

Nate told his friends that his book had been long-listed for a fairly prestigious award. He tried to downplay it, but he was in fact extremely pleased. To celebrate, they made him drink a glass of a dessert wine that Hans insisted was considered good luck in Germany.

They walked from the restaurant to the party. Nate didn't intend to stay long. He had a lot of packing to do.

He'd been at the party for only a little while when he saw Hannah on the far side of Cara's living room. He made her out just in time to see her see him. She flinched and immediately turned away. When Nate looked back, she was gone.

He went into the kitchen to get a drink. Hannah was by the refrigerator. He had hoped to find her. "Hi," he said.

"Hi."

Her voice was cool, her expression unreadable. He said it was good to see her. She smiled blandly and looked as if she wished he wasn't there.

Nate held a beer in one hand. In his pocket, the fingers of the other coiled and uncoiled against his thigh. He realized he wanted to tell Hannah he was sorry. Or something. But he was afraid it would come out wrong. Patronizing. He decided to do it anyway. Greer told him he overthought these sorts of things, and she was often right.

He took a breath and plunged ahead. "I wanted to say that I'm sorry. About a lot of things. Really. I was an ass."

Hannah's expression became a little less guarded. She said yeah, he kind of was. But she said it a little wryly, more amused than angry. After a moment, she started to apologize, too. "I shouldn't have written what I—" She blushed.

He realized what she was referring to. Perhaps he colored as well. "Don't worry about it," he said.

She looked away from him. But there was something arch in the way she sucked in her lips. Nate shrugged and rolled his eyes conspiratorially. She met his glance. Nate felt, more than saw, some kind of recognition of camaraderie. For an instant, the embarrassments—the disappointments—of the past were a grim joke that they alone shared.

He noticed that her hair was subtly different, still straight and falling past her shoulders but a little more fashionably cut. She was wearing more makeup than he remembered as typical for her. She had on a shortish skirt. She looked good.

Not long ago, Aurit had told him that Hannah was seeing a documentary filmmaker. Naturally, this had bothered him a little. Documentary filmmakers were the most pretentious people in the world. He'd always thought so. The thought of some jackass filmmaker enjoying Hannah's intelligence, her humor, her maturity irritated him. He felt that only he, Nate, was smart enough to fully appreciate the value of her special merits. Which was insane.

He wondered now if she was still seeing the filmmaker. It would probably be weird to ask.

"I heard about your book," he said instead. "Congratulations."

"Thanks."

"I know it'll be terrific."

"That's nice of you to say."

Then silence—amiable enough, but soon a bit anxiety-provoking.

"So . . ." Nate began. There was something he wanted to say, but he didn't know what it was. For lack of anything else, he asked if she'd seen Peter. She shook her head. "He's here for the weekend," Nate said. "He'll be happy to see you."

He thought she blushed again. He wondered if that had been the wrong thing to say. But why? Perhaps it had just reminded her of things. Then he too remembered the night she'd met Peter. The restaurant, the conversation, her apartment after. He'd held her and he'd felt—he'd felt something so strong and so sad. Had he told her he loved her that night? He had loved her that night.

Suddenly, he was lightheaded. He gripped his plastic cup too tightly, and it began to crumple in his hand. Beer overflowed onto his shoe.

"Careful," Hannah said, smiling. Then, unexpectedly—he

thought they were just getting started—she said she should get going. "My, uh, friend is in the other room. We've actually got to take off. Tell Peter I said hello. I wish I'd seen him."

Nate left soon after. On the subway home, memories poured forth: long nights spent talking in the chairs by her window, in his bed, a lot of laughter, the easy but deep rapport, sex that at its best was full of such feeling, such intensity. He felt a sense of loss, the force of which surprised him as much as the fact of it. He'd thought about Hannah so infrequently since they'd broken up.

At home, he was met with a dry papery smell. The moving boxes, stacked in shadowy piles along the walls.

He began to pace. *Of course* Hannah never seemed more appealing than she did now, when she was out of reach, when he was about to move in with Greer. And yet he felt sure it was more than that, what he was feeling. The affection he felt for Hannah was real and spontaneous and familiar. It was what he had felt when they were together—at their best moments.

But he had been unhappy with her. That was why they'd broken up.

He retrieved a half-filled box from the ground and placed it on his desk, intending to pack up his file cabinet. He didn't. After a moment, he walked to the window. When he opened it, a blast of cold air rushed in. He let it wash over him, making the hairs on his arms stand up.

Even now, it was hard for him to say why he'd been unhappy with Hannah.

After a moment, he closed the window. He sat down at his computer. When he turned off the light and got into bed, it was nearly three. He still had trouble falling asleep.

At least, he thought as he turned over yet again, he'd be busy tomorrow. Maybe Greer would come help him pack. Clearly he wasn't very efficient on his own. Yes, that would be nice. Greer would fill the apartment with light cheer as she laughed at his

pitiful progress and at the little messes that were constantly
unearthed as he dug into the backs of his closets and moved items
of furniture that had been rooted in place for years.

With this thought, Nate began to feel better. And then he
knew. This thing he was feeling now—this sense of loss, of
longing—would fade, pass from him like any other mood. As it
should. What he and Greer had was pretty fucking good. Moreover, he liked his life, his friends. He was pleased with his progress on the new book; perhaps that was, for him, more important
than anything else. He was, whether or not he deserved to be,
happy.

In a few days, it would be as if this night never happened, the
only evidence of it an unsent e-mail automatically saved to his
drafts folder. ("Dear Hannah . . .") He'd no more remember the
pain—or the pleasure—of this moment than he would remember,
once he moved into the new apartment, the exact scent of the air
from his bedroom window at dawn, after he'd been up all night
working.

Acknowledgments

I was lucky to have incredibly supportive early readers. I am indebted to Melissa Flashman and Ryan Ruby, who read the book chapter by chapter as it was being written. Ryan, your line edits were terrific, and I'm grateful for the many conversations we had about Nate. Mel, your early enthusiasm helped me believe in the book. I'll always be incredibly grateful to you for that.

I'd also like to thank Stacey Vanek Smith, for her support not only of this novel but of previous attempts. Stacey, I will always think fondly on our long phone calls about Isabel and Abby and Tom, before Nate was a glimmer in anyone's eye. Carlin Flora also read more drafts than any person should have had to. Carlin, I have benefitted in both fiction and life from your sensitivity and insight into character and relationships.

Michelle Orange, Meline Toumani and Gary Sernovitz were also generous enough to read and respond very thoughtfully. Megan Hustad also provided excellent feedback.

I'd also like to thank Anthony Madrid, whose response to my first draft helped to shape the second. Also thank you for years and years of the most wonderful friendship and conversation imaginable. You taught me so much. I wouldn't recognize the person I'd be if I hadn't met you in Tucson all those years ago.

Thanks also to Dan Ray, Lou Rouse, Matt Bonds, and Myles Perkins for letting me listen in on years of guy talk.

I am very grateful to my literary agent, Elyse Cheney, who pushed me to make the novel as strong as it could be and who read it far too many times to count. In addition, Sarah Rainone is a sensitive, insightful, and creative editor, and I am indebted to her wonderful editorial skills. Thanks also to Alex Jacobs, who worked tirelessly on behalf of this novel, and read and responded to drafts at various crucial moments, and to Tania Strauss, who offered a refreshing new perspective.

I'd been told that editors don't really edit these days, but that couldn't be more false when it comes to Barbara Jones, my wonderfully sensitive and astute editor at Henry Holt. Thank you also to Joanna Levine, Kenn Russell, James Meader, Vicki Hare, David Shoemaker, and everyone else at Holt, with additional heartfelt thanks to the person who had to input my obsessive markings on the text. Also, I'm so grateful to Tom Avery, whose enthusiasm has meant so much, and to everyone at William Heinemann and especially Suzanne Dean. Speaking of Britain, thanks also to Natasha Fairweather.

I also want to thank my brothers, Zev and Steve Waldman. Zev, your line edits were terrific. Steve, I couldn't have had a more consistent and kind champion than you've been for so many years. My cousin Wilhelmina Waldman has also been a huge support over the years.

And of course a huge thank-you to my parents, who never once suggested that I get a "real" job and who have always been incredibly kind and supportive. Your love and patience have seen me through too many crises to count.

Finally, thanks to my amazing husband, Evan Hughes, from whom I have learned so much, about writing and everything else. Evan always treated my fiction writing as the most important thing I could be doing. He is a brilliant editor and a wonderful observer of people and has endured endless conversations about Nate and company. Evan, to say I couldn't have written this book without you is true—and beside the point. I can't begin to imagine my life without you.

About the Author

ADELLE WALDMAN is a freelance journalist and book reviewer. A graduate of Columbia University's journalism school, Waldman worked as a reporter at the *New Haven Register* and the Cleveland *Plain Dealer*, and wrote a column for the *Wall Street Journal*'s Web site. Her articles have appeared in the *New York Times Book Review*, the *New Republic*, *Slate*, the *Wall Street Journal*, and other national publications. She lives in Brooklyn.

JUL 1 9 2013

28 DAYS